The Politics of Foundations

T0304214

The Politics of Foundations explores the roles and visions foundations have of, and for, themselves in the new Europe.

The leading contributors to this volume go beyond a quantitative profile of foundations in Europe, and probe deeper into their role and contributions in meeting the economic, cultural, environmental and educational needs of European societies. The book includes a mapping and appraisal of foundation visions, policies and strategies, and an overall assessment of the current and future policy environment in which they operate. The volume combines the detailed comparative analysis of current challenges facing foundations, with individual country studies on Austria, Belgium, Czech Republic, Denmark, Estonia, France, Germany, Greece, Hungary, Ireland, Italy, the Netherlands, Norway, Poland, Spain, Sweden, Switzerland and the United Kingdom and also includes a comparative view from the United States.

This valuable reference will be of interest to researchers and students of foundations, policy-making, comparative politics and international business, as well as policy-makers and professionals.

Helmut K. Anheier is Director of the Center for Civil Society at UCLA's School of Public Affairs, where he is also a Professor of Public Policy and Social Welfare. He is also Centennial Professor of Social Policy at the London School of Economics, UK. **Siobhan Daly** is Senior Lecturer in Politics at Northumbria University in Newcastle upon Tyne, UK.

Routledge research in comparative politics

The Politics of Foundations

A comparative analysis

Edited by Helmut K. Anheier and Siobhan Daly

LONDON AND NEW YORK

First published 2007
by Routledge
2 Park Square, Milton Park, Abingdon, Oxon OX14 4RN

Simultaneously published in the USA and Canada
by Routledge
270 Madison Ave, New York, NY 10016

Routledge is an imprint of the Taylor & Francis Group, an informa business

Transferred to Digital Printing 2008

Typeset in Baskerville by Wearset Ltd, Boldon, Tyne and Wear

British Library Cataloguing in Publication Data
A catalogue record for this book is available from the British Library

Library of Congress Cataloging in Publication Data
A catalog record for this book has been requested

ISBN10: 0-415-70167-8 (hbk)
ISBN10: 0-415-47984-3 (pbk)
ISBN10: 0-203-02818-X (ebk)

ISBN13: 978-0-415-70167-9 (hbk)
ISBN13: 978-0-415-47984-4 (pbk)
ISBN13: 978-0-203-02818-6 (ebk)

Contents

viii   *Contents*

Figures

Tables

Contributors

Frank Adloff, University of Goettingen, Germany.

Zoltan Aszalos, Metaforum Centre, Budapest, Hungary.

Claudio Beccarelli, One marketing services AG, Zürich, Switzerland.

Paolo Canino, Instituto per la Ricerca Sociale, Milan, Italy.

Stefano Cima, Istituto per la Ricerca Sociale, Milan, Italy.

Freda Donoghue, Centre for Nonprofit Management, Trinity College Dublin, Ireland.

Charalambos Economou, Panteion University of Social and Political Sciences, Athens, Greece.

Berta Fraguas Garrido, Fundación Colegios del Mundo Unido, Madrid, Spain.

Federica Givone, CSIL – Centre for Industrial Studies, Milan, Italy.

Barbara Gouwenberg, Vrije Universiteit Amsterdam, Amsterdam, the Netherlands.

Ulla Habermann, University of Copenhagen, Denmark.

Corine van der Jagt, Platform Gemeenschapsfondsen, Kockengen, the Netherlands.

Jerzy Kryzszkowski, University of Łodź, Łodź, Poland.

Mikko Lagerspetz, Tallinn University, Tallinn, Estonia.

Diana Leat, Cass Business School, London, UK.

Håkon Lorentzen, Institute for Social Research, Oslo, Norway.

Miguel Ángel Cabra de Luna, Fundación ONCE, Madrid, Spain.

Gautier Pirotte, Université de Liège, Belgium.

Robert Purtschert, Universität Freiburg, Switzerland.

Erle Rikmann, Tallinn University, Tallinn, Estonia.

Sabine Rozier, Université de Picardie Jules Verne, Paris, France.

Georg von Schnurbein, Universität Freiburg, Switzerland.

Theo Schuyt, Vrije Universiteit Amsterdam, the Netherlands.

Philipp Schwertmann, Migration Council Berlin-Brandenburg, Germany.

Ruth Simsa, University of Economics, Vienna, Austria.

Marek Skovajsa, Charles University, Prague, Czech Republic.

Rainer Sprengel, Maecenata Institut, Berlin, Germany.

Rupert Graf Strachwitz, Maecenata Institut, Berlin, Germany.

Stefan Toepler, George Mason University, Virginia, USA.

Sophia P. Tsakraklides, Temple University, Philadelphia, USA.

Filip Wijkström, Stockholm School of Economics, Stockholm, Sweden.

Balázs Wizner, MTA Institute of Sociology , Budapest, Hungary.

Foreword and acknowledgements

The project, *Visions and roles of foundations in Europe*, developed and directed by Helmut K. Anheier and managed by Siobhan Daly, began at the London School of Economics in 2001, moved to UCLA's Center for Civil Society in 2003, and came to completion in 2004. It was a cross-national, comparative project seeking to contribute to a better understanding of the policy environment in which foundations operate.

The impetus for the project was a discrepancy between the knowledge base and policy relevance of foundations. Indeed, at a time when we seemed to know little about the roles and visions of foundations, policymakers were calling for greater private, philanthropic involvement in fields as disparate as culture and the arts, social services, and research and education. What role could foundations play in this context? How do they see themselves and how do others perceive them? In this context, a systematic appraisal of what role foundations can fulfil seemed not only of academic value: it became a matter of some considerable practical relevance for foundation representatives and policymakers alike.

From a policy perspective, the project was thus both timely and relevant. It was timely because foundations were becoming more visible in policy debates; yet, little was known in a systematic way about the current and future role, and policy environment foundations were facing across different countries. Therefore, a comparative framework was needed not only to account for major differences and similarities across different countries, but also to reveal underlying factors that might account for policy trajectories and common challenges. Within this comparative perspective, the aim was to develop a common platform that could serve as a future benchmark for the positioning of foundations in modern societies.

The work presented in this volume is a first step towards this goal, to which researchers from a broad cross-section of countries contributed: Austria, Belgium, Cyprus, the Czech Republic, Denmark, Estonia, Finland, France, Germany, Greece, Hungary, Ireland, Israel, Italy, Liechtenstein, Luxembourg, the Netherlands, Norway, Poland, Portugal, Spain, Sweden, Switzerland, Turkey, the United Kingdom and the United States. Within a common framework, country teams compiled and updated a qualitative and quantitative comparative profile of foundations, selected a sample of foundations in each participating country, and conducted expert interviews on the current and future role of foundations.

We are indebted to many. Firstly, we would like to thank our country researchers for their hard work, and for their commitment to this research. In addition to the contributors to the current volume, we would like to thank Kjell Herberts, Nuno Themudo and Markus Wanger for their contributions to the project. We thank Lisa Carlson, who served as the research assistant of the project in 2001 and 2002; Jane Schiemann and Sue Roebuck at the London School of Economics for administrative assistance, particularly during the start-up phase; Laurie Spivak and Jocelyn Guihama at UCLA's Center for Civil Society for administrative support at UCLA; Marcus Lam for his excellent editorial and research assistance; and Ilona Iskandar for helping formatting and proofing final drafts.

We are grateful to Emmanuelle Faure of the European Foundation Center for being a great supporter of this project throughout. We thank the members of the International Advisory Committee: Gian Paolo Barbetta (Catholic University of Milan), Lord Ralf Dahrendorf (House of Lords, UK), Mme Nicole Fontaine (former Member of the European and French Parliament), Stanley Katz (Princeton University), Eva Kuti (Central Statistical Office, Hungary), John Richardson (European Foundation Centre), James Allen Smith (Georgetown University) and Volker Then (University of Heidelberg).

Support of this project from the following foundations is gratefully acknowledged: Bodossaki Foundation, Greece; Robert Bosch Stiftung, Germany; Charities Aid Foundation, UK; Compagnia San Paolo, Italy; Levi Strauss Foundation, Belgium; C.S. Mott Foundation, US; Esmee Fairbairn Foundation, UK; FIN, The Netherlands; Finnish Cultural Foundation; Fondation de France; Foundation for Swedish Culture in Finland; Ford Foundation, US; Freudenberg Stiftung, Germany; Fritt Ord Foundation, Norway; Fundación ONCE, Spain; Haniel Stiftung, Germany; Riksbanken Jubilee Fund, Sweden; Swiss Foundations, Switzerland; and Wanger Advocaturburo, Liechtenstein. Special thanks go to the Fondation de France for hosting a project team meeting at their offices in Paris in 2002.

Finally, we thank the hundreds of foundation representatives who participated in the many expert interviews and focus groups that were part of this project. Their willingness to share information and to reflect on the roles and visions of foundations contributed immensely to this research.

Part I

Studying the politics of foundations

1 Philanthropic foundations in modern society

Helmut K. Anheier and Siobhan Daly

Philanthropic foundations are typically discussed in terms of the contributions they make to charity, research, culture and the arts, health care, humanitarian assistance and other worthy causes. They are also recognized for their role in bestowing public recognition for artistic, scholarly, altruistic and other forms of excellence. Their function, therefore, is to allocate, on a voluntary basis, private resources for public benefit and status.

Yet, leaving aside taxation and similar systems, foundations are not the only institutions for converting private funds to public use. What sets foundations apart from other ways of philanthropic giving – such as individual giving to religious, charitable or other causes – is the legally highly regulated and institutionalized form of donating, managing, expending and distributing private resources (usually money) they take for supporting some recognized public purpose. Establishing a philanthropic foundation is a socially as well as a culturally and legally visible act. It is also usually seen and presented as a laudable initiative.

Yet foundations are also inherently political institutions – a characteristic that has received much less attention when compared to the growing scholarship on their charitable and philanthropic activities (see Anheier and Toepler 1999; Lagemann 1999; Hopt and Reuter 2001; Schlüter *et al.* 2001).[1] This political nature, however, rests much less on party politics in the conventional sense, but implies a rather different, more fundamental way of the 'political'. Exploring these political aspects and their implications is a major focus of this volume.

What makes foundations inherently political? For one, foundations represent private agendas that operate in public arenas outside direct majoritarian public control (Karl and Katz 1987; Anheier and Toepler 1999; Prewitt 1999) – a characteristic that makes them distinct and perhaps even somewhat unusual institutions. Indeed, foundation historian Nielsen describes them as 'strange creatures in the great jungle of American democracy', and wonders that foundations 'like giraffes, could not possibly exist, but they do' (1972: 3).

The political nature of foundations derives from their very constitution and their institutional location in modern society which affords them far-reaching independence. Put differently, foundations are political because their legitimacy, including their very existence and range of permissible forms and operations, depends on political preferences and the regulatory and institutional frameworks they entail. Such preferences cannot be taken for granted, and have indeed significantly varied and changed over time. What is more, such preferences may be more or less codified in law, more or less explicitly part of public debates.

Independence, politically, legally, culturally and socially sanctioned, is at the centre of the political nature of foundations. Anheier and Leat (2006) argue that foundations are among the freest institutions of modern societies: free in the sense of being independent of market forces and the popular political will. This enables foundations to ignore political, disciplinary and professional boundaries, if they choose, and to take risks and consider approaches others cannot. As quasi-aristocratic institutions, they flourish on the privileges of a formally egalitarian society; they represent the fruits of capitalistic economic activity; and they are organized for the pursuit of public objectives, which is seemingly contrary to the notion of selfish economic interest.

While modern foundations exist in democratic societies, they are themselves not democratically constituted. There is no 'demos' or membership equivalent, and no broad-based election of leadership takes place. Unlike market firms, membership-based nonprofit organizations or government agencies, foundations have no equivalent set of stakeholders that would introduce a system of checks and balances. Expressing primarily the will of the donor, the organizational structure of foundations does typically not allow for broad-based participation and decision-making outside the limited circle of trustees. No shareholder or membership represents the interest of the organization, its clients or beneficiaries.

Thus, the political nature of foundations rests on their triple independence of market forces, the ballot box and outside stakeholders. Of course, such independence is not absolute, and only relative to the greater dependence of other institutional forms such as the public agency or the private business firm. However, the critical point is that the politics and policies that allow for such greater independence and make the legal, social and cultural space for foundations possible cannot be taken for granted. As we will see, countries vary greatly in the extent and the terrain of political space allocated to foundations. Nor is this space constant over time. Foundations indicate, perhaps more than any other type of nonprofit organizations, long-term directions and shifts in the relationships between public and private responsibilities, and between private wealth and the public good.

Yet why should modern societies make space available for independently endowed private actors in the public domain? Why do some societies allow public agendas formed and implemented by private foundations, while others do not and attach many restrictions? Indeed, the political space for foundations is more than a legal or formal one. In the institutional reality of modern societies, this space is shaped by political ideologies, visions and models, and enacted through roles and, ultimately, justified by expected contributions.

In this book, we will explore these various visions and roles that describe the political space of foundations. We will do so from a comparative perspective, and draw in the experiences of a relatively large set of countries. These countries have in common that they are market economies with a democratic system of government. However, they vary in their history, level of economic development, and political-administrative system. Most importantly, they vary in the history of foundations, the current political space they allocate to them, and the overall importance of private philanthropic institutions. This book seeks to explore these differences.

In preparing the ground for the comparative analysis this book offers, it is useful to take a brief look at history first (see Smith and Borgmann 2001). Historically, foundations are among the oldest existing social institutions, showing great longevity. Even though historians have traced the 'genealogy' of foundations back to antiquity (Coing 1981), Plato's Academy in Greece and the library of Alexandria in Egypt, modern foundation history has medieval roots.

Throughout the Middle Ages, foundations were largely synonymous with religious institutions operating in the fields of health and education, and operating as orphanages, hospitals, schools, colleges and the like. An integral part of feudal social structures, the governance and operations of foundation boards frequently combined both aristocracy and clergy. Indeed, foundations were the prototypical institutional mechanism for the delivery of educational, health and social services under the feudal order. Beginning with the High Middle Ages, however, we find a stronger presence of the emerging urban middle class among founders of foundations, which were often linked, and dedicated, to particular trades or crafts guilds (Schiller 1969). Gradually, the rising urban middle class, professionals and industrialists began to replace gentry and clergy as the dominant donor group – a trend that grew with the process of industrialization in the nineteenth century.

However, as Archambault *et al.* (1999) show, not all countries experienced growth in the number and influence of foundations during the industrialization phase. Being identified with the *ancien regime*, foundations and associations remained banned in France after the Revolution of 1789, and faced a highly restrictive legal environment until the twentieth century. Indeed, the state kept a watchful, frequently distrustful eye, on foundations in many countries. For example, in Austria, the state repeatedly attempted to appropriate foundation assets to fill budget gaps at various times from the seventeenth to the nineteenth century, and transformed private university foundations into governmental institutions during the eighteenth and nineteenth centuries.

However, in many European countries, and not only in the United States, the latter part of the nineteenth and early twentieth century was generally a period of growth and expansion for foundations. By contrast from 1914 to 1949, the European foundation world suffered greatly from the political and economic upheavals, in particular from the impact of inflation, wars and totalitarian regimes, which led the former German President, Roman Herzog (1997: 37–38) to speak of a persisting 'cultural loss'. Only since the 1980s have European foundations expanded in numbers and asset size, although, as we will see below, this trend is not uniform across the continent.

By contrast, the American experience has been very different. Significantly, while Europe's foundations faced great uncertainty and frequent decline, the American foundations moved to the forefront of organized philanthropy. The most important development occurred in the United States at the beginning of the twentieth century with the emergence of large-scale philanthropic foundations. Historians like Karl and Katz (1981; 1987) have shown that the first of these new foundations did not adopt the more traditional charity approach of directly addressing social and other public problems, but aimed at exploring the causes of such problems systematically in view of generating long-term solutions rather than just alleviating them (see Bulmer 1999; McCarthy 1989). Given the significance of this new orientation of foundation work and the large amount of resources that went into it, the first of these foundations came to symbolize a new era of institutional philanthropy pushing the more traditional aspects of foundation work to the background.

Accordingly, as Anheier and Toepler (1999) argue, the modern foundation is often perceived as a genuinely American invention – a tendency that holds two potential dangers. First, we may overestimate the actual economic importance of foundations relative to government spending in the USA. Although foundations held nearly $460 billion in assets in 2003 (Renz and Lawrence 2005), total foundation assets represent only a very small fraction of the national wealth in that country. Against this background, Salamon (1992: 17) long ago observed, 'although the overall scale of foundation assets seems quite large, it pales in comparison to the assets of other institutions in American society'.

The second potential danger lies in downplaying other philanthropic traditions and styles. From a comparative perspective, countries have developed a rich tapestry of foundation types and can look back to a long history of philanthropic traditions; foundations may assume different forms and play different roles in European countries or Australia and Canada than in the United States.

Yet the social roles foundations can assume, and the broader political visions behind the space allocated to them have not been systematically explored. Indeed, from a comparative perspective, few types of organizations have received less attention by researchers and policy analysts than foundations. While cross-national studies of business firms, government agencies and service-providing nonprofit organizations are increasingly becoming available, little is known in a systematic way about the current and future role and policy environment of foundations.

Paradoxically, at a time when we seem to know relatively little about the potential of foundations, policy-makers are calling for greater private, philanthropic involvement in fields as disparate as culture and the arts, social services, and research and education (see, for example, European Commission 1997; 2005). What is more, not only politicians, but also representatives of corporate interests and civic leaders, frequently stress the role foundations, along with other forms of philanthropy, could play in building and servicing civil society.[2]

Purpose

Our purpose is to present a systematic analysis of the current and future role of foundations in Europe and the United States, and the political context in which these roles are shaped. This analysis includes a mapping and appraisal of foundation visions, policies and strategies, and an overall assessment of the current and future policy environment in which they operate.

The analytic questions that guide our research are as follows: do political expectations of foundation roles and visions reflect what this set of institutions wants to achieve or contribute in a given social and political context? Do roles and visions reflect each other, and form distinct patterns or combinations? Finally, is the political space of foundations reflected in their overall size and scope as well as in their actual and potential contributions? In approaching these questions, we will, *en route*, pose others as well:

- What political space do foundations have, and how do they fill it?
- What is the nature of current debates? Who defines the topics, what drives the agenda, and for what end?
- To what extent is the current policy situation faced by foundations a break with the past, and how far does it represent continuity with existing historical patterns?
- How do foundations perceive their current and future relationships with the state, the voluntary or third sector, and with businesses?
- How do foundations perceive their resources and competencies, as well as the obstacles and constraints facing them?

Before proceeding to deal with these questions, however, it is first necessary to consider methodological aspects, in particular the definition of what constitutes a foundation, and issues concerning country selection, sampling and data collection.

What is a foundation?

The definition of foundations varies from one country to the next. Anheier (2001) and Hopt and Reuter (2001) underline the 'rich tapestry' of foundation forms that complicates our understanding, as it produces a highly complex, sometimes confusing, terminology and legal treatment. Indeed, what is defined as a foundation in one country may not qualify as such in another. Moreover, not all organizations labelled 'foundation' are in fact foundations. In Central and Eastern Europe, many foundations are either membership associations or corporations. The German political foundations such as the Friedrich-Ebert-Stiftung or the Konrad-Adenauer-Stiftung are registered associations with no significant assets of their own; their operating budgets are largely covered by annual subventions from the German Government (Beise 1998). In the Netherlands, the distinction between foundation (an asset-based entity) and association (a membership-based entity) has become largely indistinguishable in the fields of education and social services. In Switzerland, some foundations are primarily investment trusts for families, pension schemes for corporations or local sickness funds.

The definition of foundations varies from one country to another not along one primary axis, but frequently in several dimensions. There are legal definitions that reflect either common-law traditions with an emphasis on trusteeship (United States, United Kingdom, Australia), or civil law traditions (e.g. Switzerland and Germany), with the important distinction between legal personalities based on either membership or assets (Van der Ploegh 1999; Hopt and Reuter 2001; Schlüter *et al.* 2001, Appendix 1; van Veen 2001; Bater and Habighorst 2001).[3] Other definitions bring in additional aspects, such as type of founder (private or public), purpose (charitable or other), activities (grant-making or operating), revenue structure (single or multiple funding sources), asset type (own endowment or regular allocations), and the degree of independence from the state, business or family interest.

To cut across this terminological tangle, we propose a modification of the structural/operational definition developed by Salamon and Anheier (1997) for nonprofit organizations generally. Accordingly, a foundation has the following characteristics (Anheier 2001):

- It must be an *asset-based entity*, financial or otherwise. The foundation must rest on an original deed, typically a charter that gives the entity both intent of purpose and relative permanence as an organization.
- It must be a *private* entity. Foundations are institutionally separate from government, and are 'non-governmental' in the sense of being

structurally separate from public agencies. Therefore, foundations do not exercise governmental authority and are outside direct majoritarian control.

- It must be a *self-governing entity*. Foundations are equipped to control their own activities. Some private foundations are tightly controlled either by governmental agencies or corporations, and function as parts of these other institutions, even though they are structurally separate.

- It must be a *nonprofit-distributing entity*. Foundations are not to return profits generated by either use of assets or commercial activities to their owners, members, trustees or directors as income. In this sense, commercial goals neither principally nor primarily guide foundations.

- It must serve a *public purpose*. Foundations should do more than serve the needs of a narrowly defined social group or category, such as members of a family, or a closed circle of beneficiaries. Foundations are private assets that serve a public purpose.

- *Self-understanding and identity*. Given the great diversity of foundation forms and foundation-like institutions, the foundation should have an organizational identity or self-understanding as a 'foundation', i.e. as distinct from operating nonprofit, fund-raising organizations and other types of fund-distributing organizations.

Grant-making foundations are usually regarded as the prototype of the modern foundation, which is largely a reflection of the US experience and its post-war dominance in the field of philanthropy (Toepler 1999). Whereas in the USA, over 90 per cent of the existing 60,000 foundations are grant-making, the majority of foundations in Europe are, as we will see, either operating, or pursue their objectives by combining grant-making activities with the running of their own institutions, programmes and projects. Historically, of course, foundations were operating institutions primarily, e.g. hospitals, orphanages, schools and universities, although many did distribute money (alms-giving) and contributions in kind (food, land or wood, for example). By contrast, the sharp distinction between grant-making and operating foundations emerged much later historically, and is for both the USA and Europe largely a product of the nineteenth and early twentieth centuries (Karl and Katz 1987; Bulmer 1999).

Behind the complexity of forms, there are nonetheless several basic categories:

1   Grant-making foundations, i.e. endowed organizations that primarily engage in grant-making for specified purposes. Examples include the Ford Foundation in the USA, the Leverhulme Trust in the United Kingdom, the Volkswagen Stiftung in Germany, the Bernard van Leer Foundation in the Netherlands and the Carlsbergfondet in Denmark.

2   Operating foundations, i.e. foundations that primarily operate their

own programmes and projects. Examples include the Institut Pasteur in France, the Pescatore Foundation in Luxembourg, which runs a home for senior citizens, and the Hospitalstiftung in Germany, which for centuries has operated a health care establishment.

3   Mixed foundations, i.e. foundations that operate their own pro-grammes and projects and engage in grant-making on a significant scale. Examples include the Fundación March in Spain, the Calouste Gulbenkian Foundation in Portugal and the Robert Bosch Stiftung in Germany.

Nongovernmental organizations and nonprofit organizations generally would differ from a foundation in the sense that no asset base and original deed would be required. They would be based either on membership, i.e. associations, or on some other corporate form, such as a limited liability corporation or cooperative. Operating foundations and grant-seeking foundations are closer to the corporate nonprofit form than they are to grant-making foundations.

Of course, as indicated above, as with any comparative definition, some problems remain. There are four major areas where the definition pro-posed here encounters difficulties: first, where the label 'foundation' is used to disguise some other organization; second, where foundations engage with a market economy and change into primarily economic actors; third, where foundations become instruments of the state; and fourth, where they become a dynastic means of asset protection and control. In selecting the foundations for this analysis, we have addressed these issues at the country level rather than by establishing generic prin-ciples beyond the definition and typology suggested above.

Despite some limitations, the definition proposed above provides us with a benchmark against which we can examine the position of founda-tions in different European countries, as the authors do in the various country chapters. In this way, the definition and contextual discussion is useful for the comparative analysis of foundations that we will approach in the next chapter. Similarly, we limit comparisons to three categories of foundations, i.e. grant-making, operating and mixed, although other forms exist as well. Nonetheless these three forms capture the basic dis-tinctions that can be made between foundations cross-nationally, and the country chapters address more specific types in the context of particular cases.

Roles and visions

The presence of nonprofit organizations in countries worldwide has been explained with reference to market and/or government failure: voluntary organizations emerge to 'fill gaps' in order to address unmet needs, particularly those outside of the mainstream in societies (Weisbrod 1988).

Another explanation of why voluntary organizations exist centres on perceptions of their trustworthiness. In situations of information asymmetry, in other words, where consumers lack the information to judge or scrutinize the performance of producers or service providers, consumers will tend to place more trust in nonprofit organizations. In contrast to the private sector, voluntary organizations are seen to be more trustworthy as the need to make a profit is not their central motivation (Hansmann 1987). A third strand of thinking, associated particularly with interpretative sociologists (or institutionalists) (see Halfpenny and Reid 2002: 540), and theories such as social origins theory (Salamon and Anheier 1998), underlines the effects of environmental factors on the development and nature of voluntary organizations, notably the impact of historical, institutional and sociological factors.

The reasoning that underpins prominent theoretical arguments is relevant to most types of nonprofit organizations, including foundations. Whilst these theories can inform our thinking as to why foundations, along with other nonprofit organizations exist, we seek to move beyond this question to explore not only why they exist but what continues to make them acceptable to, if not tolerated by, the societies they operate in. Thus, we focus on the roles of foundations with a view to understanding the grounds upon which the legitimacy of foundations is based. In the previous section, we indicated how patterns of growth in foundations are influenced by various factors, notably the history, economic performance and politics of a country. In a similar way, influenced by the thinking of the interpretative sociologists (or institutionalists) in particular, we posit that the roles foundations fulfil are likely to be affected by the policy environment in which they operate. The 'visions' we have articulated represent different political scenarios, with a view to determining which best reflects the actual environment in which foundations function.

Roles

What roles do foundations fulfil? Put another way, what do foundations claim to do, and what contribution do they make to societies? Various suggestions have been made in the literature as to what types of roles foundations play.

Prewitt (1999: 20–29) explores four key purposes for foundations: redistribution, efficiency, social change and pluralism. According to Anheier and Leat (2002), the promotion of *pluralism* is variously seen to involve foundations promoting diversity and social experimentation, protecting dissent and civil liberties and acting as an alternative actor to the state in certain policy areas, thereby also serving to limit its dominance. Prewitt (1999: 28–29) argues that foundations are particularly well placed both to facilitate and to promote pluralism. Their independence means that they are not subject to the same constraints as the public sector or the market, which leaves them open to supporting less mainstream concerns. As such, in a related way, promoting innovation is also viewed as a specific niche for foundations as they are seen to be well placed by virtue of their independence to take risks on funding innovative projects. Thus, foundations are *social innovators*. However, the extent to which foundations have the vision and ability, particularly over the long term, to sustain and to build on innovative efforts remains open to debate (see Anheier and Leat 2002, 2006; Anheier and Toepler 1999: 16).

The role of foundations in affecting *social change* has also been interpreted in a variety of ways, ranging from influencing – and changing in a radical sense – popular opinion on social issues, to supporting new ideas and new needs. However, although Prewitt acknowledges that foundations do have the potential to affect social change, he also emphasizes the importance of not exaggerating the extent of the social or policy change which foundations have had the power to influence. In this regard, the analysis of foundations in the United States is divided. Although some observers support Prewitt's view, others are both critical and suspicious of the amount of influence foundations seek to exert over society (Roelefs 2003). At the same time, by contrast, it has been argued that foundations have an important role to play in the preservation of traditions and cultures. A rather narrow interpretation of this role may involve foundations in preserving aspects of a country's culture, but a broader interpretation may envisage foundations seeking to oppose change, as much as they seek to bring it about.

The notion of redistribution implies that foundation giving enables the redistribution of money from the wealthy to the less well-off sections of society. However, Prewitt also questions assumptions about how redistributive foundation grant-making actually is. There is no clear evidence to support the claim that grant-making provides for more redistribution than if the money was given to the government via taxation. Indeed, much foundation giving is not redistributive in its aims at all. What is more, Prewitt disputes the suggestion that foundations' spending (via grant-making) is more cost effective and efficient than government spending. The efficiency of private companies is judged via the profits they make. Similarly, the efficiency of governments is judged by voters at elections. However, there are no clear mechanisms of accountability by which the efficiency of foundations can be evaluated. This undermines the viability of efficiency as a means of justifying the contribution of foundations. In all, it has not been clearly established that there are more advantages to be derived from resources remaining in the control of foundations than of governments or citizens. However, foundations remain tolerated so long as the attempts to 'do good' outweigh any attempts by foundations to abuse their position (Boris and Wolpert 2001: 69–70). In the United States at least there is a degree of consensus that the roles foundations fulfil should be acknowledged, as should the types of challenges they encounter in seeking to bring about change (Boris and Wolpert 2001: 69–70).

Focusing on the redistributive function of foundations, particularly in the American context, means that the predominant role of European foundations in the running of their own programmes and services tends to be overlooked. Generally, as the nation state developed, the role of foundations changed from that of a traditional, religion-based charitable institution to a somewhat more pluralist provider of quasi-public goods, used by and for special groups and interests. The extent to which this happened, however, varies from one country to the next (see below). Yet it tended to manifest itself in the form of 'gap-filling' in areas that are not addressed by the state. In this way, the role of foundations has long been to *complement* the state.

In Europe, governments have also displayed a preference for creating or sponsoring foundations to fulfil certain functions. This strategy may be adopted as a means of dealing with issues that are controversial or politicized, such as the Swiss foundations that were created to manage the financial dealings on accounts held by Holocaust victims and their families (see Anheier and Toepler 1999: 18). This type of scenario provides one example of how foundations may *substitute* rather than complement the role of the state.

Both of these scenarios may involve a role for foundations in the delivery of services but, as Prewitt (2001: 364) argues, this role is viewed as distinct from the role played by other nonprofit organizations in this area:

> What distinguishes service delivery philanthropy from direct charity is that the former, as a foundation project, is normally justified as testing out a model or promoting an innovative strategy that can be adopted elsewhere.

Altogether, based on our review of the roles that have been suggested in the literature on foundations, and taking existing empirical profiling of foundations in Europe into account, we identified seven key roles worthy of exploration in our research. The following roles provide the framework for this part of our analysis:

Complementarity

Foundations serve otherwise under-supplied groups under conditions of demand heterogeneity and public budget constraints.

Substitution

This role expects foundations to take on functions otherwise or previously supplied by the state. In this role, foundations substitute state action, and foundations become providers of public and quasi-public goods.

Redistributive role

This role refers to the idea that the major role of foundations is to engage in, and promote, redistribution of primarily economic resources from higher- to lower-income groups.

Innovation

Foundations are engaged in promoting innovation in social perceptions, values, relationships and ways of doing things, a function which has long been ascribed to them.

Social and policy change

This role suggests that foundations seek to promote structural change and a more just society, fostering recognition of new needs, and the empowerment of the socially excluded.

Preservation of traditions and cultures

Foundations oppose change and preserve past lessons and achievements likely to be swamped by larger social, cultural and economic forces.

Promotion of pluralism

Foundations promote experimentation and diversity in general; protecting dissenters/civil liberties against the state; challenging others in social, economic, cultural, environmental policy.

Visions

Against the background of the analysis of European foundations, Anheier (2001) proposes seven models, each of which groups countries together in accordance with the importance and role of foundations, and the nature of their relationship with the state and business sector. This classification is informed by social origins theory (Salamon and Anheier 1998; Anheier and Salamon 2006), which posits that the size or scale of a country's non-profit sector and its position vis-à-vis the state is influenced by a range of factors, notably historical development and 'social forces'. The social origins theory is based on modifications of Esping-Andersen's analysis of the welfare state (1990) to incorporate the nonprofit sector. It identifies four more or less distinct models of nonprofit development or 'nonprofit regimes', each characterized not only by a particular state role, but also by a particular position for the nonprofit sector; and, most importantly, each reflecting a particular constellation of social forces. *We suggest that nonprofit regime types, as well as the policies and the policy-making style associated with them, help account for cross-national differences in the nonprofit sector scale and structure but are also useful for casting the roles and visions of foundations.*

Table 1.1 differentiates these regimes in terms of two key dimensions: first, the extent of government social welfare spending and, second, the scale of the nonprofit sector. In the *liberal model*, represented by the USA and the UK, a lower level of government social welfare spending is associated with a relatively large nonprofit sector. This outcome is most likely where middle-class elements are clearly in the ascendance, and where opposition either from traditional landed elites or strong working-class movements has either never existed or been effectively held at bay. This leads to significant ideological and political hostility to the extension of government social welfare protections and a decided preference for voluntary approaches instead. The upshot is a relatively limited level of government social welfare spending and a sizeable nonprofit sector.

The *social democratic model* is very much located at the opposite extreme. In this model, exemplified by Sweden, state-sponsored and state-delivered social welfare protections are extensive and the room left for service-providing nonprofit organizations is quite constrained. Historically, this type of model emerged most likely where working-class elements were able to exert effective political power, albeit typically in alliance with other social classes. This is particularly true in the case of Scandinavian countries like Sweden, where working-class political parties were able to push for extensive social welfare benefits as a matter of right in a context of a weakened, state-dominated Church and a limited monarchy. While the upshot is a limited service-providing nonprofit sector, however, it is not necessarily a limited nonprofit sector overall, as shown above. Rather, the nonprofit sector performs a different function in social democratic regimes: an advocacy and personal expression, rather than a service-providing, role. In Sweden, a very substantial network of volunteer-based advocacy, recreational and hobby organizations turns out to exist alongside a highly developed welfare state.

In between these two models are two additional ones, both of which are characterized by strong states. However, in one, the *corporatist* model present in Germany, for example, the state has either been forced or

Table 1.1 Third sector regime types

Public sector social welfare spending	Third sector size (economic)	
	Small	Large
Low	Statist	Liberal
High	Social Democratic	Corporatist

Source: Salamon und Anheier 1998.

induced to make common cause with nonprofit institutions, so that non-profit organizations function as one of the several 'pre-modern' mechanisms that are deliberately preserved by the state in its efforts to retain the support of key social elites while pre-empting more radical demands for social welfare protections. This was the pattern, for example, in late nineteenth-century Germany, when the state, confronting radical demands from below, began to forge alliances with the major churches and the landed elites to create a system of state-sponsored welfare provision that over time included a substantial role for nonprofit groups, many of them religiously affiliated (Anheier and Seibel 2001).

The *statist model* is the fourth possible model. In this model, the state retains the upper hand in a wide range of social policies, but not as the instrument of an organized working class, as in the social democratic regimes. Rather it exercises power on its own behalf, or on behalf of business and economic elites, but with a fair degree of autonomy sustained by long traditions of deference and a much more pliant religious order. In such settings, limited government social welfare protection does not translate into high levels of nonprofit action, as in the liberal regimes. Rather, both government social welfare protection and nonprofit activity remain highly constrained.

Like the third sector at large, so has the importance and scale of foundations across Europe been influenced by various historical, social and political forces,[4] although as Table 1.2 shows, we are able to introduce further specifications to the regime types suggested by Salamon and Anheier (1998). For instance, the salience of foundations, and the prominence of grant-making foundations in the UK reflects how, historically, charitable giving was cultivated in the UK, with legal regulation provided since the Statute of Charitable Uses of 1601. By contrast, the suspicion with which foundations have been traditionally regarded in France, combined with the efforts of the state to maintain a monopoly on public services, explains the complex state regulation of foundations (Archambault 2001).

Given that the prevalent institutional and legal environment is fundamental to the development of foundations, grant-making foundations in particular (Toepler 1998), its restrictive nature explains why grant-making foundations have not flourished in France. Similar observations could be made of other countries too, notably those which are representative of the peripheral statist model (Ireland, Greece).

In Scandinavia, foundations traditionally worked in a form of partnership with the state, though in the post-war era they found that they were somewhat sidelined by the emergence of the welfare state. This provides some basis for explaining why some of the larger operating foundations became incorporated into the delivery of services within the welfare system, whilst grant-making foundations remain in the minority. Similarly, representative of the civil society-centred corporatist model, in the Netherlands, following the Second World War, the number of operating foundations grew as part of the development of the welfare state. Although the state sought to assume responsibility in the area of social welfare, for the most part it did so through public funding of these activities rather than through the performance of these tasks (Burger *et al.* 2001: 195). Finally, the prevalent political, social and economic context can be seen to matter to the extent that in the Mediterranean-corporatist and post-socialist statist models, long periods of non-democratic government prevented the development of grant-making foundations in particular.

These models suggest various ways in which different types of foundations relate to the state, as well as the differences and similarities between the size and nature of foundation sectors in Europe. Informed by social origins theory, we posit that the closer examination of the position and scale of foundations can best be explained through a structural explanation that accounts for the influence of a range of social, historical and economic factors. The importance of such an exercise notwithstanding, our aim is to move beyond the use of models for the purposes of classification in order to capture the dynamics of relations between foundations and key actors – notably the state, the corporate sector and nonprofit organizations – as well as between foundations themselves. In this way, we seek to capture the challenges facing foundations, especially in the light of broader changes that have altered the context for philanthropy.

We argue that these relationships can best be understood by the investigation of what we term the 'visions' of foundations. The visions reflect the models used to articulate the position and scale of foundations. We draw upon the following somewhat stylized visions as 'markers' for what are undoubtedly more complex sets of political preferences. These 'visions' provide the framework for this part of our analysis (Table 1.2):

- In the *social democratic model*, foundations exist in a highly developed welfare state. As part of a well coordinated relationship with the state, operating foundations either complement or supplement state activities.
- In the *state-controlled model*, foundations are ultimately subservient to the state. Restrictive laws, complicated administrative procedures, and extensive oversight establish a relatively tight control regime for foundations.
- In the *corporatist model*, foundations are by and large in some form of subsidiarity relation with the state. Operating foundations are part of the social welfare or educational system, and many combine grant-making and operative dimensions.
- In the *liberal model*, foundations form a largely parallel system next to government, frequently seeing themselves as alternatives to the mainstream and as safeguards of non-majoritarian preferences.
- The *peripheral model* sees foundations in a minor role, and as largely

Table 1.2 Third sector regime types and foundation models

Regime type	Foundation model	Countries	Overall importance	Characteristics		Borderline issues
				Operating foundations	Grant-making foundations	
Social democratic	Social democratic model	Sweden, Norway, Denmark, Finland	High	Larger operating foundations integrated in public welfare service delivery	Many smaller foundations set up by individuals; large company foundations; social movement	Complex borderline between business and foundations
Corporatist	State-centred corporate model	France, Belgium, Luxembourg	Low	Close supervision of foundations by state; emphasis on public utility	Few grant-making foundations, primarily operating, quasi-public umbrella foundations	Complex borderline between state and foundations
	Civil society-centred corporate model	Germany, Netherlands, Austria, Switzerland, Liechtenstein	Medium	Operating foundations part of welfare system, close state links, subsidiary	Grant-making foundations somewhat less prominent many fixed foundations	Complex borderlines between state and foundations, and foundations and business
	Mediterranean corporate model	Spain, Italy, Portugal	Medium	Long history of operating foundations linked to	Delayed development of grant-making foundations;	Complex relationship with state/religion

				dominant religion, parallel to public welfare provisions	rapid recent development after autocratic experience
Liberal	Liberal model	UK, USA	High	Fewer operating foundations	Prominence of grant-making foundations; long history of independence	Relatively clear boundaries, indirect state involvement
Statist	Peripheral statist model	Ireland, Greece	Low	Foundations are service-providers to compensate for public sector short-fall	Few grant-making foundations	Complex historical links to dominant religion, patriarchy, immigration patterns
	Post-socialist statist model	Central and eastern European countries	Medium	Delayed development; operating foundations dominate, parallel to public welfare provision	Very few domestic grant-making foundations; rapid recent development	Complex borderlines between state and foundations, and foundations and business

insignificant yet ultimately worthwhile institutions as long as they do not challenge the status quo.

- In the *business model*, foundations become instruments of corporate citizenship, and assist business interests in reaching out to communities and customers by serving the public benefit in enlightened but ultimately self-interested ways.

Country selection and approach

As indicated above, our aim is to produce a comparative profile and analysis of the roles and visions of foundations, and relate the political positioning of foundations to their actual size, scope and overall importance as a sector. To do this, we engaged the participation of researchers from as broad a selection of European countries as possible and included the United States as a comparative yardstick to contrast the European experience.[5]

Our research questions are conducive to a case-study approach (Yin 2003). As outlined above, we focus on how foundations interpret their roles in societies, and also on how and why the roles they fulfil are influenced by opportunities and challenges in the prevalent policy environment. As such, the case studies are illustrative, but also exploratory. We assume that expectations of foundation roles and visions should be grounded in informed assessments (by foundation leaders, representatives and experts) of what this set of institutions wants to achieve and contribute in a given social and political context. We further assumed that roles and visions reflect each other, and would fall into distinct patterns or combinations. Finally, we assumed that the political space of foundations is reflected in the size and scope of foundation sectors.

Our methodological approach, based on these assumptions, aimed at collecting comparative and comparable information of such expectations, the patterns they form, and their relationship with 'reality'.

We began by enlisting researchers in all participating countries. The first major task for the project researchers was to compile and update a comparative profile of foundations in each European country in terms of types, size, areas of activities and changes over time. Each country profile was also required to include a mapping of concepts, cultural facets and other factors influencing the qualitative understanding and position of foundations in different countries.

Drawing upon the form of the foundation as our unit of analysis (as defined above), each country study undertook a multiple-case design. Following Yin (2003: 46), we view the multiple-case design as an issue of research design, rather than as a method that is distinct from a single case study (see Lijphart 1971; 1975). The purposeful, rather than random, selection of cases against the background of our empirical profiling of the sector allowed each country researcher to select a range of cases conducive to advancing our understanding of the roles and visions of foundations, as well as their position in, and contribution to, society more broadly. It also gave the country researchers flexibility in their selection of cases, allowing them to make their selection of cases in terms of age, size and type of foundations within the wider context of their own knowledge of the foundation sector in each country.

Given the nature of the research questions and the objectives driving the study, semi-structured interviews were the most appropriate method of investigation. In the course of the interviews, respondents assessed each of the roles and visions outlined in the previous section in a country-specific context. With the help of these responses we sought to determine the extent to which foundation representatives and other relevant interviewees were aware of, and understood, the different roles and visions, as well as whether they sought to articulate them in terms of foundation activities.

In this way, we also tried to discern whether foundation representatives identified gaps between expectations of foundations, on the one hand, and the behaviour of foundations, on the other. Similarly, using the framework set out above to investigate the visions of foundations, in interviews with foundation representatives and other key stakeholders, interviewers aimed at fathoming which scenario best reflects the prevalent policy environment in which foundations operate.

In addition to our investigation of the specific roles and visions we probed broader, but related, themes: To what extent do foundations see themselves as part of a 'foundation sector' or as part of a nonprofit sector? How distinctive are foundations perceived to be? Should foundations be more or less accountable to government? Is there a need to create more foundations in a particular country? Do foundations influence public policy and if not, should they have more influence? How well are foundations understood by the public and/or by government? What efforts need to be made to be more transparent and open about their activities? Finally, the interviews were concluded with a series of open-ended questions about what foundations identify as the main issues and challenges facing them in the immediate and long term. Ultimately we specifically sought to discern how these themes and challenges are likely, in the interviewees' opinion, to affect the roles of foundations in the future.

The selection of each set of cases for interview and analysis followed the same procedure in each country:

First, against the background of a detailed empirical profile of the foundation sector, a selection of foundations was made in each country: 25–30 for countries with larger foundation sectors and 10–15 for countries with smaller foundation sectors. Cases were selected according to the range of categories of foundations outlined above. We also sought to include a balanced number of established and recently created foundations in each case selection.

Second, each of these initial case selections was subject to a peer review process in an effort to guard as far as possible within our chosen method against problems such as bias in the selection of cases. This was followed by a preliminary analysis of annual reports and other relevant material with the aim of gaining a more in-depth knowledge and understanding of each of the cases selected.

The third step involved the identification from the initial selection of a subset of foundations, including a range of large, medium-sized and small entities, as well as those that were typical and atypical of the foundation sector in a particular country. For countries with larger foundation sectors, 12–15 cases were selected, whilst countries with smaller foundation sectors identified 8–10 cases for further analysis via interviews.

In order to gain a broader perspective on the roles and policy salience of foundations, interviews were also conducted with 'experts' in the field in each country, as well as with policymakers, members of umbrella organizations and government organizations.

Finally, in each country the cases selected were contacted for the purposes of conducting semi-structured interviews. Following the completion of this phase of the research, all of the interviewees were invited to attend a Country Workshop to further discuss the findings from the interviews. For each country study, a report was produced.[6]

Conclusion

The use of a common framework for the investigation of the roles and visions of foundations means that although we treat each country study as a single case study, it is also possible to engage in a cross-case comparison of the findings. The exploratory nature of our study demands that we treat each of the roles and visions that make up our theoretical framework as markers by which we can demonstrate where similar results are evident. However, one could argue that our framework made our research conducive to the identification of commonalities across the countries included in the study. Despite the diversity of foundations, in terms of forms, activities, even the legal and fiscal regulations under which they function, the comparison reveals some of the common themes, issues and challenges that emerged throughout the study. Yet, it also permits the exploration and comparison of more nuanced differences in how roles and visions are interpreted across the cases included in the study. Hence, it invited both comparisons of similarities as well as an analysis of the more subtle differences that emerged from the research.

We are aware of the limitations of our approach. In particular, we cannot explore different trends and patterns for specific types of foundations. What is more, overall, given our choice of a case-study approach we are aware of the limits of any generalizations that can be discerned from such a comparative analysis. Our conclusions are posited in the spirit of 'analytic generalization', rather than broad empirical generalizations (Yin 2003). Nonetheless, we believe that our findings place us in an enlightened position to suggest some of the likely implications that follow from the present study for foundations. A comparative perspective is needed in order to understand what the major differences and similarities are across different countries, and what some of the underlying factors are that might account for policy trajectories and common challenges facing foundations.

Notes

1 Some foundations like the 'political foundations' in Germany (Beise 1998) or the 'conservative foundations' in the USA (National Committee for Responsive Philanthropy 2004) are more directly involved in the political process.
2 See for example the proceedings of the Sixth Global Forum on Reinventing Government, issued by the Ministry of Government Administration and Home Affairs, Seoul, Korea in 2005; or the sessions of announcement of the World Economic Forum (www.weforum.org/site/knowledgenavigator.nsf/Content/Philanthropy?open).
3 For an overview of the legal framework and taxation treatments of foundations in European countries, see: European Foundation Centre (2002) *Foundations in the European Union: Profiling Legal and Fiscal Environments*. Brussels, European Foundation Centre.
4 For an overview, see Smith and Borgmann 2001.
5 The following countries were included in the project on which this book is based: Austria, Belgium, Czech Republic, Denmark, Estonia, Finland, France, Germany, Greece/Cyprus, Hungary, Ireland, Italy, Liechtenstein, the Netherlands, Norway, Poland, Portugal, Spain, Sweden, Switzerland, United Kingdom and United States. Although every effort was made to be as comprehensive as possible with the country selection, and to bring all country studies to a conclusion, practical considerations meant that not all countries could be presented in this volume. However, we are confident that the selection is sufficiently broad to provide for a broad comparative examination of the roles and visions of foundations across Europe.
6 These reports form the basis of each of the country chapters in the present volume. The comparative analysis in Chapters 2, 3 and 4 draws upon the findings presented in the country reports *and* the country chapters from the present volume.

References

Anheier, H.K. (2001) Foundations in Europe: A Comparative Perspective. In Schlüter, A., Then, V. and Walkenhorst, P. (eds) *Foundations in Europe*. London: Directory of Social Change.
Anheier, H.K. and Leat, D. (2006) Creative Philanthropy: Towards a New Philanthropy for the 21st Century. London and New York: Routledge.
—— (2002) From Charity to Creativity: Philanthropic Foundations in the 21st Century. United Kingdom: Comedia.
Anheier, H.K and Salamon, L.M. (2006) The Nonprofit Sector in Comparative

Perspective. In Walter W. Powell and Richard Steinberg (eds) *The Nonprofit Sector: A Research Handbook*. 2nd Edition. Yale University Press, in press.

Anheier, H.K. and Seibel, W. (2001) *The Nonprofit Sector in Germany*. Manchester: Manchester University Press.

Anheier, H.K. and Toepler, S. (eds) (1999) *Private Funds and Public Purpose, Philanthropic Foundations in International Perspective*. New York: Plenum Publishers.

Archambault, E. (2001) France. In Schlüter, A., Then, V. and Walkenhorst, P. (eds) *Foundations in Europe: Society Management and Law*. London: Directory of Social Change.

Archambault, E., Boumendil, J. and Tsyboula, S. (1999) Foundations in France. In Anheier, H.K. and Toepler, S. (eds) *Private Funds, Public Purpose: Philanthropic Foundations in International Perspective*. New York: Kluwer Academic/Plenum Publishers.

Bater, P. and Habighorst, O. (2001) Tax Treatment of Foundations and their Donors. In Schluter, A., Then, V. and Walkenhorst, P. (eds) *Foundations in Europe: Society Management and Law*. London: Directory of Social Change.

Beise, M. (1998) Politische Stiftungen. In Bertelsmann Stiftung (ed.) *Handbuch Stiftungen*. Wiesbaden: Gabler.

Boris, E.T. and Wolpert, J. (2001) The Role of Philanthropic Foundations: Lessons from America's Experience with Private Foundations. In Anheier, H.K. and Kendall, J. (eds) *Third Sector Policy at the Crossroads: An International Nonprofit Analysis*. London: Routledge.

Bulmer, M. (1999) The History of Foundations in the United Kingdom and the United States: Philanthropic Foundations in Industrial Society. In Anheier, H.K. and Toepler, S. (eds) *Private Funds and Public Purpose, Philanthropic Foundations in International Perspective*. New York: Plenum Publishers.

Burger, A., Dekker, P. and Veldheer, V. (2001) The Netherlands. In Schlüter, A., Then, V. and Walkenhorst, P. (eds) *Foundations in Europe: Society Management and Law*. London: Directory of Social Change.

Coing, H. (1981) Remarks on the History of Foundations and their Role in the Promotion of Learning. *Minerva*, XIX (2), 271–281.

Esping-Andersen, G. (1990) *The Three Worlds of Welfare Capitalism*. Princeton: Princeton University Press.

European Commission (1997) *Promoting the Role of Voluntary Organisations and Foundations in Europe*. Luxembourg: Office of Official Publications of the European Communities.

European Commission (2005) Giving More for Research in Europe. The role of foundations and the non-profit sector in boosting R&D investment. Report by an Expert Group on measures and actions to promote the role of foundations and the non-profit sector in boosting R&D investment. Brussels: European Commission.

Halfpenny, P. and Reid, M. (2002) Research on Voluntary Sector: an overview. *Policy and Politics*, 30 (4): 533–550.

Hansmann, H. (1987) Economic Theories of Nonprofit Organization. In Powell, W.W. (ed.) *The Nonprofit Sector: A Research Handbook*. New Haven: Yale University Press.

Herzog, R. (1997) Zur Bedeutung von Stiftungen in unserer Zeit. In Bertelsmann Stiftung (ed.) *Operative Stiftungsarbeit*. Gütersloh: Verlag Bertelsmann Stiftung.

Hopt, Klaus J. and Dieter Reuter (eds) (2001) *Stiftungsrecht in Europa*. Cologne: Carl Heymanns Verlag.

Huber, E., Ragin, C. and Stephens, J. (1993) Social Democracy, Christian Democracy, Constitutional Structure and the Welfare State. *American Journal of Sociology*, 99 (3), 711–749.

Karl, B.D. and Katz, S.N. (1981) The American Private Foundation and the Public Sphere, 1890–1930. *Minerva*, XIX (2), 236–269.

Karl, B. and Katz, S. (1987) Foundations and the Ruling Class. *Daedalus*, 116 (1): 1–40.

Lagemann, E.C. (1999) (ed.) *Philanthropic Foundations: New Scholarship, New Possibilities*. Bloomington: Indiana University Press.

Lijphart, A. (1971) Comparative Politics and the Comparative Method. *American Political Science Review*, 65 (3), 682–693.

Lijphart, A. (1975) The Comparable Cases Strategy in Comparative Research. *Comparative Political Studies*, 8 (2), 158–177.

McCarthy, K.D. (1989) The Gospel of Wealth: American Giving in Theory and Practice. In Magat, R. (ed.) *Philanthropic Giving: Studies in Varieties and Goals*. New York and Oxford: Oxford University Press.

National Committee for Responsive Philanthropy (2004) *Axis of Ideology Conservative Foundations and Public Policy*. Washington, D.C.: National Committee for Responsive Philanthropy.

Nielsen, W. (1972) *The Big Foundations*. New York: Columbia University Press.

Prewitt, K. (1999) The Importance of Foundations in an Open Society. In Bertelsmann Foundation (ed.) *The Future of Foundations in an Open Society*. Guetersloh: Bertelsmann Foundation.

—— The Foundation Mission: Purpose, Practice, Public Pressures. In Schlüter, A., Then, V. and Walkenhorst, P. (eds) F*oundations in Europe*. London: Directory of Social Change.

Renz, L. and Lawrence, S. (2005) *Foundation Giving and Growth Estimates*. New York: The Foundation Center.

Roelefs, J. (2003) *Foundations and Public Policy: The Mask of Pluralism*. Albany: State University of New York Press.

Salamon, L. and Anheier, H.K. (1998) Social Origins of Civil Society: Explaining the Nonprofit Sector Cross-Nationally, *Voluntas*, 9 (3): 213–248.

Salamon, L.M. (1992) Foundations as Investment Managers. Part I. The Process. *Nonprofit Management and Leadership*, 3 (2), 117–137.

Salamon, L.M. and Anheier, H.K. (eds) (1997) *Defining the Nonprofit Sector: A Cross National Analysis*. Manchester: Manchester University Press.

Schiller, T. (1969) *Stiftungen im gesellschaftlichen Prozeß*. Baden-Baden: Nomos.

Schlüter, A., Then, V. and Walkenhorst, P. (eds) (2001) F*oundations in Europe*. London: Directory of Social Change.

Smith, J.A. and Borgmann, K. (2001) Foundations in Europe: the Historical Context. In Schlüter, A., Then, V. and Walkenhorst, P. (eds) *Foundations in Europe*. London: Directory of Social Change.

Toepler, S. (1998) Foundations and Their Institutional Context: Cross Evaluating Evidence from Germany and the United States, *Voluntas*, 9 (2): 153–170.

Toepler, S. (1999) Operating in a Grant Making World: Reassessing the Role of Operating Foundations. In Anheier, H.K. and Toepler, S. (eds) *Private Funds and Public Purpose, Philanthropic Foundations in International Perspective*. New York: Plenum Publishers.

Van der Ploegh, T. (1999) A Comparative Legal Analysis of Foundations: Aspects of Supervision and Transparency. In Anheier, H.K. and Toepler, S. (eds) *Private Funds and Public Purpose, Philanthropic Foundations in International Perspective*. New York: Plenum Publishers.

Van Veen, W.J.M. (2001) Supervision of Foundations in Europe: Post-incorporation Restrictions and Requirements. In Schlüter, A., Then, V. and Walkenhorst, P. (eds) F*oundations in Europe*, London: Directory of Social Change.

Weisbrod, B. (1988) *The Nonprofit Economy*. Cambridge, MA: Harvard University Press.

Yin, R.K. (2003) *Case Study Research: Design and Methods* (3rd edn). London: Sage.

2 Comparing foundation roles

Helmut K. Anheier and Siobhan Daly

In this chapter we offer a comparative description and analysis of foundation roles, drawing on material presented in the various country chapters in Part II of this book.[1] In line with our analytic questions and assumptions, we will first discuss roles and visions separately, and prepare the ground for the next chapter which will explore how they relate to each other as well as to the overall importance of foundations cross-nationally.[2]

In the collection and analysis of the data, we sought to assess the extent to which:

- foundation representatives and other stakeholders are aware of and understand the different roles;
- roles are reflected in the visions of foundation representatives and stakeholders;
- roles guide foundations in their activities, particularly in their grant making;
- the aspirations associated with particular roles are feasible in terms of resources, capacity, approach and competence.

These criteria serve as useful markers for the analysis of foundation roles. However, it is necessary to state that some of the roles outlined in the previous chapter do not feature dominantly in the vernacular of the foundation representatives and stakeholders. Annual reports rarely prove an informative source of the types of roles foundations seek to fulfil. In the interviews conducted in countries such as Switzerland and Greece, some respondents struggled to define specific roles for foundations, and in the UK, some representatives rejected being pressed into articulated roles. To the contrary, foundations readily identify with specific areas of activity such as 'education' or 'research'. This sense of identity is reinforced by the tendency of foundations in some countries, such as Denmark, to underline their uniqueness, rather than their position as part of a sector or group of similar entities.

By themselves, these observations are useful findings as they provide preliminary insights into how foundations view themselves and the world around them. Nonetheless, the results of the interviews and workshops conducted in each of the countries included in this study demonstrate that the role statements allowed the interviewees to articulate the nature of the broader relationship between foundations and the state, between foundations and civil society, and among foundations themselves. By using the roles in this way, our research is not simply about imposing preconceived perceptions of roles on interviewees. Rather, it is about providing them and us with the analytic tools necessary to articulate the normative goals of foundations and how these goals can translate into practice. We will now discuss each posited role in detail.

Complementarity

The complementarity role suggests that foundations serve otherwise under supplied groups under conditions of demand heterogeneity and public budget constraints. The idea of being involved in 'doing what the state doesn't do' and 'filling gaps' in areas that have been overlooked resonates clearly with foundations across Europe. The majority of foundation representatives and other relevant stakeholders interviewed readily associate this role with foundations (see Table 2.1).

Indeed, the complementarity role of foundations is similar to the subsidiarity principle, which established a division of labour between public and private institutions. It stipulates that decisions should always be taken at the lowest possible level or closest to where they will have their effect, for example in a local area rather than nationally, and through private rather than public action. In government, subsidiarity has been generally understood as a principle for determining how powers should be divided or shared between different levels of government. In essence, it justifies non-intervention by the state in individual affairs. In social policy, it states that government should only become active if citizens, private organizations and local communities are unable to tackle social problems.

When the language used to describe the role of complementarity is explored in greater detail, the diverse interpretations of what it means to

Table 2.1 Complementarity

Complementarity	Country
Role pronounced/applies	Austria, Belgium, Czech Republic, Finland, France, Germany, Greece, Hungary, Ireland, Italy, Netherlands, Norway, Poland, Portugal, Spain, Sweden, Switzerland, United Kingdom
Somewhat	Denmark, Estonia
Less so, not at all	United States

complement the state become apparent. There are three main ways in which foundations address gaps in state-led services or activities. First, foundations may complement the role of the government by providing financial resources for the provision of certain services. As a foundation representative from Denmark indicated, this may also take the form of foundations engaging in a *bargaining* scenario with the government:

> We do not normally go into bargains. But sometimes an application needs more support than we are prepared to give. If we then give half of the amount asked for, we tell the applicants to find the rest somewhere else – to look for other foundations or to ask the local authorities maybe. This often has 'inspired' the authorities to offer further support, because they do not want the applicants to lose all the good money from us. But we never put this as a condition for a donation.

By contrast, the language used to convey the role of foundations in complementing the state in Portugal emphasizes *partnership* with the government, which involves foundations bringing their experience and competence to public organizations and operating in areas that have been neglected by the government. Similarly, in Belgium, the King Baudouin Foundation is also keen to underline its position as a partner of the government:

> [W]e are a partner of the State but they do not control us. . . . We are in touch with all political cabinets, all public powers. According to the programmes, it is clear we have some close relationships. These are partners, truly partners.

However, particularly when acting as 'partners' of the government, one of the challenges foundations face in complementing the role of the state is finding a balance between doing enough to ensure that apparent gaps are filled and not overstepping their original intentions for getting involved in a particular area. One foundation representative in France, for example, emphasizes the importance of being clear about what foundations intend, or do not intend, to support. For this particular individual's foundation, this involves concentrating on projects and avoiding giving support to more core expenses.

Second, foundations may address the needs of certain sections of society. The notion of foundations 'filling gaps' is often prevalent here. For example, in Sweden the IRIS corporation (owned by the Foundation for the Visually Impaired) assists the Association for the Visually Impaired in order to be able 'to act where society has not been able to live up to its responsibility' (see Chapter 21).

Third, foundations, normally operating or mixed foundations, may be engaged in the provision of services, such as running schools, hospitals, orphanages. Indeed, in the transition to democracy in Central and Eastern Europe and the Baltic States, foundations were earmarked by governments to provide such services. Hence, as one foundation in Estonia suggests, foundations played an important role in the deconstruction of the former Communist state apparatus:

> [T]he state got hold of many functions, which actually had no need of being governed by the state. At the same time it would have been very complicated to privatize them in the form of business enterprises. Take the hospitals. Health care services are not looked upon as business, but as a function guaranteed by the state.... There was one alternative – to turn the hospitals into foundations. It was the result of highly rational considerations.

Across the countries examined, complementarity is about cooperation through partnership, bargaining, and supporting the state via grant-making, catering for specialist needs and 'filling gaps' where the state has failed to act or has not acted in a sufficiently responsible way. Clearly, the majority of interviewees in the countries included in the analysis are aware of this role. However, it is also clear that how this role comes to be articulated into the visions of foundations differs from one country to the next. As we will discuss in Chapter 3, underpinning these subtle, yet diverse interpretations of the complementarity role are issues about the nature of the relationship between foundations and the state and the implications prevalent policy environments have on this relationship.

Substitution

This role expects foundations to take on functions otherwise or previously supplied by the state. In this role, foundations substitute state action, and foundations become providers of public and quasi-public goods. In general, as Table 2.2 illustrates, foundations do not appreciate the idea of being involved in substituting the state.

Table 2.2 Substitution

Substitution	Country
Role pronounced/applies	–
Somewhat	Czech Republic, Estonia, Hungary, Netherlands, Portugal, Spain, Sweden, Switzerland, United Kingdom
Less so, not at all	Austria, Belgium, Denmark, Finland, France, Germany, Greece, Ireland, Italy, Poland, United States

However, the feasibility of avoiding such a role is becoming more and more difficult. Foundations in Western Europe are concerned about the implications which changing roles and responsibilities of governments in the provision of public services have for their autonomy. In the Netherlands, for example, some foundations expressed their fears that being 'forced' to take over certain responsibilities compromises their autonomy (see Chapter 17). Such concerns were particularly resonant in the UK:

> We are legally required not to substitute but it's so grey now and government changes the rules so often, so now it's really hard to find a distinctive role.

> We're trying to figure out how we add value and not substitute for public services.

What is more, in Central and Eastern Europe, whilst foundations were viewed as a 'lifeline' by governments in the early years of the democratic transition (see Pinter 2001: 289), foundations, in the Czech Republic and Hungary, for example, underline the need for greater clarification of the division of responsibilities between foundations and the state. As a representative of the Partners Hungary Foundation stated:

> [W]hen the state does not wish or cannot fulfil some of its own roles, these may be taken over on the basis of contracts by NGOs, but these roles must continue to be state roles by definition, and have to be covered from the central budget.

Throughout Europe, similar challenges are facing foundations, the only difference being the context in which these challenges have to be addressed. Whilst the Western European cases address the task of (re)defining their roles in the context of broader reforms in public services, foundations in Eastern Europe seek to (re)define their role in the democratized regimes. The nature of the relationship between foundations and the state dominates the analysis of the complementarity and substitution roles, and has serious implications for the roles, autonomy and visions of foundations throughout Europe. It will be possible to flesh out these issues in greater detail when examining the visions of foundations in Europe. At present, it suffices to emphasize their pertinence to the examination of the roles of foundations in complementing and substituting the state.

Preservation of traditions and cultures

We propose this role as one where foundations oppose change and preserve past lessons and achievements, likely to be swamped by larger social, cultural and economic forces. However, this role is often taken to be

Table 2.3 Preservation of traditions and cultures

Preservation of traditions and cultures	Country
Role pronounced/applies	Finland, Italy, Switzerland
Somewhat	Austria, Belgium, Denmark, Germany, Greece, Hungary, Netherlands, Norway, Poland, Portugal, Spain, Sweden
Less so, not at all	Czech Republic, Estonia, France, Ireland, United Kingdom, United States

specific to a foundation's objectives and activities, such as where foundations are created to preserve the memory of prominent figures in arts and
culture or to make a private art collection available to the public. Indeed,
in the countries where this role is considered salient, (see Table 2.3), such
as in Finland and Italy, culture and recreation accounts for a high concen-
tration of foundation activity.

The role also evokes negative connotations of foundations being back-
ward-looking and not at all progressive. This is contrary to the urgency
some respondents in countries such as Switzerland and the UK place on
improving internal governance, transparency and accountability among
foundations. For example, in Ireland one foundation representative
declared:

> [I]t's absolute rubbish and completely wrong because to do some
> good foundations have to move away from this.

In this regard, the reluctance of interviewees to associate foundations with
the preservation of traditions and cultures can be juxtaposed usefully
against the prevalent climate of encouraging more strategic and transparent thinking among foundations (Breitneicher and Marble 2001: 508–601;
Burkemann 2004). This, in turn, provides some explanation of why the
interviewees are somewhat reluctant to associate with this role. Foundations want to be seen to be progressive, efficient and forward-thinking
institutions, as is particularly apparent in the analysis of the roles of
innovation and social and policy change below.

Redistribution

This role suggests that the major function of foundations is to engage in
and promote the redistribution of primarily economic resources from
higher to lower income groups. The role is rooted in the wishes of early
philanthropists, particularly in the nineteenth century, to give something
back to society, which normally involved a focus on addressing symptoms
of problems based on traditional notions of charity (see Anheier and Leat

2002). There is no denying the historical significance of this role for foundations in Europe, something that is noted by stakeholders in Switzerland and Denmark, for example. Hence, foundations such as the Egmont Foundation in Denmark and the Charitable Association of Copenhagen include the alleviation of the poor among their purposes. In the former case of Switzerland, the relevance of this role today is thought to be specific to foundations engaged in development aid on an international scale; for example, it was associated with the Limmat Foundation's operations in Latin America.

However, in terms of the awareness of this role amongst our interviewees (see Table 2.4), we find that the idea of the role of redistribution giving legitimacy to foundations is not widely accepted, in particular in the United States (see Chapter 23). Even in countries where a majority of stakeholders argue that this role is pronounced, such as in Greece, stakeholders associate this role with ensuring equal entitlement for all, rather than transferring wealth from the rich to the poor.

The preference of some foundations to treat redistribution as a de facto feature of foundation giving, rather than as a specific role, is explored in some of the interviews, notably in the Czech Republic and Sweden. As a representative of a Swedish foundation argues:

> This [redistribution] might not be the primary purpose in establishing a foundation; that the intention of the donor is to redistribute his or her wealth. I do not believe so. . . .
>
> If a very rich person makes a donation, a redistribution of wealth is in the nature of the transaction itself. And it is this redistribution that constitutes the basis for tax-exemption for foundations. This is the reason why they are tax-exempt; it is a way of paying your taxes. The law requires some kind of redistribution to grant the foundation tax-exemption.

Table 2.4 Redistribution

Redistribution	Country
Role pronounced/applies	Greece, Spain
Somewhat	Czech Republic, Estonia, Belgium, Poland, Sweden
Less so, not at all	Austria, Denmark, Finland, France, Germany, Hungary, Ireland, Italy, Netherlands, Norway, Poland, Portugal, Switzerland, United Kingdom, United States

This interviewee lends some credence to the claim that foundations seek to justify the tax exemptions they receive through redistribution – here by suggesting that the act of giving is redistributive in itself. As discussed in Chapter 1, there are problems with this line of argument, of course, such as the fact that it is not always evident that foundations' activity is really redistributive, i.e. they may support the better off as well as the less well off sections of society. Moreover, it is unclear whether funding by foundations is any more redistributive than if foundations had been taxed in the first instance (Prewitt 1999: 21).

The feasibility of foundations in European countries being capable of fulfilling a redistributive role is also fundamental to explaining why respondents are, overall, reluctant to identify with this role. Interviewees in countries with smaller foundation sectors, such as Austria and Hungary, questioned the feasibility of this role in the context of the limited financial resources of small and medium-sized foundations. Moreover, the prevalence of 'fundraising foundations' (e.g. in Portugal and Ireland) places further emphasis on the role of foundations in mobilizing resources, rather than redistributing them.

Overall, our research suggests that redistribution is a feature of foundation giving, although it is not a principal characteristic across European countries. From the perspective of the diversity and complexity of the European foundation landscape, redistribution is best treated as a (potential) feature of foundation giving, but not as a prevalent guiding role.

Social and policy change

This role involves foundations in promoting structural change and a more just society, fostering recognition of new needs, and the empowerment of the socially excluded. Whilst redistribution is associated with traditional notions of charity, the social and policy change role is linked with philanthropy, i.e. addressing the root causes of problems (Prewitt 1999: 23). The (potential) role of European foundations in social and policy change has not (as yet) proved as controversial as in the United States (see Chapter 1), although more recognition is being given to how some foundations do, or can, influence the policy process (for example, on the UK, see Davies 2004; Burkemann 2004). What is more, in the early 1990s foundations in Eastern Europe who were seeking to promote social change were accused of 'social manipulation', with foreign-funded foundations branded as 'agents of the "imperial West"' (Pinter 2001: 284).

In our research, as Table 2.5 illustrates, we found that this is a role that is specific to some (albeit few) foundations' objectives.

In Poland, for instance, the Stefan Batory Foundation and the Helsinki Foundation are engaged in a joint programme 'Against Corruption', which has launched various initiatives such as the drafting of anti-corruption legislative proposals, information and education campaigns and legal aid for people who have encountered corrupt practices. In Denmark, whilst the

Table 2.5 Social and policy change

Social and policy change	Country
Role pronounced/applies	Denmark, Hungary, Poland, United States
Somewhat	Belgium, Czech Republic, Estonia, Germany, Greece, Ireland, Netherlands, Portugal, Spain, Switzerland, United Kingdom
Less so, not at all	Austria, Finland, France, Italy, Norway, Sweden

Plum Foundation includes the resolution of conflicts in its statutes, the Health Foundation seeks to affect social change in improving individuals' health and quality of life. However, in countries such as Sweden and Italy, where this role is less pronounced, making an impact on social and policy change is linked more with associations than foundations. In France, foundations appear to place more emphasis on their role in listening to the types of changes people would like to be made, rather than actively engaging in this role. However, some foundations, notably the Fondation Léopold Mayer, seek to bring about deep-seated changes in society.

The majority of foundations in each of the participating countries identified the *potential* for foundations to pursue this role, but many also questioned just how well placed foundations are to fulfil such a role – as well as the types of difficulties it creates for foundations. This was particularly the case among the British foundations interviewed:

We want to move towards influencing policy but the Board is still struggling with equating policy with politics. They say it will influence by example rather than lobbying but we need to engage in a position to influence politics.

Why would anyone listen to us? We aren't service providers so we don't have that sort of knowledge and the knowledge we do have we don't really organize or use properly. What do we really have to say?

In Hungary, the interviewees strongly supported this role for foundations, but questioned the overall likely impact foundations can have in this area. Some interviewees argue that even powerful organizations such as the Soros Foundation, for example, did not receive significant recognition of their role until the middle of the 1990s when political actors began to recognize the importance of civil society actors:

Foundations have made a great effort in the past ten years to achieve social and policy change. However, their overall impact is not significant.

On the other hand, some respondents from Portugal believe that foundations are ideally positioned to fulfil this role by virtue of their independence:

> What primarily distinguishes a foundation from government and business is its high degree of freedom to take decisions and its particular timetable to implement the corresponding actions and programs. As independent institutions, foundations do not depend on any political process, or on any past or future constituencies, on the market or publicity/propaganda.[3]

The notion of social change is itself contentious as it embraces various ideas ranging from changing how we think about, and address social issues, to the promotion of radical structural change (Anheier and Leat 2002). Although foundations identify with addressing what are essentially social issues in relation to other roles such as complementarity and innovation, with one exception of a foundation interviewed in Belgium, they appear unaware of how to maximize their potential to fulfil a social change role via the functions they already serve. The key issue of how well-placed foundations are to affect social and policy change (the latter in particular) is not always linked to the need for foundations to be more strategic in their operations. As Breitneicher and Marble (2001: 581) argue, a foundation's operations are made strategic by its links to and understanding of the public policies that form, influence and may even decide the outcomes and effect of a foundation's grant-making. The independence of the foundation form may have little or no bearing on the ability of foundations to affect social and policy change without the strategic understanding of the environment in which foundations operate. This may, in part, explain why this role is viewed as a potential, rather than a wholly realizable goal for many foundations.

Promotion of pluralism

As indicated in Chapter 1, the promotion of pluralism can take a variety of forms. This role was presented as one where foundations are engaged in promoting experimentation and diversity in general; protecting dissenters and civil society liberties against the state; challenging others on social, economic, cultural and environmental issues. In some cases, the very presence of foundations is also viewed as a sign of pluralism itself (see Chapter 23).

In federal countries such as Germany and Switzerland, this role is associated with foundations engaged in 'bridge-building' activities between communities and areas (see Table 2.6). For some foundations, for example in Austria, Denmark and the Netherlands where foundations attach particular salience to this role, the promotion of experimentation and diversity is linked with the freedom and autonomy of foundations. For instance, one Danish interviewee stated:

Probably we have a significant role because we freely choose what we want to support. We have as such no rules and no regulations apart from our statutes. and we can intervene in a quick and efficient way when it is needed, and in areas where our state cannot support. This is why our role might seem more important than our contribution in numbers might actually justify.

Differences in the importance attached to this role amongst foundations in the Czech Republic and Hungary reflect the gap between the ideal roles envisaged largely by foreign-funded foundations, on the one hand, and the issues of sustainability and survival that preoccupy other foundations, on the other.

In the Czech Republic, for instance, this role is awarded particular importance by the larger foundations, funded by foreign resources:

The importance of foundations lies in principle in pluralism and this presents a counterbalance to the one-sided bias in the support provided by the state. . . . A maximum plurality of democratic and stable institutions is always crucial.

Smaller foundations and particularly those of Czech origin attach less salience to this role. The feasibility of foundations in Hungary, particularly those dependent on state funding, fulfilling a role in the promotion of pluralism is thought to be problematic:

Many of the Hungarian foundations are dependent on the state budget, since they receive very limited private money. This somewhat questions [their] independence and [their role in the promotion of] pluralism.

As also underlined by interviewees in France and Portugal, the diversity of the foundation landscape across Europe means that we must recognize that foundations may neither be willing nor have the capacity to fund the

Table 2.6 Promotion of pluralism

Promotion of pluralism	Country
Role pronounced/applies	Austria, Denmark, Estonia, Netherlands, Poland
Somewhat	Czech Republic, Finland, Germany, Greece, Hungary, Italy, Portugal, Spain, Switzerland, United States
Less so/not at all	Belgium, Ireland, France, Norway, Sweden, United Kingdom

'unusual or the unexpected', nor the 'diversity and differentiation' (Prewitt 1999: 28–29) we may associate with the promotion of pluralism.

Innovation

This role suggests that promoting innovation in social perceptions, values, relationships and ways of doing things has long been a role ascribed to foundations. The majority of foundations in a majority of countries included in the study identify with the innovation role (see Table 2.7). As discussed in Chapter 1, this is consistent with the common expectation that foundations are ideally placed to facilitate innovation, take potentially controversial risks and act as philanthropic venture capital (Anheier and Toepler 1999: 15).

By itself, however, the broad consensus that innovation is a salient role for foundations does not tell us very much. In countries where this role is pronounced, interviewees question the meaning of innovation and what it means to be innovative. Moreover, reflecting the different interpretations of the term innovation, different types of examples of innovative activities emerge across the countries included in the study. Using the four criteria that Kanter (1983) identified as common to successful innovation, we can explore the foundation representatives' interpretations of this role. These criteria include:

1   There exists a degree of *uncertainty* in relation to both the process and outcome.
2   Innovations are *knowledge-intensive* in that the principal actors have knowledge of the definition of the situation, the process and likely outcomes.
3   Innovations tend to be *controversial* as they may deviate from established interests.
4   Innovations tend to *reach across established boundaries* in organizations, fields and sectors.

Table 2.7 Innovation

Innovation	*Country*
Role pronounced/applies	Belgium, Czech Republic, Denmark, Estonia, Finland, France, Germany, Ireland, Italy, Netherlands, Poland, Portugal, Spain, Sweden, Switzerland, United Kingdom, United States
Somewhat	Austria, Greece, Hungary
Less so, not at all	–

Uncertainty

Our research found that the ability of foundations to take risks (economic or otherwise) is associated with their ability to support projects in the long term. Supporting new activities, particularly in the area of research and development, features amongst the examples of foundations acting innovatively. For instance, in Switzerland the Technopark Foundation plays a role in the Technopark Zurich, which provides support for market-oriented entrepreneurial activities. Similarly, for the Carlsberg Foundation in Denmark, supporting new ideas is also key to foundations encouraging innovation:

> I am convinced that researchers working with basic research without a conception of a specific solution beforehand are the ones that start new thinking – if they are creative that is! By supporting them we will do innovation a great favour. . . .

Although the foundation representatives interviewed in Sweden struggled overall to give substantive examples of foundations acting innovatively, the ability of foundations to be more flexible and steadfast in their commitments than the public sector authorities in particular was underlined.

Knowledge intensive

Reflecting this latter viewpoint, some stakeholders associated the innovative role with foundations being capable of doing a better job than the government in fulfilling roles such as complementarity and substitution. Indeed, in Greece, interviewees did not view innovation as a separate role performed by foundations, but rather as a special characteristic associated with foundations that distinguishes them from the state. Interpretations of this role among foundation representatives in the Czech Republic underlined how the state lacks the ability and interest to be innovative. This in turn creates an opening for foundations:

> The Czech civil society suffers from imitating what the state is doing, the way the state provides care. Foundations are able to come up with new issues, give them support and sponsor pilot projects, unprofitable care, programmes that are linked to systemic changes.

The application of existing ideas/expertise in new fields of practice (which could be termed knowledge intensive innovations) is often considered more feasible for foundations than supporting completely new ideas, (typical of uncertain innovations) (see Chapter 17).

In Belgium, Greece, France and Sweden for example, the innovation role appears intertwined with the role of foundations in complementing the state. For those Belgian foundations that have developed close working relationships with the government, innovation involves the identification of new social needs, finding new ways to address these needs and making this information available to the government, with the intention that they will act upon it:

> One of the roles of the foundations is to find a niche that is not covered by the State, develop this niche and, at a certain point in time, tell the authorities that they can adopt this approach. We perform the work because we think it is an important niche, then we try to fit it into the state system.

Crossing boundaries

Ideas about innovations are also linked to practices as well as activities. In this regard, crossing established boundaries in organizations, fields and sectors is often viewed as key to foundations acting in an innovative way. In the UK, for instance, this is linked to the need for foundations to be more accessible and progressive in their outlook:

> Foundations need to be more outward looking – not so internally focused. Awareness among the public and government is very, very low. We're just not maximizing our impact. We could be acting in a complementary fashion to think tanks and working with other foundations.

Of the four major examples of foundations engaged in innovative activities in Germany (Quandt, Freudenberg, Bertelsmann and Bosch), these cases share two characteristics in common: their openness to horizontal networking and collaboration with other civil society actors and the emphasis they place on reviewing their goals and activities at regular intervals.

Innovation as controversial

The extent to which acting innovatively may also be controversial does not feature highly on the stakeholders' agenda. Rather, stakeholders are more concerned with how feasible fulfilling an innovation role is for the bulk of European foundations. Our interviews, in Italy and Austria for example, revealed that foundations are aware that they are often not up to the task of acting in an innovative way. The lack of professionalization and transparency as well as sometimes the constraints posed by the founding deeds are also identified as obstacles to foundations acting innovatively. What holds foundations back from being innovative is as salient an issue of how innovative they are, as one respondent in the Dutch research points out:

All foundations feel that they are innovative, active, well known and playing a major role in society. From the outside the image is quite different: 95 per cent of the board members are male, over 55 years old, part of the 'old boys' network, not granting any projects that might endanger the foundation. They are complaining that they do not receive any interesting project proposals or grants, but they do not want to go public because they are afraid to receive too many grant requests. How can they expect them if nobody knows of their existence?

In all, the willingness of foundations to take risks is associated with funding research or activities that are new. It is also linked with actions that are simply different to what the state does, or rather to how public sector institutions choose to carry out certain responsibilities. Beyond these factors, innovation for foundations also implies changes to prevalent practices. Although awareness of how foundations can be innovative is pronounced amongst the majority of cases included in the study, there are serious questions about the feasibility of this role for European foundations. These are clearly linked to broader issues about transparency, economic resources, the need for greater professionalization and the desire to be loyal to the wishes of the founder, on the one hand, versus the wish to alter the vision of a foundation as circumstances dictate.

Conclusion

The analysis of the roles of foundations across Europe reveals on the whole that foundations wish to be seen as innovative entities, independent though complementary to the state, with the potential to affect social and policy change. The idea of foundations being redistributors of wealth does not hold water among the stakeholders consulted. Similarly, the notion of foundations as preservers of traditions and cultures is largely associated with the specific activities of certain foundations in the area of arts and culture – given that this role evokes connotations of ineffectiveness and a lack of progressiveness in the world of foundations. The promotion of pluralism functions less as a guide to foundation practices as much as it is associated with the very presence of foundations as symbolic of the democratic nature of European societies and the opportunities this affords for foundations (see Table 2.8)

Foundations face complex challenges that require more strategic reflection and action. The diverse notions of cooperation through partnership, bargaining and various means of supporting the state underline the need for greater clarification of the relationship between foundations and governments. The salience of this issue is reinforced by the juxtaposition of the broad reluctance of foundations to be engaged in a substitutive role, on the one hand, versus the impression that changes in

Table 2.8 Roles – a summary

Role	Awareness	Roles reflected in visions	Roles guide foundation	Feasibility
Complementarity	High	Yes: but diverse interpretations of what this role involves	Yes: but is role of government influencing role(s) too?	Medium: a particular role for grant-making foundations in sustaining this role?
Substitution	Medium	Reluctantly	No	Medium: support among some experts Encourages debate about resources and responsibilities among foundations.
Preservation of traditions and cultures	Medium	Specific to some foundations as main activity in arts and culture	Specific to some foundations where they are engaged in this role as main activity	Foundation-specific
Redistribution	Low	Some historical significance	No: range of factors motivate donors	Low
Social and policy change	Medium	Some doubts about ability of foundations to sustain this role and likelihood of success	Potentially: but need to address challenges	Medium
Promotion of pluralism	Medium	Specific to some contexts (e.g. federalism in Germany and Switzerland)	Not a guide: viewed more as a feature of foundations' existence in democratic societies	Medium
Innovation	High	Taking risks Using knowledge to be more efficient/effective than government Reaching across boundaries	Yes: but diverse interpretations of innovativeness	Medium: need to maximize potential

the policy environment via government initiatives and declining public spending are forcing foundations to consider this role more seriously, on the other. The analysis of the roles of social and policy change and innovation raise the important question of how foundations can maximize their potential. Despite the extensive, though diverse nature of cooperation between foundations and the state that the complementarity role suggests, most foundations do not appear to link the roles they currently fulfil with the ability to affect social and policy change. This is all the more surprising given that foundations tend to see themselves as more innovative than the government in the performance of certain activities. Overall, then, the examination of the roles of foundations emphasizes the merits of reflection amongst foundations. The need for self-reflection is also becoming more urgent in the face of changing government policies and initiatives. In this regard, it is clear that the feasibility of foundations' aspirations cannot be divorced from the policy environment in which they function. Thus, we turn to the analysis of the visions of foundations in the next chapter.

Notes

1 The country chapters are abridged versions of country reports which were produced for each study as part of the broader project from which this book draws. We have drawn upon material from these reports *and* the chapters for the purposes of the comparative analysis.
2 The analysis in this chapter will focus on European countries primarily, and will have less to say about how the United States fits in, other than mentioning its positioning for the various roles and visions specifically. The reason for this is that the chapter by Toepler is devoted to a USA–European comparison, which frees the present chapter to focus on Europe.
3 The quotation here is from the report on the Roles and Visions of Foundations in Portugal produced by Nuno Themudo.

References

Anheier, H.K. and Leat, D. (2002) *From Charity to Creativity: Philanthropic Foundations in the 21st Century.* United Kingdom: Comedia.
Anheier, H.K. and Toepler, S. (1999) Philanthropic Foundations: An International Perspective. In Anheier, H.K. and Toepler, S. (eds) *Private Funds and Public Purpose, Philanthropic Foundations in International Perspective.* New York: Plenum Publishers.
Breitneicher, J.C. and Marble, M.G. (2001) Strategic Programme Management. In Schlüter, A., Then, V. and Walkenhorst, P. (eds) *Foundations in Europe.* London: Directory of Social Change.
Burkemann, S. (2004) Influencing Public Policy. *Alliance Extra,* June.
Davies, J.S. (2004) The Foundation as a Political Actor: The Case of the Joseph Rowntree Charitable Trust. *Political Quarterly,* 75 (3), pp. 275–284.
Kanter, R.M. (1983) *The Change Masters.* New York: Simon and Schuster.
Pinter, F. (2001) The Role of Foundations in the Transformation Process in

Central and Eastern Europe. In Schlüter, A., Then, V. and Walkenhorst, P. (eds) *Foundations in Europe*, London: Directory of Social Change.

Prewitt, K. (1999) The Importance of Foundations in an Open Society. In Bertels-mann Foundation (ed.) *The Future of Foundations in an Open Society*. Guetersloh: Bertelsmann Foundation.

3   Comparing foundation visions

Helmut K. Anheier and Siobhan Daly

As discussed in Chapter 1, the visions of foundations refer to the broader objectives, purpose and context in which foundation roles are cast. Visions encompass both 'models' based on political and cultural preferences and projection towards what is seen as desirable in terms of *Realpolitik*. This, in turn, reflects what foundations can do, rather than what they ideally should do. The analysis of the visions of foundations is complementary to the examination of the roles of foundations, as here we seek to probe deeper into the normative basis of the roles cast and the policy implications they entail.

Similar to the analysis of the roles of foundations, we sought to determine whether foundation representatives and stakeholders:

- are aware of the particular scenarios represented by each vision;
- understand the differences between the different visions or models;
- seek to articulate these visions and to put them into practice;
- actually create appropriate roles for foundations around these visions.

What is more, similar to the investigation of the roles of foundations, statements which correspond to the description of each of the models or visions were put to interviewees. However, in some countries, foundation representatives found it particularly difficult to articulate the visions of foundations. Various reasons for this are put forward across the countries examined. In the case of Ireland, Donoghue suggests that the number of grant-making foundations is so small that it is impossible to identify a definitive model. What is more, in the case of the UK, Leat (see Chapter 7) identifies several reasons why foundations have difficulty in articulating visions: notably a dominant tradition of 'doing not talking' among British foundations and a tendency not to question what foundations do, backed up by a prevalent notion that 'foundations do not necessarily see it as their role to have roles and visions'. In Finland, the conservative nature of foundations is suggested by one interviewee as a reason why foundations do not emphasize their visions.

This poses a challenge for our analysis of the visions of foundations in

Europe. In particular, we face the dilemma of deciding whether it is possible to articulate models that reflect the position of all, or at least a majority of foundations in each individual country. For instance, this dilemma presented itself in the research conducted in Sweden. In discussing the visions of foundations, some interviewees pinpointed visions of society that appear to be evident in particular foundations. However, Wijkström (see Chapter 21) also argues that:

> It is important to acknowledge the possibility that larger visions might be associated with a foundation both on an implicit as well as a more explicit level.

On a more practical level, the absence of an awareness of visions, combined sometimes with an unwillingness to see their relevance, means that it has not always been possible to determine where particular models are either pronounced, somewhat evident or not evident at all. Although in most countries, the interviewees were willing to discuss the differences between the different models, in other countries such as Norway, Greece and Sweden, the discussion was mainly framed in the language of the social democratic and liberal models. None of the other models was deemed to be relevant.

However, despite the initial lack of awareness amongst some respondents of some or all of the models we use to articulate particular visions of society, we find that the probing of these models with interviewees allows us in most cases to construct a picture of how foundations interact with other actors, such as policy-makers. In so doing, we are also able to examine the opportunities and constraints foundations encounter in seeking to carry out activities and, indeed, to fulfil certain roles.

We accept that the visions of a foundation may be more implicit than explicit, upon its founding and in its operation. However, with the material available to us, we seek to explore the roles and positions of foundations as part of a larger vision of society. In all, the analysis of the visions of foundations in this way allows us to explore the strengths and weaknesses of how foundations see their role in society, as well as allowing us to explore the policy implications of these roles.

Social democratic model

In the social democratic model, foundations exist in a highly developed welfare state. As part of a well coordinated relationship with the state, operating foundations either complement or supplement state activities. The popularity of the role of foundations in complementing the state is reflected in how most interviewees felt that the social democratic model reflected their position vis-à-vis the state (see Table 3.1).

However, the fact that welfare states across Europe, (including central

Table 3.1 Social democratic vision

Social democratic vision	Country
Vision pronounced/applies	Belgium, Czech Republic, Finland, Greece, Hungary, Italy, Netherlands, Poland, Portugal, Spain, Switzerland
Somewhat	Ireland, Norway, Sweden, UK, United States
Less so, not at all	Denmark, Estonia, Austria

and eastern Europe, albeit for different reasons; see Wagener 2002), have been in a state of transition has not gone unnoticed by foundations. Nonetheless, we approach this issue with some caution. First, the concerns expressed by the interviewees about broader changes to welfare states must not be overstated, as the extent to which foundations are aware of such changes varies significantly, both within countries and from country to country. In Sweden, for instance, although some of the foundation representatives (to varying degrees) displayed an awareness and understanding of these issues, it is less clear just how prepared foundations are for prospective changes and their potential consequences for the roles foundations play.

Second, whilst it is not our intention to suggest that foundations form an overwhelmingly significant part of the agenda of governments in rolling back welfare states, our research does draw attention to the fact that foundations have featured as part of this scenario and that it is perceived to have implications for European foundations. First, governments have looked favourably on the form of the foundation as a useful tool for fulfilling certain goals. Second, the role(s) of foundations in complementing and substituting governments has increased in importance, raising concerns among foundations about maintaining their autonomy, on the one hand, and meeting pragmatic needs regarding funding, on the other.

In Norway, for instance, the traditional omnipotence of the Norwegian welfare state is undergoing a state of transition which entails a recognition of the need to further develop civic engagement and a culture of giving to fulfil needs where the state may withdraw (see Chapter 18). The Cultiva foundation is an example of how previously public capital takes the form of a foundation, to support grant-giving in the area of culture in the community. Savings banks were converted into foundations with the surplus earned from the market being distributed as grants for public purposes. Similar action has also been taken by government in Italy.

In the United Kingdom study, however, the notion of foundations being used as a tool by governments evokes negative connotations about the 'colonization' of foundations by the government where the latter 'is interested in anyone who has money to allocate to chosen purposes, anyone who can be persuaded to do useful things' (see Chapter 7). As discussed in relation to the substitution role in the previous chapter, these types of concerns are rooted in the reluctance of foundations to act in place of the state, rather than as complementary to it.

However, in this environment, pragmatic concerns about sustaining a foundation's activities may often outweigh concerns about cultivating roles and the autonomy of a foundation being compromised, as one interviewee from a community foundation in the UK stated:

> There are problems in taking government money, but they are seen as practical ones about compliance processes and volume and about the costs of grant making – avoiding sweat shop grant making rather – rather than matters of principle.

This is also a point that resonates among the foundations interviewed from central and eastern Europe. The financing of foundation activities is a very influential factor in the way foundations articulate the nature of their relationship with governments. In Hungary, for instance, some foundation representatives appear to attach more importance to obtaining funding from the government, than they do to maintaining their independence. Similarly, in Poland, the idea of foundations working in close cooperation with the government was supported mainly by foundations in receipt of state funding, such as the Nobody's Children Foundation. Yet, political actors are divided as to whether foundations should be funded by the state, although they remain supportive of foundations complementing the state. The following respondent represents the viewpoint of the Alliance of Democratic Left political party:

> [F]oundations should support public funds and be complementary to them. They should be really non-governmental not neo-governmental.

The comparative analysis of the social democratic model captures real and present concerns amongst foundations. These can be viewed in the broader context of changes in welfare states that have taken place over the past decade (for example, see Cochrane *et al.* 2001; Ascoli and Ranci 2002). However, the themes and debates raised here enjoy different levels of prominence across European countries, depending on factors such as the size and scale of the non-profit sector, the traditional roles assumed by foundations and the size and scale of government initiatives and policies towards both the reform of public services, and foundations.

State-controlled model

In the state-controlled model, foundations are ultimately subservient to the state. Restrictive laws, complicated administrative procedures and

Table 3.2 State-controlled vision

State-controlled model	Country
Vision pronounced/applies	–
Somewhat	Austria, Czech Republic, Spain, United States
Less so, not at all	Belgium, Denmark, Finland, Greece, Hungary, Ireland, Italy, Netherlands, Poland, Switzerland, United Kingdom

extensive oversight establish a relatively tight control regime for foundations. This model evokes contrasting viewpoints on how much control can and should be exerted over foundations (Table 3.2).

The countries where this vision is *somewhat* apparent in Table 3.2 do not reflect support for the subservience of foundations to the state, as much as foundation representatives in these countries underline prominent issues concerning the state supervision of foundations. Although 63 per cent of interviewees in Spain disagreed with this model, many also thought that it reflected the situation in Spain given the legal restrictions and complex bureaucratic procedures foundations have to contend with. Similar concerns were expressed by foundation representatives in the Czech Republic who felt that the present system of regulation was excessively bureaucratic and far exceeds the legitimate interest of the state.

The Netherlands and Denmark represent contrasting situations where foundations enjoy (and see no reason to 'meddle' with) the absence of overtly strict controls on foundations. Other countries raise fundamental questions about just how important is the legal and regulatory framework in which foundations operate. Given that the provision of legal and fiscal regulations are but two factors that contribute to the development of a culture of philanthropy in a country, the case of Ireland demonstrates one way in which state regulation may prove important. The legal and regulatory environment has not been conducive in the way of facilitation and incentives for the formation of foundations (see Chapter 15), though in recent years there have been moves towards improving this situation.[1]

The alteration and/or creation of laws governing foundations is topical in many countries across Europe, including Poland, Portugal, Italy, Switzerland and the United Kingdom. In recent years, particularly following the events of 11 September 2001, the policy salience of the regulation of the environment in which foundations function has increased. In the United States the Patriot Act encompasses 'Voluntary Best Practices' for US-based charities to prevent their abuse for the purposes of financing terrorism. Regarding the prevention of the abuse of non-profit organizations for financing terrorism, although European countries and the

European Union have not followed the United States with such high-profile proposals, some efforts are being made to address this issue (Daly and Anheier 2005). Overall, despite the reluctance of the foundation representatives interviewed to associate with this role, there is a case to be made for some form of state 'control' over foundations that does not pose a threat to their autonomy.

Corporatist model

In the corporatist model, foundations are by and large in some form of subsidiarity relationship with the state. Operating foundations are part of the social welfare or educational system and many combine grant-making and operative dimensions.

The notion of foundations operating in some form of subsidiarity relationship with the state tends to be associated with countries that previously have been associated with the corporatist model, notably Germany, Netherlands, Austria and Switzerland (see Anheier 2001 and Chapter 1; see also Table 3.3).[2]

However, as also discussed in Chapter 1 (see Table 1.2), between each country, and indeed within each country, relations between foundations and the state take varied forms and foundations enjoy different levels of independence, as well as dependence on the state. The nature of relations between foundations and the state in these countries does not only reflect a corporatist vision. In Switzerland, for example, the roles foundations fulfil are articulated around the corporatist, social democratic, liberal and business models. Similarly in Germany where over 50 per cent of foundations are active in the social sector, many foundations tend to see themselves as part of the social, health and education sectors with close connections to the public sector. However, there is also a 'liberal subsector' of foundations which stresses its independence from the state.

Where foundations have, as the corporatist vision suggests, been part of the social welfare or education system, they have experienced changes in the nature of their relations with the state. In the Swiss case, for example, changes in public administration, particularly the popularity of new public

Table 3.3 Corporatist vision

Corporatist vision	Country
Vision pronounced/applies	Austria, Germany, Netherlands, Spain, Switzerland
Somewhat	Belgium, Czech Republic, Estonia, Greece, Hungary, Italy, Poland, Portugal
Less so, not at all	Finland, Ireland, United States

management, means that operating foundations now find themselves in a situation where contracts for the provision of services such as in health and social care are negotiated with public authorities. These contracts not only include agreements on the nature of the goods/services to be provided, but also stipulate certain quality criteria and standards that the foundation must adhere to.

Similarly, in Germany the traditional embeddedness of foundations, along with other non-profit organizations involved in the fields of social services and health care, in the social corporatist system is also facing specific challenges. Foundations have tended to fulfil complementarity roles, but perceptions of changing definitions of what constitutes the responsibilities of the state combined with the desire to cut public expenditure mean that many foundations now identify with fulfilling a substitutive role. The way in which some foundations have reacted to these changes is characterized by a move towards the liberal model. This has involved a rediscovery and revitalization of the original goals and ideals of the foundation founder, often with the aim of modernizing the foundations form and goals and maximizing opportunities for fundraising from other sources.

By contrast, the use of foundations as tools for the outsourcing of service delivery has not been awarded much precedence in the Austrian context. Indeed, there are notable examples of foundations who continue to enjoy close cooperative relationships with the state, such as the Caritas Socialis Private Foundation (CS). Overall, however, this finding says more about the less significant role played by foundations in Austria compared to Germany, than it does about the corporatist model. As will be seen, foundations in Austria identify with the peripheral model.

Throughout the countries of central and eastern Europe, there are mixed responses to the corporatist model as a potential scenario for foundations. On the one hand, foundations and policy-makers in Hungary, for example, underline their intention to lobby for a system of subsidiarity, while also campaigning for the independence of the non-profit sector as a whole. On the other hand, the potential negative consequences of such a model are reported:

> The corporatist model would have a negative effect on the sector as after a while foundations would act as business entities, following lobby interests. There is obviously a need for state presence, but the state should be a partner to the operation of NGOs.

On the one hand, we find countries where the model is heading towards being dismantled. On the other hand, there are countries where it is being given further consideration, in some shape or form. In the other countries, the nature of ties between foundations and the government tends to take a variety of forms, with the majority of foundation representatives in Greece, for example, coming to a consensus that the Greek case falls between the social democratic and the corporatist models.

The same countries as before remain associated with the corporatist model. However, it is also clear that traditional subsidiary relationships between foundations and the state are changing, particularly in Germany and Switzerland, for example. As a result of changes to the existing policy environment, foundations will have to rethink relationships with the state and the funding of foundations' activities is pushed to the top of the agenda. These factors are not a consequence of the roles foundations undertake. Rather, they are indicative of how changes in the surrounding context in which they operate have a direct and indirect impact on what foundations do. It is clear that being aware of the environment in which foundation goals and roles are cast is salient to achieving objectives and fulfilling certain roles.

Liberal model

In the liberal model, foundations form a largely parallel system next to government, frequently seeing themselves as alternatives to the mainstream and safeguards of non-majoritarian preferences. As Table 3.4 shows, the liberal vision is very popular amongst foundations.

The liberal vision evokes the idea that foundations should, in the words of one Spanish foundation representative, seek to 'support civil society before the public authorities by acting as a counterweight to the public sector'. This sentiment was also echoed in the Italian case study. In this sense, the liberal vision tends to cluster in two key dimensions; first, around the role foundations play in complementing the state and, second, around the roles of foundations as innovators, agents of social and policy change and the promotion of pluralism.

First, some foundations' interpretation of the liberal model is rooted in the belief that foundations may support unpopular and possibly controversial issues and, in their support for issues outside of the mainstream

Table 3.4 Liberal vision

Liberal vision	Country
Vision pronounced, applies	Belgium, Czech Republic, Denmark, Estonia, Finland, France, Germany, Greece, Ireland, Italy, Ireland, Netherlands, Norway, Poland, Portugal, Spain, Switzerland, United States
Somewhat	Austria, Hungary, Norway, Sweden, United Kingdom
Less so, not at all	–

may develop useful expertise in certain areas ranging from working with ethnic minorities, to providing pastoral care for prisoners, to the protection of animals.

The perceived demise of the social-democratic model is also leading, according to some interviewees in Sweden, to the prominence of a scenario which corresponds with the liberal vision. In this sense, the idea of foundations as an 'alternative to the mainstream' is also envisaged in how foundations are assuming more complementary *and* substitutive roles. As is evident from the analysis of the social democratic and corporatist models in particular, the nature of relations between foundations and the state, as well as the positioning of foundations vis-à-vis the state is becoming all the more complex. Our research indicates that the salience of the role of foundations as alternatives to the mainstream is increasing, as the interpretations of what constitutes the roles and responsibilities of the 'mainstream' are in a state of flux.

Second, the functioning of foundations in the context of a liberal vision is also associated with the roles of innovation, social and policy change and the promotion of pluralism. The association of this vision with the role of innovation has particular resonance in the Italian context whereby foundations are seen as innovators (e.g. in the social field) with the ability to experiment with new models that can then be transferred to the public sector and within the non-profit sector. Similarly, in Germany, for instance, the goals of the 'liberal sub-sector' of foundations cluster around these roles. The Bertelsmann Foundation is identified as part of this group of foundations in Germany:

> The Foundation sees itself as a reform workshop, starting initiatives to counteract social stagnation. It works on the basis that the state on its own is not in a position to break down encrusted political, economic and social structures. The main idea is to close 'initiative gaps' and thereby take a leading role. In this way, the idea of innovative action is linked to the possibility of utilizing extensive expertise and resources to force the targeted actors into action, instead of just aiming to persuade them through discourse.

Yet, despite the noble aspirations of many foundations, the reality of the frustration often encountered by foundations in seeking to act as a protector of non-mainstream issues and preferences is again reflected by some respondents in Estonia. Although some interviewees went so far as to interpret the liberal model in relation to the ability to influence social change, one interviewee relates the obstacles that may be encountered:

> [W]e have tried to influence legal initiatives, we have interacted with MPs and [a certain] Committee of the Parliament. I am sorry to say that it has been a rather hopeless effort. They argue that our target

group is so small and a change of legislation would not influence more than twenty people at the most. . . . And then finally . . . the act was changed anyway, but one of the few paragraphs that were not changed was exactly the one we had suggested to be changed. . . . [Some civil servants] totally ignore your professional competence and their attitude is decided by other factors.

In the protection of minorities, foundations may achieve success in different ways, such as through the support for innovative knowledge-intensive or risky initiatives. However, the gap between the feasibility and potential of foundations affecting social change more broadly in these areas is evident in the Estonian case. Moreover, the role of foundations as an alternative to the mainstream is becoming increasingly embedded in traditional roles fulfilled by foundations such as complementarity and substitution. In all, the liberal vision is gaining in relevance across European countries, in the context once again of the changing scope and responsibilities of government, rather than in the sense that foundations are in a position that is parallel to government gaining in their ability to be more innovative and to affect social and policy change.

Peripheral model

This model sees foundations in a minor role and as largely insignificant yet ultimately worthwhile institutions as long as they do not challenge the status quo. The peripheral model says more about how foundations measure their position relative to other actors in the non-profit sector, the private sector and the state, than it does about the size and importance of foundations in a particular country per se.

This is evident in the contrasting positions of two countries with relatively small foundation sectors (see Table 3.5). The general agreement of Austrian foundations with this model is rooted in the interviewees' perceptions of the position of foundations within the traditionally corporatist state. The tendency of the corporatist tradition to embrace strong government and a selection of large, influential institutions has not led to

Table 3.5 Peripheral vision

Peripheral vision	Country
Vision pronounced, applies	Austria, Finland, Hungary
Somewhat	Czech Republic, Portugal
Less so, not at all	Estonia, Germany, Greece, Ireland, Italy, Netherlands, Spain, Switzerland, United Kingdom, United States

substantive engagement with civil society, nor have foundations become a powerful lobby with the ability to challenge the status quo. By contrast, despite the relatively small size of the foundation sector in Ireland, for instance, interviewees underlined the potential of the ability of foundations to challenge the status quo: 'they're [foundations] minor, but sure if you don't challenge the status quo, there's no point.'

There are also divergent opinions regarding the power of the presence of foundations as a sector and the opportunities that are created when foundations act as part of a network. For instance, amongst the smaller Portuguese foundations the inability of foundations to affect social change is associated with the peripheral presence of foundations, although membership of umbrella organizations such as the Portuguese Foundations Centre offers them a potential opportunity for influencing policy. Yet the potential of such networks for increasing the influence of foundations is not held in equal regard across Europe. In Denmark, for instance, most foundations prefer to network on an informal level, rather than in the context of a formal organization. Although widely rejected amongst the stakeholders, the peripheral model does provide some valuable insights into how foundations value their importance and how they rate the importance of the roles they seek to fulfil.

Business model

In the business model, foundations become instruments of corporate citizenship and assist business interests in reaching out to communities and customers by serving the public benefit in enlightened but ultimately self interested ways. Although this vision of foundation relations with the corporate world was widely rejected by our interviewees, the development of relations with the corporate sector was identified as a key priority for foundations in Greece, Hungary, Ireland, Finland and the Netherlands (see Table 3.6).

In Switzerland, a sharp divide emerged amongst the interviewees. Nearly half of the stakeholders interviewed in Switzerland disagreed with

Table 3.6 Business vision

Business vision	Country
Vision pronounced, applies	–
Somewhat	Belgium, Estonia, Finland, Italy, Portugal, Switzerland, United States
Less so, not at all	Austria, Czech Republic, Denmark, Greece, Ireland, Netherlands, Poland, United Kingdom

this model. On the one hand, there was a disavowal of corporate foundations which reflects a more general perception that these foundations are motivated by self-interested rather than altruistic purposes. On the other hand, it is also argued that there are mutual benefits for foundations and businesses to be derived from corporate giving and corporate foundations.

Despite the calls for increased cooperation between foundations and the corporate sector, some foundations seem less certain about the potential benefits of cultivating better relations with business. In Estonia, for example, foundation representatives reported how differences in organizational culture and operations made cooperation between business and the foundation sector very difficult. In the United Kingdom, one foundation representative underlined how it may be 'safer' to work with non-profit organizations rather than the corporate sector. Foundations in Denmark, for instance, argue that the activities that interest foundations tend to aim for a longer-term impact, whereas the corporate sector is more concerned with the short-term impact activities such as sponsorship provides. There are lessons to be learned here, not only for foundations but for governments in seeking to understand what motivates foundations:

> I think the politicians ought to consider this matter very carefully – sponsorships from business companies and donations from foundations are not the same thing. We [the foundations] have a totally different agenda. Even if projects would be in need of 'prompt money', this is not a policy we want to promote. This kind of operation will diverge from our visions as a foundation.

Although foundation representatives are keen to display their outright rejection of the business model, it raises underlying issues about how foundations engage with the corporate world. Given the predominance of concepts such as corporate social responsibility, the increasing interest of European foundations in developing relations with the corporate sector is particularly timely. However, this does bring certain challenges for foundations that stem from different cultures of operating and ideas about the aims and nature of charitable giving. From the point of view of foundations, it means reassessing their operations and addressing issues surrounding transparency and standards of professional practice. For the corporate sector, it is about balancing their philanthropic objectives with their own interests. Nonetheless, as a viable alternative to government funding, it is likely that every effort will be made by foundations to ensure that these challenges can be addressed.

Conclusion

The analysis of the visions of foundations encompasses the wider context in which foundations' roles are articulated. In this chapter, it has been

Table 3.7 Visions – a summary

Visions	Awareness	Seek to put visions into practice	Create roles for foundations around these visions
Social Democratic	High	By complementing the role of the state	Yes: complementarity role, but pressures for greater substitution role evident.
State controlled	Low	No: concerns about the impact of the legal and fiscal environment	No: but need to consider consequences of too much and too little regulation
Corporatist	Medium	Yes: but foundations face challenges in maintaining existing relationships	Yes: traditionally, complementarity, but there are also trends towards substitution
Liberal	High	Yes	Two main clusters: 1 complementarity 2 innovation, social and policy change, promoting pluralism

possible to explicate the opportunities, obstacles and challenges foundations encounter in seeking to implement their goals. These are summarized in Table 3.7.

The analysis of the social democratic and the corporatist models underlines how prevalent changes in the structure and organization of welfare states are having an impact on the roles of foundations. In particular, the rolling back of the welfare state and the dismantling of existing subsidiarity relationships has made access to funding a key priority for many foundations.

As in the case of some British community foundations and some of the examples from central and eastern Europe, pragmatic concerns about financing take precedence over normative ideals about maintaining autonomy. Foundations are looking beyond governments for support, although relations with the corporate sector do appear to be in need of development. What is more, as it becomes clear that governments view foundations as favourable tools for certain functions, we see how concerns about the blurring of the complementarity and substitution roles expressed in the previous chapter are rooted in perceptions and experiences of the prevalent policy environment.

Despite the relatively small size of the foundation sector in certain countries, foundations as a whole do not wish to be seen as peripheral organizations who cannot affect change. They also do not wish to be controlled by the government. Nonetheless, the necessity of a cohesive regulatory environment for foundations emerges in our research. It is important for the generation of a culture of giving in a country. It may also be viewed as salient to foundations' visions of the liberal model, as an encouraging legal and fiscal framework is fundamental to creating an appropriate enabling environment for foundations.

The majority of foundations wish to see themselves as existing parallel to the government and as an alternative to the mainstream. Amidst fluctuating policy changes and initiatives, the positioning of foundations in this vision is becoming more difficult to articulate. This is evident in how one Swedish respondent's liberal vision encompasses both the complementarity and substitution roles. In all, fluid clusters of roles and visions do not emerge in different countries. Nonetheless, our research does suggest some important trends and patterns in how roles and visions combine. We turn our attention to these combinations in the next chapter.

Notes

1 The Department of Community, Rural and Gaeltacht Affairs published a consultation paper on the regulation of charities in 2003 and then asked an independent expert to report on responses to this consultation in 2004. See Department of Community, Rural and Gaeltacht Affairs (2003) Establishing a Modern Statutory Framework for Charities: Consultation Paper. Available at: www.pobail.ie/en/CharitiesRegulation/ConsultationPaperonCharitiesRegulationfile,4024,en.pdf; Breen, O.B. (2004) Establishing a Modern Statutory Framework for Charities. Report on the Public Consultation for the Department of Community, Rural and Gaeltacht Affairs. Available at: www.pobail.ie/en/CharitiesRegulation/ExternalReportonPublicConsultation/file,4534,en.pdf. It is expected that a Charities Bill will be considered by the Irish Parliament in 2006.
2 The Dutch research concentrated on endowed foundations. Many of the operating foundations which have a subsidiarity relationship with the state tend to be both controlled and funded by the government. Thus, they are not included in the Dutch research, nor are they included here.

References

Anheier, H.K. (2001) Foundations in Europe: A Comparative Perspective. In Schlüter, A., Then, V. and Walkenhorst, P. (eds) *Foundations in Europe*. London: Directory of Social Change.

Daly, S. and Anheier, H.K. (2005) Preventing the Abuse of Nonprofits to Finance Terrorism – the EU Response. *Alliance Extra*, March.

Ascoli, U. and Ranci, C. (eds) (2002) *Dilemmas of the Welfare Mix: The New Structure of Welfare in an Era of Privatisation*. New York: Kluwer Academic/Plenum.

Cochrane, A., Clarke, J. and Gewirtz, S. (eds) (2001) *Comparing Welfare States*. London: Sage.

Wagener, H.-J. (2002) The Welfare State in Transition Economies and Accession to the EU. *West European Politics*, 25 (2): 152–174.

4 Combining roles and visions
Patterns and implications

Helmut K. Anheier and Siobhan Daly

Introduction

Roles and visions are mutually reinforcing in terms of their ability to help us understand what foundations do and why they carry out specific roles. As the previous two chapters have shown the roles foundations aspire towards, as well as those which underpin their activities, are interlinked with extrinsic factors, notably the policy environment and intrinsic factors such as the size and resources of foundations.

From the outset, it has been our aim to explore whether and how roles give legitimacy to foundations. In this chapter, we probe further to see what insights our study provides into what appears to motivate foundations to aspire towards certain roles. Thus, we begin this chapter by examining the more specific claims to legitimacy that underpin the roles of foundations. These claims to legitimacy form a justifying function, i.e. they allow us to be clearer about the grounds upon which foundations justify the roles they fulfil.

We then examine the extent and nature of the changes that have occurred in the policy environment in recent years and the impact which these changes have had on how foundations position themselves vis-à-vis the state, and the market, in European societies. These changes are encapsulated by the restructuring of welfare states in Western European societies and by the establishment and evolution of the post-communist state in eastern Europe and the Baltic States. Although the impact of these broader changes on foundations has not been widely discussed, the results of our study suggest that it is important to contextualize their implications thus far and the types of issues they are likely to raise in the future for foundations. Against this background, in conclusion, we explore the different ways in which roles and visions interlock and how the mapping of roles and visions links with the nonprofit regimes identified in Chapter 1. In this way, we seek to show how these are changing times for foundations, with many grappling with new roles and new needs.

Roles and the basis of legitimacy

Our findings appear to confirm established perceptions and expectations of the types of roles foundations are most likely to identify with. As discussed in Chapter 2, our analysis reveals on the whole that foundations wish to be seen as innovative entities, independent though complementary to the state, with the potential to affect social and policy change. As discussed in Chapter 1, the argument that foundations, as distinct from other nonprofit organizations, fulfil specific roles is underpinned by the emphasis that is placed on the distinctiveness of the foundation form. In particular, the independence of the foundation, especially its financial independence, is seen to give foundations the freedom to act in an innovative way. Even in the performance of functions that are similar to those of other nonprofit organizations, such as service delivery, it is argued that foundations can again be set apart by virtue of the emphasis they place on incorporating innovative techniques and measures into this type of activity.

Roles give legitimacy to foundations, and our analysis shows that the distinctive characteristics of the foundation form are coveted by the majority of stakeholders. However, in this section, we also posit that these roles are underpinned by various claims to legitimacy. We draw upon the four bases of legitimacy identified by Brown (2001), which include moral, technical and performance, political and legal forms of legitimacy.[1]

The roles of Europe's foundations appear to be predominantly based on claims to a form of moral legitimacy. As such, despite foundations' overwhelming claims of innovativeness it appears that it is a sense of 'doing good' that continues to prevail. There is a sense of duty in complementing the state towards 'filling gaps' that have been left by the state, through the provision of services, partnerships or catering for specialist needs. Despite their concerns and protestations that they do not want to be seen to be substituting the role of the state in certain areas, the tendency of foundations to be resigned to the possibility of having to fulfil this role – rather than an outright refusal of this role – also suggests a prevalent sense of moral obligation to meet certain needs in society.

Attempts to 'do good' are also complemented by claims based on the technical expertise and knowledge of foundations. The intertwining of roles such as complementarity and innovation reinforces the perception that, in service delivery for example, foundations seek to do more than 'deliver services', but rather seek to try out innovative ways of doing things. Thus, as discussed in Chapter 2 in relation to the innovation role, some stakeholders argue that foundations can carry out certain responsibilities in a more efficient way than the state. As one policy-maker from Austria stated:

> The Caritas or similar organizations are definitely better at distributing food than the state or the municipalities. There are

several reasons for this, not least due to their flexibility in the employment of people and personal commitment.

Foundations not only seek to 'do good' but, in certain country studies, notably Belgium, Greece and Sweden, they also believe that they can do things more effectively than other actors, notably the state. Claims to legitimacy based on the expertise and competence of foundations rest on the types of activities in which they are engaged. Even in relation to the preservation of traditions and cultures, for example, foundations underline how their specialist knowledge of a particular area of arts and culture may be particularly advantageous. As one representative of the Maurice Carême Foundation in Belgium stated:

> [T]he state can't do our job. It's impossible. We know our job but it's impossible to find people in the public administration who know Carême, Plisnier or Ghelderode very well. We need some specialists and voluntary work is essential.

Although beyond the scope of the present study, the careful examination of the performance of foundations would allow us to evaluate these claims. For present purposes, they serve to reinforce the perception that foundations are distinctive by virtue not only of the roles they fulfil, but by the innovative way in which they perform these roles.

As Brown (2001) argues, moral legitimacy is often interlinked with political legitimacy, whereby the claims made by organizations are based on principles and practices such as democratic representativeness, participation, transparency and accountability to those on whose behalf they act. In relation to the promotion of pluralism, foundations profess themselves to be ideally positioned to *strengthen civil society* or to *build bridges* between different elements of society. However, among the interviewees who support this role and a role for foundations in social and policy change, it is the independence and autonomy of foundations, specifically the fact that they are not dependent on political processes or answerable to any constituencies that makes them particularly amenable to this type of function. In the course of our research, we did find that many foundations are concerned about how little awareness there appears to be among the general publics of European countries regarding what foundations do. However, efforts to improve transparency and accountability appear more intertwined with enhancing claims to legal legitimacy, rather than political legitimacy.

Claims based on the legal form of legitimacy do not relate to specific roles foundations fulfil. Rather, they pertain to broader concerns and issues raised in the course of the interviews about regulation, transparency and accountability. On the one hand, improved transparency and accountability is about improving both practices and public perceptions of foundations. For some foundations in Germany, it is also, significantly, about giving legitimacy to the initiatives and activities of foundations. In practice, providing for better transparency and accountability has involved activities such as the development of 'codes of practice' by trans-European bodies such as the European Foundation Centre (EFC) and in individual countries. For instance, in Spain, the Fundación Lealtad's principles for Transparency and Good Practice represent one initiative which aims to demystify the activities of foundations in the eyes of the public and, indeed, of politicians. Similarly, in Portugal the Portuguese Centre for Foundations has played a key role in lobbying for improvements to the legal framework in which foundations operate as this is seen as integral to the improvement of governance and transparency. Yet, although these initiatives present a very positive picture of efforts to improve governance amongst foundations, they are not wholly representative of all founda-tions. The Danish interviewees reserved the prerogative to privacy – for some it is part of their assertion of autonomy – and saw no need for a more stringent regulatory environment. Moreover, in the Netherlands, our research has found that some Dutch foundations remain reluctant to 'go public' for fear of being unable to deal with the number of grant applications likely to follow the publicizing of their activities!

What is more, weak legal legitimacy may undermine other claims to legitimacy by foundations. In the eastern European cases and Estonia the legal and moral legitimacy of foundations has been undermined by the manipulation of the foundation form for untoward means. In Hungary, for example, the fact that foundations enjoyed more favourable tax con-ditions than other nonprofit organizations in the early years of the trans-ition meant that thousands of foundations were rapidly created; by businesses as a means of evading tax or by professionals in order to facili-tate the continuation of an activity that had been carried out under the auspices of a state institution. In particular, the creation of *fake* founda-tions and the scandals that follow their discovery highlight the weaknesses of prevalent legal and regulatory systems. What is more, they lead to a climate of mistrust surrounding *genuine* foundations.

Within this framework, it is possible to posit a more nuanced interpre-tation of how foundations perceive their position in societies. The claims to legitimacy suggest that independence and innovation are not the only underlying dimensions to the roles foundations fulfil. Rather, claims per-taining to the roles foundations aspire towards are, more often than not, countered by concerns about feasibility, capacity and sustainability in the long term. The fact that foundations continue to pursue certain roles, despite these concerns, suggests a need to probe deeper into what moti-vates foundations to carry out specific functions in what are sometimes dif-ficult circumstances. Our analysis suggests that understanding the sense of moral obligation that appears to pervade foundations is important, as is the extent of the technical expertise which foundations believe they possess. What is more, the influence and role of the state also feature, as does the wider legal and regulatory environment in which foundations operate. In the next section, we examine the types of changes that have had an impact on the roles of foundations in recent years, and those which are likely to affect the role of foundations in the future.

Foundations and the policy environment: the restructuring of welfare states

In recent years, three trends in the restructuring of welfare states have had particular repercussions for the nonprofit sector: marketization, new partnerships and an enabling role for the state (Lewis 2004). Overall, the impact of these changes on foundations specifically has been overlooked. The results of our analysis, particularly our analysis of the visions of foundations in Chapter 3, suggest some ways in which these factors have affected foundations, or indeed, are likely to affect foundations in the future. The changing role of the state has had the most obvious impact.

The influence of *marketization*, and, in particular, the principles of new public management on nonprofit organizations has been most clearly visible in the contracting out of services by governments to the nonprofit sector. Indications of how outsourcing by governments has affected foundations are evident from the study, though dominant patterns are not forthcoming. To take one example: the trend towards the commissioning of tasks, that were previously the responsibility of the state, to nonprofit organizations in Spain led to some suggestions that operating foundations need to think carefully about a substitution role in order to guarantee their financing in the long term.

The impact of New Public Management (NPM) is evident in that the pressures of increased regulation and mechanisms of accountability that have accompanied it in many countries are being felt by foundations across Europe. In particular, as mentioned in relation to the Swiss case in Chapter 2, foundations who agree contracts with public-sector authorities must not only commit to the provision of services, but to meeting standards of quality and supervision.

In recent years, nation states and the European Union have also awarded increasing importance to the development of new partnerships between the state, the market and nonprofit organizations as an alternative, first to the classic structures of the welfare state and, second, to the 'contract culture' which emphasized the market and nonprofit sectors as proxies for the state (Lewis 2004: 177). Of course, the notion of nonprofit organizations working in various forms of partnership with the state has long been the norm in many European countries (see Salamon *et al.* 2003). In the UK, the 1998 Compacts (for England, Scotland and Wales) signified a new style of partnership between the government and the nonprofit sector, which recognized the independence, purposes and needs of nonprofit organizations. Their real significance lay, however, in the fact that 'for the first time, a purposive stance towards the third sector per se [became] mainstreamed into central government's public policy agenda' (Kendall 2000: 542). Similar agreements have been forthcoming in France in 2001 and in Estonia. The Estonian Civil Society Development Concept (EKAK), originally supported by the Estonian Parliament in 2002, and most recently the subject of an implementation plan for 2004–2006, sets out the government's commitment not only to developing civil society, but also to specifying the 'mutually complementary' role of public authorities and non-governmental organizations, including foundations (Mänd 2004).

But where do foundations fit in these scenarios? The complementarity role of foundations explicitly encompasses a form of partnership for some foundations, but one that involves cooperating with public sector organizations with a view to sharing experience and expertise in certain areas, particularly those that are seen to be neglected by the government. On the one hand, this may entail more traditional forms of partnerships with national and municipal authorities that involve close cooperation with the state in fields such as health and social care. On the other hand, where the complementarity role is linked with efforts towards innovation, the emphasis of the partnership may be on generating specific outputs. It is not at all clear from our research that foundations attach any importance to the development of more formalized partnerships with governments.

It is the trend towards *an 'enabling' role for the state*, underpinned by an emphasis on 'active' rather than 'passive' welfare that, both explicitly and implicitly, has had the greatest repercussions for foundations.

One of the most salient challenges facing foundations in the context of the restructuring of welfare states concerns, to paraphrase one of our interviewees, how to 'add value' whilst at the same time avoiding a wholly substitutive role. This is a challenge that resonates throughout each of the country studies. Foundations increasingly speak of the added pressures and responsibilities that have emerged as a result of broader public sector reforms.

However, in some instances, the way in which foundations interpret their roles appears at odds with the broader trend towards a more enabling role for the state and the pressures that some foundations believe follow from this. For example, the ability of foundations to identify and develop activities in certain 'niche' areas, with a view to the government taking eventual responsibility for these tasks, resonates in discussions of both the complementarity and innovation roles. There are clear instances of where this approach has worked well in the past such as the role that the World Wildlife Fund (WWF) played in generating interest and then action on environmental issues in Switzerland.

However, as a form of 'strategy' it sits uncomfortably with how some foundations feel compelled to engage in areas where the state is perceived to have withdrawn or to have decreased funding. As the Dutch study chose to focus exclusively on grant-making foundations, it is possible to discern the impact which broader changes in the welfare state have had on this type of foundation in particular. On the one hand, foundations underline their reluctance to engage in a complementarity role. On the other hand, they emphasize how due to perceptions of the decline of state involvement in areas such as health, education and research, they are forced to focus at least part of their grant-making on organizations that were previously supported by the government (see Chapter 17). In the UK grant-making foundations have been predominant and the boundaries between state and foundations have been clearly demarcated. Yet, our analysis has shown how some foundations were particularly vocal about fears of government interference in their activities, through perceptions of government interest in the destination of foundation grant-making or, again, through having to take up the slack where government withdraws (see Chapter 7). Similarly, in the Swedish study, foundations express their frustration at what they view as the increasing expectations of governments and municipal authorities that they will fulfil 'public sector' roles, on the one hand, and having to cope with a move towards a more restrictive fiscal and regulatory environment on the other (see Chapter 21). The trends identified in these countries do not suggest that governments are on the look out to take on responsibilities in the niche areas identified by foundations. Rather, the move towards the enabling state appears to have increased expectations of the type and nature of roles that foundations can fulfil. This trend is less about enhancing or giving greater recognition to the roles of foundations. Rather it is more about decreasing the burden borne by the state.

The combined analysis of the restructuring of welfare states with some of the findings from our research suggests some ways in which the context for philanthropy has changed, and also how it has affected the roles of foundations. Above all, it suggests the need for a widespread reassessment of the role and contribution of philanthropic foundations across Europe. The widespread support for the complementarity role, combined with a reluctant engagement by some in activities that tend more towards substituting rather than complementing the state, suggests that foundations are sometimes motivated by more charitable rather than philanthropic objectives. To be sure, foundations assert their role as innovators and their independence (as representative of the pluralist nature of society). However, the broader picture suggests that this independence is under threat from increasing expectations of the types of roles foundations can fulfil, particularly of the gaps they can fill where the state withdraws. As such, then, it is the distinctiveness of foundations that is under threat.

A post-communist model?

The challenges facing foundations in eastern Europe and Estonia cannot be understood within the framework of the restructuring of (western) European welfare states. Rather, the underlying issues and themes facing these foundations need to be considered against the background of the fall of Communism and the pursuant democratization of Hungary, Czech Republic, Poland and Estonia. In the early years of the new democracies, foundations appear to have served two principal functions. First, on the one hand, governments tended to view the foundation form as a means of helping to transform the state. Similar to other countries, foundations identified strongly with the role of foundations in complementing the state. Typical of other interpretations of this role, this may take the form of making grants to nonprofit organizations to fulfil certain tasks, particularly those that involve meeting needs that are not addressed by the state, and foundations running their own programmes or services.

Second, on the other hand, foreign-funded foundations sought to contribute to building civil society, and ultimately to contribute to building democracy in these countries. The representatives of the foreign-funded foundations interviewed for this study underlined in particular the importance of roles such as social and policy change, innovation and pluralism, specifically the role of foundations as a 'counterbalance to the one-sided bias in the support provided by the state'.

However, in various ways, the state is central to the future development of foundations in these countries. For some it is integral to their survival. The role of foundations as innovators is often interlinked with the expectation that, although foundations take the initiative in certain areas, they do so with a view to giving way to the state in the performance of certain roles. The idea of the complementarity role involving the identification of niches which can then be taken over by the government resonates in the Czech study, where it was felt that 'the state needs to improve its ability to take over from foundations the financial support for successfully launched projects' (see Chapter 8). Similarly, in the Hungarian study, the idea of foundations acting as innovators is intertwined with them singling out areas in which the state needs to take further action.

At the same time, interviewees in these countries readily spoke of examples of where activities of foundations had ceased because of a lack of long-term private or public funding. In Hungary, these concerns tend to manifest themselves in calls for the need for greater clarification about the responsibilities of foundations, on the one hand, and those of the state, on the other. For some foundations, particularly those involved in health and social care in Hungary and Poland, maintaining a close relationship with the state (and the resources this brings) is fundamental to their survival. This outweighs any concerns about compromising their independence or being engaged in a substitutive function. However, interviewees question the extent to which foundations dependent on financial support from the state can legitimately claim to encourage pluralism, or to be representative of the plurality of institutions that exist parallel to the state. In the Hungarian case, and Estonia too, this suggestion appears rooted in suspicions of what agenda governments envisage for foundations, particularly those that they create. As one interviewee from Estonia stated:

> [W]hat has happened lately is that the government creates foundations for the financing of all kinds of projects that in fact belong to the functions of the state. The foundations should be independent bodies but for instance [a foundation established by the government] is 100 per cent dependent on the Ministry of [name] ... quite irrespective of who belongs to the board.

The need for greater coordination between foundations and the state, between foundations and business and, indeed, between foundations and other foundations resonates clearly throughout these cases, whether in the form of a liberal vision, or less so, in the form of a corporatist or social democratic vision. Key themes regarding the shortage of resources and the sustainability of roles over the long term are particularly discernible in the cases from this region; dealing with these issues is fundamental to enhancing coordination efforts between all relevant stakeholders. Although the changes in the recent context may differ from those of western European countries, the thematic nature of the challenges facing foundations in eastern Europe and Estonia are similar. Avoiding substitution, maintaining independence and, above all, clarifying the nature of relations between foundations and the state, are themes that resonate across all of the European countries included in our analysis.

Conclusion

The comparative analysis of foundations through qualitative methods has allowed us to probe deeply into how foundations perceive themselves and the world around them. As such, the diversity of arguments and opinions that emerge from this research mean that we are less able to draw rigid conclusions about the roles and visions of foundations. Some patterns and tendencies have emerged from our research that point to a complex picture, and suggest a time of change ahead for foundations in most of the countries examined.

Two scenarios dominate how roles are articulated around particular visions of society, or rather, how roles and visions interlock. First, awareness of the social democratic vision, as reflective of the policy environment in which foundations function, was particularly high amongst the foundation representatives and other key stakeholders. To a lesser extent, awareness of the corporatist model was also significant in those countries traditionally associated with this vision. These visions are inextricably linked with the role of foundations in complementing the state, which may take a variety of forms including partnership/bargaining, filling gaps and provision of services. These scenarios are underpinned by a wide-spread reluctance on the part of foundations to engage in a substitutive role – although an underlying sense of wanting to 'do good' and, for some, the practical need to survive, means that many foundations find themselves engaged in this type of role.

Second, the high level of awareness of the liberal model amongst the stakeholders is rooted in assertions about the autonomy of foundations (and the accompanying advantages of this independence). Different sets of roles tend to be created around this vision. On the one hand, interpretations of this model associate the liberal vision with foundations who seek to be innovative, have an impact on social and policy change and/or aspire towards the promotion of pluralism. On the other hand, for some stakeholders it is about the role foundations fulfil in complementing the state, such as in the support they give to programmes aimed at minority-oriented issues. Perhaps more specifically, it is about the expertise, experience and initiative that foundations believe they bring to this role, which is rooted in claims to a form of technical legitimacy.

The mapping of countries exclusively against these scenarios has proved complex. Countries do not always cluster exclusively around certain role/vision combinations. There are sub-sectors of clusters within certain countries. For example, the chapter on Germany reveals two 'foundation worlds', one grounded in a corporatist tradition, the other closer to the liberal model characteristic of the USA and the UK. There are also cases reflecting actual or potential frictions between the role/vision pattern of a country and its overall nonprofit regime and foundation model.

The different ways in which the roles and visions of foundations appear to combine are representative of the uncertain environment many foundations appear to find themselves operating within. As has been discussed throughout the analysis of roles and visions, this uncertainty is generated by a combination of changing roles of governments and new policy initiatives that are forcing foundations to rethink what roles they can or wish to fulfil, as well as how they function. What is more, it has been affected by uncertainty about funding in some countries. The legal and fiscal environment also contributes to what foundations do and how effective they are. The correct legal and fiscal context is fundamental to creating an appropriate enabling environment for foundations to prosper.

The complex policy challenge for foundations is suggested in Table 4.1. It shows that some foundations in some of the countries covered find themselves at odds with the overall nonprofit regime type and the foundation models we outlined in Chapter 1. Other countries, however,

Table 4.1 Role-vision clusters and regime types

Role-vision cluster	Nonprofit regime type			
	Liberal	Social Democratic	Corporatist	Statist
Complementarity – social democratic		Finland	Belgium, Netherlands, Poland, Portugal, Spain	Czech Republic, Hungary, Italy
Complementarity/ substitution – social democratic (in diminishing form)	United Kingdom, (USA)	Norway, Sweden		
Complementarity – social democratic/ corporatist			Switzerland	Greece, France
Complementarity – corporatist			Austria, Germany, (Netherlands)	
Innovation/social and policy change/ promotion of pluralism – liberal	USA, UK	Denmark	Germany	Estonia, Ireland

demonstrate more congruency. Finland, a social democratic nonprofit regime and foundation model reveals a role-vision pattern (complementarity – social democratic) that is in line. Norway and Sweden are also largely congruent cases, although the combination of complementarity and substitution introduces a potential policy tension with government.

For other countries, however, there are major disparities between what foundation representatives 'envisage' in terms of roles and visions, and the realities of existing nonprofit regimes types and foundation models. For example, Estonia and Ireland, both examples of a statist tradition, cast the roles and visions of foundations very much in a liberal tradition that seems closer to that of the USA. The German case reveals a split result, and parts of the country's foundations are in the complementarity – corporatist patterns, others in the innovation/pluralism – liberal one, suggesting that German foundations are passing through a period of policy debate and possible reforms.

Finally, the statist nonprofit regime type, with the two sub-models of the peripheral statist and the post-socialist statist foundation models, is the one where most changes could be expected. As Table 4.1 shows the various countries of this type are spread across most role–vision patterns, suggesting not only significant 'disconnects' between policy and foundations, but perhaps also that statist models are at the brink of profound reform.

Gaps between the awareness and understanding of roles, on the one hand, and the feasibility of foundations to meet certain expectations or, indeed the need for foundations to modify expectations are influenced primarily by the nature of relations between foundations and the state. Support for the complementarity role tends to cluster around the social democratic and corporatist visions, but the role of foundations in substituting the state is gaining in salience. As discussed in Chapter 3, in countries where the social democratic vision is relevant, this has raised fears among some foundations about their autonomy being compromised, but pragmatic needs of survival and sustaining activities have led some foundations to engage in substitution by accepting government grants to provide certain services, for example.

Similarly, in countries which have traditionally embraced the corporatist vision the form of relationship between foundations and the state appears to be changing, on the one hand, towards the negotiation of contracts for the provision of services and, on the other, towards initiatives that enhance the independence of foundations. In these contexts, perceptions of changing responsibilities and roles of governments have reinforced notions of foundations substituting rather than solely complementing the state.

Moreover, as the distinction between public and private responsibilities becomes more complex, some foundation representatives indicated that there are signs of a shift towards a liberal model in which the complementarity and substitution roles are more pronounced. This also suggests a shift in the liberal vision too, from one where foundations not only act in parallel to the state, but also in place of the state in terms of its traditional responsibilities. The other roles that foundations envisage in the liberal vision such as innovation, social and policy change and the promotion of pluralism also raise salient questions about whether the opportunities necessary to create these roles are being created, both by foundations themselves and within the wider political system.

Our research has consistently shown that foundations wish to be seen as innovative entities, functioning in a scenario where they act as an alternative to the mainstream, consistent with the liberal vision. In this scenario, it is their independence and autonomy that defines them and their particular contribution to society. By contrast, the similar high levels of awareness of the social democratic vision, and the emphasis this scenario places on complementing and/or substituting the government defines foundations vis-à-vis the state. The dilemmas and trends some foundations identify regarding foundations being reluctantly cajoled into assuming roles that are not their key priorities somewhat compromises assertions about independence and autonomy. The signs are that this will continue in the broader scenario of the restructuring of European welfare states.

Finally, let's take a brief look at transnational issues, in particular in relation to the European Union (EU). In recent years, there has been a significant shift in relations between foundations and the EU, which has not coincidentally coincided with the increased importance awarded to linking the EU institutions with citizens. The White Paper on European Governance (European Commission 2001) proposed opening up the policy-making process to include third-sector organizations, while the proposed constitution for Europe went one step further in providing the foundations for a legally recognized civil dialogue. These developments contrast sharply with the largely ignored 1997 Communication and the stalled attempts to create a European Association Statute and a European Foundation Statute (see Kendall and Anheier 2001).

However, overall, changes in relations with the EU have provided more challenges than opportunities for foundations. Indeed, against the background of the results of the various country studies, it appears that foundations represent true latecomers on the European scene. Many foundations, including those in the new member states, have neither adequate knowledge nor pronounced interest in engaging in activities at the European level. From a policy perspective, the challenge is twofold. On the one hand, foundations and their representatives need to make a case for a future role for foundations in front of a European Commission that, while pro market, seems politically closer to statism and corporatism than liberalism; on the other, foundation representatives need to harness the interest of those who wish to be European foundations, and see benefit from moving outside the confines of national state models.

Note

1 Brown (2001: 63) defines legitimacy as follows: 'Civil society organizations are legitimate when their roles and activities are accepted as appropriate to their contexts'.

References

Brown, L.D. (2001) Civil Society Legitimacy: A Discussion Guide. In Brown, L.D. (ed.) *Practice Research Engagement for Civil Society in a Globalizing World.* Hauser Center for Nonprofit Organisations and CIVICUS: World Alliance for Citizen Participation.

European Commission (2001). European Governance: A White Paper. COM (2001) 428 final.

Kendall, J. (2000) The mainstreaming of the third sector into public policy in England in the late 1990s: whys and wherefores. *Policy and Politics,* 28 (4): 541–562.

Kendall, J. and Anheier, H.K. (2001) The third sector and the European Union policy process: An initial evaluation. In Kendall, J. and Anheier, H.K. (eds) *Third Sector Policy at the Crossroads: an international nonprofit analysis.* London: Routledge.

Lewis, J. (2004) The state and the third sector in modern welfare states: independence, instrumentality, partnership. In Evers, A. and Laville, J.-L. (eds) *The Third Sector in Europe.* Cheltenham: Edward Elgar.

Mänd, K. (2004) Estonian Government strengthens ties with civil society. *E-Seal 12,* November.

Salamon, L., Sokolowski, S.W. and List, R. (2003) *Global Civil Society: An Overview.* Baltimore, MD: Center for Civil Society Studies, The Johns Hopkins University.

Part II

Country analyses

5 Austria

Ruth Simsa

Introduction

In comparison to other countries, the Austrian foundation sector is relatively underdeveloped and its overall influence is insignificant. Yet, at the same time, private foundations are a controversial subject of public discussion and debate. They are viewed as a means of accumulating capital whilst simultaneously taking advantage of the benefits of reduced taxation without necessarily having a public purpose. This situation has arisen due to the presence of different laws governing foundations – one of which allows for the establishment of foundations for purely private purposes. This law has led to public debate about the legitimacy of tax exemption for private purpose organizations created by wealthy individuals, an issue which remains on the political agenda. What is more, the new law is also seen as a useful tool for reorganizing nonprofit organizations (NPOs) that used to be incorporated as associations. It enables these organizations to operate more flexibly and to be less controlled by public agencies. Overall, as a consequence a majority of the foundations in Austria have not been established for charitable reasons. The focus of this chapter will be on foundations which serve public purposes.

The main function of charitable foundations in Austria is to complement the state's activities. The role of foundations in fostering pluralism is also popular as foundations support minority groups or activities. Furthermore, many foundations act as promoters of innovation in research or development and some try to preserve traditions. Overall we find that charitable foundations do not really have the potential to challenge the status quo. Austria is characterized by a corporatist system, and foundations are not significant actors in this system. Nonetheless, there is an emerging trend whereby the state's responsibilities are outsourced to private organizations. To a certain extent, foundations are regarded to be one tool of privatization. On the one hand, there are foundations that cooperate closely with the government. On the other hand, there are foundations that have been co-founded by either the local or by the federal government. However, the foundation sector is quite heterogeneous and others continue to work independently.

A profile of foundations

Historical development

Similar to other countries, the development of foundations can be linked to charitable beliefs espoused by the Christian church, combined with increasing prosperity and the emergence of a middle class. From the fifteenth century onwards, the role of the church declined and foundations were placed under the authority of the state.

Although the age of the Enlightenment and secularization was hostile towards foundations, a core group survived. In the nineteenth century, the social values espoused by the medieval foundations became important again. Foundations regained their administrative autonomy and the idea of creating foundations enjoyed renewed popularity. Many new institutions with a wide range of purposes were established. During the twentieth century, there were consistent patterns of growth in the number of foundations (Mraz 1999: 49).

The period of economic crisis which followed the First World War had drastic effects on the sector. Only those foundations with a very high capital base survived. During the Nazi regime, the foundation sector was subject to drastic changes; 2,400 institutions, mainly those created by Jewish donors, were closed down without their assets being transferred to other charitable establishments. Only an insignificant part of the assets were returned after the war.

The 1975 federal law for foundations and funds was a significant development. It consolidated the multitude of existing regulations into clear guidelines for the establishment and operation of foundations. Due to the corporatist system in Austria, the negotiation and implementation of policies are characterized by tight control through chambers and parties and by a permanent coalition between the two major parties. As discussed below, the reform of the law did not, however, result in key opportunities for foundations to play an important role in this system.

Legal issues

There are two laws concerning foundations. The first one is the Bundes-Stiftungs- und Fondsgesetz (BStFG, the Federal Foundations and Funds Act) of 1974, which limits foundations to serving a charitable purpose only. Under this law, foundations had to have the following characteristics: (1) asset character, (2) charitable purposes, (3) permanence. There are approximately 475 charitable foundations registered under this act.

In the 1980s the existing law was considered inappropriate because of its charitable purpose limitation. More and more Austrian capital was being directed to foundations in countries with more liberal regulations. Thus the law for the establishment of private foundations called the Privatstiftungsgesetz (PSG, the Private Foundations Act) of 1993 was introduced. The PSG does not limit foundations to serving a charitable and public purpose. The main reason for the introduction of the new law was to make the Austrian capital market more attractive to investors through the provision of tax advantages. As a measure of its success, 2,300 private foundations have been established in recent years.

Although the new PSG was not meant to replace the charitable BStFG, there is a tendency in this direction. As the PSG requires less supervision from the government, (Grafl 2000: 9) funders seem to prefer it.

Empirical profile

Restricted transparency and access to the legal deeds of foundations, combined with the fact that the PSG embraces foundations created for charitable and non-charitable purposes, means that we lack complete information about the empirical profile of Austrian foundations. Table 5.1 presents our best estimates of the number of foundations in Austria today. In our interviews, experts estimated that approximately 5 per cent of the 2,306 private foundations have charitable purposes. In total, we estimate that approximately 600 foundations have been established for charitable purposes. It is not possible to acquire reliable information about the assets of Austrian foundations.

Regarding the classification of foundation activities according to the International Classification of Non-Profit Organizations (ICNPO), the dominance of social services is evident. Organizations engaged in this area make up almost 42 per cent of all charitable foundations in Austria. The second largest group is education and research, constituting almost one third of foundation activity. With almost 11 per cent, culture and recreation ranks next, followed by those not elsewhere classified with just below one third, and health, with more than 6 per cent (see Figure 5.1).

Both the quantitative data and the analysis of the legal and historical situation show the important role of the PSG. The sector increased dramatically after the establishment of the new law. On the other hand, it also shows that if you take into consideration just charitable foundations, the sector is quite small in the Austrian context. Thus, in examining the

Table 5.1 Estimated Number of Foundations in Austria

PSG-foundations (private and charitable purpose)	Charitable PSG-foundations (estimated)	BStFG-foundations	Foundations regulated by federal law	Total number of charitable foundations (estimated)
2,306	115	214	261	590

Charitable Foundations (ICNPO)

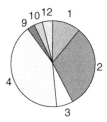

Group	No.
Culture and Recreation	1
Education and Research	2
Health	3
Social Services	4
Environment	5
Development and Housing	6
Law, Advocacy and Politics	7
Philanthropic Intermediaries, Voluntarism Promotion	8
International	9
Religion	10
Business and Professional Associations, Unions	11
(Not elsewhere classified)	12

Figure 5.1 Charitable Foundations in Austria (ICNPO) (sources: Grafl, 2000: 70f; author's own research; Salamon and Anheier 1992: 18).

roles of foundations in Austria, it is necessary to bear in mind that the sector holds neither a very distinctive nor a visible position.

Foundation roles

Foundations are part of a small subgroup of numerous associations and cooperatives that make up the Austrian NPO-sector. For example, a representative of a charitable foundation characterizes foundations as follows: 'They are no more than a drop in the ocean, rather a little rivulet.'

The following analysis, based on the framework outlined in Chapter 1, illustrates how foundations, however comparatively small in number they may be, view their role(s) in Austrian society.

Complementarity

In terms of awareness and practice this is the most important role for Austrian foundations. They are addressing gaps within the social system and complement the state's activities wherever it does not cover existing needs or where foundations are the better instruments to address certain needs. Some areas are particularly vulnerable to financial crisis and foundations play an important role in these fields. For example the Dr. Maria-Schaumayer Foundation's purpose is to promote women's scientific careers. The Kindertraum private foundation is also involved in complementing the state's activities. In close cooperation with private and corporate sponsors, it aims to fulfil the wishes of ill children, which would be much too costly to be part of the state's expenses.

The attitudes towards foundations fulfilling this role are divided. While the majority of both experts and representatives holds the opinion that complementarity is one of the most important roles for foundations, others disagree. The latter group argues that the Austrian welfare system is strong enough to deal with all aspects of social services and that foundations have too little influence to be a supportive force for the state.

Substitution

Generally, the role of substituting the state is not one that is predominantly performed by Austrian foundations. The question of replacing the state is not really relevant within the strong domestic welfare-state structure and the comparatively small amount of capital at the disposal of foundations. Nonetheless, some experts suggest that because of their flexibility and commitment, foundations might be more suitable than state bodies for dealing with certain tasks, especially in the fields of social services and culture. Overall, there is a low but slightly growing awareness of this role, whereas in practice it is still not wholly relevant.

Innovation

The dichotomy between preservation and innovation is often raised in connection with foundations. It is also evident among the stakeholders interviewed. While some institutions are viewed as promoters of progress, which is mainly true for those engaged in research and development projects, others are clearly perceived as cultivators of tradition and of past achievements, especially in the cultural sector.

While foundations describe themselves as innovative, external experts question this portrayal of foundations. Some foundations, however, make important innovative contributions, for example, in the promotion of culture and art such as the Arnold-Schönberg Centre or in research. Foundations also seek to act innovatively in the development and application of new working methods, for example the Anton Proksch Institut in addressing drug addiction, or the development of new means of social care by the Caritas Socialis Private Foundation. Our analysis of individual cases showed that innovatively oriented foundations are often more effectively managed, they act more strategically and more economically than other foundations. However, generally, foundations have rather small effects on social innovations.

Preservation

The role of foundations in maintaining traditions is estimated to be rather insignificant. Indeed, many foundation representatives appeared indifferent about this role. Within the group of experts, the mood tends towards opposing the idea of foundations preserving traditions and cultures. Yet there are some foundations fulfilling this role, particularly in the field of arts and culture in maintaining the memory of renowned artists' works. Some foundations fulfil both innovative and preserving functions, for example, a foundation which preserves the work of Arnold Schönberg and supports, at the same time, the development of innovative theories and methods in cooperation with the University of Music and Drama of Vienna.

Redistribution

Austrian foundations are generally not viewed as suitable instruments for this role. For one, their financial resources are not viewed to be sufficient. Experts also hold the opinion that the PSG is obstructive to the redistribution of funds because of the possibility of having exclusively private purposes. Both of these attitudes are held by an overwhelming majority of representatives and policy makers.

Social and policy change

Many of the interviewees wish foundations to fulfil this role, but there is doubt about the feasibility of this role for foundations in Austria. Apart from one exception among the experts interviewed, the awareness of this role is very low. It is a role that is associated with specific cases rather than with Austrian foundations in general. For instance, a representative of the 4 Pfoten Private Foundation states that one of the organization's aim is to change society's attitudes about the protection of animals. Similarly, the Caritas Socialis Private Foundation seeks to contribute to social change by increasing awareness and understanding of hospices. These foundations are motivated by the goal of changing society (or at least certain aspects of it), but as yet this is not a role that is prominently associated with foundations in Austria.

Pluralism

Foundation representatives, policy makers and other stakeholders view promoting pluralism as a very important role for foundations. In particular, foundations are viewed as an important agent for encouraging and supporting cultural diversity – hence the tendency to associate cultural-oriented foundations, such as the Arnold Schönberg Centre Private Foundation, with this role. Quite simply, by giving grants to particular purposes and target groups, foundations are also seen to play a key role in fostering pluralism in all fields of activity.

Visions and policies

We analysed the visions of foundations by comparing the ways in which foundations see themselves, their role in society and their underlying values, with those of experts and policy makers. For the most part, foundations' current roles fit into the system of visions conveyed by foundation representatives, experts and policy makers.

The social democratic model, where foundations are envisioned to be providers of public goods and social services, is the most important both as a role and as a vision, shared by foundation representatives and experts. For example the Anton-Proksch-Institut (API), a therapy centre for drug and alcohol addicts, works in close cooperation with the federal and regional authorities and other research institutions in relation to prevention and treatment issues. While this foundation believes that social services should broadly remain the responsibility of the state, the representative interviewed also underlined the experience and knowledge gained by foundations from working in a particular area. In this way, foundations can complement but not substitute the state.

Austria clearly reflects the corporatist model. In this context, foundations are viewed as a helpful tool for cooperation in terms of implementing and running public services, and in many areas cooperation with the government is pretty tight. Social services and culture are, in terms of funding and scope of activities, dominated by public institutions. However, since foundations are perceived to be more flexible, innovative and cost-efficient than public bodies, the government looks for new ways to organize the provision of several services, such as in the area of health care. The example of the Caritas Socialis Private Foundation, an institution that works largely independently but in close cooperation with the government in the provision of social care is illustrative of the relevance of the corporatist model. This foundation, financed mainly by public resources, runs some nursing homes in Vienna as well as developing new projects and approaches to social care. In this way, the foundation sees itself as an independent 'development partner' of the public authorities, but its activities are deeply embedded in the broader welfare system.

Nonetheless, it should also be noted that despite the presence of some key examples of foundations functioning as part of the corporatist system, the peripheral model reflects the current situation of foundations in terms of their significance in Austria. Indeed, most statements of experts and foundation representatives point out that Austria reflects the peripheral model regarding the number of foundations, their financial contributions and their impact on society; a situation which is also reflected in the visions of most interviewees.

The liberal model reflects the situation in Austria only to a small, but nonetheless relevant extent. The liberal model envisions foundations as a visible force independent from both government and market, supporting issues that form an alternative to the mainstream. For example, the Köck Privatstiftung's support for projects in Montessori pedagogy through the provision of financial aid and expertise is underpinned by a vision of a limited role for the state and the encouragement of private initiatives and philanthropy. However, foundations lack cohesiveness as a sector and the financial capacity to act as a viable force that functions parallel to the government.

Finally, the business model is present to the extent that some corporations, especially local savings banks, fund community projects. However, it is definitely a minor feature of the foundation sector. Besides sponsorships, corporations are not largely involved in contributing to public affairs.

There is a tendency towards opposing the state-controlled model, where foundations are ultimately subservient to the state. Nonetheless, corporatism and strong governments characterize the current broader situation for foundations. In relation to museums or social insurance, for instance, Austria's tradition lies in public institutions that are tightly controlled by the Parliament. There is only one example of a large museum, the Collection Essl, that is exclusively privately financed through a private foundation.

The general vision of society in which foundations' roles are cast is a democratic one that includes a state covering individual risks and providing (at least basic) services and rights within a welfare state and an engaged civil society. A strong civil society is regarded as an important factor reflecting a functioning democracy based on a pluralistic and open society. Foundations' ideal roles include the function of being a tool to finance and guarantee the permanence of projects and to strengthen the nonprofit sector rather than performing substitutive functions, as they lack the financial capacity to support such a goal.

Current developments and emerging issues

The relevance of NPOs is increasing in Austria, both in respect to expectations and *quantitatively* in relation to employment, financial capacity and the provision of services. The background for this development is the trend towards the privatization of public responsibilities.

Tax law is a topic that is likely to remain on the agenda. On the one hand, this concerns fiscal benefits for private foundations which have problematic effects on distribution as well as on transparency. Here tax exemptions are given without a reasonable degree of public control and they are given to rather wealthy people. On the other hand, tax allowances on private donations for public benefit purposes are not given in Austria contrary to practice in most other European countries. Experts argue that the harmonization of tax systems and tax rates needs to feature more prominently on the EU agenda.

Experts and foundation representatives alike pinpoint an emerging scenario whereby the state is perceived to be withdrawing from certain responsibilities and outsourcing public services. This is likely to enhance the importance of the nonprofit sector as foundations and other organizations will have to address the needs that subsequently arise. Thus, new ways of strengthening civil society are being explored, with the creation of community foundations (which have yet to emerge in Austria) being quite topical in this respect.

Further, cooperation between foundations will become more important. There is no coordinating umbrella organization for charitable foundations comparable to the Association of German Foundations, for example. The foundation sector is a loose system of institutions which operate in parallel to each other. However, there is an umbrella organization of private foundations, which acts as a lobbying tool for its members.

Finally, Austrian foundations also identify the need to cooperate on an international level in their fields of activity. Until now they have not done this to a large extent. One exception is the 4 Pfoten Private Foundation, which seeks out intensive international lobbying and cooperation. It is also expected that international foundations will enlarge their presence in Austria. The European Foundation Centre is not very well known to Austrian foundations, either to policy makers or experts.

Conclusion

Austria has a rather vital civil society in terms of associations and other NPOs but its foundation sector plays a rather subdued role. Furthermore, with the 1993 law, a new function of foundations as instruments of the capital market, tools to accumulate assets while enjoying almost the same tax privileges as charitable foundations was created. This situation could be interpreted as a challenge for both the civil society and the state to put more effort in strengthening the charitable foundation sector. Particularly with regard to strategies of the EU, a harmonization of tax laws regarding foundations is necessary and would be helpful for strengthening the position of foundations as a contribution to civil society. Finally, it can be posited that steps towards an internationalization of activities, cooperation, and regulation of the foundation sector by the European Union could contribute to a strengthening of the role of foundations in the future.

References

Grafl, Th. (2000) Das Osterreichische Stiftungswesen-Rechtliche Aspekte und Quantitative Dimensionen, Diplomarbeit WU Wien.

Mraz, S. (1999) *Die Rolle des Stiftungswesens im österreichischen NPO-Sektor*, Diplomarbeit WU Wien.

Simsa, R., Kern, M. and Haslinger, R. (2003) *Visions and Roles of Foundations in Austria*, Projektbericht, Wien.

Prewitt, K. (1999) 'The Importance of Foundations in an Open Society'. In Bertelsmann Foundation (ed.) *The Future of Foundations in an Open Society*, Gütersloh: Bertelsmann Foundation Publishers.

Salamon, L.M. and Anheier, H.K. (1992) 'In search of nonprofit sector I: Question of definitions', *Voluntas*, 3 (2): 125–151.

6 Belgium

Gautier Pirotte

Introduction

Foundations in Belgium make up a very small part of the nonprofit sector. Approximately 70,000 nonprofit organisations (NPOs) and 50,000 associations are listed in the country (Salamon *et al.* 1999; Mertens *et al.* 1999). As of August 2002, 340 foundations were registered with the relevant departments of the Ministry of Justice under the title of Public Utility Establishments (PUEs). Recently, they have been renamed as Public Utility Foundations (PUFs).

Despite a new rigid legal framework (see below), the foundation form remains very ambiguous in Belgium as the term covers two or three different entities:

1 foundations in the strict sense, i.e. those recognised by the law under the name of a 'Public Utility Foundation' (PUF);
2 nonprofit-making organisations (NPOs) using the term foundation in their name, e.g. the André Renard Foundation or the Jacques Brel Foundation;
3 a number of other organisations which are neither PUFs nor NPOs but which likewise bear the name of a foundation, e.g. the CERA Foundation.

The reform of the old law on associations sought to clarify the legal and conceptual connotations of the term 'Foundation'.

The Belgian foundation sector is very heterogeneous. Foundations vary, not only in terms of their mission but also in relation to their financial and/or human resources. The majority of Belgian Foundations are operating or mixed foundations, combining an operative dimension and grant-making activities. Since the end of the 1970s, there have been various changes in Belgian (civil) society. Moreover, the reform of the welfare state is likely to have some influence on Belgian Foundations. As the comparative international study by Salamon *et al.* (1999) showed, the nonprofit sector in Belgium is very dependent on public grants. In

Belgium, 77 per cent of the NPOs' income is made up of public grants, 18 per cent of private grants and 5 per cent of donations. The welfare state was built within a society which, since the creation of the independent Belgian state, has been segmented by the process of 'pillarisation'. The role and place of Foundations must be understood within this particular context. A *pillar* is a set of organisations linked by philosophical (laic or Catholic) or political (Social Democrat, Christian Democrat or Conservative) allegiances. Even if this pillarisation process has seemed to be in crisis since the end of the 1970s (Swyngedouw 1999; Vrancken 2000), it has long meant that Belgium has been characterised by a segmented society ruled by a quite weak State which is forced to bargain with different and often opposing interests.

A profile of Belgian foundations

Historical development

There are four key dates in the historical evolution of the Belgian foundation sector: 1831, 1921, 1975 and 2003. In 1831, Article 27 of the Belgian Constitution ratified the right of association without citizens being subject to any 'preventive measure'. Although the right of association was recognised by the Constitution of the newly independent Belgium in 1831, it could not be exercised fully during the nineteenth century because of the absence of implementing statutes. The laws of 24 May and 27 June 1921 enabled the participation of an ever-growing number of associations in Belgian society. The legislature not only provided a legal framework for nonprofit-making associations, it also established a legal system for foundations – defined originally as Public Utility Establishments (PUEs). This was similar to that which existed in Anglo-Saxon law, where the trust institution had enabled communities to benefit from the generosity of certain private individuals.

On 29 December 1975 the King Baudouin Foundation was created, the most important Public Utility Foundation (from both a financial and political point of view) in Belgium. The King Baudouin Foundation is also important for the evolution of the sector and for the dynamism of philanthropic activities in Belgium (see below). The roots of this Foundation can be found in a State initiative (the King, the Parliament and the Government acting together) with the aim of creating an autonomous entity, free from pillar allegiances and partisan interests that could serve as a link between citizens and the State. The King Baudouin Foundation is perpetually searching for a specific identity for PUFs.

The fourth important date for the field is 2003. The new legal dispositions relative to 'Associations without lucrative goals' and 'Public Utility Foundations' came into effect on 1 July 2003. The new requirements in relation to keeping accounts were introduced on 1 January 2004. Belgian legislation relating to PUFs (formerly PUEs) has been modified in an attempt to clarify the confusion that arose from associations adopting the name 'Foundation' without being structured as a Public Utility Establishment.[1]

Legal issues

Despite the reforms supported by the recent law of 2003, the main part of the current legal framework has been inherited from the law of 1921. The term Public Utility Foundation is still defined as a legal act emanating from one or more natural or legal persons which consists of permanently allocating assets for the achievement of a specific and public benefit goal. The aim of the public utility foundation must be nonprofit-making and of a philanthropic, religious, artistic, scientific or educational nature. The foundation does not have members and neither the founders nor any individual can gain financially from the operations of the foundation. The founding act (its constitution) must be approved by the government (i.e. by the Ministry of Justice in practical terms) in the form of a royal decree of approval. PUFs can therefore be described as *private* entities endowed with financial assets earmarked for objectives for the *public* benefit.

The new law only uses the word *foundation*, the term *establishment* being considered too vague. This name will henceforth be reserved for foundations recognised by royal decree. Legal action against 'false foundations', which will force them to change their name, is provided for. The law establishes two categories of foundations: small and large, with each category having specific accounting requirements. These two categories are still rather vague at present and should be put into specific effect by a royal decree in the future. Whilst small foundations must contend with simplified accounting procedures, large foundations have to keep accounts in accordance with the 1975 accounting law. Foundations which meet at least two of the three following criteria at the closing of their accounting year comply with this stipulation: (1) five full-time equivalent staff; (2) total revenue of €250,000 not including exceptional income or VAT; (3) balance sheet total of €1,000,000 of assets.[2]

An empirical profile

As mentioned above, the PUF concept in Belgium covers a variety of institutions for which it is difficult to find a common denominator. We can underline the following patterns in the growth of the PUF sector: 24 of the 340 registered PUFs were established before the Second World War; 81 were created during the 1940s, 1950s and the 1960s; 74 PUFs were established in the 1980s and 82 during the following decade.

Given that a PUF can be established by an individual or by an entity,

Table 6.1 Distribution of PUFs in Belgium according to founder's origin

Founders	Number of PUFs
Individual(s)	245
NPO or PUE	53
Profit-making entity	16
Public authorities	6
Not declared	20
Total	340

such as a profit-making company, we have divided this latter category of founders into three sub-categories: nonprofit-making entity (NPO or PUE), profit-making entity and public authorities.

Table 6.1 above shows that the vast majority of Belgian PUFs are created by an individual. In contrast to widespread practice in other countries, Belgian enterprises create very few PUFs. Indeed, this type of initiative has never been a tradition in the Belgian corporate world. However, the recent development of corporate funds which we will discuss below, seems to indicate positive developments in this regard.

The number of personnel employed by the foundations varies greatly, ranging from zero to several hundred. Some foundations do not have any volunteers and in many cases do not see any need to have voluntary personnel, while others see their activities and their image as depending exclusively on volunteer work. Unfortunately, we only have partial data on the assets currently held by PUFs, due to the Ministry of Justice only carrying out assessments since 1995. These recent approximations show that the assets of PUFs vary greatly between €3,000 and €40 million! Moreover, despite the legal provisions in force, PUFs often neglect to submit their accounts regularly. The examination of the data available from the Ministry of Justice did, however, enable us to reconstruct the amount of total annual revenues and expenditure of a sample of approximately 100 PUFs from the figures for the years 1995–1997. For this period, the amount of expenditure of the PUFs in the sample totals €58 million on an annual basis. By way of comparison, the Belgian gross national product was around €219 billion in 1997.

Roles of Belgian foundations: between complementarity and innovation

All of the foundations interviewed see themselves as complementary to the state, satisfying needs not met by the public authorities in their individual sectors of activity such as education, culture, social welfare and health. Furthermore, some claim to have been established in order to fill gaps in policy or an under-exploited niche.

The role of foundations in complementing the state can be illustrated in part by the activities of the King Baudouin Foundation. Since 1989, the King Baudouin Foundation has benefited from an annual allowance given by the National Lottery. Today this allowance represents up to 30 per cent of the foundation's income. Despite this important financial state support, representatives of the King Baudouin Foundation stressed the independence of the Foundation. Its purpose is not to replace or compensate for the activities of the authorities, but it does work quite closely with the government as a 'partner of the state'.

Some older foundations, mainly those established prior to the 1970s, had a different interpretation of the position of foundations vis-à-vis the state, their task and role in the welfare system, and their relationship with other nonprofit organisations. For example, the Louise Godin Foundation is one of the oldest Belgian Foundations which manages a centre for children with psychological problems, as well as a home for children who are having difficulty with their schooling. Although initially based on the endowment of its founder Louise Godin, the institute's activities are supported by the Walloon Agency for People with Disabilities (a Regional Agency) today. This foundation defines itself as an operating entity that *must* be financially supported by the State. In contrast to the discourse of the King Baudouin Foundation, the leader of the foundation we met does not underline the need for independence vis-à-vis the state:

> We accept donations and legacies. But it is quite rare [that we receive them]. We regularly question notaries about it but they tell us most legacies are dedicated to the Red Cross, the Friends of Animals, etc. People are most prone to give money to these kinds of associations than to us. Anyway, I am not ready to go and see every notary of the place with my bag because I don't think that's my job. In our case, the State has a role to play. I don't think we must live on charity!
>
> (Louise Godin Foundation)

Other foundations, whilst defining their roles within this complementarity relationship with the state, define themselves more as an initiator rather than as a simple operating organisation. In this regard, the roles of complementarity and innovation are intertwined.[3] In the Belgian context where foundations have developed very close relationships with public powers, innovation mainly consists of revealing social needs, introducing new solutions (or new methods) of dealing with these needs and, then handing responsibility over to the State. For example, as one representative related:

> [O]nce the authorities took up the initiative in environmental matters..., we put this cause to one side. At the beginning of the eighties, however, there was the reform of the state; we did not know

what was going to come under federal or regional jurisdiction, especially with regard to the environment. That's why we intervened in this sector.

(King Baudouin Foundation)

Only a few foundations, where the grant making activity is a little more developed, for example, the King Baudouin Foundation and Foundation for Future Generations, identify with the redistribution of economic resources. Nonetheless, some foundations, while unpretentious, nevertheless plan to redistribute their profits in the future. For example, the Folon Foundation aims to give associations (especially for people with disabilities) parts of the profits collected by the Museum dedicated to this artist's works.

Although foundations define their role at the junction between innovation and complementarity to the State's activities, the role *social and policy change* does not evoke much reaction from foundations. Yet, the idea of influencing the political agenda surfaces regularly:

We do not want change for its own sake; we want to induce lasting change. We always work with the aim of development over the long term and remedy in the short term. We're not calling for a revolution; what we do want is to get certain issues put on the political agenda!

(King Baudouin Foundation)

The role of foundations in preserving traditions and cultures is mainly associated with maintaining the memory of an individual or of their life's work. For instance, our selection of cases included two foundations created in honour of two well known artists: the painter Jean-Michel Folon and the poet Maurice Carême. In both cases, the creation of a foundation for an artist, whatever his discipline and notoriety, is viewed above all as a way of ensuring their work's durability, to prevent their work from being scattered and to protect the rights of (future) beneficiaries.

Visions: corporatist and social democratic model denied?

Due to the mixed nature of the Belgian foundations, combined with their sometimes close relationships with public authorities and the welfare state context, we would expect the corporatist model to be predominant. This initial observation seems correct because this model fits very well with the Belgian case, particularly as it is characterised by a segmented civil society. Nevertheless, we also stressed above that the traditional organisation of civil society is experiencing a period of flux in parallel to the apparent decline of the welfare state. Moreover, given that many foundations insisted on a complementary role vis-à-vis public authorities, the social democratic model also appears to be relevant to the Belgian context.

Finally, the tendency amongst most foundations to underline the necessary independence of the foundation sector suggests the relevance of the liberal model, although it does not fit well within the Belgian context.

In contrast to the topic of roles, none of the models of visions proposed appeared to satisfy our interviewees. This can be explained, on the one hand, by a lack of awareness and often misunderstanding of the models discussed and, on the other hand, by the visions' lack of relevance to the situation encountered in Belgium. More often than not, the visions expressed by the foundations combined various elements of the models.

No foundation sees itself as an agent implementing the public policies of a highly developed and centralised welfare state:

> It is us who take the initiative without referring to the State. I know that I have support; they think what I am doing is good, and I have very good relations with the ministries. We live in a State that has great respect for our activities; there is no control on the part of the State.
>
> (Maurice Carême Foundation)

Nevertheless the social democratic model seems to fit very well with situations where foundations are integrated into the welfare system and carry out activities on behalf of the public authorities. For some of the interviewees, if they complement the public authorities' activity, this means that the state should not be permitted to define or even influence their projects, attitudes, behaviours. This is why the social democratic model, the state controlled model and even the corporatist model – all of which suppose different degrees of state influence over the operations of the foundations – are simply but firmly rejected. Unsurprisingly, the state-controlled model is also rejected unanimously.

The corporatist model poses more problems and ambiguities for those we spoke to. They were particularly bothered by the word corporatist and the suggested role of arbiter assumed by the state:

> I do not like the name and when I see the definition, it isn't this either: I don't think the State acts as an arbiter with us because we are a private foundation, working with our own resources.
>
> (King Baudouin Foundation)

> It is us who take the initiative without referring to the State; the State gives us grants on the basis of our activity reports but I do not have to submit my initiatives and achievements, I am completely free!
>
> (Foundation for Morale Assistance to Prisoners)

This model in which the state acts as an arbiter between the different private interests thus appears, like the social-democratic model, to contradict the assertion constantly made by the heads of the foundations that they have complete independence in the running of their operations.

It would appear that only small foundations, involved in very specific activities (such as the Foundation for Morale Assistance to Prisoners, and the Foundation Maurice Carême promoting artists), fall within the scheme of a liberal model. These foundations seem to be aware of their situation:

> The State cannot do this [promoting poets and artists], it's imposs-ible! First, because it is impossible to find civil servants as specialised as us in this field! The work requires specialists and one thing that is for sure is that volunteer work remains essential in this regard! Fur-thermore, it may not quite be the role of the State; I think that indi-viduals who perform small jobs do them better. And then, you have to be reasonable – I don't think the State has the resources, either! Private initiatives therefore remain essential.
>
> (Maurice Carême Foundation)

Foundations claim that, despite their initial orientations, they are above any ideological orientation. In this context, the non-political stance declared by the leaders of Belgian foundations appears as a challenge to the pillar system.

The dominant emerging discourse insists on autonomy, self initiative, innovation and ability. But this vision is facing the ambivalence of the rela-tionships between foundations and a weaker, but omnipresent state. They reject defined models where the state would be an attentive partner, a referee with subsidiary power, a controlling agent with firm and clear leadership. Nevertheless, our analysis indicates the relevance of the corporatist or the social democratic models where the State plays a role of an arbiter or partner. Even if many PUFs are trying to work with their own assets, the Belgian Government as well as the Cultural Communities or the Economic Regions are still important and solid financial and political partners.

Current developments and emerging issues

Within the Public Utility Foundation Sector, two major trends have recently emerged. First, the management of new funds by existing founda-tions is one of the most salient initiatives to emerge in recent years. This practice, called *protected assets*, functions as follows: a founder delegates all or part of his assets to an existing institution which will be responsible for allocating it to a purpose determined beforehand by the founder. The assets allocated in this way are not given any distinct legal personality.

With the encouragement of philanthropy being one of the essential functions of the King Baudouin Foundation, it has developed different formulae within its *Funds and Philanthropy* programme to enable the implementation of various forms of generosity. Apart from donations that it receives directly, the King Baudouin Foundation also manages around 70 funds on behalf of private individuals (nominative funds), associations (specific funds) and companies (corporate funds).

A second trend, which is also relevant to the Belgian nonprofit sector, appears to be related to the foundation sector's heterogeneity. With some exceptions, we noticed a real lack of political clout exerted by most of the foundations in Belgium. Regarding their ambitions to play an independent role between state and society (or, specifically between public authorities and beneficiaries) this lack of political clout could be a problem, especially if Belgian foundations really want to influence social or cultural (comprising education) policies. This situation can certainly be explained by the heterogeneity of the sector and the economic weakness of most of the foundations. Nevertheless, and even if the heterogeneity of the sector represents an obstacle, it would certainly be beneficial to create a space for the consultation of foundations in Belgium, a kind of summit structure able to defend the interests of foundations in the country. Some leaders of Belgian foundations find that 'it's sometimes easier to meet at European level than in our own country' and feel the need to 'establish ourselves as interlocutors for the public authorities'.

Conclusion

There are several key points to be emphasised from this chapter. First, all of the foundations interviewed claim to play a complementary and an innovative role. However, they do not attach importance to social democratic or corporatist models of relations between the state and civil society organisations. What is more, both these models seem to fit well with the evolving Belgian context. Belgian foundations favour a more liberal model, underlining their high level of autonomy vis-à-vis the state. They do not attach much importance to the role of the state which is, in fact a regular political and financial partner of foundations. We must remember that some of them were created as a result of a state initiative.

Has the federalisation process affected the foundation sector in Belgium? This is a large and complex question that needs further analysis. We should emphasise that the identity of Belgian foundations has not been really affected by federalisation. Of course, we note that since 1980 (when the federalisation process grew in importance) more foundations were created in Flanders and the Walloon Region. But more than half of the PUFs are still located in the Brussels region. The fact that the administrative supervision is still in the hands of the federal Ministry of Justice offers greater stability. Moreover, at least for the foundations included in this study, the main aim is to develop activities on a national scale.

As for the foundations' identity and the scale of their activities, are

Belgian foundations ready for Europe? Most of the time, the leaders of Belgian foundations stress their international/European ambitions, whatever their human or financial capacity. A manager of the King Baudouin Foundation said: 'We are a European Foundation working in Belgium!' To develop their ambitions, Belgian Foundations need more human and financial resources. The director of Child Focus claimed:

> It's clear for us that our European ambitions is limited by our financial constraints. Despite these financial limits we created a European Federation and this poor federation helped us to develop international contacts. We created a small specific financial committee to find new funds for this Federation. We can say that we are on the international scene but with no financial capacity.

These latter findings suggest that new dynamics are emerging inside the Belgian foundation sector (in terms of networking, empowerment of philanthropic activities, etc). Nonetheless, mainly due to the new legal framework that recently came into force, not to mention the state of flux that prevails regarding the pillarisation process and changes to the welfare state, it is possible to speculate that the roles and visions of foundations will continue to evolve and change in the future.

Notes

1 The main reason behind the legislature's decision to modify this statute is the fact that it contains provisions that are contrary to European law. Indeed, Section I, concerning NPOs, stipulated that three-fifths of the members had to be Belgian nationals; this infringes Article 6 of the Treaty of Rome, which forbids discrimination based on nationality. Belgium received formal notice from the European Commission in this regard in 1998. The aim is also to achieve greater transparency within the association sector and curtail the inappropriate use of PUFs and NPOs (fronts for commercial businesses, organised crime, etc.).
2 Finally, the new law introduces a new institution, the 'private foundation' (commonly referred to as the 'family foundation') to preserve the family character of an enterprise by using the technique of title certification. This mainly concerns persons with very substantial assets who do not wish to have such assets divided up between their heirs.
3 In Belgium, foundations often take the initiative in place of the State. What is more, many foundations increasingly find themselves embracing this type of role, such as the National Fund for Scientific Research. Created in 1928 by several Belgian scientists and industrialists to promote scientific activities, the support of this foundation is becoming more and more crucial for the durability of a large part of public scientific activities in Belgium in response to the decline of public policy dealing with scientific research.

References

Chambre des Representants, Session 1920–1921, 98, 23 March 1921.

Chambre des Representants, Document 1854/9-98-99, bill amending the 1921 law.

Fondation Roi Baudouin (2000) *Statuts de la Fondation Roi Baudouin.* Bruxelles: Fondations Roi Baudouin.

Fondation Roi Baudouin (2001) *Rapport Annuel 2001.* Bruxelles: Fondation Roi Baudouin.

Mertens, S. *et al.* (1999) *Le secteur non marchand privé – Résultats d'une enquête-pilote: Panorama statistique et éléments de comparaison internationale.* Bruxelles: Fondation Roi Baudouin.

Salamon, L.M., Anheier, H.K., List, R., Toepler, S., Sokolowski, W. and Associates (1999) *Global Civil Society. Dimensions of the Nonprofit Sector.* Baltimore: The Johns Hopkins Comparative Nonprofit Sector Project.

Swyngedouw, M. (1999) Les rapports de force politiques en Belgique. In Martiniello, M. and Swyngedouw, M. (eds) *Où va la Belgique. Les soubresauts d'une petite démocratie européenne.* Bruxelles: L'Harmattan, pp. 45–58.

Vade Mecum de Droit Administratif (Vade Mecum of Administrative Law) (1992) *Service Corporations,* no. 8, 1992.

Vrancken, D. (2000) *Le crépuscule du social.* Bruxelles: Labor.

7   United Kingdom

Diana Leat

Introduction

In the United Kingdom there is no legal distinction between charitable foundations and any other type of charity. Nevertheless, the term 'foundation' is generally, though not exclusively, reserved for endowed, or sometimes fundraising, grant-makers. It is not widely used to refer to wholly operating endowed or non-endowed charities. Reflecting these popular definitions, the research on which this chapter is based focused primarily on grant-making foundations, but also includes some part-operating foundations and a small number of non-endowed grant-makers.

British foundations constitute a diverse and in many respects divided world. A small number of large foundations control the vast majority of assets, income and grant-making, with the remainder spread between a much larger number of smaller foundations. What little is written about foundations is largely based on the characteristics and activities of the small number of larger foundations controlling the majority of assets and income. Foundations also vary in age and origins. Unlike some other European countries, foundations in the UK are largely secular in origin and interests. However, a significant proportion (in number) of foundations have a religious orientation and give for religious education and social activities. Jewish foundations, for example, tend to give exclusively to Jewish groups and causes.

Traditionally, foundations have assertively maintained their independence from the state and jealously guarded their privacy. Among the larger foundations this scenario has changed in recent years. Many of these foundations now provide a range of information about their activities. However, in general, the existence and activities of foundations are not widely known among the general public and, as this research demonstrates, within government. Foundations have traditionally favoured 'doing over talking'. There has been little pressure for them to identify and legitimate their roles. In this study a number of respondents found it difficult to articulate the roles and visions of foundations in the UK, and some appeared to find the question irrelevant at best and irritating at worst. What is more, foundations emphasize their individuality and independence. It is debatable to what extent foundations may be described, or see themselves, as a distinct sector. Nonetheless, as discussed below, foundations increasingly find themselves having to reconsider established assumptions and ideas about what foundations do, largely in response to broader societal and political influences.

A profile of foundations in the UK

Historical development

Three key interrelated themes underpin the historical and legal development of foundations in Britain in recent centuries:

- the secularization of philanthropy,
- the changing roles and responsibilities of the wealthy, and
- the changing and ambiguous relationship vis-à-vis the state.

By the end of the Tudor period, philanthropy had moved from personal giving for pious purposes, regulated by the ecclesiastical courts, to largely secular giving regulated by the Court of Chancery. The industrial revolution of the eighteenth and nineteenth centuries caused enormous social upheaval and exacerbated existing problems of social welfare, as well as adding new ones to the list. Nineteenth-century industrialists and other wealthy people contributed to social welfare at home and abroad (e.g. in the anti-slavery society) as well as to the arts and the environment (Chesterman 1979).

Prior to statutory provision on any scale, foundations largely saw their roles as providing for the poor, elderly and sick, as well as funding education, religion and the arts. Whilst foundations were restricted largely to giving under the six heads of charity law, with the creation of the welfare state in the mid twentieth century, foundations began to more clearly distinguish between their roles and those of the state.

For the first three-quarters of the twentieth century foundations emphasized five key principles in their work (Leat 1992): 'doing what the state doesn't do'; pump-priming innovation; unpopular causes and risk taking; and providing emergency funding. These principles have gone hand-in-hand with traditional practices which stress being responsive rather than proactive; making smaller short-term grants; giving grants for specific projects rather than for core funds, and often for capital rather than revenue purposes. In this way, foundations distanced themselves from the state and limited their responsibilities. Pump-priming was a nice idea if there was a nearby well with water, but in a terrain in which statutory funding had largely dried up it was increasingly seen as an ineffective use of resources. Traditional foundation roles were further confused when government turned the tables on foundations and adopted the role of innovator and pilot funding. The introduction of the National Lottery distributors with resources vastly greater than even the richest of foundations created further disturbance of the status quo.

Legal issues

In legal terms, charitable foundations do not differ from other types of charity, i.e. there is no specific legal form for foundations. Very broadly, the governance of charitable organizations in Britain takes three main legal forms: (1) the unincorporated association, (2) the incorporated association and (3) the trust.

The preamble to the 1601 Statute of Charitable Uses forms the basis of the legal definition of charitable purpose today: the relief of poverty, the advancement of education, the advancement of religion and other purposes of public benefit (but see below for proposed changes). Various commentators have noted the close relationship between the definition of charitable purposes and the provisions of the state poor laws, but its actual wording allowed for purposes unrelated to poverty.

By the end of the nineteenth century charities, including foundations, enjoyed a range of legal and fiscal privileges, but at the same time were required to submit to state supervision (however limited) via the Charity Commission. All of these advantages carried forward into the twentieth century. Despite the advent of the welfare state, charities were still encouraged, and still expected to submit to supervision in return for fiscal and legal benefits.

The 1960 Charities Act increased the powers of the Charity Commission, in particular by increasing its powers to take remedial action in cases of misconduct (e.g. by freezing a charity's bank account), and extending its powers to modernize the purposes of a charity. The Charities Act 1992 and 1993 required foundations to publish an annual report (something relatively few foundations had previously done and to which some foundations objected). It also required foundations to keep accounts in the form specified in regulations to be based on a recommended accounting practice (SORP 2). Foundations were required to make their accounts available to any member of the public on request, for a 'reasonable fee', and both annual reports and accounts were to be available for inspection by the Charity Commission. In addition the 1992 Act gave the Charity Commission statutory powers to demand information from charities and to hold formal enquiries, as well as legal authority to exchange information with other government bodies, including the Inland Revenue. The Act made it a criminal offence to fail, persistently and without reasonable excuse, to fulfil the requirements of the Act. The 1992 Act also broadly increased foundations' freedom in handling their investments and income. These provisions of the Act concerning accountability and openness by foundations marked the end of an era of privacy for foundations.

As will be discussed below, in the twenty-first century more fundamental changes have been set in motion with two major government reviews of the meaning of charity and of the role of the voluntary sector in public service delivery.

An empirical profile

The data on foundations are patchy and largely restricted to the minority of relatively rich foundations that command the lion's share of assets and income (Fitzherbert *et al.* 1999). Furthermore, estimates of numbers and known names for Scotland and Northern Ireland are included in various guides but the data are less robust than those relating to England and Wales (see for example Griffiths *et al.* 2002; CAF 1999).

There are around 9,000 endowed, grant-making foundations in the UK giving an estimated £2 billion per annum (approximately €2.6 billion). The total figure given is further swelled by the contribution (around £280 million or €350 million in total) of a dozen large operating charities which give grants in the course of their work (Pharoah and Siederer 1997). With total voluntary sector income estimated to be around £16 billion (approximately €20.8 billion), foundations are, in financial terms, both a relatively insignificant part of the sector and provide only a small part of overall voluntary sector income. According to the Association of Charitable Foundations (ACF), foundation spending is also insignificant in relation to total government spending.[1] The majority of foundations are independent 'private' foundations created by individuals within families. There is a small number of corporate foundations, a growing number of government sponsored grant-makers, and patterns of growth in the development of community foundations.

Different types of foundation in the UK

ENDOWED FOUNDATIONS

By definition, endowed foundations make up the bulk of all charitable grant-making foundations. Endowed foundations vary radically in size and level of grant-making activity. Some foundations are run solely by family members, others include non-family members on their boards.

CORPORATE FOUNDATIONS

Only a minority of corporate foundations are endowed. More commonly, corporate foundations have no permanent endowment but rather receive regular transfers from the associated companies. Corporate giving has been growing in recent years, but now appears to be declining. As in other European states, there has been growth in the number of foundations created as a result of banking, and other corporate sector, privatization, mergers and reform.

COMMUNITY FOUNDATIONS

Community foundations are relatively new to the UK. They first appeared in the late 1970s and have doubled in number (from 15 to 31) in the last decade (Community Foundation Network 2002; see also Humphreys 1997). Part of this growth has been funded by American, and a few British, foundations. These aggregate figures, as in so many areas of the foundation world, conceal huge variation between individual community foundations. Community foundations have found a special place in the new policy environment acting as an 'agent' for some large central government grant-making programs to local areas. Some community foundations have also been instrumental in accessing European Social Fund grants.

FUNDRAISING GRANT-MAKERS

Fundraising foundations are not new. Many of the established foundations today were funded by public subscription. Fundraising foundations have also increased in recent years. Data on them is patchy and the various guides tend to treat them erratically.

GOVERNMENT-INSPIRED GRANT-MAKING FOUNDATIONS

From 1995 the total amount given in grants by non-endowed charitable organizations was increased by the Saturday National Lottery, and more recently by the New Opportunities Fund distributing the proceeds of the mid-week lottery. The effects of this level of grant-making on other foundations and on grant recipients has been controversial, but there now seems to be some consensus that the Community Fund in particular has taken some of the load off foundations working with smaller organizations. In addition to the Lottery Boards there is a small but growing number of grant-making charitable organizations set up as a channel for the distribution of government funds.

OPERATING GRANT-MAKERS

It has been estimated that the largest 11 operating grant-makers made grants of £256.2 million in 1996–1997 and had a total income of £486.5 million and assets of £369.3 million (Pharoah and CIU 1998).

Foundation assets

Estimates of the total assets of foundations are difficult to obtain, £30 billion is a broad estimate. Assets are very unevenly distributed between foundations. For example, in 1995–1996, only three foundations had assets of over £500 million and a further four had assets over £300 million (based on data in Pharoah and Siederer 1997: 94).

Table 7.1 Estimates for total grant expenditure in the UK in the main subject areas

	£ million	% of total grants expenditure
Social care	233	25
Health	174	19
Education	155	17
Arts/culture/recreation	95	10
Religious activities	76	8
Development/housing	42	5
Environment/animals	30	3
Philanthropy/volunteering	30	3
Science and technology	24	3
Civil society/law/advocacy	23	3
International	20	2
Social science	14	2
Subtotal classified	916	100
Uncoded to main subject	64	
Total grant-making	980	

Source: Vincent and Pharoah 2000: 25.

Foundation activities by grants made

Despite foundations' emphasis on innovation as a key part of their role, the evidence from a pioneering study by Vincent and Pharoah (2000) suggests that the majority of grants by number and total value go to social care, followed by health and education (see Table 7.1). Religious activities attract a substantial minority of grants, and the rest are spread thinly over a wide range of areas. Science and technology attract the lowest number of grants but the highest mean grant size.

Vincent and Pharoah's (2000: 64, 72, 73) survey revealed strong patterns of fashions across foundations. Local foundations tend to share the same main priorities as local authorities, which indicates that foundations are frequently either substitutes for council responsibilities or provide leverage to public funding. There are significant gaps between grant-makers' stated preferences and their overall patterns of giving. However, the fact that the broad priorities of foundations do not appear to be addressing new issues, less popular causes and less mainstream needs does not necessarily imply that they have no innovative capacity (Anheier and Leat 2002).

Patterns in foundation growth

The formation of foundations appears to have been at its peak during the 1960s and 1970s. The ACF Annual Review for 1996–1997, commenting on the possibility of a review of charity taxation, suggests that general taxation levels are the key factors in foundation formation and growth (ACF 1997).

During the 1990s a small number of foundations became substantially richer as a result of stock market gains, take-overs and mergers. In 1997–1998, the composition of CAF's top 500 table changed by 10 per cent with 50 new entrants to the table (and obviously the same number of exits).The grant-making total of new entrants was £28 million higher than that of exits. Overall, a larger number of trusts reported a decrease, rather than an increase in grant-making, and many kept their grant-making at the same level (Pharoah and CIU 1998).

One of the most significant developments affecting foundation income was the abolition of Advance Corporation Tax (ACT) credit. This was not intentionally directed at foundations but had indirect and unintended effects by significantly reducing many foundations' investment income.

There is anecdotal evidence to suggest that interest in individual/family foundations is growing. However, there is no systematic evidence to suggest that this expression of interest is being realized in foundation formation. Community foundations appear to be growing in number and will certainly grow in terms of flow-through funding as a result of grant-making on contract to government. More generally, there appears to be some tendency to reach for foundations as a solution to political problems.

Foundation roles

The majority of endowed grant-making foundations saw themselves as one of a group of similar organizations, but views on whether or not this constituted one sector varied. The opinion of one person that 'some would self select into a sector – ones that see themselves as developing good practice, ones that see themselves as professional' was echoed by others. Similarly, several respondents suggested that there are really two sectors, made up of large and smaller foundations.

Endowed grant-making foundations saw themselves as part of the wider voluntary or nonprofit sector, but as distinctive from other voluntary organizations in terms of their not having a major service providing role, their financial independence and lack of members. None of the foundations interviewed used the language of civil society to describe how they would identify themselves.

Operating foundations were much more ambivalent about to which sector, if any, they belonged. They saw themselves as having as close, if not closer, identification with the wider nonprofit sector than with the sub-sector of foundations. Community foundations seemed clearer in identifying themselves as a distinct group or sector, with 'a foot in both grant-maker and grant-seeker camps'.

The overall impression was of organizations very much aware of their individuality, but also with some more or less strong sense of identification with others in the foundation world.

All foundations, except the community foundations and one other foundation, saw themselves as national organizations even though some of them also gave overseas (see below).

Those outside the foundation world were generally less likely to see foundations as forming a sector. Some saw foundations as a sub-group within the voluntary sector, noting the separation of ACF and the National Council of Voluntary Organizations (NCVO) and contrasting that with the Independent Sector in the USA that includes both grant-makers and grant-seekers.[2]

Roles

The foundations interviewed generally found it difficult to articulate any distinctive role, and some found the probing of the question irritating and 'academic'. One foundation commentator said:

> I don't see it as a relevant question. Foundations don't see it as their role to have roles and visions.

Some noted that there were various formulaic answers to the question of foundations' roles but these did not really say anything. Those outside foundations broadly shared these views.

Endowed foundations saw their distinctiveness as lying in the fact that they are not, generally, beholden to government and public opinion, that they do not have to fundraise and as a result are freer to take risks and to fail. Some saw these characteristics as a means of distinguishing them from the rest of the voluntary sector, which is perceived as being increasingly driven by the government and fundraising agenda.

Community foundations saw their distinctiveness as lying in the fact that they are local fundraisers and grant-makers, as well as having a role in promoting dialogue across sectors. However, the purposes of fundraising, grant-making and dialogue were harder to elicit.

In relation to specific roles, the following observations can be made.

Complementarity

The majority of foundations were keen to emphasize that they saw their roles as complementing that of others, including government. Those outside foundations shared this view. As noted above, the overall pattern of foundation grant-making suggests that foundations give money in very much the same fields as local and central government.

Substitution

Substitution was a much more complex matter. Although most foundations rejected this role in theory, most also commented that this was more difficult to avoid in practice. It was felt that government had 'changed the rules', cutting back on services, involving the voluntary sector in providing services on contract, and taking on the role of 'experimenter'. In this situation, foundations argued that 'avoiding substitution is no longer viable'. However, in some foundations staff commented that trustees still acted as though they believed that if the foundation demonstrated the value or viability of a project, the state would take over longer-term funding. The issue of substitution and relationships with statutory funding was for many foundations the most difficult and pressing issue.

The majority of foundations, and other commentators, but perhaps significantly not government officials, were fearful of the 'colonization' of foundations by government:

> If you look at all the recent developments and reviews, when you strip away all the warm words you realize it's about what's in the government's interests. All the rest is just a side-show. If Whitehall doesn't want to play it won't.

The role of community foundations in grant-making on behalf of government was an interesting example here. Community foundations shared with other foundations a reluctance to substitute for statutory services but had been happy to become an agent of government in delivering various grant-making programmes. Community foundations welcomed the flow-through funding, visibility and legitimacy that grant-making on behalf of government was perceived to bring. Endowed foundations do not feel these needs, and some reported that they too had been approached to undertake such programmes and had refused.

Redistribution

Although some staff saw redistribution as playing some part in foundations' roles, this was not viewed as a key role, nor one to which trustees would sign up. One foundation director commented:

> Foundations should, in general, try to help the poor and more marginalized so to that extent it's a redistributive role. But it's a bit fanciful to see them as engines of redistribution, though I would definitely say they ought to be champions of social justice.

Innovation

Innovation was the single most common term used, by foundations and others, to describe the roles of foundations. Foundation representatives identified a wide range of innovations they attributed to foundations. But several foundations questioned what the term really meant and whether foundation grant-making actually reflected this role. There were also questions regarding the viability of innovating in the light of the changes outlined above, including the activity of an interventionist government creating innovation fatigue with a constant flow of new programmes and initiatives. Nevertheless, foundations saw greater risk-taking as one of their ideal roles.

Social change

A minority of foundation staff saw the major role of the foundation in terms of social change and policy influence, providing new ideas, acting in some respects like, or with, think tanks. A small number of others were exploring this type of role 'as part of searching for ways to have more impact'. But there were problems in adopting this role: foundations' traditional emphasis on being apolitical, combined with 'a history and culture of reticence'; trustees' tendency to equate policy and politics, and to shy away from developing networks for policy influence; lack of research and knowledge:

> Why would anyone listen to us? We aren't service providers so we don't have that sort of knowledge, and the knowledge we do have we don't really organize or use properly.

More generally, the majority of foundations did not see themselves as having much, if any, policy influence. In part, this was attributed to politicians' lack of understanding and knowledge of foundations. But some foundations asked:

> Whose fault is that? Foundations don't encourage people – politicians or others – to understand them, and mostly they don't try to influence policy.

Some foundations, as well as commentators, were unhappy with any notion of social change and policy influence:

> Foundations aren't government so why is it their job to change policy – that's government's job and foundations' resources are peanuts compared with government.

Despite this, some foundations saw greater policy relevance and involvement as one of their ideal roles.

Preservation of traditions and culture

Only one foundation described preservation as one of foundations' roles. Given the roles of foundations in preserving architectural and cultural heritage (such as the arts) this was perhaps surprising.

Pluralism

Safeguarding pluralism was not frequently seen as a key role. Some described it as a 'lowest common denominator position – scraping the barrel'. Nevertheless, most foundation respondents saw the existence of foundations as an important expression of individualism and acceptance of individual interests. Some of those who put forward this sort of argument acknowledged that this could be seen as encouraging ineffectiveness.

In general, foundations saw themselves as having different roles from government, but some found it difficult to lay down clear rules on this. Some saw the freedom to offer an alternative agenda to government, to be 'quirky', to challenge and to fail as the main differences from government. Foundations with general purposes also saw themselves as different from specialist agencies – within and beyond government – in that they were free to think outside the usual policy boxes and divisions, to make new connections and, at best, to offer a holistic approach.

Innovation and complementarity were the two most common roles attributed to foundations by others. Some, inside and outside government, also raised questions relating to substitution, but as one official commented 'we're getting onto very dangerous territory here'. Those outside the foundation world generally shared the view that foundations have little policy influence. The view that, with the exception of community foundations, and perhaps a handful of influential, usually larger, foundations, 'foundations are not on the radar of politicians and officials' was common. It was also noted that foundations were barely considered within the government's Strategy Unit review examining roles of the voluntary sector.

Foundations generally saw their proper or ideal relationship with government as one of complementarity. Yet some wanted a more equal and involved, but still distanced, relationship with government in which foundations capitalized on their resource independence and knowledge in order to better contribute to agenda setting and policy development. In addition, some foundations wanted to see more risk-taking, more idiosyncrasy, more learning and foundations being more outward looking and cooperative.

Are the roles of foundations in the UK changing? There have been some changes in practice and there was a sense of a desire to do something different but, at the same time, there was a feeling of being overwhelmed by 'so many problems and too much to do'. Lack of staff, a cultural resistance to spending time thinking, the flow of government initiatives and the growing complexity of the political and policy environment created a temptation for some to 'just hunker down and retreat into our own world'. In addition, some staff felt constrained and frustrated by the time required to get trustees to address roles, think about and then accept change.

Foundation visions

Interviewees did not identify with the models used to articulate visions, arguing that these were too neat and simple. Most foundations broadly subscribed to a liberal model in which foundations are independent of government and market and provide alternatives to the mainstream. However, few foundations claimed to be 'a visible force'. Most also saw themselves as fitting under a social democratic model in that they saw their activities as complementing or supplementing government activity. The liberal and social democratic models were seen as compatible insofar as alternatives were also seen as supplements. The foundations with corporate links and the community foundations also saw themselves as fitting under the business model enabling business to serve public benefit.

An underlying theme in all interviews was the changing role of government and, by implication, the changing roles of foundations. There was a more or less strong fear that foundations were being moved from a broadly liberal model towards, at best, a corporatist model or, at worst, a state-controlled model, which has the potential to co-opt them and their resources into the agenda of government.

Relationships with business, in many ways, raised the same issues: in theory some foundations recognized the need to work in collaboration with others but feared co-option by business. Community foundations, aiming to fundraise and increase dialogue between sectors, were more likely to see closer relations with business as desirable. A number of foundations bemoaned the lack of collaboration within the foundation world and between foundations and nonprofit organizations. In an ideal world collaboration would be driven by the needs of beneficiaries rather than by old principles, notions of sectoral separation and the sensitivities and needs of donors.

Current developments and emerging issues

Foundations have traditionally prized not only their independence from the state but also their differences from each other. They have also emphasized doing rather than talking, and the importance of maintaining the lowest possible overheads. Among the larger foundations these views have begun to change over the last ten years in particular.

Cultural changes

In 1990 the national Association of Charitable Foundations (ACF) was established with 30 members. In 2002 ACF had grown to 300 members. ACF has been effective in encouraging foundations to talk to each other and has led various initiatives to set standards and encourage good practice. It has also played a significant role in raising the profile of foundations with government, by lobbying for foundations' interests in various policy and legislative changes.

Possibly related to the activities of ACF, over the last decade a growing number of larger foundations have employed paid, professional staff. This in turn may have encouraged a greater interest in and questioning of foundation roles and effectiveness. Nonetheless, although foundations and commentators saw ACF as representing foundations, they noted that ACF membership was only a very small and particular part of the foundation world. Community foundations saw themselves as represented by the Community Foundation Network (CFN), and to a lesser extent by ACF.

While the dominant culture of foundations probably remains one of gift-giving – small, one-off, short-term grants with little if any monitoring and evaluation – to 'worthy' causes, some foundations have changed their approaches in the last two decades and now give more substantial, longer-term, strategic support, including funding for core costs. As this research demonstrates, foundations today are still grappling with defining their proper role, and especially their relationship with the state, in a changed and still changing context.

Terms such as 'venture capital', 'outcome funding' and 'social investment' are now used in some quarters, although it remains to be seen whether these ideas will gain wider currency and be put into practice. Other changes in the foundation world include discussion of ethical investment (although it is unclear how widely this is practiced).

Since 1997, the New Labour government has introduced various initiatives impinging on foundation roles. Until the recent creation of the Office of the Third Sector (2006), the Active Communities Unit (ACU) was responsible for the voluntary sector. Of particular relevance to foundations, the ACU's objectives included the development of productive partnerships between government and the voluntary and community sector at local, regional and national levels as well as the development of a modern regulatory framework for the sector, and to encourage good practice (Siederer 2002).

A number of themes emerge in foundations' discussion of emerging issues.

Monitoring, evaluation and accountability

Almost all foundations were grappling with monitoring and evaluation. No one saw the pressures for monitoring and evaluation diminishing over the coming years and some, especially those outside the foundation world, saw those pressures as likely to increase.

Monitoring and evaluation were seen as linked to accountability. But foundations, and others, generally had problems defining accountability:

> To whom should they be accountable? We all keep repeating this mantra but what does it mean?

Foundations, and to a lesser extent other commentators, did not agree that they should be more accountable to government, but several suggested that they should be more accountable to beneficiaries. Greater accountability to government was seen as being incompatible with foundations' innovative and creative roles:

> Our one great privilege is our lack of accountability but we should take advantage of that.

At the same time, some foundations recognized that lack of accountability allowed them to be inefficient and ineffective. Community foundations believed that they had to be more accountable to the communities they claim to serve, including, and especially, donors. Some outside the foundation world distinguished between transparency and accountability, suggesting that foundations should be more transparent, but not necessarily more accountable.

Another key issue for the future was the implications of the Community Fund 'saga'. In 2002 the Community Fund gave a grant to an asylum seeker organization; this was picked up by a tabloid newspaper and the Fund received thousands of complaints, and questions in Parliament. There were anxieties about future public scrutiny of all grant-makers, and about the Fund's future priorities in grant-making. Any changes in the Community Fund's priorities in grant-making were seen as likely to have further uncertain implications for demand on foundations.

Declining income

Above all, foundations were concerned about declining income as a result of changes in ACT, as discussed above and now, more significantly, declining stock markets. For some the combination of issues to do with substitution and 'doing more with less' was leading to the consideration of new, more policy-oriented approaches, building on the foundation's existing knowledge base. The changes in the Cabinet Office Strategy Unit report *Public Action, Private Benefit – A Review of Charities and the Wider Not-for-Profit Sector* were seen as significant in 'giving foundations even less excuse not to be inventive and interesting and social change oriented' (see below).

Governance

The governance of foundations did not appear to be a major issue for either foundations or other stakeholders. Board management relations were mentioned by some of the larger foundations. These respondents noted the difficulty of encouraging Board members to understand the complexity of grant-making, to accept that it required time, money and skills, and to focus on making hard choices to achieve a sustainable difference. Various respondents suggested that greater professionalization would create dilemmas regarding costs and bureaucratization which were culturally difficult for trustees.

Public and political understanding of foundations

The two topics on which foundations and others were in almost total agreement were public and political lack of understanding of foundations. But several respondents questioned whether foundations want to be understood, and what efforts they make to encourage better understanding.

General European and cross-border issues

With one exception the foundations giving internationally did not typically fund in Europe, and there was much more emphasis on funding in the Third World. The major challenges of cross-border giving identified included the difficulties of obtaining adequate knowledge of the organization requesting funding, as well as of the needs and the context; assessment and monitoring, and evaluation of international projects or initiatives.

The possibility of getting better value for money was pinpointed as a particular opportunity presented by international giving. The UK voluntary sector was seen as increasingly overcrowded, homogeneous, and business-oriented in methods. For these reasons, some foundations already giving internationally were considering expanding such giving.

With three exceptions, only the larger foundations were aware of the existence of the European Foundation Centre (EFC) and none had close links. Among those larger foundations aware of EFC there was some interest in the concept; but foundations' and trustees', lack of European orientation, as well as the cost of EFC membership were viewed as obstacles to greater involvement.

The three exceptions to this scenario were the two community foundations interviewed and one foundation working extensively in Europe and more widely. Interestingly, the two community foundations identified EFC with the Community Philanthropy Initiative (CPI) at the EFC (in reality, a project within EFC). The international foundation saw the EFC as a potentially important institution that was starting to change in the right direction. Some of those outside the foundation world, including those in government, were only vaguely aware of EFC. Others were generally more knowledgeable, and more critical.

Among foundations there was very little knowledge of the European Code of Practice, the European Foundation Statute, or any other European foundation issue. The only exceptions were the one foundation specializing in international funding and, to a lesser extent, community foundations with contacts with CPI at the EFC.

Among smaller foundations there was also a fear that pan-European initiatives would further marginalize smaller organizations. Those outside the foundation world were more likely to be aware of European initiatives but did not typically have any detailed knowledge or strong views.

Only two foundations identified European matters among their list of most important policy issues. Both of these foundations pointed to the increasing difficulty of separating UK and European problems and policies. These foundations suggested that increasing foundation involvement in wider Europe required legal changes, and cultural change to get 'Trustees beyond their conservative comfort zones'.

British foundations appear to adopt a highly pragmatic approach to wider European involvement – broadly consistent with their traditional emphasis on doing not talking. Where there are easy mechanisms for involvement and/or where there are tangible benefits, British foundations seem to become involved in wider European issues. There are, however, signs of change. Some foundations noted a desire to engage with European colleagues in discussions on specific policy and practice issues. But issues to do with costs, time and overheads were cited as potential barriers.

Future policy issues

Respondents varied in what they saw as the most important policy issues in the coming years. Foundation responses were as varied as those of other commentators. However, responses clustered under four broad headings.

Demonstrating effectiveness

Demonstrating effectiveness covered a variety of sub-themes, including the need for greater emphasis on, and development of practice in evaluation, accountability, learning and dissemination. Addressing issues of effectiveness was seen as a crucial policy issue not only in relation to external perceptions and pressures, but also for foundations' own quest for ways of dealing with the implications of their own likely reduced income. The most important policy issues identified by community foundations tended to be more specific and concerned with their own development needs. They included endowment building, expanding activities and becoming self-sustaining.

Relating to government

Relating to government was a theme running through a number of responses and has been discussed above. It included the issue of substitution; foundations and policy influence; carving out new roles and relationships in the light of new 'hyperactive' government policies and styles; and helping grant recipients bid for funding.

Legal and tax frameworks

For a minority of foundations one key policy issue was getting the legal and tax frameworks right. Others, mostly outside the foundation sector, saw addressing legal and tax frameworks as an opportunity to make space for new models of funding, including loans, investment in social businesses, and venture philanthropy.

Responding to new needs in the light of reduced public spending

Over half of all foundations interviewed saw public spending as one of the most important policy issues for foundations. Some pointed to the changing nature of poverty and exclusion, suggesting that some exclusion is becoming acceptable, and pointing to the lack of interest in income poverty at policy and practice level. Giving to individuals was another issue here, given the reduction in financial support for refugees and asylum seekers introduced at the beginning of 2003. These matters were seen as particularly important in the light of proposals to generate greater public involvement in Big Lottery Fund priorities in giving. Decreasing foundation income created further dilemmas here.

Conclusion

In recent years the foundation world has changed in various ways. There have been changes within individual foundations with the employment of paid staff. It is important, however, not to overstress the professionalization of the foundation world which is largely confined to the small number of wealthier foundations.

Despite some spectacular increases in assets and incomes, the majority of foundations experienced losses as a result of a change in Advance Corporation Tax, and all now live in a low interest economy.

New players have come in, including the Community Fund (now part of the Big Lottery Fund) dwarfing all other social welfare foundations.

Foundations have faced further change with a succession of re-interpretations of existing charity law by the Charity Commission, as well as changes in the rules governing campaigning. More radical changes in charity law, redefining the very notion of charity, are now underway. External regulation of foundations has also changed in the last ten years and looks set to change further.

Proposals for radical reform of the Charity Commission and its renaming as the Charity Regulation Authority, and for a new Standard Information Return from large charities (income or expenditure above £1 million) seem likely to cause some controversy among foundations. Some have argued that any further reporting burden will deter potential foundation creators. Others may take issue with the information required (ACF 2002: 6).

In the past foundations relied on the mantra that their role was to 'do what the state doesn't do' (Leat 1992), supporting unpopular causes, funding innovation and taking risks. In recent years, that mantra is increasingly seen as providing an inadequate guide to action. Almost all foundations were grappling with the issue of substitution: what it means in the changing policy context and whether, and how, to avoid it. Foundations and other stakeholders saw this as likely to be an ongoing issue, becoming more rather than less difficult.

Foundations' future relationships with government have to be seen in the context of the Cabinet Office Strategy Unit's *Public Action, Private Benefit – A Review of Charities and the Wider Not-for-Profit Sector*, published in 2002, which was accompanied by the Treasury's *Cross Cutting Review of the Role of the Voluntary Sector in Public Service Delivery*. The very fact that these reviews were conducted is significant in itself, highlighting the current Labour government's interest in the nonprofit sector and its role in public service delivery. Significantly, too, the review of charities has an introduction by the Prime Minister rather than the more usual departmental minister.

The Treasury's *Cross Cutting Review of the Role of the Voluntary and Community Sector in Service Delivery* has potentially significant, though mostly indirect, implications for foundations. Two recommendations are of particular indirect relevance to foundations: first, that the costs of contracts for services should reflect the full cost including any relevant part of overhead costs and, second, moving to a more stable funding relationship and ensuring that the sector is equipped to work effectively in partnership with government.[4] As part of its 2002 Spending Review the government announced a new £125 million fund – Futurebuilders – designed to help voluntary organizations undertake public service delivery, and to modernize themselves.

There are various interesting issues here. First, these measures may go some way toward removing some of the tensions for foundations in meeting requests to fund core costs which could, arguably, have been seen as part of the costs of delivering a contract with local or central government. Second, government appears to have involved foundations very little in advising on the needs of the sector in terms of capacity building. Third, and perhaps most significantly, the emphasis on 'partnership' between voluntary organizations and government, and on the roles of voluntary organizations in public service delivery, potentially leaves foundations in an ambiguous space. Are foundations also assumed to be included in public service delivery? If voluntary organizations and government are now partners where does this leave foundations? Are they included in the partnerships, are they too to be modernized or are they to be left to do their own thing?

At present it seems that foundations are not generally being invited to join the cosy party between voluntary organizations and government. This may be a mixed blessing. It may give foundations the potential freedom to develop truly distinctive roles. But if foundations want to develop distinctive, independent roles they need to provide a confident defence of their public value, beyond serving the agenda of the current government, and to be clear about why they deserve to be listened to.

Notes

1 See www.acf.org.uk.
2 www.independentsector.org.
3 www.hm-treasury.gov.uk/Spending_Review/spend.

References

ACF (Association of Charitable Foundations) (1997) Promoting the effectiveness of UK grant-making trusts, *Annual Review 1996–97*. London: ACF.
Association of Charitable Foundations (1997) *Trust and Foundation News*, June/July.
Association of Charitable Foundations (2002) *Annual Review 2001–02*. London: ACF
Association of Charitable Foundations (2002) Briefing paper on *Public Action, Private Benefit – a Review of Charities and the Wider Not-for-Profit Sector*. Cabinet Office Strategy Unit report – September 2002.
Anheier, H.K. and Leat, D. (2002) *From Charity to Creativity, Philanthropic Foundations for the 21st Century*. London: Comedia.
CAF (Charities Aid Foundation) (1999) *The Directory of Smaller Grant Making Trusts 1998–1999*. Tonbridge: CAF.
Chesterman, M. (1979) *Charities, Trusts and Social Welfare*. London: Weidenfeld and Nicholson.
Community Foundation Network (2002) *Review of the Year 2001–02*. London: Community Foundation Network.
Fitzherbert, L., Addison, D. and Rahman, F. (1999) *1999/2000 A Guide to the Major Trusts, Vol. 1 The Top 300 Trusts*. London: Directory of Social Change.
Griffiths, D., Traynor, T., Walker, L. and Wiggins, S. (2002) *A Guide to Scottish Trusts, 2002–2003*. London: Directory of Social Change.
Home Office (1989) *Charities: A Framework for the Future*. London: HMSO.
Humphreys, G. (1997) Community Foundations in Review 1995–6. In Pharaoh, C. and Smerdon, M. (eds) *Dimensions of the Voluntary Sector*, 1997 edition. West Malling: Charities Aid Foundation.
Leat, D. (1992) *Trusts in Transition*, York: Joseph Rowntree Foundation.
Pharoah, C. and CIU (1998) *Dimensions of the Voluntary Sector*, 1998 edition, Tonbridge: Charities Aid Foundation.
Pharoah, C. and Siederer, N. (1997): Number, income and assets – new estimates. In Pharaoh, C. and Smerdon, M. (eds) *Dimensions of the Voluntary Sector*, 1997 edition. West Malling: Charities Aid Foundation.
Siederer, N. (2002) Joined-up government website announced by revamped ACU, *Trust and Foundation News*, June/July/August 2002: 4.
Villemur, A. (ed.) (1995) *Directory of Grant Making Trusts 1991*. Tonbridge: Charities Aid Foundation.
Vincent, J. and Pharoah, C. (2000) *Dimensions 2000*, Volume 3: Patterns of Independent Grantmaking in the UK. West Malling: Charities Aid Foundation.

8   Czech Republic[1]

Marek Skovajsa

Introduction

Czech foundations are a part of the package of institutions and social values that returned to Czech society with the fall of communism. An older domestic philanthropic tradition combines with models adopted from Western liberal democracies to produce specifically post-communist types of foundations. Czech foundations are also significant actors in the process of post-communist transformation and it is precisely this transformation that provides the key to a deeper understanding of the roles Czech foundations want to, and do, play.

The 360 (approximately) Czech foundations officially registered as of 2004 display unequal levels of professionalism and differ in their ability to think systematically about the ways in which they should operate in the existing social setting. The roles and visions of Czech foundations are best seen in conjunction with the perception of the roles they expect the state to play. The memories of an overbearing communist state made the desire for a sharp distinction between state and civil society in the early 1990s quite strong and led to the pre-eminence of the liberal vision. Yet the story is more complex. After having retreated from many areas, the post-communist state has been undergoing a process of reconstruction and the original liberal preference for a minimal state has gradually given way to a broader and more realistic assessment of its role. The foundations soon realized that they are partners of the state rather than an opposition to it. Furthermore, the fact that they received substantial support from the state made it impossible for them to mistake independence from the state as total isolation from it. This is why, in the present study, the dominant liberal vision of foundations as independent products of a self-organizing civil society amalgamated with the view that foundations should occupy a position of subsidiarity vis-à-vis the state and fulfil complementary functions where the state is less efficient. Thus, the complementarity role in respect of the state and the liberal vision, followed by the corporatist one, are the most popular visions among Czech foundation stakeholders. By the same token, roles of substitution or redistribution and the state-controlled vision that depict the position of foundations as marginal or dependent on the state are strongly rejected.

A profile of foundations in the Czech Republic

Historical development

The present state of the foundation sector in the Czech Republic is the outcome of its development since the fall of communism in 1989. This is a fact even if the tradition of giving to, and through, foundations in Czech society stretches all the way back to the early Middle Ages. The promising development of the Czech non-profit sector in the twentieth century was thwarted by two totalitarian interludes, the Nazi occupation in 1939–1945 and the much longer period of Communist rule in 1948–1989.

After the collapse of communism, the foundation sector became both a symptom and an agent of the deep social transformations affecting Czech society. Its post-1989 development can be divided into three phases characterized by varying growth rates, levels of regulation and changes in the policy environment (cf. Frištenská 2000):

- 1990–1992: rapid, but weakly regulated growth in a liberal and supportive policy climate;
- 1993–1996: continuing and still weakly regulated growth combined with a difficult relationship with the government;
- 1997–present: slow growth, efficient legislative regulation, balanced relationship with the government, restructuring of the sector.

The state's assistance to foundations is quite unique. Through a project known as the *Foundation Investment Fund* (FIF), the government distributed the sum total of €41 million (CZK 1,333 billion) to 73 foundations. In this way, it more than doubled the total volume of endowments registered by all Czech foundations (see Table 8.2). At the same time, the foundation sector itself began to mature. In 1997, the Czech Donors Forum, an association of grant-makers, was established to offer advice to foundations, to defend their interests in the legislative arena and to cultivate philanthropy among the general public and corporate donors.

Legal issues

Foundations in the Czech Republic are legally defined by the Act No. 227/1997 on Foundations and Foundation Funds, which took effect in January 1998. It provided the basis for the much more effective regulation and oversight of foundations than before and caused a sharp decrease in the total number of foundations registered (from 5,238 in December 1997 to 274 in 1999; see Table 8.1). The present Czech law defines the foundation as 'a special property association established pursuant to the law to accomplish generally beneficial objectives'. The normative view that underlies the definition of foundations in the Czech legal system is clearly that of grant-giving foundations. The assets registered as foundation endowments must be kept intact and only the proceeds originating from them can be used for grant-making and administrative expenses. All grant-making has strictly to correspond to the foundation's declared publicly beneficial purpose. However, the clause setting the minimum foundation endowment at roughly €15,600 (CZK 500,000) falls short of making sure that all foundations have an income sufficient for the effective promotion of public benefit goals. The foundations, as private entities independent of the government, are prohibited from receiving grants from the state (transfers of funds within the FIF program do not count as such). The revenue from a foundation's property that is part of its endowment and listed as such in the Foundation Registry is exempt from revenue tax. All other revenues are subject to normal treatment in accordance with the Czech law. Tax deductions are provided for both individual and corporate donors to foundations.

There are two other forms of non-profit legal entities in the Czech Republic that arguably fulfil the criteria of the structural/operational definition of foundations (Anheier 2001). The 'foundation funds' are property associations that differ from foundations as defined by the Czech law in that no part of their assets is transformed into an 'eternal' endowment. The 'public benefit corporations' which, despite their official name, are not membership-based, operate their own programmes and provide publicly beneficial services that are specified in their statutes.

An empirical profile of Czech foundations

There were strong patterns of growth in the Czech foundation sector after 1989 until the 1997 Foundation Act, which reduced the total number of foundations by more than 90 per cent. Table 8.1 documents the varying growth rates for foundations, other foundation-like entities (foundation funds and public benefit corporations) and civil associations as major recipients of foundations grants.

Available data on the growth of the total size of foundation endowments and their sources is shown in Table 8.2. More than 50 per cent of foundation endowments were donated to Czech foundations by the government.

Complete and reliable data on the fields of activity in which Czech foundations make grants or operate their own programmes are almost inexistent. Table 8.3 shows the breakdown of grant money distributed in 1998–1999 among the ICNPO fields of activity for the sample of 64 foundations that participated in the second round of the FIF.

In sum, the development of the Czech foundation sector has been

Table 8.1 Growth of the Czech NGO sector, by year and type of organization

Year	Type			
	Foundations	Foundation funds	Public benefit corporations	Civil associations
1990	N	–	–	3,879
1991	N	–	–	9,366
1992	1,551	–	–	15,393
1993	2,768	–	–	21,694
1994	3,800	–	–	24,978
1995	4,253	–	–	26,814
1996	4,392	–	1	27,807
1997	5,238	–	52	30,297
1998	94*	71	129	36,046
1999	274*	695	560	38,072
2000	307*	735	557	42,302
2001	330*	784	701	47,101
2002	338*	825	762	49,108

Sources: Czech Bureau of Statistics, Albertina Monitoring Service.

Notes
Figures with * from: Buzková 2002: 14.
N = data not available.
– = the given type of NGO did not yet exist.

Table 8.2 Endowment total of Czech foundations, by year and source (in € millions/CZK millions)

	Endowment total	From the state		From private sources	
1999	69/2194	38/1220	56%	30/974	44%
2001	71/2274	38/1220	53%	33/1054	47%
2002	76/2425	40/1290	53%	35/1135	47%

Sources: 1999 – Müller 2000: 33; 2001, 2002 – Buzková 2002: 16.

Table 8.3 Grants given by 64 Czech foundations that participated in the second round of the FIF, in years 1998–1999, by field of activity

	ICNPO field							
	1	2	3	4	5	6	7	8
Grants disbursed (%)	19,7	16,5	11,8	17,4	4,6	5,8	11,8	6,0

Source: adapted from Müller 2002: 28.

Notes
Volume total of grants disbursed: €20,913,000 (CZK 669,200,000).
Number of foundations: 64.

short, but quite dynamic. With the 1997 Foundations Act foundations acquired clear identity of assets engaged primarily in grant-making and strictly separated from the state. At the same time, however, the state has contributed more than 50 per cent of the total endowments owned by Czech foundations today. The available data show that the activities of Czech foundations concentrate in the ICNPO fields of culture and sport, social services, education and health.

Roles of Czech foundations

In this section the primary aim is to explore foundation representatives and stakeholders' interpretations of the roles foundations should perform in Czech society. Second, the aim is to determine what roles Czech foundations are able to perform given the existing constraints on their operation, such as legal requirements on the size of their assets. As will be shown, the role expectations of some foundations are not matched by their capacities for actual role performance. And, conversely, foundations perform roles which they do not consider of primary importance to themselves simply because these roles are feasible and they are pushed towards them by the prevalent policy environment.

Complementarity to the state

The notion that the role of foundations is complementary to that of the state was the most widely accepted of all of the roles. According to foundation representatives, the state is responsible for the large-scale production of public goods, whereas foundations should operate in those areas and situations, where the state is unable to serve legitimate needs, because they are too narrow and weakly represented. As the executive secretary of a large foundation focusing on education stated:

> In the area of education the state can't measure up to us. We can much better than any state institution or the school itself find the people who deserve to be supported. . . . The state's concern is with quantity and the foundations' with quality. It should be so in all spheres of society. It's useful this way.

The feasibility of foundations engaging in the complementarity role is heavily dependent on the resources a foundation has available. The general under-funding of Czech foundations makes it very difficult for them to perform the complementarity role successfully, even in a narrowly defined area, over a longer period of time. For instance, a corporate foundation established to support orphans after they leave their institutions had to abandon its original objectives because of the lack of support from its founder and potential sponsors, local entrepreneurs. Although this is a

rather extreme example it illustrates well the potential setbacks foundations may suffer when they try to complement the state.

Substitution

The vast majority of all interviewees believe that foundations should not
substitute the state in fulfilling the obligations it has towards its citizens.
The state should not be offered help where it clearly fails to meet its fundamental duties, as stressed by a member of the management board of a
regional foundation:

> Foundations should be the complement of the state, they should not
> substitute the state in the duties it has in relation to its citizens,
> because we pay our taxes to the state, not to foundations.

The negative view of the substitutive role is particularly typical of foreign-
funded foundations and foundations that emphasize their belonging to
civil society and independence from the state. Only for a specific group of
foundations is substitution acceptable. They believe that the state is
unable to meet its responsibilities in certain areas but the problems
cannot remain unattended. These are the foundations operating in fields
where the state's role is, or used to be crucial, such as health care or
culture. For example, a number of foundations raise funds or supply
special equipment for state-owned hospitals. Even more emphatically than
in the case of the complementarity role, foundations are aware of their
limitations when the substitution of a function previously exerted by the
state is at stake. With the resources they have they cannot substitute the
state in the large-scale funding of service provision. Furthermore, foundations, as private entities, do not have access to many legal instruments the
state can use to get things done efficiently. The feasibility problem would
be serious, were it not for the foundations' general unwillingness to function as a substitute for the state.

Innovation

The role of foundations as promoters of innovation in society has been
verbally agreed to by most interviewees in our research. Unlike the complementarity and substitutive roles, the foundation stakeholders were less
explicit about *how* Czech foundations acted in an innovative way. Innovation is very important in the opinion of representatives of foreign-funded
foundations, yet one can infer from the examples they gave, and from
the practice of their foundations, that it often consists of importing tried
and tested attitudes and practices from Western societies. The foundations that have incorporated into their visions the idea that they should
be agents of innovation are the largest and most active foundations,

especially foreign-funded ones. However, there are also major foundations, significantly those working in such fields as the preservation of
national culture, health or social care, that do not consider experiment-
ing and innovation to be an important aspect of their activities. For the
representatives of these foundations, it is more essential to make certain
services possible. This view coincides with an acceptance of the substitution role.

The feasibility problem in the case of innovativeness is linked to the
need for foundations to be able to sustain new practices and attitudes over
a certain period of time, if they are to take roots in society. This means
that large and sufficiently endowed foundations are suited to the promotion of innovation in broader social areas, whereas smaller foundations
can contribute to innovation only in very narrowly defined fields.

Redistribution

Many foundation representatives have a cautious attitude towards a view of
foundations as instruments of social redistribution given that equality in
access to basic goods was one of the cornerstones of the official ideology
sustaining the communist regime. For most of them redistribution is
much less important than the roles of complementing the state, promoting innovation or pluralism. In the opinion of an interviewee, the President of the Management Board of a foreign-funded foundation
redistribution is a rather trivial feature of all foundation giving, but
cannot be considered a full-fledged role of foundations in society:

> No foundation is established to redistribute income, but all do it.
> However, this is not their primary purpose.

Redistribution was considered essential solely in the case of corporate
foundations in which both their representatives and other stakeholders
identify with the need for mechanisms of redistribution across social
classes. Nonetheless, in practice many of the activities, programmes and
support schemes of foundations, particularly of the larger entities are
clearly aimed at the redistribution of resources.

Social and policy change

Foundation stakeholders stressed many times how important it is to
change the practices, attitudes and values instilled by decades of communist domination. However, the empowerment of excluded social groups
failed to elicit strong acceptance due to associations that were made by
many interviewees between the concept of social justice and the communist ideology. One noteworthy exception to this rule is the way in which
foundation stakeholders frame their approach to the Roma minority,

which is viewed as a social group in need of foundations' support. This entails changing the policy climate and the attitude of the state.

> The state will never provide protection to those minorities which it does not need or which it does not want to integrate, but foundations are in a position to do it. (Director of an umbrella organization)

Representatives of foreign-funded foundations are more willing to include the promotion of social and policy change, understood as support for the efforts/activities of socially excluded groups among the main elements of a vision for their foundation.

Notwithstanding financial constraints, which are less serious here than in the case of the previously discussed roles, a further obstacle to the feasibility of this role is an insufficient ability to exert influence on the legislative and policy-making processes which have the power to alter the position of particular social groups. This shows how important it is for foundations to develop a coordinated relationship with policy-makers and to become partners in the policy-making process that the government takes seriously.

Preservation of traditions and cultures

The preservation of past traditions and cultures is a less important role for representatives of most Czech foundations. In post-communist societies traditions might be linked to their communist past or strongly opposed to it. However, in their vast majority, Czech foundation stakeholders take traditions to mean something else. Nonetheless, the views on how important it is to preserve non-communist traditions are very different. For the representatives of a foundation that had previously been based in western Europe and supported members of the anti-communist dissident movement, the preservation of past traditions has only a secondary role. On the other hand, one older foundation that was created at the beginning of the twentieth century views the preservation of patriotic and national traditions as its supreme obligation. Preservation was frequently contrasted with innovation and the support it received was clearly lower. The feasibility of this role in general depends on the nature and importance of the tradition in question.

Pluralism

Czech foundations are well aware of the potential to promote, through their grant-giving or programmes, pluralism and alternatives to the mainstream:

> The importance of foundations lies in principle in pluralism and this presents a counterweight to the one-sided bias in the assistance pro-

vided by the state.... The maximum of plurality in democratic and stable institutions is always essential.

(Member of the management of a major foreign-funded foundation)

Yet, for some interviewees, the most important task for foundations is above all to serve the public benefit irrespective of whether they achieve it in the same, or different way than the state. Representatives of foundations that work within a policy area, such as health care or culture, with the strong participation of public institutions, do not find this particular role very appealing.

Pluralism is most valued by the foreign-funded foundations. As in the case of innovation, alternative practices may mean 'those imported from the West'. Yet, some representatives of foreign-funded foundations offered a different understanding of why pluralism is important. They believe that it is a substantive value in modern democratic society that keeps in check the power of the state and increases the efficiency with which various objectives can be attained. The promotion of pluralism frequently accompanies complementarity and innovation. One large foreign-funded foundation aims to promote new and alternative approaches to pressing social issues, such as the situation of minorities or care for the terminally ill with an expectation that they will be taken over by the state. A systematic effort to introduce alternative ways of doing things is costly and therefore only major foundations can afford it. That is why larger foreign-funded and other well established foundations can promote alternatives more successfully and over longer time periods than smaller ones.

Roles of Czech foundations: summary assessment

The role expectations of Czech foundation stakeholders focus around the idea that foundations are actors of civil society and as such independent of the state. They are expected to do what the state is not supposed or able to do. The actual roles of Czech foundations, however, display subtle, but significant differences. Since foundations are not as (financially) strong and independent of the state as they would like to be, the complementarity role remains their strongest role. All of the other ones are less prominent. One can distinguish two senses of complementarity to the state: one is an autonomous complementarity, when foundations act out of their own resources, the other is a delegated complementarity, when foundations complement the state or the European Union using money they have received in areas and for purposes determined by these donors. To better understand the way Czech foundation stakeholders perceive the roles of Czech foundations we proceed to focus on the different visions of the place of foundations in society.

Visions of Czech foundations and related policy issues

In this section we explore how Czech foundation stakeholders understand the various predefined visions, which capture the nature of the various positions (and roles) of foundations in society. These visions are discussed in turn, with a view to determining what policy implications can be derived from them and what they tell us about current issues in the Czech foundation sector.

Liberal vision

This is the most widely accepted vision of all. It is also the model most resembling the concept of a strong, decent and self-organizing civil society. Part of its attractiveness lies, without doubt, in the étatist nature of the former communist regime. The representatives of foundations and other non-profit organizations were naturally biased towards emphasizing the independence and autonomy of their sector. The liberal vision is not only connected with such roles as promoting social change, innovation and pluralism, but also with complementarity. The foreign-funded and many domestic foundations, large and small, construct their self-under-standing around the liberal model and there is no exaggeration in saying that this vision lies at the core of their identity.

The major policy concerns related to the liberal vision that were raised in the research interviews have to do with the conditions under which foundations can form an autonomous force in society. Foundation representatives desire better tax treatment of foundation donors and the introduction of 1 per cent revenue tax transfers to NGOs as they expect these steps to increase the financial independence of the non-profit sector and to reduce the role of the state. They also realize that more coordination within both the non-profit and the foundation sectors is required to increase the chances of foundations succeeding in ambitious projects and influencing the legislative and policy-making processes in ways that are favourable to the public interest.

Corporatist vision

The corporatist model is the second most popular vision among foundation stakeholders, which is a sign that they acknowledge that Czech foundations often cooperate closely with the government in the fields of social services provision, health care and education. It is striking that this vision is quite popular although the Czech Republic can hardly be considered a typical example of corporatism. The provisions of the existing law discourage foundations from running their own programmes. Thus, foundations as a rule do not provide services directly, but give grants to operating non-profit organizations. Quite often these grants complement funding from the government or regional self-administrative bodies. The legal bias against operating foundations makes it necessary to understand the subsidiary relationship between foundations and the state within the corporatist model in the Czech case in a specific way. Foundations are 'backup sources' of funds for operating NGOs where the state is unable to contribute. If they wish to use their resources effectively, foundations have to cooperate with the corresponding public agencies. A community foundation included in our sample has developed close working contacts with various municipal and regional institutions. Due to its involvement in the regional policy-making process, it has a better chance to attract funding from among the entrepreneurs from the region.

The foundation representatives supporting the corporatist model emphasized that closer coordination and better communication with government agencies is needed to make it efficient. Representatives of foundations that intend to operate their own programmes stressed that these foundations should not be put in a disadvantageous position by the law. However, if this demand were to be met the whole philosophy and fundamental premises of the Czech foundation law would have to be revised and radically changed.

Business vision

Most foundation representatives believe that the business model does not offer an adequate account of the actual and ideal place of foundations in society. This is true even of the representatives of corporate foundations, who agreed that foundations can be useful instruments of corporate citizenship, which was one part of the description of this vision, but were not willing to admit that companies support foundations to serve self-interested objectives, which was its other part. An exceptional case of successful cooperation between a foundation and the corporate sphere was provided by a community foundation that has established good working contacts with the regional corporate sector (the foundation's supervisory board is composed of its representatives) and serves as an agency through which corporate money is channelled to recipients in their region.

Some salient policy concerns were raised in conjunction with the business vision, notably that the tax treatment of corporate donors should be improved and there is a need to strengthen the tradition of corporate giving more generally. Foundation stakeholders also stressed that long-term partnerships have to be sought between foundations and the corporate sector, offering stability of income to foundations and a positive image to companies. The umbrella organization of Czech foundations, the Czech Donors Forum, has a special programme that aims to promote corporate philanthropy and closer cooperation between foundations and companies.

Social democratic vision

There are very few indications that this vision is accepted by a significant portion of Czech foundations. One reason is that it accords an important position to operating foundations, but as mentioned above Czech foundations are in this respect severely restricted by the law. Given that the law casts foundations as non-operating, purely grant-making entities, they can only intervene in the welfare system on a significant scale as grant-makers. This makes them more independent of the state than the social democratic model assumes. Most Czech foundation representatives are not inclined to identify with the social democratic model precisely because they think that it accords too strong a role to the state, leaving little space for the free activity and initiative of foundations. It is a matter of fact, however, that many foundations engage in the kind of activity that can be described as complementing the state in the framework of a developed welfare-system. This is particularly the case regarding foundations which operate in the health care sector.

Since the social democratic model is not accepted as a point of departure for foundation practice, no fundamental policy issues concerning it were expressed in the interviews. Three major obstacles stand in the way of a more thorough implementation of this model in Czech society: legal bias against operating foundations, the non-existence of public foundations and the fact that it is impossible for foundations to receive grants from the state.

State-controlled vision

Unsurprisingly, given how the liberal model supplies many foundation representatives and policy-makers with a framework for their understanding of foundations, the idea that foundations should be ultimately subservient to the state encountered strong resistance among our interviewees. Some foundation representatives believe that the current foundation legislation is too strict, far exceeding the legitimate concern of the state. Nonetheless, the notion of a state-controlled model for foundations, far from being merely academic, reflects the continuing tension in the relationship between foundations and the government. The state (especially the Parliament, and Ministry of Finance) is not willing to give up a portion of its revenues to contribute to the financial independence of the non-profit sector via the improvement of the tax treatment of foundation donors and the introduction of optional 1 per cent revenue tax transfers to NGOs. Such measures would increase the amount of funds that foundations can incorporate into their endowments or use for grant-making. But both would at the same time cut a slice off the sum total of resources over which politicians exert control.

Peripheral vision

It comes as no surprise that no foundation representative in our sample agreed that foundations are largely insignificant. Even the most sceptical among them believed that with all existing limitations, such as the insufficient size of their endowments, foundations can perform very important roles, at least in specific social domains. The policy-makers, too, rejected the view that foundations are marginal and insignificant. Rather, they see foundations as forming an influential segment of the non-profit sector, with clearly defined responsibilities and opportunities for social eminence.

As shown in the preceding subsections, the way in which the foundations' relationship to the state is defined appears as a key feature not just of roles, but also of the visions explored in our research. The most strongly accepted vision of the place of foundations in society is the liberal one. The interviewees felt that all the other visions did not describe so accurately what their foundations are and should be doing. The two most unpopular visions, the state-controlled and the peripheral one, are in direct contradiction with the liberal vision. The corporatist, social-democratic and business visions, although not directly opposed to the liberal vision, address those aspects of the foundations' activities that are more technical and down-to-earth than the general distinction between the state and civil society. These visions seem to become more appealing to foundations at later stages of the post-communist transformation, when concern with concrete policy problems prevails over broad ideological disputes. In particular, there are indications that the corporatist model that involves a relationship of subsidiarity between foundations and the state is becoming increasingly important for Czech foundations.

Current developments and emerging issues

It is no exaggeration to say that the Czech foundations presently face a turning point in their post-1989 history. As the support from foreign (US and European) sources is waning, they are confronted with the necessity to rely on themselves, on their ability to articulate attractive visions, on their administrative capacity and on managerial skills more than ever before. The decision of the government to give a considerable financial injection to Czech foundations through the FIF is not likely to be repeated and foundations cannot reckon on any other form of state subventions. The most urgent task is that of laying bases for the self-sustainability of the Czech foundation sector.

If foundations play a significant role at all, then they certainly play it in the non-profit sector. As some observers put it, they form the 'elite' in the Czech non-profit sector, its best organized, trained and most active segment. Moreover, they are quite aware of their relative strength compared to other NGOs:

> The foundations have gotten ahead of the rest of the non-profit
> sector. They were the only ones to be able to form an association and
> so [to] find some common goals, they also have an ethical code.
>
> (Director of an umbrella organization)

Czech foundations, even the big ones, are not in a position to fully substitute from their own resources the financial assistance provided by foreign donors that will cease with their withdrawal. In this new situation those foundations which want to maintain their privileged position within the non-profit sector can either try to transform themselves into a type of implementing agency for EU funds or programmes, or they should content themselves with the role they can perform with the resources available to them. Since foundations are not able to compete with the state or the EU in terms of funds paid out to other non-profit organizations, they have to direct their giving to areas neglected by the state where smaller resources can produce large benefits. The promotion of pluralism or policy and social change are relevant here.

There is also no exaggeration in stating that the accession to the EU represents a milestone in the development of the Czech foundation sector. Foundations and other NGOs are learning how to apply for European grants. Yet, Europe does not figure high on the list of themes around which the Czech foundations build their visions. Czech foundation stakeholders in their majority do not see Europe as a field of operation that would open up new possibilities to them, nor are they aware of the opportunities provided by initiatives such as the European Foundation Centre or the European Foundation Statute. Europe is associated predominantly with prospects for more generous funding from EU funds and programmes. Only the leading foreign-funded foundations have a systematic strategy for adapting to the expected changes and the new constraints and opportunities that are likely to arise from the accession process.

Conclusion

Czech foundations were more successful in creating appropriate visions and roles for themselves the more they were able to adapt in the post-communist situation to the models guiding the operation of foundations in Western societies, the liberal model in particular. As a consequence, foundations have concentrated on roles that they as independent forces can perform better than the state-controlled entities or the state itself: to complement state activities where they are insufficient, to promote pluralism, to introduce innovative practices. Although Czech foundations orient themselves towards the liberal model more than towards any other, the slow but steady increase of the influence of the corporatist model can also be detected, although the political context in which this happens is not typically corporatist. Rather, it shows the tendency of

Czech foundations to enter, as grant-makers, into a relationship of subsidiarity with the state.

As discussed in the previous section, Czech foundations are in their vast majority not ready for Europe. With rare exceptions, they have left Europe out of their visions and failed to reflect on the roles they can play in the enlarged European Union. The main domestic challenge Czech foundations are facing at present is that of learning to rely more on themselves, not only on their economic resources, but also on their creative potential in order to administer their assets more efficiently and to seek out new sources of income. The cultivation of philanthropy in the general public and in the private sector is a mandatory option not just for foundations, but for every Czech NGO. In terms of the production of viable visions that can guide their activities foundations should improve the mechanisms that assist them in identifying the issues that call for their concern. They also need to follow closely, and influence the changes in the policy environment in all of the areas in which they operate.

Note

1   I would like to express my thanks to Dr. Miroslav Pospíšil, whose collaboration was essential in the initial phase of the research project and who gave me useful feedback on various sections of the research report on which this chapter is based.

References

Anheier, H.K. (2001) 'Foundations in Europe: A comparative perspective'. In Schlüter, A., Then, V. and Walkenhorst, P. (eds) *Foundations in Europe*, London: Directory of Social Change.

Buzková, M. (2002) *Polarizace nadačního sektoru v České republice po roce 1997* [The Polarization of the Foundation Sector in the Czech Republic after 1997], Unpublished material of the Czech Donors Forum.

Czech Donors Forum (2001) *Adresář nadací v České republice* [Directory of Foundations in the Czech Republic], Prague: Czech Donors Forum.

Frištenská, H. (2000) 'Vývoj organizované filantropie v ČR po roce 1990' [Development of Organized Philanthropy in the Czech Republic after 1990], www.donorsforum.cz 22.3. 2003.

ICN (2002) *Statistika počtu neziskových organizací v letech 1990–2002* [Statistical Overview of Czech Non-Profit Organizations 1990–2002], Praha: ICN.

Müller, J. (2000) *Ekonomické prostředí pro občanský neziskový sektor v České republice* [Economic Environment for the Civic Non-Profit Sector in the Czech Republic], Prague: Czech Donors Forum.

Müller, J. (2002) *Kapitalizace českých nadací* [Capitalization of Czech Foundations], Prague: Czech Donors Forum.

9 Denmark

Ulla Habermann

Introduction

In a small country like Denmark, with only five million inhabitants, there are as many as 14,000 foundations. However, at first glance, foundations in Denmark are usually quite anonymous entities. With few exceptions they do not seek to publicize their activities. It is not unusual for foundations with large assets not to publish an annual report. This lack of openness is reflected in how little research has been carried out in the field. Foundations are under-researched and we lack insights into the way foundations act and function (Lynge Andersen 2002). In a way this also reflects the lack of interest that society, including the press and the politicians, has shown in foundations.

The largest 70 foundations in Denmark have more than half of the total assets of all foundations at their disposal (Lynge Andersen 2002). This means that the country is cluttered with small charitable institutions, often with so little resources that they find it difficult to live up to the expectations of their own statutes. The few foundations (some of them included in this research) that do have large assets have the opportunity to play an important role in society. To a certain extent, these foundations set up partnerships with each other, with voluntary organizations, with businesses, with the state and with local authorities.

Ironically they do not openly admit to their power and they seem to play down their own importance, partly for reasons of modesty and partly to protect their own interests. What is more, the eight foundations interviewed for this study do not want to be taken for granted. They do not automatically want to take up a role of complementarity in their relationships with the state. They are very conscious of setting their own agenda and of formulating their own visions. However, although they do not want to complement the state, in recognizing broader changes in society they are often forced into the role of complementarity.

A profile of foundations

A short history of foundations in Denmark

In Denmark, foundations and charitable institutions[1] have existed since the Middle Ages. Traditionally, foundations were connected to the Catholic Church and its charitable work, for example poor relief and caring for the sick. After the reformation in 1536, foundations adapted to the new societal order by permutation[2] (Møller 1987). In the late nineteenth century, philanthropy became the bourgeois answer to addressing prevalent social problems. Donor contributions were particularly visible in charitable provision and in the promotion of art and science.[3]

In the twentieth century, under the influence of the emerging industrial society and an opening up of the democratic process, new foundations adopted a sense of social responsibility. The foundations of this period competed and collaborated with the emerging welfare state.[4] However, corporate foundations did not constitute a significant presence until the 1950s (Lynge Andersen 2002). Many of the bigger Danish foundations were founded as late as after the Second World War. From 1960 until 1980 patterns of considerable growth in the number of foundations can be identified. During this period, the number of foundations more than doubled from 4,099 to 8,852. Increased attention was paid to the regulation of foundations, and this was followed by changes in legislation.

Legal issues

There is no legal definition of 'foundation', but the law is based on the following characteristics:

- assets must be irretrievably separated from the means of the founder;
- there can be one or more aim(s);
- an autonomous board has the authority of disposal over the assets;
- the foundation is legally regarded as having independent legal personality;
- no person outside of the foundation has ownership of the assets.

Furthermore, the law requires that a foundation has specific statutes, a board, a certain amount of capital, and that it sets up rules for annual reports and revision. Until 1984 Denmark had no proper law governing the field of foundations. However, in the 1970s public debate about foundations had gained such momentum that the government set up a committee to look into the matter of the 'secret life of the foundations'.

The work of the Foundation Commission, established initially by the Social Democratic government in 1978, resulted in the following four laws:

- *The Registration law* (Registreringsloven, 1983) according to which all foundations with a capital of more than 50,000 Danish crowns (approximately €7,500) were obliged to register. An evaluation of the bylaws of the foundations was also carried out. For new foundations (founded after 1985) the capital requirements were 200,000 Danish crowns. In 1991 this increased to 250,000 Danish crowns (approximately €36,000). However, in 1992 the Registration Law was abolished on the grounds that it was too bureaucratic.

- *Law on corporate foundations* (Lov om erhversdrivende fonde, 1984) and *Law on charitable foundations and certain associations* (Lov om almennyttige fonde og visse foreninger, 1984). These two laws on charitable and corporate foundations (from 1984) ensure that distributions are made according to the bylaws and that assets are not simply accumulated. Furthermore, the aim is to support the charitable foundations and to underline the different nature of charitable and corporate foundations.

- *The taxation law* (Fondsskatteloven, 1986). The aim of the taxation law was to place corporate foundations (erhversdrivende fonde) on a par with business co-operatives in relation to taxation rules. This means that all income from all sorts of activities (interests, inheritance, gifts, fees and profit due to appreciation), and not only surplus must be taxed. This, however, does not affect the charitable foundations, which are exempt from paying taxes.

Empirical profile

As it is no longer obligatory to maintain a central registration of foundations in Denmark it is difficult to assess the exact number of foundations. The Ministry of Justice, being responsible for the legislation on foundations, estimates that there are about 11,000–12,000 foundations in all. Experts in the field estimate a total of 14,000 foundations, and of those the biggest 69 foundations have half of the (total) capital at their disposal.[5] No single source can provide the exact number (Lynge Andersen 1999). In the KRAK register, which is broadly considered the most reliable information source, foundations are registered according to their purpose and activities.[6] A large number of Danish foundations tend to be grant-making, i.e. they distribute grants to applicants. But some of the bigger foundations also have operating activities, i.e. they initiate their own projects or programmes. Usually foundations in Denmark work on their own according to their statutes, but in some cases they engage in joint ventures to support larger projects.

Table 9.1 indicates which purposes and fields of activity are the most common destinations for foundation grant-making. In 2002 giving focused on predominantly social and health issues closely followed by educational issues. The table also shows a total of 22,265 foundations in 1988 and 14,308 in 2002 indicating a dramatic decline in numbers. But the picture is not so

Table 9.1 Danish foundations registered in KRAK 1988 and 2002 (total number of entries)

	1988	2002
Social issues and health	8,930	5,640
Education	3,716	4,320
Research	1,593	1,372
Religion	726	314
Culture, sport, environment	2,179	1,182
Private enterprise foundations	4,539	940
Others	582	540
Total	22,265	14,308

simple. In 1988, several foundations with more than one target group appeared several times in the register under different headings. Furthermore, the most likely reason for the decline is that it is no longer obligatory to enter the central register. Foundations with either very small assets or with no public purpose tend to choose not to register. Therefore, the number of foundations has probably not declined so dramatically – but fewer foundations choose to have their details recorded and published.

The eight foundations interviewed for the qualitative part of this study cannot represent all Danish foundations. Moreover, the interviews cannot be used as an expression of the attitudes of Danish foundations as such. However, on the whole they certainly form a distinct part of the Danish foundation scene. They are financially important and they set an exemplary role in terms of conduct. In the following analysis, the interviews,[7] annual reports of foundations (where available) and other written material have been examined and interpreted according to the specific issues of interest in this study, namely the roles and visions of Danish foundations.

Foundations roles

The notion of 'roles' is not easily accepted by the representatives of the Danish foundations included in this study, nor do they easily identify with certain roles. Moreover, one might expect the roles of foundations in a highly developed (social democratic) welfare state setting, as in Denmark, to be characterized by a close and well-coordinated relationship with the state. However, the foundations do not always see this relationship as so straightforward.

Complementarity

Although this role is not one that the foundations favour, it is one that they often have to accept in a welfare state context. The foundations seem to be very much aware of what their role means in this respect:

> We are very much aware not to go in and fill the gaps caused by government cuts.

They do not want to be substituting the state, but they acknowledge that, in practice they cannot always avoid the role of complementarity. This sometimes implies bargaining for the best possible solutions in a time of economic cutbacks. Foundations guarantee some of the money on the condition that the state or local authorities pay the rest. These kinds of bargains can be conducted in many ways. Some negotiate openly with the public authorities, others are more discrete:

> We do not normally go into such bargains. But often the authorities have been 'inspired' to offer further support.

Some foundations strongly express their concern regarding the policy direction of the government towards social services and culture. On the one hand, they feel an obligation to create a basis for a solid debate and to find new ways of working in these areas. On the other hand, they often feel that they and their well-documented projects and ideas are not taken seriously:

> It is extremely depressing to watch how little room for creativity is left in the public sector.

Redistribution

This role is not considered to be relevant to Danish foundations. On the one hand, they are well aware that the form of the foundation as such is often meant to benefit 'those in need'. The Charitable Association of Copenhagen – one of the smaller foundations in this study – was founded with the purpose to 'help the needy and deserving poor – especially those who have no other way of getting the needed support'. Indeed, hundreds of small foundations have redistributive purposes in their statutes, and they give out small donations to special groups of deserving poor. On the other hand, as acknowledged by foundations such as the Charitable Association of Copenhagen, this role seems to have less importance in a welfare state, which traditionally has worked to guarantee the absence of poverty. The foundations do not see it as their role to further redistribution on a societal basis, although they do want to identify groups of people that need support and to focus on issues that need attention. In any case, foundations do not have enough resources to fulfil this role per se even if they wished to. Redistribution in Denmark is financed by taxes not by private funds.

Innovation

During the interviews the foundations identify easily with being portrayed as 'creative entrepreneurs', as supporters of risky projects and promoters of new ways of thinking. It was agreed that foundations should act as alternatives to the mainstream and promote innovation, particularly in areas where neither government nor markets seek to act innovatively. The Egmont Foundation, for example, is very clear on this matter by stating in its Annual Report (2001) that vision, dynamism and innovation are essential requirements for supporting projects.

For the most part, however, this role must be seen as part of the way in which the board of directors interpret the will of the founder in relation to their specific activities. Furthermore 'innovation' is a traditional means of role-perception in the Danish voluntary sector. It belongs to the narrative of voluntary organizations during the twentieth century and can be seen as a part of the debate that underlines the need for nonprofit organizations to be autonomous. (Lorentzen 1993, Henriksen 1996, Habermann 2001). Independence is perceived to be fundamental to the ability of foundations to act in an innovative way.

Social and policy change

The role of promoting social and policy change is in many ways related to the innovation role. Although the idea is supported in the interviews, only one foundation has a written formulation about the idea of social change. Clause 4 of the statutes of The Plum Foundation outlines the role of the foundation in the resolution of conflicts and states as its charitable purpose: the provision of support that will lead to the rapid resolution of such conflicts. Other foundations seek to bring about change for specific groups such as minorities or children (the Egmont Foundation and the Health Foundation), or they seek to make changes in the environment (Realdania). Yet critics of foundations are often deeply sceptical of what they see as the increasing influence of the foundations on the political scene in Denmark. They view the donations of foundations as a double-edged sword. For example, on the one hand, the foundations can build museums and opera houses and promote social change. On the other hand, they seldom, if ever, give money for operating these institutions and partly expect the state to pay these expenses. This has potential negative consequences for some observers:

> The foundations will undermine the public policy debate on culture. It is a re-feudalisation. We are returning to the donations of princes and the church. It will turn out to be a democratic problem.
>
> (Krogh Andersen 2002)

Preservation of traditions and culture

Some foundations are more or less founded with this purpose, while others focus their activities on maintaining national heritage, and still others have a penchant for monument building, as evident from the interview with the Realdania Foundation:

> [I]n ten years time we want people to say that Denmark would not have looked this way if it had not been for us.

Foundations often interpret the statutes to support projects of renovation and maintenance, or the extension of museums, for example. This, then, seems to be a 'traditional' role for foundations. Yet, regardless of their good intentions, and even if foundations strive to make their contributions important rather than spectacular, these projects can be controversial.

Pluralism

Promoting experimentation and diversity in a democratic society is a role that can be viewed as a consequence of foundations wanting to be an alternative to the state. It is possible that foundations want to provide something extra, but they also want to ensure that different opinions and political views are expressed. Foundations are keen to play a part in contributing to the plurality of society. They see themselves as working differently, more efficiently and more flexibly than the authorities and most of them have the funds to pursue their cause independently:

> Probably we have a significant role because we freely choose *what* we want to support. We have as such no rules and no regulations apart from our statutes. And we can intervene in a quick and efficient way when it is needed, and in areas where the state cannot support. This is why our role might seem more important than our contributions in numbers actually justify.

The foundations are very much aware of these different roles and which roles they prefer to identify with. But they are not always in agreement about which roles are more important than others. On the one hand, the foundations define themselves as being part of civil society as they are autonomous entities that express and carry out the will of individuals – in this case the founder. On the other hand, the foundations stress their individuality. Hence it follows that the foundations do not seem to have developed a common foundation identity. Moreover, they do not seem to want such an identity – particularly when it comes to defining their relationship vis-à-vis the state. Nonetheless, the foundations demonstrate during the interviews that they in fact do have a similar sense of self-understanding, which gives them more in common than they themselves might be aware of. This common self-understanding includes the following elements: to be self-contained, to have autonomy/freedom, to express certain values and address certain causes, and – not least – to make an important contribution to society. These factors influence the way they see their roles in society and the way they articulate their visions.

Foundations visions

One way of evaluating roles is to probe deeper into the visions of foundations and to look at what foundations can do, and not what they ideally want to do. The two vision-statements that were generally supported in all of the interviews correspond with the self-image of the foundations in relation to their roles. These visions were formulated as follows:

- foundations should be a visible force independent from both government and market;
- foundations should provide alternatives to the mainstream and safeguard minorities.

Consistent with the liberal vision, the foundations feel free to do what they think is important. The foundations often want to be seen as pioneers within the context of their own objectives. They focus on special areas of interest in order to bring out their message more clearly. This, they believe, also allows them to be able to make a real difference by concentrating their efforts and donations on single issues for a period of time. Furthermore, they are convinced that the projects they support would not have happened without their contributions.

However, it can be difficult to articulate a liberal vision in the present welfare state model influenced by social democracy. Moreover, the expectation of the government that the foundations should take on a more complementary role does not make the situation any more straightforward. The tentative and somewhat ambivalent attitudes amongst foundations toward the complementarity role become clearer when visions are discussed. The board of the Velux Foundation has publicly expressed their concerns that the government is only interested in the short term 'utility value' of the foundations. This is seen to be indicative of a lack of understanding of the broader role(s) of foundations in a changing society and their commitment to their individual charters and (long-term) objectives (see Velux Foundation Annual Report 2002). The foundations are very careful not to let public cuts rule their own policies:

> [T]he minister of Culture, to take an example, cannot expect us to cover the cuts he made at the National Museum. [But at the same time where this potential situation arises, partnerships seem to be a

solution:] We see partnerships of many kinds as very important. We want to work with small companies as well as with the (local) authorities and with universities. We want our partners to feel that our common efforts have been important and responsible in every way, that the process has been worthwhile and that different interests have been respected.

The foundations consistently underline their cooperation with other partners – the public sector and/or other foundations – as vital to the significance of their role. They generate networks and work hard to implement their ideas together with different partners. This does not in their view contradict their assertions of autonomy, independence and individuality. Yet, clearly, perceptions of changes in the broader policy environment have had implications for the roles and operations of Danish foundations.

Current developments and issues

Discussions concerning roles and visions of foundations are topical at present. Three issues that emerged from the research are particularly pertinent: new government policies, the challenges of internal governance, and foundations in an international context.

New government policies and the autonomy of foundations

During the last ten years, Danish politics has been underpinned by the principle of involving citizens, business and voluntary organizations in a more active and responsible way. This means that the foundations are likely to be asked or expected to play a much more visible role than before and also that the resources of foundations will be crucial for society in a more direct way. On the one hand, it is recognized that the foundations have a favourable position in society because they have the freedom to choose between areas of activity. On the other hand, there is a potential for conflict between the traditional and preferred scenario, and the prevalent policy environment where foundations, either by their own choice or by necessity due to government policy are likely to become a more visible force in society.

The interviewees were concerned about the cut-backs in social services and culture and see this situation as growing more critical. Foundations have to become more strategic in the way they choose their partners and as to what kind of projects they support. Furthermore the implementation of the projects is more important, because it is becoming harder to ensure that public money will be available to continue successful projects.

Another scenario following on from these considerations is that in the future it may be more difficult to disassociate the work of the foundations from the work of the state. This would, according to the foundations, be an alarming situation for both parties. The foundations find it acceptable to try out new ideas and finance projects that in the first instance may be difficult to accomplish in the public sector. They also often make a suggestion – or even stipulate conditions – to share the expenses for such projects, or aim to have projects continued with public money, if they prove to be a success. But there must be limits to the extent to which projects are 'forced upon' the foundations:

> The public sector should not to a large extent be allowed to influence the ideas and visions of the foundations. Public bureaucracy must never take power or gain influence here.

Internal governance issues facing foundations

Foundations often find it difficult to adapt the will of the founder to the changing societal environment. Developments in society mean that some foundations simply are not able to give out all the grants meant for special causes because the target group no longer exists. The specific wording of the statutes makes it necessary to apply for an alteration to the statutes which is difficult to obtain. It is also the case that some foundations have very small assets and strive to find meaningful ways to distribute their money. In local communities foundations with small funds are often joined together in order to make their resources go further. Foundations in Denmark do not favour cooperation as part of an umbrella organization, but rather they prefer to cooperate in a more informal way mainly because existing legal regulations are relatively flexible and easy to operate within.

Another concern is the relationship between foundations and the general public. In Denmark foundations have traditionally been satisfied with the role of doing good, following the will of the founder and keeping a low profile in the public eye. In our information age a more open attitude towards the broader environment is inevitable, but only six of the eight foundations interviewed for this study have websites, which give the public access to some – often carefully chosen – knowledge. Furthermore two of the interviewed foundations do not publish an annual report. This lack of transparency can only contribute to an unwanted air of secrecy and in the long run bring about unnecessary criticisms.

Foundations in a European/international context

On the whole the foundations in this study have a limited interest in European and international matters. The statutes often limit, or even forbid donations outside of Denmark. This makes it irrelevant and of little interest for the boards of foundations to be interested in international and European affairs. Some foundations have engaged in giving outside of

Denmark by interpreting the statutes in a global setting: an example is the Egmont Foundation which identified as a priority the need to support democracy in the new member states of the European Union. Only one foundation is clearly international by virtue of the will of the founder (the Plum Foundation).

The foundations interviewed were to some extent aware of proposals for a European Foundation Statute. Only one of the Danish foundations interviewed is a member of the European Foundation Centre. None of the other seven interviewed foundations had any plans to join the 'club', as they said. They resent the sense of exclusiveness and the notion of a 'European elite', which does not fit well with the image of modesty and altruism in the self-understanding of (some) foundations, nor do they attach importance to the information and discussions that may result from membership.

Conclusion

To some extent and in spite of an individualistic sense of self-image, Danish foundations have a similar way of thinking. They have the same ideas about their roles and activities in society and they share values of responsibility towards the common good. An example is the recurring theme of the autonomy of foundations. The narratives found in the interviews (and in the annual reports) often raise issues of freedom, creativity and responsibility to society. This corresponds to agreement on roles and visions, which are underpinned by ideas of autonomy, innovation and acting as alternatives to the state; as well as the rejection of the roles of redistribution and of being peripheral to society. What is more, foundations do not wish to be an instrument of the state. Foundations clearly do not want to fill gaps left by the government, but in practice they find this difficult to avoid, especially when it comes to helping individuals.

Despite their claims of autonomy, foundations are highly influenced by what goes on in society – by the activities of the government, universities, political parties and think tanks. The present government has expressed great interest in partnerships with foundations and, more than ever before, the public and the media emphasize the need for more knowledge and more openness about the 'secret world' of foundations. In this environment, there is clearly a need for more information about foundations and more open dialogue between foundations and the media, the government and the public. To these ends, it would appear to be in the interest of all parties – the public, the government as well as the foundations to reinstate the Registration Law (abolished in 1992) so as to ensure that debates about partnerships, responsibilities and future possibilities are based on statistical facts and not on myths. Foundations would also benefit from further cooperation amongst themselves, for example, by expanding existing informal arrangements to include more (smaller) foundations, in order to ensure legitimacy and high standards among all foundations and to discuss future legal issues and partnerships. Furthermore, in order to enhance the transparency, and to lessen the mystery surrounding foundations, the obligation for foundations to publish annual reports may be given more consideration. As stated at the outset of this chapter, many gaps remain in our knowledge and understanding of foundations in Denmark. For several reasons, foundations have not been of political interest until now and gaining access to the field has been complicated. As this chapter has shown, we can no longer afford to ignore foundations, nor can foundations afford to be isolated actors in a society that demands more than a philosophy of doing good.

Acknowledgements

Comments from Finn Terkelsen, The Tuborg Foundation and Hans Edvard Nørregård-Nielsen, The New Carlsberg Foundation.

Notes

1 In the Danish language different names were used, such as *stiftelser, legater, fonde, selvejende institutioner*. Before the foundation laws from 1984 all names were used at random according to the preference of the founder. The new laws did not insist on the use of the word *fond* (foundation) – although after 1985 it was requested that *fond* should be a part of the name of the foundation eventually put in brackets, e.g. 'Elmersens legatstiftelse (fond)'. (Lynge Andersen 2002).
2 Permutation: if the purpose of the foundation is evidently out of step with the norms in society alterations in the bylaws may be permitted.
3 Brewer J.P. Jacobsen (The Carlsberg Foundation) always made a clear distinction between the two. All his life he was active in both fields, but in charity matters he preferred to be anonymous (Glamann 1994).
4 The Egmont Foundation of 1920 belongs to this new type of foundation, concentrating on helping single mothers and their orphans. It managed to become one of the biggest private foundations in this field of philanthropy in Denmark.
5 In 2002 total assets were estimated to be approximately 200 billion Danish crowns (approximately €28.6 billion) (Krogh Andersen 2002).
6 Since 1988 the KRAK-Publishers has published a directory on charitable foundations (*KRAKS fonds- & legatvejviser*). In 2002 the eighth edition was printed. Until the abolition of the Registration Law in 1992 the directory based its information on the former central register. After this date, it is based on a voluntary system of registration.
7 The interview data come from interviews with chairmen of the boards and executive directors of the foundations. The interviewees have read the manuscript and relevant corrections and comments have been incorporated in the text. There has, however, been no interference with the way the data has been used or interpreted. The author thanks the foundations for interviews gladly given and for the interest shown towards the project.

References

Bordt, R.L. (1997) *The structure of women's non-profit organizations*, Indiana: Indiana University Press.

Glamann, K. (1976) *Carlsbergfondet* [The Carlsberg Foundation]. København: Rhodos.

Glamann, K. (1994) *The Carlsberg Foundation since 1970*. Copenhagen: Carlsberg.

Habermann, U. (2001) *En postmoderne helgen? Om motiver til frivillighed* [A postmodern saint? – on motives for volunteerism]. Lunds University. Lunds Dissertations in Social Work.

Held, V. (ed.) (1996) *Justice and care. Essential Readings in Feminist Ethics.* Boulder, CO: Westview Press.

Henriksen, L.S. (1996) *Lokal frivillig organisering I nye omgivelser* [Local voluntary organisations in a new context]. Aalborg: ALFUFF.

Hornby, O. (1988) *'With Constant Care...' A.P. Møller: Ship owner 1876–1965.* København: Schultz Forlag.

Jansen, H.M. (1993) *Fra almisse til sygekasse. Dansk sygeforsorgs historie* [From alms to health insurance. The history of Danish sick benefits]. København: Sygekassernes Helsefond.

Jensen, K.W. (1996) *De glade givere* [The cheerful givers]. København: Gyldendal.

Kauffman, E. (1973) Erhversdrivende selvejende institutioner [Corporate foundations]. (3. udgave).

Krogh Andersen, M. (2002) A series of articles on foundations in *Denmark, Weekend Avisen* on the following dates: 12.07.02, 28.06.02, 14.06.02, 25.05.02, 17.05.02, 23.02.02.

Kryger, M. (1988) *Patron of Culture and Scholarship.* Børsen. June 20th.

Lorentzen, H. (1993) *Frivillighetens integration* [Integration of Voluntarism]. Oslo: Institut for Samfunnsforskning.

Lynge Andersen, L. (1996) *Fonde og foreninger I* [Foundations and associations I]. København: Gadjura.

Lynge Andersen, L. (1998) *Fonde og foreninger II* [Foundations and associations II]. København: Gadjura.

Lynge Andersen, L. (1999) *Fra stiftelse til fond*, København: Handelshøjskolen.

Lynge Andersen, L. (2000) 'Stiftelser over broen. I', in Foldgren and Nielsen (red) *Retten (om)kring Øresund* [Foundations across the bridge. In Foldgren and Nielsen (ed.) Law in the Oresund-region]. København: Jurist- og Økonomforbundets Forlag.

Lynge Andersen, L. (2002) *Fra stiftelse til fond* [From charitable institution to foundations]. København: Gjellerup.

McCarthy, K.D. (ed.) (2001) *Women, Philanthropy and Civil Society.* Indiana: Indiana University Press.

Mogensen, J.C. (1924) *Den frie fattigforsorg i Kjøbenhavn og Kjøbenhavns understøttelses – forenings historie* [Voluntary poor relief in Copenhagen and the history of Copenhagen´s charitable association]. Kjøbenhavn: Axel Andersens Forlag.

Møller, P.O. (1987) *Fonde* [Foundations]. Handelshøjskolen i København Hovedopgave.

Nørregård-Nielsen, H.E. (2002) *Ny Carlsbergfondet ved hundredåret for dets oprettelse* [The new Carlsberg Foundation in a century]. www.carlsbergfondet.dk/nycarlsbergfondet.

Olivarius, J.H. (1910) *Stiftelser* [Charitable Institutions]. København: Indenrigsmin-
isteriet.

Pedersen, J. (1956) The Carlsberg Foundation. København.

Selle, P. (2001) 'The Norwegian Voluntary Sector and Civil Society in Transition.
Women as a Catalyst of Deep-seated Change'. In K.D. McCarthy (ed.) *Women,
Philanthropy and Civil Society*. Indiana: Indiana University Press.

The Carlsberg Foundation. Annual reports (2001), (2002) and (2003). Carlsbergfondet, Årsskrift 2001, 2002 and 2003. www.carlsbergfondet.dk.

The Egmont Foundation. Annual reports (2001) and (2002). Egmont Fonden,
Årsskrift 2001 and 2002. www.egmontfonden.dk.

The Health Foundation – Annual Report (2001) Sygekassernes Helsefond,
Årsskrift 2001.

The Health Foundation – Jubilee publication 1973–1998. Sygekassernes Helsefond, Jubilæumsskrift 1973–1998. www.helsefonden.dk.

The Realdania Foundation. Annual reports (2001) and (2002). Fonden Realdania,
Årsrapport 2001 og 2002. www.realdania.dk.

The Velux Foundations, Annual reports (2001) and (2002). Veluxfondene,
Årsskrift 2001 og 2002. www.VELUXfondene.dk.

10 Estonia

Mikko Lagerspetz (with Erle Rikmann)

Introduction

The restoration of the market economy and democratic institutions in Estonia began in 1991, when the country became independent. Since then, ideas about the relationship between the emerging foundation sector and other parts of society – notably the government and the for-profit sector – have been developing at a rapid pace. They are partly based on the revolutionary popular movements' discourse of the late 1980s, on ideas originating from the United States (US) and Western Europe, and on the (mostly implicit) expectations of politicians and other stakeholders. Inevitably, the everyday work of the foundations presents them with new challenges and possibilities, sometimes demanding painful compromises. This chapter examines foundations in Estonia today and how they see their place in society.[1] We will show how the foundations make efforts to combine their ideals with the realities of their everyday work and explore how common ideas and visions, but also controversies develop within the field of non-profit organisations.

A profile of foundations in Estonia

Historical development

Despite Estonia's short existence as an independent state (1918–1940 and again from 1991), associational life, foundations, and the co-operative movement have a rather long history in the country. Urban merchants and craftsmen had traditionally been organised in guilds, which also participated in city administration. The first associations of a voluntary, modern type were created by the German-speaking middle classes (such as the Freemasons; cf. von Wistinghausen 1997) and the land-owning nobility (such as Economic Societies) in the late eighteenth century. The nineteenth century saw a mushrooming of literary, cultural and educational societies, along with the beginnings of a co-operative movement (Jansen 1993). These societies rapidly became some of the primary vehicles that the Estonian national movement had at its disposal when seeking to gain popular appeal and official recognition for its objectives. In the 1920s and 1930s, much of the associational life was closely connected to the nation-building process. The newly independent country was successful in mobilising its citizenry for voluntary work within cultural community centres, education and defence organisations. In 1940, almost all of these organisations were forced to cease their activities because of the incorporation of Estonia into the Soviet Union. Along with private companies, the Communist authorities disbanded foundations, and their assets were nationalised.

After the most sombre period of Stalinism, several cultural, sports and health care organisations were revived, and there was renewed interest in cultural and leisure activities from the early 1980s onwards (Saar 1993). The importance of these embryonic forms of civil society in the revolutionary process of 1987–1991 cannot be overestimated. In 1989, a law on Freedom of Association was enacted, which formed the legal basis for the establishment both of political parties and of different kinds of non-governmental organisations (NGOs). Following independence (from 1991), a rapid growth in the number of registered organisations has taken place, especially since the late 1990s (Lagerspetz *et al.* 2002; Trummal and Lagerspetz 2001).

Legal issues

There are two main laws dealing with NGOs in Estonia: the Non-profit Associations Act and the Foundations Act. Both came into force on 1 October 1996. Prior to this date, organisational activities were regulated by an Act on Non-Governmental Organisations from 1994, which made no distinction between foundations and other forms of NGOs. Foundations can be established by any physical or legal person, including government agencies. There is no minimum amount of assets required.

According to the Estonian Income Tax Act, non-profit associations and foundations do not pay taxes on their income. The Ministry of Finance keeps a list of public interest NGOs, which (in February 2000) included 840 organisations, of which 92 were foundations. The list is regularly updated. A corporate body can make tax-exempt gifts and donations to public interest NGOs in an amount not exceeding 3 per cent of the total amount to be paid in social tax, or 10 per cent of the profit of the latest year. An individual has the right to deduct gifts and donations up to 5 per cent of his or her income. The decision of whether to grant public benefit status to an organisation is preceded by an assessment by a government official. However, our interviewees with first-hand experience of the procedure deemed it to be rather haphazard and insufficiently formal. Moreover, not all organisations were aware of the possibility of applying for this status at all. In January 2000, corporate income tax was abolished in

Estonia. As a result, there are no special financial incentives for business corporations to donate money to NGOs or to establish their own foundations.

In December 2002, a more general legal document was enacted by the *Riigikogu*, the Estonian Parliament. The document called *The Concept for the Development of Civil Society in Estonia* (EKAK) is an official statement of the principles of cross-sectoral co-operation.[2] Internationally, there are several recent examples of similar documents (White 2002). Among the best-known are the British Compacts on Relations between Government and the Voluntary and Community Sector. A distinctive feature in Estonia has been the fact that the initiative for creating such a document came from the NGO field itself, not from the government (Liiv 2003).

The representatives of foundations we interviewed in the course of this study tended to regard the legislative framework in a positive light. At the same time, they pointed out that both civil servants, managers of private enterprises and the foundations themselves were not sufficiently aware of the potential advantages offered by the existing legislation and were thus unable to make proper use of it for their own benefit.

An empirical profile

The non-profit sector presently consists of three types of organisations: non-profit associations *(mittetulundusühingud)*, foundations *(sihtasutused)* and non-profit partnerships *(seltsingud)*.[3] Jointly, they are all referred to as non-profit organisations *(mittetulundusühendused)*. As of 1 June 2004, a total of 20,084 non-profit membership organisations and 601 foundations were registered in the Central Database of Registry Departments of Courts. As the total population of the country is less than 1.4 million, this makes for an average of more than 14 registered organisations per one thousand inhabitants. However, it is important to add that real estate associations (apartment, garage and cottage associations) make up about half of the total amount of NGOs.[4] The official data does not allow us to estimate the exact number of functioning civil society NGOs in Estonia, since registers also list many organisations which are not active in practice.

Most foundations in Estonia can be classified as operating foundations though their functional difference from non-profit associations is not always clear. The same applies to those foundations, which explicitly work for the benefit of a distinct group, i.e. a geographically or otherwise defined community. There are also several important foundations that have been established by the central or local governments, although their legal status as (theoretically) private entities is the same. The government-initiated foundations are both grant-giving and operating. The rationale for establishing these entities includes a wish to decentralise governance, to guarantee the independence of specific policy areas, to enable partnership with private capital, and to allow the participation of non-political professional people in decision-making.

The Central Business Register, which keeps the register of the different types of non-governmental organisations, does not collect information about their activities nor about the size of their financial assets. Information on economic activities has been collected annually by the Statistical Office by means of mail surveys of a sample of NGOs, the representativeness of which may, however, not be very good. A research project with the aim of developing and testing a new questionnaire for use with NGOs was launched in November 2002 by an institute for applied social research, the foundation PRAXIS.[5] A pilot mail questionnaire was sent to 215 foundations, but the response was more disappointing than expected: no more than 32 respondents (15 per cent) replied. According to the pilot survey, the size of the foundations' economic activities in terms of income during 2002 ranged from zero, or 39 Estonian crowns (€2,5) to 31.6 million (€2,025,000). The arithmetic mean was 4.09 million (€280,000), but becomes much smaller (2.64 million, or €180,000) if the foundations with current participation either by the state, local government or public universities are excluded. The most numerous and most resourceful group of foundations were those whose functions can be classified in Group 6 of ICNPO (Development and housing). In this group, the foundations with the participation of either the state or other government-related bodies operate with the largest amount of finances.

Foundations (and more generally, the non-profit organisations) in Estonia are operating in an environment with appropriate legislation, free of undue restrictions. At the same time, it is important to note that no clear administrative practice has yet emerged when public benefit status is being granted to an organisation; the registering authorities do not record details of organisations on grounds other than their legal form. Both of these problems relate to the novelty of non-profit activities in the country. They also indicate that NGOs have themselves not yet been able (or active enough) to influence governmental bodies in these issues. The adoption of EKAK, the parliamentary document on principles of the relationship between government and the third sector, is both a sign of growing consciousness among the NGOs, and of growing attention to them among politicians.

Foundation roles

When asked to rank the roles in order of importance, the *promotion of pluralism, innovation*, and *social and policy change* are the roles that the representatives of foundations appear to value the most. *Complementarity* was the least popular of the possible roles. However, the interviews and the group discussion point to the fact that the different roles are in practice intertwined and can be difficult to distinguish from each other. As the following response suggests, showing initiative or innovation in a field neglected by the government may form a part of a strategy of social change: after positive results have been shown, it may, in theory at least be easier to convince the decision-makers of the need to continue the activity.

Respondent: There are several roles. One role could really include the preservation of cultural traditions, of all kinds. But on the other hand, highly innovative ideas can be promoted or initiated. This is an important activity that we practise little and that could be the norm. And of course, it would be good to co-operate here with the state. One can initiate models of a kind, and if they work out well, the government can take over.

Question: This is the way that [your foundation] works?

Respondent: We used to try to do that. And there were several projects that would have been worth taking over by the government but they failed to do it. For instance, the teacher training that we supported, development of critical thinking..., the programme should have been taken over by the government, as we ran out of resources. We could not continue, we are not the government, but it was actually a part of the government's duties, but they did not consider it worthwhile to continue, which was a pity. There are plenty of similar examples.

(Individual interview/representative of a foundation, 310303)[6]

If the initiative does not result in a change of policy or interest by the relevant authority, the foundations may find themselves forced either to put an end to the new activity, or to continue it with insecure and insufficient funding. The decision to complement the work of the public sector can be the result of the pressing needs of a neglected social group, e.g. those with disabilities, or those living in less developed regions of the country. The foundations taking care of such functions sometimes do not find the situation just or satisfactory. As one of our respondents put it:

> [T]he work we are doing should actually be done by [the corresponding government agency], as is the case in other countries both far and near. But as the state lacked any understanding of the need, and perhaps it also lacked the resources, a foundation was established for the purpose.
>
> (Group discussion/representatives of foundations, 200303)

Overall, foundations are engaged in what can be described as fulfilling the role of complementarity vis-à-vis governmental bodies, even if that does not coincide with what the foundation representatives consider their proper or preferred role, as indicated above. Indeed, it emerged from a group discussion with all of the interviewees that most of the foundations saw complementing the functions of governmental bodies as a central element of their everyday work. For the foundations established by the government this was not problematic: they were themselves direct results of public sector management reforms, which included a *substitution* of governmental agencies by bodies with the legal form of a foundation. This was seen as a logical continuation of the post-socialist transformation of society. The dominance of the state over all social life was to be overcome, but not all functions previously performed by the state could be taken over by private enterprises.

A second role that was often touched upon by the representatives of foundations was that of *redistributing resources.* A majority of the organisations in our sample were not grant-giving – they were running their own projects, relying on volunteers and directly employing workers. During the feedback workshop (in which the respondents had an opportunity to comment on our preliminary findings) we witnessed the following controversial exchange:

Participant 1:   I mean, the redistribution of money as such does not add to what we could call the overall wealth of society. . . . The money just moves to another location, but no new values are being created.

Participant 2:   But you see, there is a difference between merely transferring the money of a rich person to another person, and doing it through an, . . . an energetic and innovative foundation, which means that the money might find a more proper addressee. I do disagree with the view that redistributing money does not create new values.

(Workshop 310303)

The conversation also shows two widely different views of the need for innovation and pluralism. As Participant 2 points out, one of the rationales for establishing a foundation is, indeed, the fact that they add new dimensions to decision-making on resource allocation. Here, foundations can rely on committed individuals and expertise that may be unavailable for other agencies. Participant 1, a representative of a government-related foundation, is unwilling to accept such an argument.

For the foundations created by the government, the main rationale for adopting this organisational form lies in its flexibility of governance, compared with traditional governmental bodies. Similarly, when making their choice between the forms of the foundation and the non-profit association, the grassroots-initiated organisations were attracted to this legal form for exactly the same reason.

The interviews and discussions underline differences between private and government-initiated foundations. Whereas all participants acknowledged the role of foundations as complementing the functions of the state, the representatives of purely private foundations tended to emphasise their capacity for innovation, and to present their activities as ways of challenging and influencing existing policies. Paradoxically, they are often themselves heavily dependent on project grants from the government. We should keep in mind that most of even the private foundations active in Estonia are not financially independent in their activities; this is one of the most important differences between them and many of their Western European counterparts. For this reason, their practical activities always seem to include compromises between their preferred roles and those which they are compelled to perform in place of, or in some form of conjunction with, the financing – governmental – agencies.

Foundation visions

In terms of the visions of foundations in Estonia, the cultivation of better relations with the business sector emerged as a key priority. Building partnerships with the business world was discussed as highly valuable in principle, even if only a minority of the respondents actually did have such partnerships. No more than five of the foundations (in our sample of 16) mentioned domestic private donors (individual or corporate) among their main financers. Differences in organisational culture and organisational resources were mentioned as a factor that could render co-operation more difficult between foundations and the corporate sector. Heavy reliance on the work of a few employees and/or voluntary workers sometimes made it impossible for the smaller foundations to keep the timetables that were proposed by the business leaders. Business leaders also tend to underestimate the amount of work and professional knowledge that is needed for administering and distributing grants.

> [T]here is not enough understanding that the culture of organisation and management is different due to the lack of resources. If you explain that, [the partners] usually will understand. But often you do not come to think about the fact that your partner in the business or government sector expects the same kind of organisational culture from you that they have themselves. This creates initial misapprehension.
>
> (Group discussion/representatives of foundations, 200303)

The strong emphasis on the need to develop co-operation with the business sector is certainly related to the foundation sector's general lack of resources, but also to its general dependency on the government. The respondents did not favour the *social democratic* and the *state-controlled* models. There were but few examples of foundations being involved in the provision of welfare services in the way referred to in our definition of the social democratic model.[7] As indicated in the previous section, foundations wishing to fulfil such a role were openly disappointed with the government, which seemed to lack both the necessary interest and the resources to meet certain needs. The *corporatist* model received mixed responses. Representatives of the foundations with guaranteed regular public financing seemed comfortable in their role of carrying out functions that had been assigned by the government.

This vision was above all challenged by the *liberal* model, which was supported by representatives from the foundations relying on private initiative. They saw themselves as an innovative force promoting pluralism in society. In contrast to the proponents of the corporatist model, those who favoured the liberal model saw it as essential that the foundations should be flexible in redefining their objectives, in order to be responsive to emerging new needs in society. This point was made by a representative of a private grant-making foundation:

> [I]f we are too careful in regulating our working principles, we might end up eliminating something important from our activities and regret it later.
>
> (Group discussion/representatives of foundations, 070303)

Some statements that were presented in the course of group discussions seem to go even further than the liberal vision in their emphasis on social change, empowerment of minorities and opposition to certain aspects of prevailing state policies. Indeed, several of the representatives of Estonian foundations see themselves as quasi-political pressure groups:

> In addition, we have tried to influence legal initiatives, we have interacted with members of the parliament and [a certain] Committee of the Parliament. I am sorry to say that it has been a rather hopeless effort. They argue that our target group is so small and a change of legislation would not influence more than twenty people at the most, it would be useless. And then finally ... the act was changed anyway, but one of the few paragraphs that was *not* changed was exactly the one that we had suggested to be changed.... [Some civil servants] totally ignore your professional competence and their attitude is decided by quite other factors.
>
> (Group discussion/representatives of foundations, 200303)

Our respondents did not doubt that foundations would continue to be a part of Estonian society, and probably become more influential than hitherto. They argued that the needs that the foundations had been created to fulfil were likely to continue existing, and that foundations were the best organisational means for responding to these needs. Another argument connected them with innovation and policy change:

> For us there remains the task of having our finger on the pulse of
> society where the development of democratic culture is concerned.
> That means if we notice shortcomings and possibilities of some kind,
> we can implement some kinds of new models in co-operation with
> other associations. Or we can encourage people to speak up.... [The
> future of foundations in five to ten years] is basically dependent on
> ourselves, on the extent to which we are able to show that foundations
> are important, a kind of island or cells of independence, which con-
> tribute to the feeling of commonality.
>
> > (Individual interview/representatives of foundations, 310303)

Foundations were often conceived of as representing a certain Western-
influenced cultural pattern, which had started to take root again in
Estonia after the end of Soviet rule. In particular, the representatives of
private foundations clearly saw themselves as part of a wider field of non-
governmental activities. Many expectations were connected to this rapidly
developing part of society. They were encouraged by the successful adoption of the EKAK. They anticipate an eventual rise in living standards,
which will create new possibilities for people to make charitable donations. However, accounts of the foundations' actual performance did not
always give support to this optimism. Above all, the either direct or financial dependence of many foundations on the government remains an
underlying source of uncertainty.

Current developments and emerging issues

The interviews, group discussions and the workshop underlined several
issues that appear crucial to the future development of foundations and to
the non-profit sector in general. Some of them were connected to the
relationships between foundations and the government and business
sectors; and a number of issues were centred around financing. Finally,
relations within the non-profit sector received some attention.

As discussed above in relation to the business model, differences in
organisational culture were regarded as a possible source of misunderstanding between foundations and partners from the other sectors. The
establishment of mutually rewarding partnerships is, however, also made
more difficult by the 'blurring' of the division of responsibilities between
different government agencies. This situation has the potential to render
it impossible for a foundation to find the appropriate partners for cooperation. The private foundations pointed to the scarcity of civil servants
with competence in their respective field of activity. Creating understanding and trust between the foundation and the prospective financing
government body was difficult and time-consuming; and when personnel
changes took place in the government apparatus, the process had to be
started anew. Moreover, some discussants pointed to a possible tendency

towards the re-centralising of the administration of government finances. In short, the state does not seem to have defined any clear policy towards the non-profit-public partnerships in general and foundations in particular. True, the EKAK is an effort at creating clarity in these policies and as such is an important step forward. However, until its principles are implemented in practice, the relative unpredictability of state policies continues to create an element of uncertainty among foundations.

Most foundations felt that the government should finance their activities more than it did. Their representatives also claimed that private giving was inhibited both by a lack of clarity regarding the overall principles of deciding on the tax-exempt status of non-governmental organisations and a lack of information on the potential advantages offered by legislation. A poor level of knowledge about the practices and regulations related to non-profit activities was considered characteristic of both the governmental and business sectors, but also of the non-profit sector itself. A problem touched upon in the course of most interviews and discussions was the actual variety of organisations registered as foundations. Some – a minority – were the result of private donations, some were effectively bodies at arm's length to the government, some were reminiscent of membership-based NGOs. Representatives of these different types of foundations mentioned 'fake foundations' as an additional type. They referred to legal entities actually established with the sole aim of tax minimisation, with little to do with public benefit purposes. The existence of such foundations was regarded as harmful for the image of the whole sector.

> A thing that the tax authorities are worried about is that the foundation has become a kind of favourite form of organisation, as was said here before, and not only for civic organisations, but for the state and also for business organisations, merely for the reason that its structure of administration is very simple.... If we think about a hospital or a theatre, we can see the public benefit, but what has happened lately is that ... the government creates foundations for the financing of all kinds of projects that in fact belong to the functions of the state. The foundations should be independent bodies, but for instance, [a foundation established by the Government] is 100 per cent dependent on the Ministry of [name]..., quite irrespective of who happens to belong to the board. Fake foundations *(libasihtasutused)* are emerging. It is even more worrying that business corporations have started to establish foundations in order to fulfil some side functions.... There is no public benefit involved in that.
> (Group discussion/representatives of foundations, 200303)

Among representatives of the foundations established by private persons and donors, one could sometimes sense an air of distrust and even envy towards those established by the government. They were also bothered by the fact that no legal or statistical distinction was made between the different types.

When discussing their most pressing problems, the foundation representatives seem highly aware that professional competence and trustworthiness are, in fact, their principal assets. At the same time as they underline the importance of meeting the expectations of their financers, they seek to guard the public image of foundations and the whole of the non-profit sector. For their future survival it is essential that their activities are perceived as legitimate by the government, by the prospective donors and by the general public as well.

Conclusion

The 16 foundations that were selected for analysis in our study were representative of the principal different categories of foundations that exist in Estonia (grant-giving, operational, corporate and community foundations). They came from different geographic locations and various fields of activity. Some of them were established before the restoration of the country's independence in 1991, but most were younger. One could, however, suggest further kinds of distinctions on the basis of the concerns expressed in the course of the interviews and discussions. The foundations can be further divided between those closely supervised by governmental bodies, those based on civic initiative (at times with the participation of local governments), and the few foundations that were genuinely private but also in possession of substantial financial assets.

A characteristic of the foundation sector in Estonia is, first, its relative distance from the business sector. True, the representatives of foundations willingly acknowledged the need for partnership with business enterprises, but not all had actually tried to create such relations. Foundations directly established by business corporations for tax-related purposes were indignantly referred to as 'fake foundations'. Here, the foundations can be seen as guarding the overall image of their sector against suspicion by governmental authorities or the general public.

A second important characteristic of the sector is its relative proximity to both the state and local governments, and to the non-profit membership associations. The close relationship with the government sector means financial dependence and the relative centrality of the roles of complementarity and substitution to the everyday practices of the foundations. However, it also necessitates a high awareness of policy issues and the need for lobbying activities. In this respect, the foundations based on civic initiative functioned in the same way as membership NGOs, and also identified themselves with the larger group of NGOs. On the other hand, representatives of the government-controlled foundations were prone to identify themselves with governmental bodies. Even the few larger, private grant-giving foundations considered it important to gain from the state at least some kind of symbolic recognition of the importance of their work.

Regarding their roles and visions of society, there was a tension between the foundation representatives' assessment of the roles and visions statements, and their everyday activities and concerns as they described them in the course of the interviews and discussion. The respondents emphasised the roles of promoting *pluralism, innovation* and *social and policy change.* These roles are compatible with the *liberal* social model, or even with a more radical vision that can be termed *participant society.* However, when facing their under-financed and state-dominated realities, the practical activities of foundations as they were described in the course of interviews and discussions seem to be determined by the tasks of *complementarity* and *substitution* of government functions, which are closer to the model of *corporatist* society.

The present roles and visions of Estonian foundations very much restrict themselves within the domains of their own society; only a few participated in international networks. It is too early to assess whether Estonia's accession to the EU has created new opportunities for cross-border co-operation. However, it is evident that most foundations lack both previous experience and the organisational and personnel resources demanded by successful international co-operation.

The sector of foundations in Estonia has emerged very recently and very rapidly, and has accompanied an overall social, political and economic transformation which has not been any less dynamic. It should not come as a surprise that the position of foundations in society cannot yet be defined in an unambiguous way. Likewise, it seems logical that the role of the non-profit sector in society has recently become the topic of an active discussion within the sector; this discussion is likely to continue for some time to come. At present, a dedicated and conscious group of activists with pioneering ambitions has emerged within the private foundations. They see themselves as guardians of democratic values and as promoters (and sometimes, importers) of modern, just and rational practices. However, their ideals are not always compatible with the harsh realities of their everyday work. Whether or not they get a chance to realise their goals is ultimately dependent on the overall development of the society, including the government and the business sectors.

Notes

1 Acknowledgements. This chapter was written by Mikko Lagerspetz on the basis of empirical research planned and conducted together with Erle Rikmann. In addition to ourselves, Katri Vallaste was a member of the Estonian research team. Liis Niinemets, Ingo Raudkivi and Anna Raud, all students of the Estonian Institute of Humanities, assisted by conducting and transcribing interviews. We are grateful to Ms. Ülle Lepp for statistical information, to the Open Estonia Foundation and the Tallinn Art Building Fond for their practical assistance, and

to the representatives of Estonian foundations, who invested a part of their time
and intellectual resources in our research project. We also wish to thank the
editors of this volume for many useful comments and suggestions.
2 The implementation plan for the EKAK for the period 2004–2006 was adopted
by the Estonian government in 2004 (Mänd 2004).
3 Non-profit partnerships are informal associations based on a mutual agreement
of common action between individuals, they do not have to be registered, and
they are not treated as legal entities.
4 These forms of co-operative ownership have emerged due to legislation which
obliges the apartment owners in a block of flats to form an association for the
management of their commonly owned real estate.
5 A think tank focussing on policy evaluation, initiated and partly financed by
George Soros. See www.praxis.ee.
6 The numbers refer to the date (dd/mm/yy) of the interview, group discussion
or workshop. The quotations have been translated from Estonian by the author
of this chapter.
7 'Foundations are part of a highly developed welfare state and cooperate with
the state to either complement or supplement the state's activities.'

References

Jansen, E. (1993) 'Voluntary associations in Estonia. The model of the 19th
century'. *Proc. Eston. Acad. Sci. Humanities and Social Sciences*, 42 (2): 115–125.
Lagerspetz, M., E. Rikmann and R. Ruutsoo (2002) 'The structure and resources
of NGOs in Estonia', *Voluntas*, 13 (1): 73–87.
Liiv, D. (2003) 'Koostöökokkulepped avaliku võimu ja mittetulundussektori vahel
– uued arengud, uued käsitlused' [Compacts between the Government and the
voluntary sector – new developments, new treatises], in: M. Lagerspetz, A.
Trummal, R. Ruutsoo, E. Rikmann and D. Liiv, *Tuntud ja tundmatu
kodanikeühiskond* [Civil society – the familiar and the unknown], Tallinn: Avatud
Eesti Fond, pp. 82–100.
Mänd, K. (2004) 'Estonian Government strengthens ties with civil society'. *E-Seal.*
Available at: www.efc.be/seal/eseal.htm.
Saar, E. (1993) 'Rahvuskesksete seltside liikmeskonna territoriaalne jaotus ja
dünaamika (1970–1989)' [The territorial distribution and dynamics of nation-
ally minded organisations, 1970–1989], *Proc. Eston. Acad. Sci. Humanities and
Social Sciences*, 42 (2): 184–194.
Trummal, A. and M. Lagerspetz (2001) *The Profile of Estonian Civil Society. A Prelimi-
nary Report on the Civicus Index on Civil Society Project in Estonia*, Washington, DC:
CIVICUS.
White, D. (2002) Social services or social politics? The significance of state-third
sector agreements for welfare state development, *Paper presented at the Fifth International Conference of the International Society for Third-Sector Research, Cape Town,
South Africa, July 7–10, 2002*.
von Wistinghausen, H. (1997) 'Näitlejad ja muusikud Tallinna
vabamüürlasloožide liikmeina' [Actors and musicians as members of Free-
masonry in Tallinn], *Akadeemia*, 9 (11): 2303–2320.

11 France

Sabine Rozier

Introduction

Traditionally, foundations in France have been regarded with indifference. However, in recent years, they have been the subject of increased interest. New initiatives are announced regularly; the French Centre for Foundations receives more inquiries from would-be patrons than ever before; a new awareness of the existence of shared interests seems to have developed among existing and potential donors and one politician has even suggested a 'foundations day'![1] Some 2,150 foundations exist in France today. France still lags far behind other countries with regard to the number of foundations compared to its total population (there are 3.5 foundations per 100,000 inhabitants).[2] It compares more favourably regarding the total expenditure of foundations, with more than €3,000 million spent annually.[3] New tax measures were adopted between 2000 and 2004 in order to encourage philanthropic giving.

The government now appears intent on encouraging foundations to act where official public establishments and local communities do not act, or where they have withdrawn. The activity of foundations is above all considered to be complementary to public authorities. The more legitimate public intervention in a particular field is considered to be, the more the representatives of foundations are inclined to play an additional role – as in the field of health (where some foundations take an active part in producing public goods). Nonetheless, independent foundations are also considered to be adept in identifying those in need and addressing social issues – even if their experts share visions and promote ways of acting that are very similar to those of public establishments and local communities. Yet, foundations are more and more at risk of being used by a state which is becoming increasingly tempted to 'delegate' public responsibilities to them.

A profile of foundations in France

Foundations will be defined here as the allocation of a certain amount of assets to a non-profit activity in the public interest. This definition includes all organizations that do not always carry the name of 'foundation' but which are legally considered to be foundations,[4] e.g. 'institute' (Pasteur), 'museum' (Social Museum), 'house' (Social Sciences House).

On the one hand, French foundations consist of a small group of powerful, old and prestigious foundations. On the other hand, there are a range of other foundations, more recently established and of various sizes which generally exist under the aegis of two large organizations: the Foundation of France[5] and the Institute of France.[6] The old and prestigious foundations are usually operating foundations: they carry out their own projects, manage their own organizations and tend to work in the fields of health, social services, scientific research and more exceptionally, education. The foundations that have been created in recent years are usually grant-making entities: they support projects conceived and run by others and focus their attention on the arts and culture, social services and assistance to local or foreign populations.

Historical development

Five principal reasons can be posited to explain why in France the foundation sector is relatively weak and the number of foundations is relatively low. First of all, the French state has traditionally been suspicious of the establishment of very large estates, in particular those accumulated by the Catholic Church (Blanc 2003: 33–39). Until the beginning of the twentieth century, foundations tended to be charitable organizations of the Catholic Church. Under monarchical rule, they appeared to be tools for the accumulation of property 'in mortmain' (*mainmorte*), and were considered to pose a dangerous counter-power to the state. This suspicion lasted under the Empire and the Republic and spread later to very large fortunes. This is why the state exerted close control over foundations until very recently. In contrast to associations, which can be established without preliminary authorization, the creation of a foundation is still subject to administrative authorization.

A second reason is due to the influence of the French State on the definition of what is the 'general interest'. The history of the construction of the general interest was both elaborated by the official elites and the spokesmen of big associations. Traditionally, the French state has a quasi-monopoly over the collection and distribution of wealth. It intends to control its 'competitors' closely. The considerable extension of the welfare state, since the second half of the twentieth century, combined with the success of associations, contributed to the weakness of foundations. The introduction of the legal separation of the Catholic Church from the state in 1905 doubtlessly slowed down the creation of foundations in the area of education. The religious foundations that survived either carried on their activities in sectors neglected by public authorities or as a complement to the public sector, in the care for the elderly or people with disabilities, for example.

A third reason for the low number of French foundations is the spectacular decline of French fortunes during the first half of the twentieth century, which before had benefited from the extraordinary expansion of capitalism under the Second Empire and the Third Republic. The estates of wealthy people dwindled for various reasons such as the introduction of income tax, the Depression, the devaluation of the currency and the blocking of the rents paid to landlords, combined with the two world wars and the increased financial needs of the state. The oldest foundations of the Institute of France are still smarting from the collapse of the largest fortunes.[7] The value of their starting capital, initially high, was reduced considerably and this halted most of their activities. They hardly survive or are slowly in decline. Only the investment of their capital in a new foundation enables them to fulfil their mission. Since the end of 1990, after the adoption of economic reforms that favoured the wealthy, big fortunes have reappeared – in good time for the creation of individual foundations!

A fourth lesser known reason for the weakness of the French foundation sector is the French inheritance tax system. A private individual cannot bequeath all of his/her fortune to a non-profit organization. By law, most of the inheritance goes to so-called 'direct heirs', that is sons and daughters (or other direct relatives) of the deceased. The Civil Code bequeaths to the direct heirs a very great part of the legacy.[8] The heirs can, in turn, take action against the recipient of a bequest which is deemed to be prejudicial to their own interests. This threatens all foundations and places existing foundations in an insecure position, which may be detrimental to their activities.

Finally, local authorities are forbidden to set up foundations. Community foundations do not exist in France. As Edith Archambault (2004: 165–181) explains:

> [T]he vitality of the associations sector [in France is due] to the decentralization which caused a number of associative and municipal initiatives, thus mixing different cultures and responsibilities. The previous inexistence of such a mixture is undoubtedly another explanation for their [foundations'] weak growth. Foundations ... seem remote and opaque organizations, related to wealth and run according to obscure rules and [they are] supposed to be not very democratic.

Legal issues

Foundations are the product of an 'act by which one or more individuals or entities decide to irrevocably assign goods, rights or resources for the realization of non-profit work, which is in the general interest' (law of 23 July 1987). In this respect, the foundation can be distinguished from the association (a gathering of individuals for a non-profit purpose). Until recently, French foundations have been characterized by the irrevocable

assignment of goods to a purpose of general interest, an unlimited existence and close administrative supervision.

Although the first of these characteristics has remained unchanged, the
two others have been subject to legal changes.

1   The existence of the foundation no longer has to be unlimited. Since
    1990, company foundations can halt their activities after their fifth
    year. Since 2003, foundations called 'foundations with usable funds'
    are authorized to dip into their starting capital, if they encounter
    financial difficulties, for example.
2   In relation to supervision, the foundations were formerly obliged to
    give a place to state officials on their board of directors. The role of
    the state official was to check the legality of the foundations' activities,
    rather than to judge the validity of projects or programs per se. Since
    the law of 1 August 2003, the role of the state official (called 'govern-
    ment commissioner') has been changed to 'observer'.

An empirical profile

Data on French foundations has long been scarce.[9] A quantitative survey
carried out by the Foundation of France and the Ministry of the Interior,[10]
and published in 2005 (*Enquête auprès des fondations*) (Blanc *et al.* 2005),
enhances the general image of the sector as one that is not very dynamic
and dominated by old operating foundations. The statistical data provided
here is drawn from the results of this study.[11]

Out of the 2,150 foundations existing in France:

1   Approximately 480 are recognized to be of public utility. This first
    group of foundations includes the largest, the oldest and the most
    prestigious French foundations, among them the Pasteur Institute,
    the Foundation of France or the Foundation Abbé Pierre. The recog-
    nition of public utility was founded under the Restoration period
    (1815–1830) to allow for the creation of intermediate bodies between
    the state and the citizens, which had been prohibited by the Le
    Chapelier Law in 1791. This recognition is still a sovereign decision of
    the state – moderated by the highest institution of administrative juris-
    diction, the State Council. It is granted today after a long process,
    following the inquiries and recommendations of French civil servants
    who are the judges of the viability of any proposed project.[12] In recent
    years, the procedure has become less cumbersome, e.g. forms were
    simplified and the tax-breaks are more advantageous. Private indi-
    viduals can deduct gifts and legacies from their taxes up to a total
    value of 60 per cent, within the limit of 20 per cent of their taxable
    income. Companies can deduct 60 per cent from their donations
    within the limit of 0.5 per cent of their sales turnover.

2   Approximately 1,600 foundations are placed under the aegis of spe-
    cific organizations. They are not legal entities but they profit indi-
    rectly from the advantages granted to the umbrella foundation
    (recognized to be of public utility). They have the right to appeal to
    the generosity of individuals and they enjoy the same tax advantages;
    thus, they can attract donors by emphasizing very beneficial possi-
    bilities of tax deduction.[13] The principal umbrella foundation is the
    Foundation of France. It harbours 550 foundations. It was created in
    1969 by André Malraux, then Minister for Cultural Affairs under
    President De Gaulle, following the recommendation of one of his
    advisers. This foundation has specialized in the sectors of health,
    research, social services and childhood support, following the wishes
    of the families, the wealthy individuals and the companies that make
    donations and bequests. The Foundation of France provides founders
    with its expertise so that they can carry out their preferred projects.

    Four other foundations recognized to be of public utility also act
    as umbrella foundations for entities which serve the same objectives as
    the parent foundation. For example, the Foundation of French
    Judaism (created in 1978), dedicated to the enrichment of the cul-
    tural, religious and artistic Jewish heritage, includes 38 foundations.
    Finally, the Institute of France (which gathers together five scholarly
    academies, among them the French Academy) is also allowed to
    receive donations. It harbours 1,000 foundations officially, but it is dif-
    ficult to know if all are still really active. The Institute of France
    embraces a multitude of foundations which offer prizes and grants,
    some very small (so many of the under-funded ones have joined
    together) and others which are much better endowed.

3   Lastly, there are approximately 70 company foundations. According
    to a statute created by a 4 July 1990 law, they can be created for a
    limited duration (five years minimum); the durability of their activ-
    ities is not guaranteed by the initial capital but by regular payments[14];
    they do not have the right to appeal to private generosity (only their
    employees can be solicited); and the companies are authorized to give
    their name to the foundation. The companies can also create a foun-
    dation under aegis of a foundation of public utility.[15]

Activities

About half of the French foundations are active mainly in the following
sectors: social services, international and culture and arts.[16] They also
intervene in health and in education and research. The foundations
under the aegis of umbrella foundations, which are the most numerous
(but also the smallest), intervene particularly in the area of culture and
arts; followed by social services, international and health. The foundations
of public utility which employ people intervene mostly in the social

services and international sectors; then in those of health and culture and arts.[17] The foundations of public utility which are not employers (they are mainly grant-making) intervene especially in the education and research sector and also in the fields of social services, international and culture and arts. The number of foundations, in particular the grant-making type, has only increased where the state is reducing its expenditures – in social services, health and employment support.

Since the 1980s, founders have shown a greater interest in the local and international care activities (sector 9 of the ICNPO). This interest rose when the 'fight against exclusion' and the development of humanitarian aid became part of the national political agenda. Interest in the health sector also rose a little. Only interest in the education and research and culture and arts sectors fell (after an increase during 1960–1969 for the former sector and during the 1970–1979 for the latter). The foundations' interests in particular sectors seem to be narrowly linked to the public authorities' concerns.

Patterns of growth

The study conducted by the Foundation of France and the Ministry of the Interior found that 7 per cent of foundations in France are over 100 years old, 15 per cent are between 50 and 100 years, and 17 per cent are between 20 and 50 years. In other words, nearly seven foundations out of ten (68 per cent exactly) are less than 20 years old and 45 per cent of the foundations are less than 10 years old.

In terms of patterns of growth, 22 per cent of the foundations came into existence before 1900. Patterns of growth accelerated during the last three decades of the twentieth century: about half were created during this period and 20 per cent of them in the 1990–2001 period. There was a clear increase in the number of foundations created towards the end of the twentieth century: about half (45 per cent) of all foundations took shape during the years 1990–2001. They are mainly grant-making foundations whose budget is relatively modest. The oldest foundations are operating foundations (some are half-operating, half grant-making). Their capital is larger and they have a high amount of annual expenditure. On the one hand, nearly 6 per cent of the foundations (budget $\geq$ €10 million) spend over three-quarters of the total annual budget of all foundations. On the other hand, 70 per cent (budget $\geq$ €1 million) spend only 5 per cent of this total budget.

Thus, contrary to perceptions, the French foundations sector is made up of young grant-making foundations. But it is clear, however, that these foundations are definitely less powerful (from a budgetary point of view) than the operating or mixed foundations.

Roles

Overall, it is perhaps unfair to say that in France the state is omnipotent, as is often declared. The French non-profit sector is rather dynamic, with approximately 880,000 associations that contribute to the general interest. By comparison, the number of foundations is particularly small: hardly more than 1 per cent of the total number of associations. However, their budget is equivalent to 7 per cent of the associations'.[18]

The question: 'What is your role and what are your objectives?' was put to a dozen foundation representatives. This small group is not representative in a statistical way, but it was selected in order to reflect the diversity of the characteristics of French foundations in terms of their legal status, duration of existence, area(s) of activity, and whether they were grant-making or operating foundations. A dominant picture of the roles and position of foundations in French society emerges from the study: foundations are linked with innovation and are perceived to complement the role and activities of the state. They refuse to 'replace' public authorities, although it appears that government officials have this in mind in a period of budgetary austerity.

Complementary role

The majority of the French foundations intend to deal with social needs that the public sector either cannot fulfil or does not have the know-how to address. They act where the state and the local authorities fail to act. They do not seek to challenge the idea of the welfare state. They do not intend to finance public goods – contrary to other countries where the subsidiarity principle allows foundations to act first. Rather, a representative of a foundation engaged in health underlined the importance of partnership between foundations and public institutions:

> We are a recognized partner of the public hospital providing housing and care.

Some foundations seek to address gaps in the market. The Post Office Foundation, for example, supports the production and the broadcasting of popular French song music which is neglected by the music industry. It promotes unknown artists rather than celebrities. Foundations choose to support projects which they know are not likely to receive funding from elsewhere. The Cartier Foundation considers that 'we have a role to play to promote artists, at home or abroad. For us it is essential to show artists who are not shown elsewhere. Very young artists who are not known yet. Or older somewhat forgotten artists'. The Pasteur Institute is proud to state that:

> [T]he great speciality of the Institute is neglected infectious diseases: much is said these days of so-called orphan genetic diseases, which

involve very few people. But there are neglected diseases with many very poor patients: AIDS, tuberculosis,... Being independent enables us to work on these types of diseases.

Nonetheless, foundations are sometimes so complementary that they closely resemble public services, in particular when they contribute to the achievement of a public service. This is the case of many foundations that manage hospitals or old people's homes. For example, at the Ophthalmologic Rothschild Foundation, the director of the hospital insisted on how similar his organization's activities were to that of public hospitals. He stressed that the mission of his hospital is almost the same as those in the public sector. The constraints he has to face are similar to those of a public hospital. The hospital receives all the patients whatever their condition or their religion.

    Foundations refuse to consider the idea of their actions replacing the activities of the state or the local authorities. They refuse to take part in the 'retrenchment' of the state. The oldest French research foundations were thus alarmed by the initiatives of the French state in 2003. During that year, the scientific community demanded more resources and more jobs. In a difficult budgetary context, the government preferred to rely on the existing foundations and to promote the creation of new foundations instead of using public money. The Minister for Research, in September 2003, underlined how the foundations reinforce investment in specialized research centres while directing their energies to causes close to the citizens' concerns. In this way, they are seen to play a major role regarding the promotion of France's standing in the world and the competitiveness of French research internationally.[19] These measures have worried the scientific community:

> It is not very reassuring to hear the ministry say: 'We do not have money, would you please take care of the researchers?' ... This is very dangerous. It is a complete inversion of the logic of research financing: the State proposes to act as complement to the foundations, and the foundations are invited to take over the State, to replace it.
>
> (Grant-making foundation)

An innovative role

In contrast to the foundations' insistence that they refuse to be subordinated to the priorities and the modes of action of the public authorities, they stressed their autonomy and the capacity for innovation that this allows. Foundations intend to act independently, by supporting original projects, as one representative of a grant-making foundation argued:

> If we appeal to people for their money, it is not to supplement public funds with our small budgets. It would not be interesting. If we invest

the funds in a new old people's home or a new project for people with disabilities, that does not mean anything. Right from the start, therefore we try to identify social innovations, to build networks and to promote innovative projects on new issues. Millions of euro are devoted to these very varied projects.

Foundation representatives deem themselves to be more receptive to the concerns of the population than the public authorities and, thus, more able to satisfy them in an effective and efficient way. They believe that they are more reactive and flexible than public agents. The public sector is considered to be too rigid, too bureaucratic. In this regard, the foundations also pay attention to their specific position. They can maintain a distance from local conflicts. They can overcome disciplinary, political or administrative cleavages. They can make people work together – people who would not have otherwise worked together. They facilitate dialogues, coordination and alliances. As such, one foundation, the Foundation of France, underlined how they always insist that the beneficiaries are consulted and involved throughout the whole initiative or project. Similarly, the Cartier Foundation attributes the success of its exhibitions and its workshops of contemporary art to the fact that there are no constraints on the curators and to the attractiveness of the possibility of having philosophers, artists and photographers work together, both for the enlightened public and the media.

The foundations seek to capture social needs, through the links established with the associations and via collaboration between experts on social trends. Hence, non-profit associations are the privileged partners of foundations, as one foundation representative argued:

> We finance the network heads, I mean the associative federations which affiliate members at the local level. We are a sort of philanthropy wholesaler: we collect and redistribute money to smaller structures. When you finance the innovation, you do not finance mammoths . . . We do not exist to help big ones. . . . Social innovation is very often the product of small associations which were created to set up new services. We help structures where the users and the donors merge. Projects made by small structures are supported by the people.

Foundations seek to remain alert to new and emerging needs in which they may have a potential role to play. For instance, one grant-making foundation's close observations and investigations of gaps in health care for teenagers led it to become involved in this particular area. The Foundation of France, for example, underlined how they draw upon committees of experts to advise them on dominant trends. Some foundations also see themselves as experimenters of innovative actions that they intend to be duplicated elsewhere, in particular in the public sector. For example, a representative of the Foundation of France stated that:

> The general logic of the foundation is to promote new solutions and, beyond their financing, to realize them and to then convince other financial agents to support them.

Sometimes, public authorities claim that they are at the origin of such projects. Yet, foundations see this claim as a kind of homage to their existence:

> When we started to deal with special care to dying patients 10 years ago, there was almost nothing, no legislation, no medical teaching. We located and financed all the people who wanted to work in this field. And it took off.
>
> (Grant-making foundation)

The sociology of innovation (Callon 1986) considers that an agent is innovating when it manages to gather many partners to its cause (Akrich *et al.* 1988). Projects which are considered to be innovative are those whose promoters manage to collect around them as much support as possible, in particular among foundations experts. Some experts work in several foundations at the same time. Thus, the projects they support are more likely to receive aid. When a project attracts the attention and the support of an institution, the rationale is that its chance of being supported by other institutions rises.

Finally, some foundations intend to play a role in the production of new ideas. For example the Foundation Charles Léopold Mayer for Mankind's Progress, a Swiss foundation established in France, intends to contribute to the well-being of humanity by capitalizing on knowledge and experiments worldwide. This is also the case regarding the political foundations. For some political parties, foundations are seen to be a tool for establishing better connections with the people. Almost all the French political parties have a foundation, e.g. the Foundation for Political Innovation of the Union for the People's Movement. These foundations seek to act as (independent) think tanks and do not wish to be seen as a party organization as such. A representative of the Foundation for Political Innovation states:

> [The foundation] is linked to a particular line of thinking and intellectual references to the right and the centre. But it is not a tool of a political party. It is supposed to be open to people and to serve the general interest. We intend to produce ideas to help imagine the future which would have useful effects in the short run. [It is a question of creating] links between ordinary people and politicians.[20]

Ultimately, foundations in France position themselves in a role which is complementary to the state, but largely in an innovative capacity. On the one hand, they see themselves as working in a position alongside, and often in conjunction with the state. On the other hand, they are independent innovative entities which identify and address gaps where foundations can take the lead, sometimes with a view to eventually handing over responsibility to the state. However, perceptions of changes regarding the role of the state also underpin how foundations perceive their role(s) in society. (Re)-defining their position and role(s) in an era where the role and responsibilities of the state is also evolving is the one of the key challenges facing foundations in France today.

Current developments and emerging issues

In the sectors where the state's and the local authorities' intervention is dominant (social services, health, education, etc), foundation officials estimate that their role is to complement the public services. They mainly intend to act where the state or public establishments are failing. They do not propose a different society or identify with a particular vision of society but insist on the need to break free from the influence of the state in the production of public goods.

> The system that works is a system based on national solidarity and on public authorities but receiving contributions of private origin. Then a balance has to be found: we each have our own opinion.
>
> (Grant-making foundation)

They also insist on the need to fight what they perceive to be the tendency towards centralization and the rigidities of the system. Thus, the former director of the Pasteur Institute (between 2000 and 2005) developed ways of acting that were more akin to those of a private company than of a public service: close cooperation with the pharmaceutical industry, little consultation with the trade unions, defence of the financial independence of the research units and a meritocratic system of wages.

However, it seems that to a certain extent foundations do follow the state withdrawal, especially in social services. For several years, a new division of roles has taken shape between the state, the market, the family and the non-profit sector. The state, confronted with budgetary constraints, tries to save money and to transfer activities to other agents. After the Second World War, France instituted a Bismarckian welfare state model,[21] which no longer really works today. Social Security was created for the workers and their families. Only those who paid contributions had rights. This system stopped functioning smoothly at the end of the 1970s. More women entered the labour market. Unemployment started to increase and today it is about 10 per cent of the working population. The population also aged. A large part of the population is permanently or temporarily isolated from the labour market and its social protection.

Public authorities thus developed a parallel system of social assistance for the poorest: state benefits, which are financed by taxes, are awarded under strict conditions. Social security benefits were formerly regarded as support for economic demand and growth. They are regarded today as a load prejudicial to the corporate sector's competitiveness. The various reforms implemented to 'save' the social protection system have failed. Successive governments tried to address the problem (such as via incentives to employment, by increasing contributions and taxes). They also tried to decrease expenditure (via restrictive policies of access to the services, by decreasing their amount, etc). But the system is still heavily unbalanced. Today, political leaders are tempted to have economic effectiveness prevail over social justice. They transfer the load of the poorest to the market, families and the non-profit sector (and in particular to associations). More and more help is requested from foundations by the associations confronted by these new needs.

Foundations are facing a new threat: that of doing what the state or local communities do not want to do any more or cannot do any more. Yet, as mentioned above, the response of the foundations' representatives to this threat was unanimous: none intends to replace the authorities. They do not have the capacity. Their budgets are too small. Moreover, they refuse to play a role that they have never wanted. Foundations which intervene in social services do not agree that they contribute to the state's withdrawal. They still think they are acting independently. At the very least, their financial autonomy protects them from too much dependence on the authorities.

But at the same time, the grant-making foundations are obliged to rely on associations which propose projects. They can build networks, shape new dynamics. But they are largely dependent on the associations' projects. However, associations often work in such a way that, paradoxically, they do reinforce the withdrawal of the State: they distribute food and clothes to the poorest, they care about their housing conditions, they fight illiteracy, they struggle against addiction (to drugs or alcohol), they are concerned with the living conditions of children, they accompany families, they help the unemployed to find a job, etc. Foundations finance projects aimed at poor people that local authorities and state do not want to help any more or cannot address any more. If one looks at the map of the foundation sector as well as how it acts, one sees that foundations play a part in this new division of roles. They help families: they facilitate, perhaps without explicitly knowing it, the transfer of the public social protection to families. They support the development of home helpers; they meet the governmental objectives of reducing the number of unemployed people, creating jobs and increasing funds for social protection.

The state and the local authorities intend to fight those who take advantage of the social protection system. This fight against fraud hides another less respectable goal: lowering the number of recipients by sanctioning those who do not comply with the new rules. These new rules consist of giving rights in return for obligations (whereas the rights used to be based on needs alone). The poor must deserve their rights: unemployed people must prove that they look for jobs actively and must accept those which are proposed to them; the recipients of the minimum income must prove that they make real efforts to be socially reintegrated. All these measures reinforce suspicion about poor people and contribute to their stigmatization. This hunt against the 'profiteers' is disguised behind a more acceptable concern: the fight against dependence, to make sure that 'work pays', to restore the dignity of the poorest and to help them to find the way of autonomy.

It is precisely in the name of the fight against stigmatization of poor people and the defence of their dignity that several foundations work in the social field. The Foundation Vivendi (which stopped its activities in 2003) intended to promote home services – and thus to help unemployed people to find a job or to build their own business. The Foundation of France refuses to take part in programmes proposed by officials of high standing. It seeks to respond to people's real needs. It sets up programmes to restore their autonomy: by consulting them at the conception and implementation stages of projects, by using their own resources and competences. The Foundation Charles Léopold Mayer for Mankind's Progress also intends to restore people's dignity and to stimulate their undertaking capacity, etc. These ways of acting are very similar to those of social public services. Over the last few years social policies have stressed recipients' autonomy, their responsible behaviour, the personalization and diversification of services. Thus, for foundations and the challenges they face: the key issue is one of breaking with the logic of dependence, of restoring people's dignity and of giving them more chances to become autonomous.

Notes

1 This suggestion was made by Olivier Dassault. He justified his initiative by saying: 'Supporting foundations means trusting private initiative and private generosity to help the state work at best in all fields: research, innovation, social services, environment, health. . . .'

2 France ranks behind Denmark, Sweden, Germany, United Kingdom, Spain, Italy, Finland. Cf. Blanc *et al.* 2005. This study includes 1,109 foundations (all French foundations except the Institute of France's): among them, 42 per cent are of public utility, 52 per cent are sheltered by umbrella foundations of public utility and 6 per cent are company foundations.

3 The estimated figure is €3,139 millions. The correct figure is probably higher since the sample did not include the Institut de France's foundations. Cf. Blanc *et al.* 2005.

4 Conversely, other organizations called foundations are only non-profit associations (like the former Saint-Simon Foundation or the Copernic Foundation).

5 The Foundation of France was established to 'receive all donations and bequests in order to manage them and to redistribute their income to organizations of general interest, in the philanthropic, educational, scientific, social or cultural fields, in order to fulfil its missions' (governmental decree, 1969).

6 It was established in 1795. It is a 'scholarly parliament'. It embraces five academies (French, literature, science, fine arts, moral and political science). It supports arts and science, manages foundations and its estates, advises public authorities and promotes French culture abroad.

7 The Institute was ruined after the First World War because of monetary devaluation. It was obliged (until 1950) to convert its donations in Government loans. Its estate is mostly made up of buildings and of transferable securities.

8 The heirs can share up to 75 per cent of the bequest.

9 Some information is known about foundations thanks to Edith Archambault's research: *Le secteur sans but lucratif. Associations et fondations en France*, Paris: Economica, 1996; 'Le secteur sans but lucratif: associations et fondations en France et à l'étranger', *Administration* 176, juillet–septembre 1997, pp. 43–49; with J. Boumendil and S. Tsyboula, 'Foundations in France', in H.K. Anheier and S. Toepler (eds) *Private Funds Public Purpose: Philanthropic foundations in an international perspective*, New York: Plenum Press, 1999, pp. 185–198.

10 As mentioned above, the foundations of the Institute of France are not included in the study (the Institute did not agree to contribute to it). But the results are relevant and can be trusted.

11 The figures date from 2001.

12 This recognition is awarded by the Prime Minister (whose decree must be signed by the Ministry of the Interior), after the Council of State has given its opinion.

13 The other tax measures established by the law of 1 August 2003 are: 1) the increase of a tax deduction on income coming from the foundations' capital; 2) private individuals can also give properties that the foundation will be allowed to use for its own purpose. The foundation will receive the income coming from these properties, during this temporary donation.

14 The 2002 law about French museums put an end to the obligation to have a starting capital.

15 At the Foundation of France (where there are about 60 company foundations, like the Cartier Foundation) or at the Institute of France.

16 Y. Blanc *et al.* (2005) has used other categories: 'social services, care and humanitarian aid' and 'arts and culture'.

17 Other figures were published by the Ministry of Interior later: 61 per cent of foundations (out of 476 foundations in 2003), were involved in the social services, health and educational fields; 22 per cent in the artistic, cultural, scientific and higher educational fields and 17 per cent in other sectors (religion, economy, environment, Army and memorials, etc.). Cf. Y. Blanc, 2003, p. 34.

18 These figures were quoted by O. de Laurens (Foundation of France) during the meeting 'Knowing French Foundations', Pasteur Institute, 31 March 2005: www.centre-francais-fondations.org/doc/connaitre_fondations_francaises.pdf.

19 C. Haigneré, 8 September 2003, on the occasion of the 20-year birthday meeting of the IPSEN Foundation.

20 F. Dhersen, UMP representative (Union pour un mouvement populaire), in Y. Bordenave, *Le Monde*, 1 November 2002.

21 It is also called the 'conservative-corporatist' model. Cf. G. Esping-Andersen, *The Three Worlds of Welfare Capitalism*, Princeton: Princeton University Press, 1990.

References

Akrich, M., Callon, M. and Latour, B. (1988) 'A quoi tient le succès des innovations?', *Annales des mines* 11, juin 1988.

Archambault, E. (2004) Pourquoi les fondations sont-elles si rares en France? In Girard, D. (ed.) *Solidarités collectives; famille et solidarités*, Paris: L'Harmattan.

Blanc, Y., de Laurens, O. and Tchernonog, V. (2005) *Enquête nationale auprès des fondations*, Paris: Fondation de France-Bureau des groupements et associations du ministère de l'Intérieur.

Blanc, Y. (2003) 'Les paradoxes des relations entre l'Etat et les fondations', *Administration* 198.

Callon, M. (1986) 'Eléments pour une sociologie de la traduction', *L'Année sociologique*.

12 Germany

Frank Adloff, Philipp Schwertmann, Rainer Sprengel and Rupert Graf Strachwitz

Introduction

Since the 1990s, foundations in Germany have undergone a remarkable renaissance. The number of new foundations created has soared, the legal framework was substantially improved (in 2000 and 2002), and public attention has focused on foundations to an extent unimaginable even 20 years ago. The reasons are obvious: the decline of the welfare state, the difficulties encountered by governments to finance any venture beyond the upkeep of the state machine, and an increased trust in non-governmental agents of public interest. It is therefore not surprising that an age-old instrument for operating and/or funding institutions and projects for the public good is seen in a positive, perhaps all too positive light.

However, the rise of foundations has not been accompanied by a public debate about the usefulness of the instrument as such. Potential caveats and limitations of the foundation form have not undergone significant academic or indeed public scrutiny. The foundation community has hardly engaged in reflection on the increased importance of their role in society and what this might mean in terms of accountability, transparency, and improvements in governance. Empirical research, though initiated in 1990 (Strachwitz 1991), and today much more developed, has still not reached a level that would permit researchers, policy makers and the general public to draw on valid and near complete information.

Moreover, we know very little as to what motivates founders (Timmer 2004) and foundation administrators. What we do know is that the foundation community in Germany is vastly more heterogeneous than, say, in the United States, due to its very long historical tradition, and its apparent diversity in size and scope. In fact it seems misleading to translate *Stiftung* as 'Foundation' at all.

Furthermore, few officers have any particular foundation-related expertise and may thus be induced to draw on contacts, predetermined notions and very general suppositions to form their vision and determine their role. Whether this is true or not, was one of the starting points of the research discussed in this chapter. Twenty-four foundations, chosen not in terms of an overall representative sample, but with an emphasis on variety, were included in the survey. As the research proceeded, it became clear that the relationship between foundations and the state was going to be the crucial divide. Whilst some foundations quite distinctly adhered to a corporatist model, others clearly did not. As this chapter will show, history and legal framework, while attempting to direct foundations towards the corporatist model, cannot prevent the emergence of a more liberal model, a scenario which indeed appears to be increasingly attractive to foundations.

A profile of German foundations

Historical development

In Germany, foundations have been part of society for many centuries (see Campenhausen 1998). Two foundations still in existence today believe they date back over 1,000 years, and a number of church foundations are probably even older. This may well be true for a number of European countries, but it is particularly striking in light of Germany's history. Issues of faith, wars and political upheaval have changed the boundaries of Germany as well as the concept of society in a radical way on several occasions. Against these odds, foundations have survived both as a concept and in concrete form, as perhaps the most stable, albeit the least known ingredient of public life.

Grant-making, operating, and endowed foundations have existed side by side as far back as foundations can be traced. Old existing foundations (since Roman times) regularly fulfil their purpose by providing legal ownership of a building or physical structure. A vast number of church foundations were *fundationes* in the sense that the original endowment was spent on building the church, where after the foundation's basic function was its legal ownership. Other foundations were created to operate hospitals, alms houses and other institutions beneficial to the community. Some were endowed with assets that would yield revenue, which in turn would benefit either a specific institution or the community at large. Thus, historically, it would not be correct to limit the foundation entity to a specific form pursuing specific aims.

The most recent history of German foundations reflects the division of the country during the second part of the twentieth century. In East Germany after 1949, foundations faced a highly unfavourable environment. The foundation form was abolished when a new Civil Code in 1975, replaced the one of 1900. By contrast, foundations in West Germany regained popularity in the 1950s, resulting in a growing number of new creations. Foundation laws were enacted in all the states of the Federal Republic and moderately favourable tax regulations came into force. Also, increasing private wealth provided a material base for increased giving.

The peak of this giving in relation to assets in private hands was reached in the late 1960s. Since this period, contrary to popular belief, there has been a slow but steady decline in charitable giving. It is interesting to note that since the Second World War, the creation of foundations by corporations and by the federal, state, and local governments has also become increasingly popular (Kilian 2003: 94 et passim).

Nonetheless, in the last 50 years there has been little discussion on foundations and their role in society. Unlike the United States, a model referred to continuously by promoters of the idea of philanthropy, there was never serious debate about whether foundations actually had a role in modern democratic society, and whether there was a need to regulate on the size, assets, pay out and scope of action of foundations. Government supervision was believed to be sufficient to ensure that foundations would not act outside the mainstream of society. Indeed, foundations were seen to be contributors to an overall corporatist structure, including the various levels of the public and the not-for-profit sectors, dominated by government. Moreover, grant-making was taken as the prime task of foundations to the extent that they were in danger of becoming quasi-public funds rather than agents in civil society.

It is only since the early 1990s that the scope of public debate has widened. New aims, such as in relation to the environment; a new generation of founders influenced by the notion of state and market failure; and the rise of the concept of civil society, have prompted new models of foundations to come into being. The first community foundations along the lines of the American model, in Hannover and Guetersloh, were created in 1996. Large charities started multiple-donor foundations to support their own work from about 1996 onwards. A number of private and corporate donors have made significant endowments available for the promotion of social change, and large operating foundations have adjusted their structure in accordance with trends in European legislation and modern management.

Legal issues

All foundations in Germany are regulated by three diverse sets of legislation: public law, civil law and fiscal law (see also Strachwitz 2001). While fiscal law is universally federal, public and civil law can be federal and state (*Länder*) law. A great majority fall under church jurisdiction as well.

Public law governs public bodies and the relationship between public and private bodies. Since the term foundation describes public as well as private entities, public law will apply to a small but highly important percentage of foundations. Public law foundations are by definition part of the state and thus not part of civil society. They are neither autonomous nor are they created in perpetuity, the creating body reserving the right to reverse its decision at any time (see Winands 2004).

Civil law provides the legal base for the great majority of those foundations that are commonly counted as members of the foundation community. However, by tradition the term foundation is neither legally defined nor is it restricted to a specific legal form. The most common legal forms for foundations are:

- The non-autonomous foundation (*nicht rechtsfaehige Stiftung*): legally a contractual trust relationship between the donor and a (most commonly sole) trustee, who becomes the legal owner while remaining restricted and bound by the statutes by contractual obligation.
- The autonomous foundation (*rechtsfaehige Stiftung buergerlichen Rechts*): a separate legal person with no outside members or owners. This form, special to German law, is ruled by specific provisions in the Civil Code (§§ 80–88, revised in 2002). It is subject to government supervision which extends to the observance of the law and of its statutes, not, however, to its internal decision making, such as the selection of grantees. Supervision is regulated in state law.
- The foundation in the form of a limited company (*GmbH*). Company legislation fully applies to this form so that technically the foundation is a (commonly tax exempt) limited company.

In addition, some bodies that appear to be foundations and are termed as such, take other legal forms, including, somewhat astonishingly, that of a membership organization (*Verein*).

Fiscal charity law applies to all legal forms of charitable activity. Only very few rules are exclusive to foundations. Major specific changes granting more extensive tax benefits towards the endowments of foundations were introduced in 2000.

Under fiscal law, both autonomous and non-autonomous foundations are entitled to fiscal personality (as are registered and unregistered associations). This renders them subject to corporate taxation and enables them to obtain exemption from taxation (which cannot be obtained by natural persons).

Since approximately 98 per cent of all foundations are tax exempt, and since there is no specific body that defines the prerequisites for exemption in a material sense (i.e. authoritatively answers the question of what is beneficial to society), the tax offices decide whether foundations conform to the notion of furthering the public good. For this, there are formal legal requirements (e.g. nondistribution, payout rules) and a list of purposes that are deemed to be of public benefit. Fiscal law is federal law, but is applied by the state governments. Thus, there exists a sphere of interpretation which is addressed in different ways by different state governments.

Under the German constitution, the established churches enjoy a special public and yet autonomous status. The close affiliation of foundations to a church has remained in place over many centuries. Today, the churches enjoy the right to legislate autonomously in foundation matters as in others and have done so. It is estimated that there are approximately 100,000 church foundations, many of which are no more than legal owners of a church building or a source of income to the local clergy, while others are highly important social service providers.

An empirical profile

As foundations are not legally required to disclose any information, statistics are incomplete. Nevertheless some reasonably reliable data are available (Anheier 2003). There exist about 15,000 foundations, not counting the 100,000 church foundations mentioned above.

In their purposes foundations are very diverse, but figures show that foundations are mainly active in the field of social services (51.3 per cent), education (35.2 per cent), research and sciences (21.7 per cent), arts and culture (21.2 per cent) and health (12.2 per cent) (Sprengel 2001: 69). Other fields of engagement (above 1 per cent) are religion, the environment, international relations, non-charitable purposes, the economy, sports and politics.

Foundations also differ in their form of activity. About 22 per cent of German foundations are operating foundations. Hence, they are running their own institutions, prizes and awards or conduct their own projects. Approximately 17 per cent are operating and grant-making (mixed) foundations (see BDS 2001: 34). Between 55 per cent and 66 per cent of foundations pursue a local or sub-national agenda that leads to a particularly high presence of foundations on a regional level.

There are many operating foundations that run their own organizations such as homes for people with disabilities, homes for the elderly or kindergartens. The work of these organizations is usually not financed by the revenues from assets but by the social and health insurance system. Many of the service providing foundations stem from the nineteenth century. Over the last two decades the relative importance of social services and education has constantly diminished for foundations, while the fields of arts and culture, sports and the environment steadily increased. In the area of social services as well as education and research, the private founders are more involved than membership organizations or volunteers. Both of these areas, in which private founders are particularly active are also highly regulated and dominated by the state. This illustrates a problem in Germany: private founders tend to invest more in state-related fields of civil society than in more autonomous areas like recreation and advocacy.

Assets and expenditure of a typical German foundation are small. Only 17 per cent have assets exceeding €2.5 million. But their income resources are diverse, as foundations may enjoy self-earned income, can be active fundraisers or receive grants from the state, etc. Foundations constitute a small entity regarding their expenditure as well. Only 12 per cent of German foundations exceed €2.5 million in their expenditure. There are no reliable data available regarding how the grants and money for projects is allocated since most foundations do not disclose any financial data.

Generally speaking, the establishment of foundations has been growing continuously since the early 1980s. Starting with 94 new foundations in 1981 this number has increased tenfold to 900 new foundations in 2001, although it decreased to about 700 in 2002 and 2003. Most of the foundations existing today were created in recent decades.

Roles and visions

Information was gathered on 24 foundations through interviews, questionnaires and the analysis of documents. Although the foundations as a whole are highly heterogeneous, it is possible to arrive at the following more generalizing statements about the self-conceptions, roles, functions and visions of German foundations. The findings show that there exists a corporatist and a liberal sub-sector within the German foundation community (see Adloff 2004). This division of the foundation sector is an empirical description as well as an ideal typical abstraction: many in-between forms are possible and recognizable. Whereas we mostly find complementary roles in the corporatist sub-sector, the roles of foundations within the liberal sub-sector vary, ranging from pluralism and innovation to the mere acquisition of prestige. In addition to dividing the foundation world in two, we also investigated the roles of many German foundations that were not anticipated in advance within the research design (i.e. the function of bridge building between societal spheres).

The roles of foundations refer closely to their embedding in society and state. Ex negativo, some similarities between German foundations concerning their roles can be recognized. No foundation supports the assumption that foundations could serve the end of redistribution between the upper and the lower strata in society; the only exception is the community foundation we researched. In addition, nobody claims that redistribution should be part of a foundation's vision. There is only a marginal approval of the role of substitution. German foundations do not wish to fill the gaps the state leaves behind when reducing its expenditures. Generally speaking, German foundations do not regard themselves as responsible for social justice to be produced by economic redistribution and for taking over the tasks that were previously the responsibility of the state.

What is more, foundations do not want to be integrated into the state-run spheres. The degree of autonomy of German foundations vis-à-vis the state has taken a very diverse shape, but no foundation aims to move closer towards the state and give up its autonomy of action. On the contrary, all foundations are prone to defend their autonomy. But despite this orientation towards autonomy, actual autonomy from state interference is very diverse among the foundations.

The corporatist sub-sector

Since the expansion of state activity in the middle of the nineteenth century, every foundation has been forced to relate to state power and actions. The majority of foundations in Germany fulfil the function of complementarity and are embedded in the system of corporatism (Anheier 1997: 242). This is true especially for foundations working in the social sector.

Foundations are embedded in social corporatism similar to the other non-profit organizations working in the fields of social services and health care (Zimmer 1997: 75). There is a long tradition of cooperation between non-profit organizations and the state in Germany that has been promoted by a specific interpretation of the principle of subsidiarity (Strachwitz 2003: 27–40). Non-profit organizations active in the fields of social services and health care had – until recently – a privileged position compared with commercial or state suppliers (Zimmer 1997: 76).

The main role or function that can be found in this sub-sector is the complementarity of state activity. As the complementary function in the social sector is at present being called into question, the difference between a complementary and a substitutive role for foundations is no longer definite. It depends essentially on the changing definition of responsibilities that should be, or should not be assumed by the state. Social scientific observers can only point out that foundations objectively are not able to substitute state activities – as their assets are too small. Nevertheless it is possible for single foundations to regard their activities as substitutive.

Foundations in Germany's social sector have fulfilled, until now, mainly complementary functions. They run social organizations, such as homes for the elderly, that often have the legal form of a limited company. Foundations of the corporatist sub-sector have reacted recently to the shrinking of the welfare state with a trend towards more liberal arrangements. This includes rediscovering the organizational form of the foundation and using it to revitalize the ideas and ideals of the original founder, or as a means of fundraising in reaction to the cutbacks in public funding. We are therefore dealing with a movement within the corporatism system towards a greater degree of autonomy for foundations.

The liberal sub-sector

In addition to the corporatist-complementary connection of foundations to the public sector there exists a foundation sector that can be described as liberal-oriented. The liberal foundation sector typically stresses its independence from the state. Representative of this sector are wealthy citizens, such as business leaders, who, via their foundation activities, wish to stress their freedom, independence and distance from the state, while at the same time showing concern for the common good. Here, the foundations are operating parallel to the state. In this regard, the proposal that 'Foundations should be a visible power, independent of the state and markets, and provide alternatives to mainstream solutions' was supported by many interviewees.

However, a strong sense of identification with the liberal section of the foundation sector in Germany does not tell us anything about what actually happens here. There is a variety of functions that are carried out by foundations in this sub-sector, as well as various self-conceptions. Moreover, the movement away from the state does not automatically lead to the field of civil society. In fact, some foundations have a tendency to express social distance from the lower strata of society and function as a means to preserve hierarchies and established social structures. Comparing foundation activities with the whole of the Third Sector, it is striking that the endowment of foundation professorial chairs and scholarships plays a considerable role and shows the self-serving character of the charitable activities of the giving elite. By contrast, the areas of culture and recreation, highly represented in the Third Sector, or the field of social movements are rarely identified in the engagement of giving elites. Also, the field of the new social movements of civil and consumer interests plays just a minor role in relation to other foundation purposes. Instead of an orientation towards civil society, links with other social sectors, such as industry, are just as likely here.

Foundations within the liberal sub-sector may just as well be an instrument for the founder to attempt to gain symbolic capital – in other words: recognition. If the founder is a company, the foundation can, in this respect, contribute to public relations goals.

A foundation can therefore be viewed as an institution for the transformation of capital types, in the Bourdieu sense (cf. Bourdieu 1998; Sigmund 2000). Through the establishment of a foundation – the classic example is in the cultural field – the financial elite can acquire cultural or symbolic capital. Newly acquired economic capital can be ennobled through the establishment of a cultural foundation. One's own distinguished taste can be shown through support of the high arts and in return one gains recognition and prestige. It is a social field that removes the law of economic interest and rewards freedom of interest (Bourdieu 1998: 154). Clearly this model of acquiring symbolic capital is suitable for individual founders as well as for company foundations refining economic capital through culture.

Innovation is another role that can be found in the liberal sub-sector. Due to the fact that just a small minority of foundations are able to employ professional staff, it is highly probable that 'conservative' attitudes strongly prevail in foundation work. The sector operates mostly through cooptation and the personal contacts of the elite which is engaged on a voluntary basis. However, there are some exceptions. These foundations can all provide examples of state-independent action serving the public benefit and explicitly aiming to provide alternatives to the mainstream by way of innovation. Beyond this, these foundations are interested in contributing to social and political change, as well as promoting pluralism. Two foundations in our sample already express their independence from the state in their choice of legal form (limited company). The ability of these foundations to act innovatively is closely linked to a high level of reflectivity, i.e. foundation undertakings are subject to a permanent process of reflection with regard to their goals and means. Thus, foundations differ from each other according to what extent they network with one another and root themselves horizontally in civil society. In particular, smaller foundations are possibly more dependent on horizontal networking if they wish to be innovative. Larger foundations are more likely to promote innovation by using vertical networking and top-down communication forms.

Two of the foundations in the sample are active in the area of promoting science; under which function this activity should be categorized is a difficult question. We assume that it does not make sense to characterize the support of the sciences as innovative per se. The promotion of science can therefore more easily be categorized in the area of the complementary role or – with an individualistic funding policy – the support of pluralism.

It is noteworthy that, as a whole, a number of movements in the direction of increased liberty can be observed in the German foundation sector. The functions within this social framework differ considerably. Clearly, one cannot speak about an innovative foundation sector in general. But, as one interviewee puts it, foundations are in the most privileged position of all: they are capable of promoting social change by providing social risk capital. However, very few do this. Thus, the liberal foundation sector cannot be restricted to the role of innovation – the possibilities that the organizational form of a foundation can offer are simply too great.

Foundations as instruments for bridge building

Foundations can serve as instruments for overcoming obstacles by building bridges between different societal spheres. This function can be found both in the corporatist part of the foundation sector, as well as in the liberal sub-sector. It differs in the spheres the foundations bridge and how they achieve it. Community foundations, for example, solve the problem of collective action by giving an opportunity to those who do not have the necessary financial means to set up their own foundation, by joining

together and pooling resources for a collective engagement. One foundation in the sample, the *Buergerstiftung Hamburg*, builds bridges by facilitating and initiating public-private partnerships. Through its legal form of a
limited company the *Deutsche Kinder- und Jugendstiftung*, it allows a number
of German federal states to be represented on the board. Other foundations are building bridges between the different levels of German federalism or are trying to close the gap between different areas of bureaucratic
responsibility. One foundation enhances ecumenical work by selecting
natural persons as board members who do not need to represent the views
of their particular church.

It is not unusual for larger tax-exempt foundations to be used to influence
different social spheres (Sigmund 2000: 344). Foundations that attempt to
affect social change with scientific expertise and to organize knowledge, can
serve as a basis for power and influence. Economic capital can be effectively
transformed into the power of social definition and conception via the institution of a foundation (cf. Berger 2001: 213). Such foundations could also
be described as institutions serving the bridging of social spheres.

Another variation of bridge building is the facilitation of discourse, for
example in the form of conferences. This kind of discourse brings
together representatives of different social groups, who would otherwise
not have the opportunity for regular exchange, for example academics,
politicians, artists and business people. In this way, foundations can play
an organizing and enabling role in creating a pluralist and, as Habermas
(1992) put it, deliberative public sphere.

Current developments and emerging issues

We investigated the visions of foundations in relation to both individual
foundations and for the foundation sector in general. First of all, focusing
on the issue of resources, it is striking that the foundations underline the
importance of whether a foundation is able to dispose of sufficient capital
resources, in order for the foundation to be able to operate on the interest
yields. There were a number of foundations in our sample who, for their
vision of a positive development, are endeavouring to build up such a sum.

A change in operational procedures is not envisaged for the future.
Moreover, it is telling that none of the foundations interviewed had operational change in mind – no foundation appeared to find their own activities in need of fundamental revision. A number of foundations suggested,
as a form of internal development, that if endowed with sufficient funds it
would also be possible to pursue goals laid down in the statutes that had
hitherto been neglected.

Regarding the sector in general, the interviewees tended to regard
their own activities and their own foundation's operations as positive
examples for the foundation sector as a whole.

As a whole, German foundations have a shared vision for a quantitative increase in foundations and a liberal model of the embedding of foundations in state and society. Within this shared targeted model, there are differences, primarily with respect to how far foundations wish to network horizontally or operate alone. All of the foundations interviewed agreed unanimously with the statement, 'Foundations should be a visible power, independent of the state and markets, and provide alternatives to mainstream solutions'. They strongly disagreed with the statement that the influence of foundations in society should be limited. The idea that foundations are undemocratic institutions enjoying too many privileges was also clearly rejected. The notion that foundations come from another time and do not fit into modern society was vehemently discarded. Taken as a whole, our interviews reveal a vision of a lively and pluralistic foundation sector that has a solid place in the democratic order, and that has the necessary means to become involved in social processes and provide its own suggestions for addressing problematic situations.

Many of the foundation representatives and experts interviewed agree that the future of German foundations lies in the deepening of civil engagement. Facing empty public coffers, the stimulation of this engagement appears to be necessary and, in this context, the establishment of foundations is the expression of civic engagement. Beyond this, there was the vision, coming especially from the experts, that foundations could represent an infrastructure for voluntary engagement. However, the financial means for this have not been available thus far and internal development in this respect is hardly possible. According to this vision, foundations could become 'points of reference in civil society' by way of being key grant-makers in certain fields of action, independent from current strategic trends. According to experts, the capability of foundations to function as central points in a civil society infrastructure distinguishes them from associations.

Within this 'civil society discourse', the function of social innovation is awarded particular importance. According to this view, the future of foundations lies in increasing the number of critical and innovative model projects and making capital available for new ideas. This vision of civil society is regularly linked to the demand that foundations become more transparent. In particular, the experts in the foundation sector have been calling for more transparent practices for many years, and this subject was also discussed in the interviews. According to critics, the public demand for greater transparency stems from the tax exemption of non-profit organizations. Greater transparency therefore has a positive effect on the democratic legitimization of foundations. Without the transparency of foundation activities, the threat exists that non-legitimate power will be exercised, with the foundations retreating back into their own private and elitist spheres.

A radical vision of civil society was opposed by a number of foundation representatives. Although the demand for greater transparency was generally accepted, the foundations did not identify a need for a closer relationship between foundations and other non-profit organizations, or for the work of foundations to have some sort of democratic legitimacy. Furthermore, they stress their operational autonomy, for example, by only being accountable to the state supervisory bodies or by practising the right to freedom of choice that does not have to be justified democratically.

The development of a positive and negative scenario in a focus group made clear that a tension between two poles has often to be balanced by the foundation.

It is striking that the visions we observed mostly refer to the actual working or governance of foundations (see Table 12.1). Improving

Table 12.1 Visions for the foundation sector in Germany

Foundation tasks	
Positive	*Negative/tensions*
Foundation as an instrument of self-fulfilment of the founder	Glorification of the founder
Pluralism among foundations	Banks as trustees: accumulation of power, marketization
Coordination between foundations and the state	Filling of gaps left by a retreat of the state; Dilution of the idea of foundations through public foundations
Clear borders towards the state	No accountability of political actions through porous borders
Identifying of new needs	Non-adaptation and non-flexibility (can lead to irrelevance of foundations)
Courage to be subjective; Support of single persons	Fear
Provision of risk capital	Too cautious, bureaucratization

Foundation management	
Positive	*Negative/tension*
Higher efficiency and innovation than the state	Bureaucratization, mismanagement, nepotism
Public relations, transparency	Lack of interest in media, no public recognition of foundations
Professionalization, high quality standards	Risk of adaptation to markets and wider environment because of professional standards
Pluralism in foundation management 'Job rotation': foundation staff should also work outside of foundations	Adaptation forces Amateurism
Commitment to the founder (in memoriam) and comparison with presence	No critical assessment of the founder

foundation management seems to be one of the most important issues. In relation to the foundation sector, the vision could be characterized as: more of the same! There is the demand for quantitatively more foundations that do not have to change. A societal vision for foundations is absent: what foundations should do in a modern world and in which direction this society should change are not very hot topics among the German foundations.

Conclusion

The analysis shows that the German foundation sector is highly heterogeneous not only in terms of structural characteristics, but also in terms of self-understanding. The crucial finding of this study, the existence of a liberal and a corporatist sub-sector, stresses the fact that the functions of foundations depend to a large extent on the way in which they are embedded in state and society. The tendency towards a more liberal and state-distanced attitude can be seen both as a risk and as an opportunity. The risk lies in the exclusive notion of foundation work. This has been described above as a prestige agency function and is underpinned by the self-serving character of the founding elite. The chance of a liberal vision for foundations is to function as an essential part of civil society, supporting civic action, providing innovative impulses and making a specific contribution to a societal development that is not solely defined and engineered by the state. This potential is yet to be fully realized, keeping in mind that a great majority of German foundations are still embedded in a corporatist vision.

The research findings demonstrate the need for a continuous and critical public discourse on foundations and their activities in a modern society. Foundations should not be permitted to remain solely responsible for their own assessment as long as they claim to serve the public good. Through public scrutiny on foundation work and discussion on how to serve the public good, demands such as more transparency and public accountability could be met without additional legal requirements. This discourse has to be accompanied by further research on foundation activities in order to provide the public and the foundations themselves with the opportunity to reflect upon and develop strategies.

The extension of a liberal foundation sector may, however, gain support from further reforms of the legal framework for non-profit organizations. This concerns, for example, the composition, interpretation and redefinition of the list of charitable and therefore tax-exempt purposes. The aim should be to remodel the relationship between state and civil society in order to provide foundations with the necessary encouragement for the further development of their position as independent agents within civil society.

References

Adloff, F. (2004) 'Wozu sind Stiftungen gut? Zur gesellschaftlichen Einbettung des deutschen Stiftungswesens', *Leviathan – Zeitschrift für Sozialwissenschaft*, Heft 2, pp. 269–285.

Anheier, H.K. (2003) 'Das Stiftungswesen in Deutschland: Eine Bestandsaufnahme in Zahlen', in: Bertelsmann Stiftung (ed.) *Handbuch Stiftungen*. Wiesbaden, pp. 43–86

Anheier, H.K. *et al.* (eds) (1997) Der Dritte Sektor in Deutschland, *Organisationen zwischen Staat und Markt im gesellschaftlichen Wandel*. Berlin.

Bourdieu, P. (1998) Praktische Vernunft, *Zur Theorie des Handelns*. Frankfurt a. M.

Berger, P.A. (2001) 'Soziale Ungleichheiten und soziale Ambivalenzen', in: E. Barlösius, Hans-Peter Müller and S. Steffen (eds) *Gesellschaftsbilder im Umbruch. Soziologische Perspektiven in Deutschland*. Opladen, pp. 203–225.

(BDS) Bundesverband Deutscher Stiftungen (2001) Zahlen, Daten, Fakten zum deutschen Stiftungswesen. Berlin.

Campenhausen, A.v. (1998) 'Geschichte des Stiftungswesens', in: Bertelsmann Stiftung (ed.) *Handbuch Stiftungen. Ziele – Projekte – Management – Rechtliche Gestaltung*. Wiesbaden, pp. 25–45.

Habermas, J. (1992) *Faktizität und Geltung. Beiträge zur Diskurstheorie des Rechts und des demokratischen Rechtsstaats*. Frankfurt.

Kilian, M. (2003) 'Stiftungseinrichtungen durch die oeffentliche Hand', in: Enrico Bellezza, Michael Kilian and Klaus Vogel, *Der Staat als Stifter*. Guetersloh.

Sigmund, S. (2000) 'Grenzgaenge: Stiften zwischen zivilgesellschaftlichem Engagement und symbolischer Anerkennung', *Berliner Journal für Soziologie*, Heft 3: 333–348.

Sprengel, R. (2001) *Statistiken zum deutschen Stiftungswesen*, Ein Forschungsbericht. Berlin.

Strachwitz, R.G. (1991) 'Hinweise zur Benutzung', in: Bundesverband deutscher Stiftungen, *Verzeichnis der deutschen Stiftungen*, Darmstadt, pp. 15–18.

Strachwitz, R.G. (2001) 'Country Report: Germany', in: A. Schlueter, V. Then and P. Walkenhorst (eds) *Foundations in Europe. Society, Management and Law*. London, pp. 133–144.

Strachwitz, R.G. (2003) 'The Principle of Subsidiarity and The Role of Faith-Based Charities in Germany', in: R.G. Strachwitz, *Philanthropy and Civil Society*. Berlin, pp. 27–40.

Timmer Karsten, S. (2004) *Deutschland: Die Stifter-Studie der Bertelsmann-Stiftung*. Guetersloh: Bertelsmann-Stiftung.

Winands, G. (2004) 'Der Staat als Stifter: Notwendigkeit, Möglichkeiten und Grenzen des staatlichen Einflusses', in: R. Strachwitz and V. Then (eds) *Kultureinrichtungen in Stiftungsform*. Guetersloh: Verlag Bertelsmann Stiftung.

Zimmer, A. (1997) 'Public-Private Partnerships: Staat und Dritter Sektor in Deutschland', in: Anheier *et al.*, *Der Dritte Sektor in Deutschland*. Berlin: Organisationen zwischen Staat und Markt im gesellschaftlichen Wandel, pp. 75–98.

13 Greece

Charalambos Economou and Sophia Tsakraklides

Introduction

Although the Greek foundation sector does not command the large resources of some of its European counterparts, it has over time made some critical contributions in social service provision, education, culture and development. Greek foundations feel that they primarily serve the purposes of complementarity, redistribution, the preservation of culture and the promotion of pluralism. Most of the foundation representatives interviewed for this study supported either a liberal democratic or a social democratic vision of state–society relations. Moreover, Greek foundation representatives are generally satisfied with the types of roles their foundations play. Their hope for the future is that they can build on, and improve what they are doing already.

This study also found that foundations in Greece are both ideologically and practically aware of their existence within the realms of both the welfare state and civil society. They do not find the two roles of service provider and civil society advocate contradictory. If it is about providing funds and services to the underprivileged, they feel their contributions are significant and supplementary to the state. This is not a new twist in the story of foundations in Greece. Though the exact arrangements and activities of foundations in Greece have undergone changes, their roles and visions have remained virtually unchanged throughout the greatest part of the twentieth century.

At present, the Greek foundation sector appears to be dealing with many of the challenges facing foundations across Europe. We agree with many Greek foundation stakeholders in their concern about their foundations' ability to more effectively cooperate with the state, business and international sectors. We suggest that one possible solution to many foundation problems is the facilitation of communication among foundations and other stakeholders, a task that this study hopes to encourage.

A profile of foundations in Greece

Historical development

Whilst the Greek foundation sector has grown in recent years, it is not comparable to the rate of foundation building at the beginning of the century. By 1938 researchers at the Greek Ministry of Economics documented the existence of 4,000 foundations around the country.[1] Though we are not aware of the exact number of foundations in existence by the 1950s, a progressive increase in the number of new foundations is evident in the 1960s and 1970s (Table 13.1). This was followed by a small decrease during the 1980s, which may have been due to a downturn in industrial development and the nationalization of many private law foundations.[2] Additionally, after the mid-1980s, EU programmes designed to fund under-developed areas of welfare and cultural activity in European countries and a general tendency for expansion in Greek civil society encouraged the proliferation of membership associations.[3]

Despite the relative growth of membership associations during the 1980s, foundations seem to exert greater influence on the Greek state largely due to their experience, professionalism, and the size of operations. This is true despite the fact that only about 10 per cent of non-profit organizations operate under the legal status of the foundation (Tsakraklides 2001a). The temporary decline in the rate of foundation establishment in the 1980s was followed by a period of higher activity in the 1990s.

Legal issues

Foundations have been defined here as 'assets' supported by non-membership-based organizations which are private, self-governing, non-profit distributing entities serving a public purpose. Legally speaking we have found this definition to fit the Greek case quite well. In everyday usage, however, the Greek word for foundation, *idruma*, is used to describe an 'operating' foundation based on an original deed, which sets out the purpose of the foundation. Such operating foundations are bureaucratically organized and operated by a full-time personnel. From the 258 foundations established between 1991 and 2003, only 93 or 36 per cent seem to provide a specific kind of service and could thus be termed *operating* foundations.

The corporate foundation is not a common foundation type in Greece even though there is a small number of very powerful such foundations. Foundations, based on endowments used to support mainly individual needs as designated by the donor, are by far the most common type of foundation.[4] These foundations can hardly be called grant-making; although they handle their original endowment they do not invest it or try to increase it in any manner. Such foundations often have no public

Table 13.1 New foundations in Greece, 1950–2003

New foundations	1950–1960	1961–1970	1971–1980	1981–1990	1991–2000	2001–present
Absolute numbers	69	107	151	128	221	37
Percentage change		55	41	−15	72	−33*

Source: Data collected by Pelleni-Papageorgiou 1993: 60–65, up to 1990. Recent data collected by authors.

Note
*Estimated.

offices. Rather, a 'contact person' is responsible for allocating funds according to the wishes of the founder. Thus, though legally designated as foundations, such legal persons are commonly referred to as 'endowments' (*klirodotimata*). About half of the foundations in this category provide scholarships. Most of the rest donate money to individuals facing dire circumstances. Larger grant-making foundations are usually linked to wealthy industrialists or corporations and provide grants to support their own projects, other foundations and/or even government works. Typical of this type of foundation elsewhere, these foundations regularly invest and multiply their endowments.

An empirical profile

Over time, one can observe significant shifts in foundation activity areas. Until the 1950s and 1960s most new foundations concentrated on welfare issues. A study of Greek welfare organizations suggested that during the 1970s services to the elderly, the blind and people with mental disabilities were overwhelmingly provided by private non-profit organizations, mostly foundations with some state help (KEPE 1985). However, foundations are gradually moving away from social welfare and health services. The expansion of the Greek welfare state has limited the need for private welfare providers, whilst globalization and the pressures as a result of entry into the European Union have increased the need for specialized education and research that public schools and universities alone cannot fulfil. Apart from the ever increasing number of educational foundations,[5] we see more foundations active in the areas of art, science, and the environment, in accordance with broader needs and trends (see Table 13.2).

Roles of foundations in Greece

The previous section suggested that two-thirds of Greek foundations provide grants primarily to individuals and much less frequently to other public and private entities. Operating and large grant-making foundations have much more broad and complex ideas about their purpose in Greek society. Thus it is mainly the opinions of their representatives that this study reflects.

Awareness

Overall, it would be fair to say that Greek foundations have some appreciation of their specific roles compared to other types of civil society organizations or the state, but that they have spent a lot less time thinking about their broader societal roles. For example, only half of foundation stakeholders interviewed could identify their foundation's realm of work (i.e. education) within the broader field of civil society or the third sector. However, the remainder felt that foundations were relatively individualistic organizations with specific goals. In fact, stakeholders were quick to point out the importance of having specific goals in order to be successful in their field of work. Thus, foundation stakeholders will only generalize on the importance of their broad area of activity, such as welfare, art and culture preservation, or education. Only when pressed further will they reflect on their role in fulfilling broader social needs.

Most foundation stakeholders point out how foundations supplement the role of the state by tending to unmet needs or caring for social groups neglected by the state. Moreover, foundations clearly differentiate their roles from those of the state. Again, during our interviews, foundation stakeholders did not, on their own – without being prompted – employ terms such as innovation and complementarity to describe their roles. What is more, they did not clearly distinguish *between the different types* of supplementary services that foundations can provide vis-à-vis the state. The perception of their roles as complementary to the state went along with a conviction that the role of the state should be to provide leadership and control, while they saw themselves as more suitable for encouraging innovation, efficiency and speed. Though innovation was not really mentioned specifically as an important role, stakeholders saw themselves as existing within an autonomous and flexible sector which allowed them to move away from established and bureaucratic ways of doing things. Thus, substitution was rejected as a desirable or necessary role: foundations and the state *are* essentially different.

Redistribution was not specifically mentioned but respondents were well aware that services were provided by the 'haves' to the 'have nots'. This role also ranks high with all endowment foundations, whose number is large but whose impact is minimal. Thus we have marked the awareness of the role of redistribution as high. The awareness of social change as a foundation role was medium; stakeholders were very concerned with the need to empower socially excluded groups and thus address social inequalities. The preservation of traditions and cultures, a role associated essentially with a specific group of foundations, was mentioned as *a priority*

Table 13.2 Establishment of new foundations, 1950–2003 in Greece, by area of activity, as a per cent of the total number of new foundations

Primary area of activity	1950–1960	1961–1970	1971–1980	1981–1990	1991–2000	2001–present
Social welfare	49.2	51.4	33.1	29.6	14.1	21.6
Health	15.9	4.6	1.9	3.1	4.5	2.7
Education	21.7	24.2	43.7	48.4	40.5	45.9
Science	5.7	7.4	.6	3.1	4.5	10.8
Religion	4.3	7.4	9.2	3.1	4.1	2.7
Art and folklore	1.4	0.9	3.2	7.8	9.1	8.1
Environment	1.4	0.9			2.3	
Foundation support		2.8	3.3	3.9	4.1	
Public works			4.6		1.8	
Various**					15.0	8.1
Total*	100	100	100	100	100	100

Source: Data collected by Pelleni-Papageorgiou 1993: 60–65, up to 1990. Data from 1991 onwards collected by authors.

Notes

*Percentage of the total foundations established that decade. Percentages do not add up to a hundred due to the rounding of numbers at the first decimal.

**This category added by authors to include all foundations which seem to engage in at least two but often more areas of activity.

especially by foundation stakeholders belonging to this group. Finally, pluralism ranked high among foundation roles because many stakeholders understood the importance of a lively and active civil society and saw their foundations as significant members of Greek civil society.

Visions and roles

The extent to which roles are reflected in the visions of foundation representatives and policy makers was not easy to evaluate. However, since – as suggested above – foundation representatives understood their work as being parallel and supplemental to the state, and that it was successful only as a result of their independence from the state, they appeared to be in agreement with both basic liberal *and* social democratic visions. Greek foundations saw their activities as crucial for social reform and for the preservation of the rights of minorities. Thus, as illustrated by Table 13.3, the visions of Greek foundation stakeholders regarding the ideal relationship between themselves, the state and business, tended to correspond with their awareness of their roles.

Practice

Greek foundation representatives and stakeholders see foundations *currently* as being complementary to the state in terms of the provision of services or the fulfilment of certain functions, but not in terms of achieving redistribution, promoting pluralism, or innovation. The promotion of pluralism, in particular, which is idealized as perhaps the most important role of foundations in modern society, is ranked lower when discussing the reality of the Greek case. Redistribution and innovation were also described as insufficiently achieved in practice. This was the best indica-

Table 13.3 Awareness, visions, practice and feasibility of roles according to respondents in Greece ($n = 25$)

Roles	Awareness	Visions	Practice	Feasibility
Complementarity	High	High	High	High
Substitution	Low	Low	Low	Low
Redistribution	High	High	Medium	Low
Innovation	Medium	Low	Low	Low
Social change	Medium	High	Medium	Medium
Preservation	High	*	High	*
Pluralism	High	High	Low	*
Other?	High (field-related)	Medium (education)	High (field -related)	*

*Insufficient data.

tion that foundations in fact felt that there should be more of a focus on these areas in terms of the foundation roles.

The discrepancy between the perception of foundation roles in modern society and their actual roles within the Greek foundation sector is indicative of the difficulty faced by foundations in realizing idealistic foundation roles. There is plenty of anecdotal and secondary evidence of this discrepancy. Many of the foundations interviewed provided very broad written statements of their purposes and activities, of which only a fraction is actually accomplished.

Feasibility

The issue of foundation practice is very closely linked to the issue of the feasibility of foundation roles. Greek foundation stakeholders were both eager and quick to point out numerous issues or problems which prevent foundations from meeting their ideal goals. The failure of foundations to meet their goals appeared to be attributed to the actions of three main actors: the state, the foundations themselves and the wider public. Of those three actors, the state received most of the blame, for example, for 'not assisting foundations', or 'not cooperating' with foundations, or 'not providing sufficient funding'. Foundations were blamed primarily for the poor standard of their personnel, lack of resources and infrastructure, lack of vision and devotion to a cause, and a backward mentality. Finally, some stakeholders portrayed the Greek public as prejudiced, uneducated on the roles of foundations, and unappreciative of their work. Overall, foundations seemed to want more from the state though they were also deeply aware of their own shortcomings.

This then appears to be a principal challenge for Greek foundations. As long as they forfeit part of their independence and assume a complementary role to the state, they put their fate at least partially in the hands of the state. Some stakeholders are beginning to question the advantages of such a relationship for Greek foundations.

Foundation visions and challenges

Several themes did emerge from this study in support of specific models of state–society relations. The ideal society envisaged by most foundation representatives was either the outcome of a distinctly liberal value system or one dedicated to social democratic goals. To the extent that these two separate worlds could overlap, there was agreement among the representatives interviewed. For example, there was a broad consensus on the importance of democratic government and the representation of all interests in the political process. Still, there seemed to be disagreement in such crucial areas as the appropriate level of state interference in civil society. As Table 13.4 suggests, the 25 respondents underlined the relevance of

Table 13.4 Average and mean scores of foundation representative agreement in Greece with state–society relationship models (5-point scale where 5 represents total agreement, $n = 25$)

State–society model	Description	Average	Mean
Social democratic	Foundations should be part of a larger welfare system and have well coordinated relationship with the state to either complement or supplement state activities in meeting needs.	3.7	4
State-controlled	Foundations should operate in assigned fields that are of primary interest to a democratically elected government, and they should have close oversight to make sure that they operate in the public interest.	1.8	1
Corporate	Foundations should enhance public benefit in areas where they are qualified to do so, and they should work largely independently but in close cooperation with the state, with an emphasis on service provision.	3.8	4
Liberal	Foundations should be a visible force independent from both government and market, and they should provide alternatives to the mainstream and safeguard minorities.	4.4	5
Peripheral	Foundations are minor institutions, yet are ultimately worthwhile institutions as long as they do not challenge the status quo.	1.2	1
State–foundation partnership	Foundations are a modern instrument of public sector reform and a milestone toward new public management.	3.4	4
Business	Foundations are an expression of corporate citizenship, and assist business interest in reaching out to communities and customers by serving the public benefit in enlightened but ultimately self-interested ways.	2.8	3

the liberal model to the Greek case, followed closely by the social democratic and corporatist models.

Foundations also agreed with the proposal that they are instruments of public sector reform and a milestone toward new public management. Some representatives feel that foundations are a tool which can be used by the state for public goals. This goes a step further than the social democratic vision by encouraging a state–foundation partnership, which may be led and administered by the state. It also acknowledges the present need for the state to find non-governmental allies.

One should note, however, that respondents were split as to whether the adherence of foundations to prescribed models or visions actually reflected the reality of the position and roles of Greek foundations. In our follow-up workshop discussion, the five foundation representatives present agreed that the Greek case actually closely resembles a social democratic/corporatist universe. We can tentatively conclude here that respondents generally identified with the need to abandon previous social democratic policies which were prevalent in the 1980s and early 1990s and to enter a new era of less state intervention.

This ideological mix of liberal and social democratic views reflects political and social tensions prevalent in Greece and in many other western democracies at present. The 1980s and 1990s were decades of welfare state expansion and populist welfare policies in Greece. By the end of the 1990s, the realization emerged that such policies were simply unsustainable and the public sector found itself buried in debts and deficits. By the late 1990s, even Greek trade unions – the strongholds of the Greek socialist party – were ready to make concessions. Thus, while socialist ideals prevail, liberal policies – especially in the economy – seem more realistic to today's foundation leaders.

This study did not produce a consensus regarding the future development of the Greek foundation sector. Twelve respondents suggested that in the following years the Greek foundation sector would develop. Seven saw a possible decline of activities due to loss of funding and other economic difficulties. Two did not predict any change. Almost all respondents thought that the involvement of the European Union (EU) would become increasingly important both in organizing the field and providing funding. Respondents of this study did, however, point out a number of challenges that foundations would have to deal with in the coming years regardless of overall trends in the development of the sector.

Whilst we address some of these challenges separately in the paragraphs below, one general point is worth making here. Though foundations clearly belong in the so-called third sector, they are subject to economic pressures similar to their for-profit counterparts. The state can protect non-profit organizations from such pressures, at least partially, and it has done so in the past. As the following section will suggest, the greatest dilemma for many Greek foundations arises because of the emerging need to become more independent and competitive – as in the liberal economic model – whilst managing to maintain as much state protection as possible – usually better guaranteed by social democratic models of state–society relations.

The first three of the challenges described below summarize directions already taken by Greek foundations to increase their competitiveness as well as their political and economic independence. The last two parts to this section discuss current difficulties in building relationships with the state and the EU.

Professionalization

The problem of professionalization was listed by seven interviewees as one of the top three problems faced by the sector. The low degree of professionalization among Greek foundations was again and again cited by foundation representatives as one of the leading causes of inefficiency, backwardness, lack of innovation, lack of public recognition and lack of funding, all of which characterize a large portion of the sector. It is also important to note that in their answers these interviewees linked the problem of professionalization with that of leadership. It is a well known fact that the Greek industrial sector is lacking professional leadership. The same seems to be true of the foundation sector.

Building a relationship with the business community

Foundation representatives and stakeholders were very concerned about the seeming inability of the state to further fund foundation programmes and activities. This study found that, increasingly, foundations seek funding from private sources. While in the past mixing for-profit business with philanthropic activity was looked at with suspicion, we found that such suspicions are eroding.

Even foundations with no direct links to business professionals or corporations have begun to forge relationships with the business community. It is becoming increasingly common for businesses to sponsor foundation projects and events. This was unheard of even 15 years ago but it is a practice that has financially rejuvenated many foundations.

Gaining public recognition

Educating the public about foundations and their roles seems to be the number one challenge for many of the interviewed representatives and stakeholders. Many representatives argued that the word foundation in Greece evokes negative connotations. At a minimum the general public has connected foundations with a few wealthy individuals. The assumption is that in indirect ways foundations serve the interests of these individuals. Finally, and perhaps most importantly, one representative said:

> [C]itizens need to understand that they should not expect everything from the state, so they should spend their time and their own money to support organizations [foundations] which are there for their own use, are flexible and provide results.

Another representative suggested that the negative opinion toward private philanthropists has been the outcome of two centuries of consistent state intervention in civil society, which slowly compromised the wonderful work of the nation's Great Benefactors.[6]

Increasing cooperation with the state

As already discussed foundation representatives felt that their most obvious partner is and should be the state. What remains unclear is the exact nature of the relationship with the state that foundations desire. Two alternate models have been suggested: the liberal and social democratic models. Though each is clearly different, foundation representatives are both unable and unwilling to make a choice for reasons already suggested earlier. Thus it remains to be seen what exact shape the foundation–state relationship will assume in the coming years.

Representatives were much clearer about their demands of the state. Foundations want a state that will be supportive and yet non-interfering. There are still frequent cases of government bias toward some foundations rather than others and many foundation leaders feel neglected due to their ideological standpoints or partisan affiliations. Two representatives clarified – and others agreed – that there needs to be complete disassociation on their part from political parties. Consensus also emerged among the foundations that the state needs to be open and receptive to the work of foundations itself, as well as to their policy recommendations.

Improving relations with Europe

Overall, foundation leaders felt that the relationship between Greek foundations and the state would depend on the EU. Some representatives predict that the EU will increasingly require higher professional and infrastructural standards from private non-profit service providers in return for funding. This could drive smaller foundations out of business. The same representatives view this change as both negative and positive. Improvement of services is of course beneficial but increasing dependency on international actors is considered undesirable.

One of the most surprising and perhaps important results of this study, however, was the lack of knowledge among Greek foundation representatives and stakeholders of developments in the European foundation world. For example, only four out of 25 respondents indicated that they were aware of the existence of the European Foundation Centre. Of those respondents three underlined its role in allowing communication between foundations. The most informed of these four respondents was quite negative about the achievements of the centre so far. Only three respondents had any knowledge of the European Code of Practice for Foundations, but they were very positive about it. Only one respondent was at all aware of the European Foundation Statute and he/she seemed to favour it.

What is perhaps even more striking is that in a country that tends to favour all forms of European integration, representatives seemed to lack any eagerness to spread their wings abroad. Only one respondent specifically suggested the need for foundations to expand their connections within the international arena. Perhaps the lack of domestic partnerships prevents the exchange of information with possible international liaisons as well.

Conclusion

The evidence presented in this chapter strongly supports the argument that foundations in Greece are and want to be complementary to the state. They do not wish to dominate any field of action but rather to provide much needed financial, organizational, scientific and other assistance. In some cases, they want to lead but only by example. The promotion of pluralism is important to them especially within the context of the liberal-democratic model, which they support. In terms of specific fields of action, foundations seemed primarily concerned with redistribution and the preservation of traditions and cultures. This is of course in agreement with what foundations actually do in Greece: welfare service provision and various cultural and educational activities. Finally, they realize that they are in a position to facilitate innovation but whether that is possible or not is incidental and not the sole purpose for their existence.

The liberal and social democratic models were the most appealing models to foundation representatives. Greek foundations want to complement the state and, to an extent, be led by the state. This does not mean they enjoy intervention in their own affairs. They seek support but only when it comes along with freedom and opportunity. What is sought, above all, is a meaningful *partnership*, with potential benefits for both parties.

Notes

1   However, many of those foundations actually referred to endowments donated directly to other public or private institutions (see section on the legal environment of foundations in Greece), and thus it would be difficult to assess how many operating and consistently grant-making foundations existed at the time even though the number was large (Zakopoulos 1968: 23).

2   We are not sure of the 'death' rates of foundations over time. However, we know that for the recent years, 1991–2003, 258 new foundations came to existence while only 15 were dissolved.

3   Membership associations were less difficult to create than foundations, and benefited from the same tax exemptions as foundations while maintaining greater independence from the state.

4   As in other European countries, in Greece all foundations are based on one or more endowments. They sometimes rely financially on these endowments completely or they invest their endowments to continue increasing their budgets. Endowments do not always result in the institution of foundations but may be also donated to other private or public legal persons, such as other foundations, public institutions. Thus any given endowment may facilitate the creation of a new foundation or may be donated to an existing foundation. The latter is performed according to the will of the donor.

5   Many of the educational foundations belong in the group of foundations that Greeks refer to as 'endowments'. Their sole purpose of existence is the distribution of usually fairly minimal funds, i.e. scholarship money.

6   The Great Benefactors were an entire class of individuals who emerged during the Greek Revolution for Independence against the Ottomans culminating in 1821. They supported the Greek state in the founding of great cultural and welfare institutions, many of which still exist.

References

Council of Europe (1994) *Recommendation No. R(94) 4: Of the Committee of Ministers to Members States on the Promotion of a Voluntary Service.*

European Foundation Centre (2002) 'Foundation Legal and Fiscal Profile: Greece', mimeo, Belgium: EFC.

KEPE (Centre for Planning and Economic Research) (1985) *Κοινωνική Πρόνοια, Εκθέσεις για το Πρόγραμμα 1983–1987* (Social Welfare: Reports on the 1983–1987 Plan), Athens: KEPE.

Marinos, Y. (Various dates, 1997–Present) *To Vima.*

Pelleni-Papageorgiou, A. (1993) *Το Ίδρυμα Ιδιωτικού Δικαίου* (The Private Sector Foundation), Athens: Sakoulas.

Salamon, L.M. and Anheier, H.K. (1998) 'Social Origins of Civil Society: Explaining the Nonprofit Sector Cross-Nationally', *Voluntas*, 9 (3): 213–248.

Salamon, L., Anheier, H. *et al.* (1998) *The Emerging Sector Revisited*, Baltimore: Johns Hopkins Institute for Policy Studies.

Stasinopoulou, O. (1996) Voluntary Care in a Mixed Economy of Welfare: Present Trends – Future Prospects, *Review of Decentralization, Local Government and Regional Development*, 4: 64–73.

Tsakraklides, S. (2001a) *Structuring Civic Action in State-Dominated Societies*, unpublished PhD dissertation, New Haven: Yale University.

Tsakraklides, S. (2001b) 'Foundations in Greece', In: Schluter, A., Then, V. and

Walkenhorst, P. (eds) *Foundations in Europe*, London: Directory of Social Change: 145–155

Wood-Ritsatakis, A. (1970) *An Analysis of the Health and Welfare Services in Greece*, Athens: Center of Planning and Economic Research (KEPE).

Zakopoulos, P. (1968) *Τα Εθνικά Κληροδοτήματα Και Αι Προς Αυτά Υποχρεώσεις Της Πολιτείας* (National Inheritances and State Obligations Toward Them), Athens: Library of Parliament.

14 Hungary

Balázs Wizner and Zoltan Aszalos

Introduction

Following the fall of communism in Hungary, the foundation sector quickly emerged. With relatively significant assets and high numbers of employees, it was seen to have the potential to work with all segments of society and the institutional system. Today, nearly 20,000 foundations are registered in Hungary. This number is surprisingly high given the limited time-span of 14 years during which these foundations have been established. However, in order to present a more accurate perspective of the foundation sector in Hungary, it is necessary to question and analyse the various, sometimes unexpected, motivations behind the establishment and operation of these organisations.

Only a few dozen really large grant-making foundations exist in Hungary and some of these are simply affiliates of large international entities. Only a handful of foundations own sufficient capital to operate independently and to provide funding to civic purposes, directly or through other nonprofit organisations. Whilst noting the presence of such foundations in the Hungarian case, this research focused on examining those organisations that are officially registered as foundations. The selection of foundations and experts interviewed during this research served the purpose of providing a broad picture of the foundation sector, a group defined in terms of legal and not functional terms. It reflected the fact that support from foreign foundation and state sources has had a crucial role in the shaping of the current structure of the foundation sector in Hungary.

A profile of foundations in Hungary

Historical development

The development of Hungarian civil society in the nineteenth and the early twentieth centuries appears to have always tried to follow patterns in western European countries as much as possible. Hungarian civil society was not strong enough to confront central power during the Austro-Hungarian Monarchy and between the World Wars but it was strong enough to resist it. Foundations did not aspire towards political influence. Rather, they specialised in the field of social services mainly as supporters of public service providers or as direct social service providers. Following the First World War in independent Hungary, under a strengthening state-controlled political system, the development slowed down, but the positive trends in growth were in fact ongoing until 1945.

The communist period did not simply destroy the nonprofit sector as an institutional system; it almost liquidated the sector's basic social and cultural components. The foundation sector suffered the most during this period, since the communist regime completely erased the foundation as a legal form and nationalised foundations' material assets.

Following the collapse of the communist regime, the combination of a desire for success and the resolve of individuals led to broad interest and involvement in the nonprofit sector. In particular, many of those who lacked faith in the state's ability to manage social problems and social services decided to take matters into their own hands to ensure positive changes. However, the association form was not really suitable for these ambitions since what people frequently had in mind was a kind of enterprise or small not-for-profit 'firm' and not a means of civil co-operation as such.

The unregulated legal environment, combined with favourable tax conditions, also contributed to the creation of thousands of foundations in the early 1990s. However, heavy media coverage on the misdeeds of fake foundations, i.e. the misuses of foundations' privileges on the one hand, and the critical economic situation of the country, on the other hand, quickly led to changes in the government's policies. Since the mid-1990s, governments have been engaged in the struggle to purge the foundation sector of fake foundations mainly through legal and fiscal measures.

Legal issues

It is possible to identify three major milestone dates in the most recent development of the legal system responsible for regulating the foundation sector. The first is 1987 when the foundation form was re-introduced.[1] Reacting to the abuse of the very liberal regulations governing the nonprofit sector, a new law in 1993 introduced the concept of public foundations. This provided a legal category for foundations that are established for the purposes of carrying out state or local government functions, and which are controlled, partly through representation in the board, by a state institution or local government.[2] These public foundations enjoy more preferable taxation conditions than private foundations.

Finally, in 1997, legal and economic experts decided to develop a comprehensive reform with a special emphasis on applying a differentiated nonprofit taxation policy for organisations engaged in genuine public benefit activities. The subsequent Act CLVI of 1997 on Public Benefit Organizations (PBO Act) distinguished three kinds of organisations: *organisations with no public benefit, public benefit organisations* and *organisations of outstanding public benefit.* The law lists the activities that entail public benefit status. However, the process of registration is bureaucratic and does not involve the substantial examination of the real activities of organisations. The law included the new regulations, which adjusted taxation to the degree of public benefit. Accordingly, in comparison with the former situation, outstanding public benefit foundations enjoy slightly better conditions in relation to taxation. The situation of public benefit organisations remained the same, while organisations of no public benefit lost all their privileges. At the same time, even a public foundation of outstanding public benefit did not have advantages in 1998 similar to those of a simple foundation during the extremely liberal period that ended in 1992.[3]

An empirical profile

In 2000, 47,144 nonprofit organisations were registered in Hungary, including 19,700 foundations. Despite the quantitative expansion of the foundation sector, only a small segment is financially stable. Less than 10 per cent of private and public foundations have full-time employees, while part-time employees are not that much more frequent either. At the same time, some statistics reveal an increasing ratio of more wealthy foundations, with a threshold of five million HUF annual incomes. Fourteen per cent of private foundations and 18 per cent of public foundations exceeded this threshold in 2000, while in 1996 these figures were 10.3 and 16.7 respectively.

In 2000, the sector's revenue was about €785.4 million, while in 1996 it was €520.8 million Euro. However, this improvement was the result of the strengthening of state supported public foundations – where revenue increased by almost 30 per cent. In addition, considering the increasing number of foundations, the average revenue of private foundations changed from about €24,400 to about €30,030. As outlined in Table 14.1, private foundations' revenue is derived primarily from private donors rather than from governmental sources, while in the case of public foundations governmental support was overwhelmingly dominant and their income from basic activities (e.g. ticket sales in case of a theatre) was also significant (as many of them were cultural institutions).

Grant-making foundations with significant capital are very rare and they are connected either to foreign donors or to the state. This situation will certainly not change in the future since the Hungarian business sector is still not explicitly committed to the development of civil society, and tends to prefer spectacular and popular events or issues as part of their public relations activity.

Table 14.1 Hungarian foundations' revenue according to different sources in 2000 (%)

| | Support | | Revenue from activities | | | Sum 100% |
	Government support	Private support	Basic activities income*	Earnings from business**	Other	
Private foundation	28.4	39.3	16.5	15	0.8	100
Public foundation	54.9	10.4	28.3	6.3	0.1	100

Source: KSH (Central Statistical Office) 2000.

Notes
*Includes income from activities meeting the foundation's purposes declared in its statute.
**Includes income from bank interest, financial transactions and other businesses which do not directly concern the foundations' purposes and from which profits are incorporated back into the foundation.

Since 2000, when they contributed about 16 per cent of the revenue of all foundations, many foreign private donors have been leaving the country, including the Hungarian Soros Foundation and other large American foundations. On the other hand, it is important not to exaggerate the effects of the withdrawal of this foreign foundation support. It is not going to influence the situation of many foundations as they are not dependent on the support of foreign donors.

As demonstrated in Table 14.2, most of the foundations are engaged in activities in the areas of culture, education and social services. In the case of public foundations, community development is a typical activity that provides an indication of the great number of local government foundations. The high number of education-oriented foundations reveals a great number of school-based foundations which support extra-services, programmes and investments in schools and more advantageous salaries for teachers.

The Hungarian nonprofit sector is also characterised by uneven regional distribution. In the central region, the ratio of organisations is about 50 per cent higher than the average. Most large, national or international organisations have their headquarters in Budapest. In sum, the enormous number of organisations does not necessarily mean that the 'civil culture' of the Hungarian society is well developed. Instead, it

Table 14.2 Distribution of foundations in Hungary according to their activities in 2000 (%)

Activity	Foundations	Public foundations
Culture	13.6	12.2
Religion	6.0	0.9
Sport	5.5	4.8
Recreation	2.6	2.0
Education	32.8	19.2
Research	3.1	0.8
Health	9.0	3.5
Social services	15.3	8.7
Emergency and relief	0.5	1.3
Environment	2.1	3.3
Community development	3.7	32.2
Economic development	1.5	2.6
Advocacy	0.5	0.7
Public safety	1.5	6.8
Multipurpose donations, umbrella groups	0.2	0.1
International activities	1.5	0.7
Business and professional associations, unions (including lobbying activity)	0.2	–
Politics	0.4	0.2
Total	100	100

Source: KSH (Central Statistical Office) 2002.

suggests that there is a search for new directions after the collapse of the old political system, and that the articulation of special interests and roles has been, and remains a difficult task. The changing legal framework was partly the cause and consequence of this situation. Therefore, it is not surprising that according to the interviewees of the current research *the Hungarian foundation sector as such does not exist.*

Foundation roles

For obvious reasons, following the collapse of communism, most of those who initiated the establishment of nonprofit organisations had neither indispensable experience nor management skills. In addition, many did not have an overall understanding of how the sector operates, since it was just in the phase of emergence. Thus it is not surprising that new, frequently self-appointed managers had no broad ideas about the role of the foundation sector and about the role of their own organisation within it.

The notion of individual foundations existing as part of a sector is very weak in Hungary, especially because foundations differ greatly from each other. Some are genuine grant-making foundations, or specific units of public institutions, whilst others are simple instruments of tax avoidance or a kind of nonprofit enterprise. A significant number of foundations are the brainchild of the ideas of Western founders or have followed the expectations of foreign supporters. They sometimes lack the ability to match their purposes to the needs of local contexts, and also lack the connections to local foundations.

However, the prevalence of an 'identity crisis' among Hungary's foundations is a general problem. In searching for financial support, many foundations had to undertake various tasks simultaneously in order to ensure the survival of their organisation. Many foundations are becoming more business-like and professional. They move toward service provision in order to supplement the foundation's budget. The identity crisis problem is particularly evident in the lack of strong umbrella organisations. Consequently, the sector's potential for promoting its interests is limited.

Foundations tend to associate themselves with the role of complementarity. During the research, foundations argued that the nonprofit organisations are usually limited to small and local issues. They do not have enough capacity to challenge the state but they do have sufficient capacity to find and address the gaps in government services.

The role of foundations in the substitution of state functions was significantly less acceptable for the foundation representatives. They emphasised that many gaps remained or appeared after the state withdrew from various spheres of services during the political transition in 1989–1990. The government was happy to transfer the responsibility of certain 'uncomfortable' tasks, such as the education of socially disadvantaged children to foundations. At the same time, the nonprofit sector was not developed enough to take over these tasks, not to speak of 'competing' with state institutions in the accomplishment of these responsibilities.

The perceived lack of capacity and resources of Hungarian foundations also explains why the foundations' role in redistribution was not rated highly. The interviewees emphasised that the already limited donor culture ceased to exist during the communist period. Very few foundations take part in the redistribution of wealth, as very few have large assets.

Foundations are also ambiguous about their ability to influence social and policy change. On the one hand, several foundation initiatives were adapted by state institutions such as in the areas of environmental protection, human rights and ethnic issues. Yet, on the other hand, one foundation leader indicated:

> Foundations made great efforts in the past 10 years to achieve social and policy change. However, their overall impact has not been significant.

Innovation is not a role that tends to be associated with Hungarian foundations. Some interviewees, in particular, the interviewed experts, argued that real innovations are very rare and mostly connected to large organisations, especially to Western grant-making foundations. By contrast others emphasised that even the adaptation of foreign patterns required innovative skills, moreover the lack of money often forced foundations to think creatively. It was added that it is not the lack of genuine ideas that is the key problem, but the lack of conditions for realising them. Accordingly, local people with excellent answers to local questions usually have had difficulties in finding opportunities to turn these ideas into practice.

In discussing the role of the preservation of traditions and cultures interviewees tended to reject rather than to accept this role. Whilst some foundations emphasised strongly the values of tradition, most organisations underlined the importance of supporting change. Environmental foundations offered a new interpretation of the term 'tradition': in their opinion, the protection of the environment cannot be separated from the preservation of local traditions and cultures. Thus, from this perspective insisting on traditions does not prevent the enhancement of pluralism; rather, it is an integral part of it. It is a widely accepted opinion that the nonprofit sector by its nature is promoting pluralism, and this shows that an idealistic image of the sector is still prevalent. However, organisations are becoming more and more aware of the problems that accompany this view. As one foundation leader stated:

> Many Hungarian foundations are dependent on the state budget, since they receive very limited private money. This questions independence and pluralism to a certain extent.

Visions and policies

The word 'vision' in the Hungarian language does not imply a social philosophy but rather an abstract and unrealistic demand of the people. The translation of the English word 'vision' as a 'realistic dream for the future' is the closest equivalent in Hungarian. However, it is not simply a linguistic peculiarity, but it also says something about the way that people think. The lack of expressed visions cannot simply be traced back to a lack of an inner drive in organisations that follow certain values. Rather, it is in part a reflection of a resistance to hollow visions imposed on society during the communist regime. As one foundation expert suggested: foundations in Hungary may have fast practical solutions to problems but they do not concentrate on constructing overarching visions. It is typical that while organisations declare the importance of independence, in practice, they are gradually getting more involved with the state sector. Certainly this explains why the relevance of the liberal model was not rated very highly in the Hungarian context. This indicates that independence is not a predominant need of Hungarian foundations. Many of them see close connections to the state as inevitable. This link is facilitated by governments that usually do not exert direct political influence, but consider the political affiliations of organisations. As such, debates about parliamentary decisions in relation to the support of nonprofit organisations can be particularly heated. Interviewees agreed that the state has to maintain a strong redistributive system, and that it has to play a key role in the distribution of public money even for nonprofit organisations. This inevitably means that the state plays a co-ordinating role. By contrast the idea of strong state control was rejected, as was the corporatist vision:

> The corporatist model would have a negative effect on the sector since, after a while, foundations would operate as business entities, following lobby interests. There is obviously a need for state presence, but the state should be a partner to the operation of foundations.

One typical statement indicated that if individual or local needs arise, foundations are more likely to furnish a prompt and adequate answer, but the state may take over in the long run. The state definitely has an important role to play in financing, controlling and providing services.

As mentioned above, foundations do not think of themselves as effective in promoting their programmes and interests on a national level, especially because of the lack of umbrella organisations and the unstable financial basis of their operations. However, they did not wish to be associated with the peripheral model, particularly as the nonprofit sector was instrumental in the creation of the new, democratic system.

Foundations are more hesitant about entering into partnerships with business than they are with the government. They were sceptical about the willingness of enterprises to become serious supporters of foundations and their ability to truly associate themselves with social issues. The most critical arguments were put forth by the foundations working in the area of the environment. In their view, corporate support can only be the path to corruption in the sense that it leads to the betrayal of the mission of the organisation. The other side of the coin is that enterprises are also suspicious of the nonprofit sector. As one expert indicated, the business sector is looking for credible, smoothly operating foundations, but there are very few of them. Nevertheless, the mutual distrust does not prevent foundation leaders from trying to learn from the business sector in their operations, particularly in the running of businesses, which serve as a financial source of funds for the foundation.

In sum, there is a trend towards the tightening of the relationship between the state and foundations. Both foundations and politicians welcome this transformation, claiming that building a partnership is indispensable. However, foundations are grappling with the need to find a balance between meeting their funding needs and clarifying the nature of their relationship with the government, whilst ensuring that their autonomy and purpose is not compromised.

Current developments and emerging issues

The development of the Hungarian nonprofit sector has arrived at a turning point today. The building of a democratic society in Hungary, the implementation of international models, and the fight against the remnants of the former regime were enough to provide a mission until now. With the fulfilment of the missions of the political transition, new goals are being formulated in which the accession to the EU and the growing competition between civil society organisations will exert a significant impact. As stated above, in this context the most pressing, and inter-linked issues facing foundations concern sources of funding and their relationship with the government.

Currently there is a temporary gap in funding for foundations, as American foundations are leaving the country and EU resources are only partly available. The involvement of the state in their financial stabilisation is definitely required, especially with respect to better tax rules. Local-based foundations would have a better chance to survive by participating in national and international umbrella organisations that would effectively represent their interests and would contribute to the formation of a more transparent sector.

One of the most pressing issues for foundations is the operation of the recent government supporting policy. A central fund, the National Civil Fund, was established in 2002 by the (socialist-liberal) government, which is at the moment the biggest supporting resource for the nonprofit sector in a wide range of areas. It addresses the representation and control of the sector, since the majority of the board members of the fund are selected through an election process conducted among nonprofit organisations. As a centralised and partly state-controlled system, the National Civil Fund is not likely to contribute to the autonomous development of nonprofit organisations as it reinforces the dependency of nonprofit organisations, including foundations on the government. Yet, ultimately, as experts on foundations argue, only a very diverse development strategy grounded in the search for various donors can produce the financial resources necessary to sustain and develop the foundation sector in Hungary.

In relation to European issues, the majority of Hungarian nonprofit organisations, with the exception of highly professional and externally funded NGOs, have not established widespread and stable relationships with European organisations. For example, only a few interviewees and politicians out of more than 30 knew about the European Foundation Centre. Most of the interviewees had a rather Euro-sceptic standpoint. The EU is seen to be too bureaucratic, concentrated and business-like and Hungarian foundations are neither strong nor well-prepared enough to represent their interests. The involvement of national ministries in the allocation of EU support evoked particularly negative sentiments in the sector since, as many argued, political relations often influence decisions on grants, and this divides the sector.

Conclusion

When faced with the phenomenon of the rapid extension of the nonprofit sector after the political transition, many intellectuals believed that liberalism achieved a victory in Hungary. However, they misunderstood the situation. Thirteen years after the transition, the following two basic lessons must be understood:

1 The emergence of the nonprofit sector or the emergence of thousands of nonprofit organisations does not mean that Hungary has a strong civil society, just as the lack of the nonprofit sector during the communist period did not mean that Hungary did not have a civil society at all.
2 Some elements of liberalism can be discovered in Hungarian society but, in general, the society is predominantly state-oriented.

As civil organisations realise that they cannot expect big endowments or donations from the private sector, they tend to undertake governmental tasks and they become service providers. Foundations tend to become predominantly service providers, since this organisational form is more suitable for such activities than an association. Complementarity, social policy change and innovation are the roles that foundations particularly associate with. The complementarity role is especially at the centre of foundations' roles, which is rather the result of a rational calculation of what foundations can do and the needs they can meet, than the result of social demand as such. Social-policy change or innovation are roles that are highly demanded of foundations but they do not believe that they are capable of having serious influence on society or on decision-makers.

Current government plans – based on the idea of subsidiarity and widely accepted by both policy makers and civil activists – offer foundations a role that is in theory accepted by these organisations. Foundations have to be aware that the Hungarian state will not develop into a highly developed welfare state in the near future. It is likely that some elements of a corporatist relationship with foundations will be realised. However, it remains an open question as to what extent the sector will incorporate into the state system, and how that will lead to additional controls. Therefore, the overall vision for foundations in Hungary is for a quasi-social democratic state where they will have a complementary role as service providers.

Notes

1 Since 1987, the Civil Code has been amended twice in 1990 and in 1993. Currently, Section 74/A to Section 74/F of the Civil Code provide the legal basis for the operation of foundations.
2 Kuti, 1998, pp. 66, 72
3 Kuti, 1998, p. 82. This research sample included five foundations with the status of outstanding public benefit, three with the status of public benefit and two without the status of public benefit.

References

KSH (Central Statistical Office of Hungary) (2002) *Nonprofit Szervezetek Magyarországon* (Nonprofit Organisations in Hungary) 2000, Budapest: KSH.
Kuti, E. (1996) *The Nonprofit Sector in Hungary*, Manchester and New York: Manchester University Press.
Kuti, E. (1998) *Hívjuk talán nonprofitnak (The Nonprofit Sector in Hungary)*, 66–72. Budapest: Nonprofit Kutatócsoport.

15 Ireland

Freda Donoghue

Introduction

Previous work on foundations in Ireland has indicated that there are more operating than grant-making foundations and that the overall foundation field is small (Donoghue 2001). Indeed, foundations are not very visible entities when we look at the Irish nonprofit sector and this lack of visibility is evident in legislation and in history. There has been some recent policy interest, namely in community foundations, which merited a mention in the Government's White Paper as a support to voluntary and community organizations (Department of Social, Community and Family Affairs 2000).

What is of most interest, however, when we examine foundations in Ireland, is to explore what foundations are, or what perceptions of them are, for, as we shall see in this chapter, the concept of foundation in Ireland is somewhat different from practice and theory in other countries. The research conducted for this chapter highlighted the definitional issues surrounding the name 'foundation'. First of all, operating foundations in Ireland do not appear to be any different from other service-providing voluntary organizations. There is no distinction to be found in law and these organizations do not, themselves, view their name as a 'foundation' to denote that they are particular kinds of voluntary organizations (Anheier 2001).

Second, however, the name 'foundation' has its own meaning in Ireland, which is an interpretation that has not appeared in the literature. Organizations in Ireland adopting the name 'foundation' do so for fundraising purposes; the term foundation conveys a sense that this is an organization which will engage in fundraising. The organization may then engage in service delivery or in grant-making, but fundraising will be the main way in which resource streams are generated into the organization. A typology of foundations in Ireland might look like that presented in Table 15.1 (adapted from the text of Anheier and Toepler 1999: 12–13).

It could be argued, therefore, that there are two main kinds of foundations in Ireland, grant-making and operating. Both of these types are

Table 15.1 Foundation types: an Irish adaptation

Types	Sources of funding	Irish Adaptation
Grant-making	Individual donors/founders	Fundraising
	Corporate	Endowment-based
	Multiple	
	Community	
Operating	Individual	Fundraising
	Multiple	Endowment-based

resourced by individual, corporate and community finance, and raised principally through fundraising and possibly in some cases also through endowment. We can, therefore, speak about fundraising or endowed grant-making and operating foundations as the main kinds of foundation to be found in Ireland, with several others such as community and corporate foundations to be found as well, although these are very limited in numbers.

This chapter will now present a short profile of foundations in Ireland, before going on to examine, in some depth, roles and visions. The chapter will then conclude with a brief look at the current situation and issues arising from that context. As will be seen, fundraising is an important defining characteristic of Irish foundations. Playing a complementary role to the state was regarded as important, although if foundations were greater in number they might have more opportunities to adopt a social change role, which was seen as a vision for the future. What is most apparent about Irish foundations, however, is their relative lack of visibility and awareness of their potential as vehicles of philanthropy.

A profile of foundations in Ireland

Historical development

Notwithstanding the relative invisibility of foundations in Ireland, it would appear that foundations are a fairly recent phenomenon. A few examples of families having endowed their wealth and setting up foundations can be found, but it appears that Irish foundations, both operating and grant-making, are not generally endowed. One early example of an endowed foundation would be the Iveagh Trust, established by the Guinness family, to provide housing in Dublin. More recent family foundations, such as the Bewley Foundation and the O'Reilly Foundation, were established in the 1960s and 1970s but these organizations tend to be associated with the families or the individuals who established them rather than with a foundation field *per se*.

During the 1990s Ireland experienced huge socio-economic changes and went from being known as the 'basket case' of Europe to become a very successful economy. At the time of writing, there is a far greater number of millionaires than in the late 1980s,[1] but there has not been any significant increase in the number of philanthropic grant-giving endowment-based foundations. Large individual donors are not very apparent (Donoghue 2002) although recent tax reforms have been enacted to encourage a philanthropic impetus (Finance Bill 2001). Be that as it may, historically the trend to establish foundations, noted elsewhere, cannot be found to the same extent in Ireland.

Legal issues

Ireland is a common law country, like the USA and the UK, having inherited its legal systems and traditions from Britain. Foundations as a separate legal entity do not exist in Irish law, however, unlike in Britain where grant-making trusts have some legal basis (Leat 2001). O'Halloran (2000) notes that there are two kinds of trusts, grant-making and operating, but trusts in Irish law do not have a separate legal personality and they can be undemocratic and cumbersome to administer over time (Law Society of Ireland 2002). Many foundations take the form 'company limited by guarantee with no shareholders' (Schlüter *et al.* 2001) and also have charity (CHY) numbers. Having a CHY number does not convey charitable status as this does not yet exist in Ireland, although that situation is currently under review (Department of Community, Rural and Gaeltacht Affairs, 2003, Charities Regulation Study Group 2004).

Attempts at reviewing charitable status, or regulating charities, have focused on fundraising organizations, which will affect foundations in the future should such legislation be passed. Nevertheless, at the time of writing, a legal distinction between foundations and associations, which exists in many European civil law countries (Van der Ploeg 1999), is not currently proposed under the legal review.

Furthermore, recent legislative changes, such as the Finance Bill 2001, were aimed at facilitating giving by both corporate bodies and individuals through tax exemptions. Coupled with the fact, as noted above, that trust laws can be quite restrictive in Ireland, some respondents in this research pointed out that foundations may be an unwieldy vehicle for facilitating giving in Ireland and may not be chosen for that purpose.

Empirical profile

The lack of knowledge about, combined with an aura of mystique surrounding, foundations are aided by a general lack of data in the public arena which, in turn, makes the size of the Irish foundation 'field', the amount of support it gives and the assets it holds difficult to gauge. Cross referencing both the list of registered companies limited by guarantee and organizations with CHY numbers, and using a list

Table 15.2 Foundations in Ireland

Type of foundation	Total	Type	
Operating	39	58	Operating
Fundraising operating	19		
Fundraising (arm of NPO)	15	15	Fundraising
Grant-making	20	24	Grant-making
Fundraising grant-making	4		
Community (fundraising and grant-making)	2	2	Community
State	1	1	State
Corporate	1	1	Corporate
Mixed	2	2	Mixed
Memorial	3	3	Memorial
Unknown	9	9	Unknown
Total	115	115	

Table 15.3 Foundations in Ireland that are also companies limited by guarantee by date of establishment

1950s	1960s	1970s	1980s	1990s	2000s
1	–	6	12	28	10

supplied by the Irish Funders' Forum (now Philanthropy Ireland), it was possible to identify 107 foundations in Ireland. To these were added a further eight foundations because they were also active in Ireland, although they were not based in the country. Table 15.2 gives a breakdown of all of these foundations by type. The three basic types of foundation, grant-making, operating and mixed, have already been outlined in this book. The following table, however, makes some modifications, most notably the introduction of the term 'fundraising' because this is an important characteristic of Irish foundations; so both grant-making and operating foundations can be subdivided into fundraising grant-making and fundraising operating.

To augment the very bare profile presented, a further exercise was conducted on foundations identified from the register of companies. Of these, 38 had been established since 1990 and 10 had been set up since 2000 (see Table 15.3).

The context of Ireland's socio-economic development during the 1990s may be one explanation for the growth in the number of foundations since 1990. Another important factor, of course, may be the currency that the term 'foundation' holds as a vehicle for seeking funds. The activity of some foundations in Ireland has also contributed to the perceived legitimacy of the term and a sense of the trustworthiness of such organizations.

To give some idea of the areas in which foundations in Ireland are active, some analysis was conducted on organizations that could be identified from the Revenue Commissioners' list of organizations with CHY numbers and these were placed in categories corresponding to the International Classification of NonProfit Organizations (ICNPO, Salamon and Anheier 1996). The largest group (29) came under health, followed by education and research (17), social services (9) and environment (6).

Foundation roles

This section will examine the roles that Irish grant-making foundations play. Limiting the discussion to grant-making foundations only must be understood in the context of organizations using the term 'foundation' to engage in fundraising to attract financial resources for service provision. There is little difference between service-providing nonprofit organizations and fundraising operating foundations. The focus of this chapter, therefore, now turns to grant-making foundations, both fundraising and endowed; the interest in this section is in exploring grant-making foundations as vehicles of philanthropy or support to nonprofit organizations.

The small field of grant-making foundations in Ireland means that a discussion of the roles which foundations have the potential to perform (Prewitt 1999; Anheier and Toepler 1999; Anheier 2001; Anheier and Leat 2002) oscillates between the roles they currently play and what role they might play if the field were bigger. As will be seen, there is some difference between the current roles played and visions of a potential role, but that difference is not based on a lack of willingness to achieve, or a lack of aspiration, and can be attributed to constraints arising from the small number of foundations in Ireland.

Table 15.4 presents the main roles that were identified by respondents to the research. Overall, research respondents thought that the importance of grant-making foundations lay in their being able to '*support* the voluntary and community sector' (emphasis added) to perform roles such as complementing state provision, being innovative and achieving social and policy change (in order of importance).

Examining the complementary role first, respondents thought that foundations in Ireland complemented the role of the state in statutory service provision but felt that this occurred in the meeting of immediate needs and not as a substitute for state services. One respondent, for example, stated that foundations played a complementary role 'up to the point of not being used by the state for functions or services that are manifestly the responsibility of the state'. Two other respondents said that foundations were involved in providing project costs whereas they argued that the state's responsibility was to provide core costs.

We might ask at this juncture what complementarity means in practice for foundations in Ireland? Many grant-making foundations provide

Table 15.4 Roles of foundations in Ireland

Roles	Awareness	Practice	Feasibility	Overall assessment
Complementarity	Some importance	Most important	Most important	Most important
Substitution	Some importance	Not important	Not important	Not important
Redistribution	Some importance	Not important	Not important	Not important
Innovation	Most important	Important	Important	Important
Social change	Most important	Some importance	Some importance	Some importance
Preservation	Not important	Not important	Not important	Not important
Pluralism	Some importance	Some importance	Not important	Not important

grants for social services and community development. Statutory funding of social service voluntary provision occurs under a grant head termed Section 65 (after s. 65 of the 1953 Health Act, which states that the state may provide funds to voluntary organizations engaged in delivering services that are 'similar or ancillary' to those provided by the state). While in practice, Section 65 grants are provided to voluntary organizations delivering services that can be innovative and new and not necessarily either 'similar or ancillary' to those delivered by statutory bodies (Donoghue 2002), the interesting thing about Section 65 is that this enshrines the complementary role in legislation. Furthermore, as voluntary activity in Ireland is assumed to be dominated by the social services or service provision (Jaffro 1996) it is not surprising, therefore, if expectations of foundations and the role they should play adopt this mantle.

Innovation was regarded by respondents as the second most important role either performed, or which had the potential to be performed, by Irish grant-making foundations although respondents held varying opinions on the strength of this role. Some respondents mentioned specific innovations, or said that being innovative was the way that foundations were viewed, but there were some interesting caveats to note arising from the interviews and the seminar. First, the full potential of innovation was seen as being constrained by the size of the foundation field. Second, the example of recent legislation (the Electoral Amendment Act 1997, which was implemented from late 2002) was seen as curtailing innovation and the role that foundations also could play in social and policy change. According to a trustee of one grant-making foundation in Ireland:

> While designed to keep an eye on political parties, some of its provisions mean that NGOs are restricted in their funding. It means that

NGOs who engage in lobbying cannot receive funds from outside of Ireland, and that donations from within Ireland are limited. Declaration of sources is a great idea, but ... [t]he Act defines 'political activity' in a way which covers most advocacy work carried out by development and human rights organizations.

Third, one respondent from a fundraising grant-making foundation thought that a recently established state foundation, the Science Foundation of Ireland (SFI), would have a large impact on the capacity to innovate because it would fund (and during the course of this research on foundations announced major grants for) scientific projects in areas that had not been adequately financed by the state previously. This respondent thought that, by comparison, private independent foundations were not, in and of themselves, necessarily innovative. In noting this, however, the respondent implicitly acknowledged that, in establishing the SFI, the state was thereby recognizing the innovative power of foundations and the need to harness some of this innovatory potential for Ireland's future in scientific research.

The role of social and policy change elicited possibly the most comment from respondents in the individual interviews. Many thought that social and policy change had not been achieved to any great extent by grant-making foundations in Ireland but there was explicit acknowledgement of those few foundations that were very important in performing this role. As one respondent aptly put it: 'Foundations are more supportive rather than out there but I would hope that a certain amount is happening that's not so publicly known.' As noted in an earlier piece on foundations (Donoghue 2001), an air of secrecy has tended in the past to surround the foundation field in Ireland. While awareness may be growing, the mystique clothing foundations has meant that little is known or understood about them. Together with the small field of grant-making foundations in Ireland, the confusion with regard to definitions, and the lack of distinction in law, an assessment of some of the roles played by foundations is harder to achieve. Some respondents to the research thought, therefore, that there had been attempts made at recognizing new needs, giving voice to and empowering the social excluded, but that these activities were attributable to only a few noteworthy foundations.

The roles that emerged as least or not important were redistribution, the preservation of traditions and cultures and the promotion of pluralism. The small size of the grant-making foundation field in Ireland was regarded as a constraint on the performance of the redistribution role. While all respondents revealed an awareness of the potential for this role, most acknowledged that this did not happen to the extent that it happened in the USA. As one respondent said:

I'm not entirely convinced ... [about the redistributive role] ... because in Ireland major funding is from outside Ireland, from the

USA, and there has been little increase in philanthropy over the last three years. Foundations could act in this manner but they don't because foundations are miniscule here.

With regard to the preservation of traditions and cultures, only one respondent (from a fundraising grant-making foundation) agreed that this role applied to Irish foundations because he stated that his organization had supported Irish language groups. Most other respondents did not agree that this role applied to Irish foundations and one respondent, from another fundraising grant-making foundation, dismissed this as a role that foundations should perform: 'It's absolute rubbish and completely wrong because to do some good foundations have to move away from this'.

Finally, with regard to the role of promoting pluralism, the general consensus among respondents was that this role might be worth aspiring to but had not been achieved by most foundations in Ireland. Again the lack of effective role performance in this area is most likely attributable to the small foundation field in Ireland and to apply this role to Irish foundations would be to overstate the efficacy of these organizations.

When respondents were asked about ideal rather than actual roles, two roles emerged as ideal for foundations, those of innovation and of social and policy change. Some respondents also expressed support for the complementary role but this was seen as being far less important than either innovation or social and policy change. The discrepancy between stated vision and practice is interesting because it reveals some of the frustration of belonging to a small group that is trying to innovate, or wants to effect social and policy change, but is constrained by its size and its lack of critical mass. It also reveals the responsiveness of these organizations to meeting needs not being met elsewhere. It should be noted that in so doing (and in performing the complementary role) foundations may also be innovative or be supporting innovative ways of meeting need. It may also be the case that the Electoral Amendment Act (1997), already referred to, might be a constraint on foundations' supporting organizations engaged in advocacy. An example was cited by a respondent of one Irish foundation which had funded some research and found its charitable recognition (its CHY number) under threat when it sought to lobby on the basis of the recommendations arising from the research findings. Yet there was also at least one example cited in the interview of foundations established to provide a funding source for advocacy groups which might not be granted CHY numbers of their own because of their lobbying activities. Establishing a foundation as a fundraising arm for their activities may therefore serve a useful purpose. Yet, foundations set up with the aim of fundraising for groups engaged in advocacy may, in the future, find their activities curtailed as a result of the Electoral Amendment Act 1997.

Visions and policies

What emerged in the analysis of the discussions with respondents about visions was the significance of the relationship with the state. This section, therefore, addresses those visions within that context. The relationship with the state and the role expectations of both parties within that relationship was found to be very important. Any vision of role performance is going to be nested in that relationship, for example whether foundations are working with the state to complement its activities, or if they adopt a social and policy change perspective and are advocating for the state to change.

An exploration of the relationship between foundations and the state in Ireland reveals tensions that have been found in examining relationships between other nonprofit organizations and state agencies (Donoghue 2002; Boyle and Butler 2003). Tensions for foundations, however, may be less explicit or certainly less publicly articulated because foundations, *qua* foundations, are not very visible. The community foundation – as a grant-making source to community-based or local organizations – is the only type of foundation to receive explicit mention in the White Paper as a type of foundation that the state is (and has been) willing to support (Department of Social, Community and Family Affairs 2000). Other grant-making foundations occupy a nebulous position and this is related to their private status. If we look at this from the perspective of foundations first this should start to become a littler clearer. While several foundation representatives recognized the role that foundations could play in complementing state activity they did not necessarily agree that this should be the main role of foundations, as has already been suggested. They stated that foundations had some part to play in a larger welfare system and should not be duplicating support or services provided by the state but they also had a strong sense that foundations needed their own autonomy. As one respondent said: 'Where a complementary relationship is possible then that is satisfactory but foundations do need their own space to be critical of the state and to support organizations that are critical of the state.' It was also thought that foundations should operate in an arena broader than that of welfare. One respondent said, 'Foundations should be there if someone creates wealth and wishes to do good. For example, what about dogs and cats? Is that for the good of the state? Who cares?'

Autonomy and independence were seen as important while recognizing that foundations could be complementary to state services. A foundation, one respondent said, 'should be independent so it can do what it thinks is needed. Once it's co-opted ... [by the state] ... it loses its whole reason for being.'

While some said that foundations were minor in numerical terms, all respondents argued that foundations were working to make a difference and pointed to examples of foundations that had made a significant impact in Ireland. Furthermore, all argued that the *status quo* needed to be challenged, or as one respondent said 'They're minor but sure if you don't challenge the *status quo* there's no point.' Another respondent said, 'It's a waste of time if they don't.'

Underpinning the relationship with the state are: (a) the small number of foundations in Ireland, and (b) the lack of clarity about what a 'foundation' is. As a result, grant-making foundations do not, as one foundation representative put it, 'even come on the radar' of the state, which can be seen in the lack of an explicit positioning in legislation or policy. Yet there has been some recognition of the role that foundations play, and it could be argued that the support they receive in that role from the state is tacit. The state appears content, therefore, to let foundations do what they do as long as they do not leave the state in the position of having to fund those activities into the future.

It could be argued that foundations are not the only kind of voluntary nonprofit organization which is overlooked in the policy arena. Despite having a White Paper since 2000, which attempted to set out the principles of the relationship between the state and voluntary and community organizations, the intervening years since its publication have seen the home of that Paper move Government Departments with a lack of policy activity accompanying that development. Furthermore, problems with its implementation have been documented (Harvey 2004), not least of which could be said to be the lack of inter-departmental, or all-departmental state commitment to voluntary activity. It appears, therefore, that although the rhetoric of support for voluntary activity continues, substantive action has not followed. Furthermore, although there is now a Unit dedicated to the White Paper in a Government Department, the relatively low profile of that Department is one sign of the relatively low priority given to this area, as also are the difficulties in the implementation of policy relating to voluntary activity.

Current developments and emerging issues

We now have one final and most important question to be considered: 'What are the conditions for foundation generation?' In other words, is there scope for a greater number of foundations in Ireland and how could this happen? Anheier and Leat (2002) note that two kinds of explanation for foundation formation have been positive, one which looks at the individual founder's motivations and the other which is focused on supply and demand.

Ireland is now a much wealthier society and it is possible that there are individuals who may be asking questions about giving which are related to public benefit, and their own beliefs and values. So, on the supply side there is enough substance to merit some development. On the demand side, it appears that structural and institutional factors such as tax incentives may not be facilitating the situation for foundation formation in Ireland (although they may not be overtly inhibiting this either). Furthermore, there is also the general lack of awareness about and debate on (a) foundations as actors, (b) foundations as vehicles for philanthropy and (c) the notion of using present wealth for sustainable futures. There are, therefore, a number of components in generating a discourse on the conditions for foundation generation, which are the state, individual donors, potential foundations leaders, foundations and business.

It is of interest to note here, in addition, that, apart from respondents from large foundations, there was not much of a European focus or an awareness of European institutions and laws which enhance or support foundation activity. Because the grant-making foundation field is small and within that there are several players which are British in origin or location, not many Irish foundations were found to be actively involved in the European Foundation Centre (EFC). It should be noted, however, that those respondents who stated that their foundations were involved in the EFC were very positive about the learning that could be achieved from peer group interaction. From the EFC's perspective, its adoption of a US-centric approach in its definition of foundations (Anheier and Toepler 1999) means that Ireland's foundation field is never going to be regarded as significant or with much to offer given the preponderance of operating foundations in Ireland. Yet, if a broader interpretation of foundations was taken, which would make sense in the European arena where operating foundations are so important (Toepler 1999), it would allow for some recognition of Ireland's peculiarities in having fundraising operating foundations which have knowingly and intentionally adopted the term foundation because its already-recognized legitimacy elsewhere gives it a credibility and a rationale for use and currency. In so doing, this could contribute towards a re-definition and a re-articulation of what constitutes a 'foundation'.

Conclusion

To summarize the discussion so far, there are a number of pertinent points arising about foundations in Ireland. These are:

- The small number of foundations.
- Little awareness of grant-making foundations as philanthropic vehicles, although 'foundation' has a currency as a fundraising sign (which could be called the semiotics of 'foundation').
- Little awareness at policy-making level about foundations, apart from community foundations (which, it could be argued, was spurred by the focus on 'community' in the White Paper, and also other community programmes and initiatives such as the Community

Development Programme, local development partnerships, and the
increasing importance of the community sector's voice).
• Ireland is now a wealthier country, yet wealth transfer as one resource
flow for the future sustainability of voluntary nonprofit organizations
has yet to happen.

Foundation formation is of particular policy significance because foundations differ from other giving structures in that they have greater permanence and are, typically, legally independent entities. At a time of social and
cultural change, as has been the case in Ireland over the past number of
years, questions could be raised about the role of foundations and why they
may (or may not) be seen as an appealing way to solve social problems.

This chapter has shown that in discussing foundations, the definition of
that organization needs to be clear, as the example of Ireland indicates.
While the foundation field is small in Ireland, and there are more operating than grant-making foundations, fundraising is an important characteristic. Despite the semiotic argument, however, foundations, as endowed
vehicles of philanthropy, whether operating or grant-making, are an
under-developed organizational form in Ireland. Furthermore, the debate
on the significance of foundations as vehicles of philanthropy needs to
happen. At the time of writing, two new grant-making foundations have
been recently established, which indicate that the discussion, although
still occurring in pockets of murmurs, is exhibiting potential to gather
momentum and become a lot louder.

Note

1 According to the *Irish Times*, 18 June 2002, there were 15,000 millionaires in
Ireland, a figure taken from the *2002 World Health Report*.

References

Anheier, H.K. (2001) 'Foundations in Europe: a Comparative Perspective', in: A.
Schluter, V. Then and P. Walkenhorst (eds) *Foundations in Europe: Society, Man-
agement and Law*. London: Directory of Social Change.
Anheier, H.K. and Leat, D. (2002) 'Towards a European Research Agenda on
Foundations: What are the Issues?', paper presented at conference on Research
on Foundations in Europe, Fondation de France, Paris, March.
Anheier, H.K. and Toepler, S. (eds) (1999) *Private Funds, Public Purpose*. New York:
Kluwer Academic/Plenum Press.
Boyle, R. and Butler, M. (2003) *Autonomy vs Accountability*. Dublin: Institute of
Public Administration.
Charities Regulation Study Group (2004) *Modernising the Charity Sector in Ireland:
Submission from the Charities Regulation Study Group to the Department of Community
Rural and Gaeltacht Affairs on 'Establishing a Modern Statutory Framework for Chari-
ties' Consultation Paper*. Dublin: Charities Regulation Study Group.

Department of Community, Rural and Gaeltacht Affairs (2003) *Establishing a Modern Statutory Framework for Charities: Consultation Paper,* December, (PRN. 810). Dublin: Department of Community, Rural and Gaeltacht Affairs.

Department of Social, Community and Family Affairs (2000) *Supporting Voluntary Activity. A White Paper on a Framework for Supporting Voluntary Activity and for Developing the Relationship between the State and the Community and Voluntary Sector.* Dublin: Stationery Office.

Donoghue, F. (2001) 'Ireland', in: A. Schluter, V. Then and P. Walkenhorst (eds) *Foundations in Europe.* London: Directory of Social Change.

Donoghue, F. (2002) *Reflecting the Relationships.* Dublin: Eastern Regional Health Authority.

Harvey, B. (2004) *Implementing the White Paper* Supporting Voluntary Action: *Report for the CV12 Group.*

Jaffro, G. (1996) 'The Changing Nature of Irish Voluntary Social Service Organisations', *International Journal of Public Sector Management,* 9 (7): 45–59.

Law Society of Ireland (2002) *Charity Law: The Case for Reform. A report by the Law Society's Law Reform Committee.* Dublin: Law Society of Ireland.

Leat, D. (2001) 'Great Britain', in: A. Schluter, V. Then and P. Walkenhorst (eds) *Foundations in Europe.* London: Directory of Social Change.

O'Halloran, K.J. (2000) *Charity Law.* Dublin: Round Hall Sweet and Maxwell.

Prewitt, K. (1999) 'The Importance of Foundations in an Open Society', in: Bertelsmann Foundation (ed.) *The Future of Foundations in an Open Society,* Guetersloh: Bertelsmann Foundation Publishers.

Salamon, L.M. and Anheier, H.K. (1996) 'The International Classification of Nonprofit Organizations: ICNPO-Revision 1, 1996', in: L.M. Salamon and H.K. Anheier (eds) *Working Paper of the Johns Hopkins Comparative Nonprofit Sector Project,* No. 19. Baltimore: The Johns Hopkins Institute for Policy Studies.

Schlüter, A., Then, V. and Walkenhorst, P. (eds) (2001) *Foundations in Europe: Society, Management and Law.* London: Directory of Social Change.

Toepler, S. (1999) 'Operating in a Grantmaking World: Reassessing the Role of Operating Foundations', in: H.K. Anheier and S. Toepler (eds) *Private Funds, Public Purpose.* New York: Kluwer Academic/Plenum Press.

Van der Ploeg, T.J. (1999) 'A Comparative Legal Analysis of Foundation: Aspects of Supervision and Transparency', in: H.K. Anheier and S. Toepler (eds) *Private Funds, Public Purpose.* New York: Kluwer Academic/Plenum Press.

16 Italy

Federica Givone, Paolo Canino and Stefano Cima

Introduction

The world of Italian foundations has undergone a phase of rapid change since the beginning of the 1990s. This chapter examines the current situation taking into account the main trends identified by some of the principal observers (Barbetta and Demarie (2001), AA.VV (2002)),[1] which include:

- the spread of a model for foundations that distinguishes the form very little from other non-profit organizations. The form is being adopted more and more by a series of non-profit organizations;
- the formation of a nucleus of grant-making foundations (previously almost non-existent on the Italian scene) based on large sums of capital as a result of the privatization of the public sector banking system;
- the choice of the legal status of foundation as a tool to privatize a number of public sector organizations, principally in the fields of culture and social services.

The Italian system of foundations is struggling to establish the cultural and basic principles of co-operation, transparency and innovation that characterize a mature and reliable foundation sector. The context in Italy is very heterogeneous and constantly changing. Therefore, it is understandable that no unitary vision of roles emerges in the present study, in terms of how they are actually performed, and of those perceived as appropriate and desirable by foundations themselves. A picture does emerge, however, of foundations engaged in providing support, in areas that are not covered by the public sector, with high quality services, characterized by excellence, stimulation and innovation compared to public sector provision.

At present the foundation sector is still too scattered and disorganized. Networks and relationships are needed to create opportunities for the structured exchange of information and to give greater recognition and a more established position to foundations in civil society. The government should ensure that foundations have the independence they need and provide appropriate legislative and fiscal assistance in order to help them to become an effective partner in the development of the new "welfare society".

A profile of foundations

Historical development

According to recent data, Italy has witnessed such a sharp acceleration in the creation of foundations that it is estimated that as many as five new foundations are created each month (Centro di Documentazione sulle Fondazioni (1999)). Despite the fact that Italy is one of the birthplaces of European foundations, the development of foundations has been lacklustre. Complex reasons which are common to many Mediterranean countries are at the root of this lack of development. These include the diffidence in the prevailing political cultures toward intermediate social bodies; centralization and the pervasiveness of the nation state; an economic and industrial structure which was either fragmented or controlled by the state, and the powerful presence of the Catholic church as an important social actor. In many cases this led to the nationalization of the oldest philanthropic institutions (e.g. the *pious works* in the form of IPABs (Public Welfare And Charity Institutions)).

The socialist, liberal and then fascist movements were similarly either not interested in, or explicitly hostile to, foundations. These attitudes prevailed until the end of the Second World War and beyond. Although the Republican Constitution (1948) guaranteed the presence of "social organisms" as a vital component of society, foundations continued to play a marginal role until recent times. Despite broad exposure to American culture after the Second World War, there was little room for modern foundations; only a handful of significant foundations were formed in the 1950s and 1960s.

A big change occurred in the 1980s and 1990s. As in many other countries, civil society became more dynamic for reasons related to economic crisis and, particularly, the emerging difficulties in the sustainability of the welfare state. The rediscovery of the principle of self-organization, combined with the relative flexibility of the regulation of private institutions under the Italian Civil Code (1942) allowed founders a variety of interpretations of the "base" model and led to a progressive broadening and diversification of the sector.

Legal issues

The "rebirth" of foundations today is undoubtedly due to a generally favourable climate towards institutions that originate from initiatives in civil society. Legislative measures were triggered in a political climate that is more encouraging of the adoption of subsidiary, horizontal models, and tax regimes that are more conducive to private philanthropy. Recent legislation has simplified and speeded up the procedures for official recognition of foundations' legal personality (Ruotolo 2001). This has effectively relaunched the use of foundations.

The main result of this new phase was the creation of grant-making foundations that originated from banks. The Carli-Amato reform Law of 1990 sought to rationalize the system by separating banking functions from the charity functions to form two different types of organization: banks (in the form of joint stock companies) and the owners of the stock (in the form of grant-making foundations). This reorganization of the public sector banking system was targeted at public sector banks (Casse di Risparmio, Banche del Monte and Istituti di Credito di Diritto Pubblico). As a result of this law, these bodies allocated their business to joint stock companies, while they themselves maintained their original philanthropic aims (Ranci and Barbetta 1996).

In addition, this new climate has resulted in a move towards the adoption of models that are widespread abroad, such as corporate and community foundations, as well as to the development of new models such as the "participatory foundations". The latter are an example of the use of foundations as an instrument by public authorities. Special legislation is used to implement specific privatization policies or to create new partnerships with the private sector (for profit-oriented, or non-profit) organizations.

The move towards the privatization of public or quasi-public sector bodies and the search for innovative and efficient operational and institutional means of service provision to the public recently gave rise to other important types of institutions in addition to the foundations of banking origin. In the welfare field, hundreds of specific groups of publicly controlled, local level welfare institutions (IPABs), are reacquiring their original status as private foundations. In the cultural fields, examples include the Opera Theatre Foundations (for example *La Scala* opera house of Milan) and other cases such as museums or institutes.

Empirical profile

There are 3,008 foundations operating in Italy, approximately 1.4 per cent of all non-profit organizations surveyed by ISTAT (national statistics office) in 1999. They account, however, for 7.75 per cent of total employment in the sector in terms of standard labour units (61,300 full-time work equivalents) and 9 per cent of paid employment (52,300 full-time work equivalents). Foundations play an even greater role in economic terms, accounting for as much as 13.8 per cent of all non-profit receipts and 13.6 per cent of expenditure (amounting to €5 billion). Finally, they receive 19 per cent of total third sector expenditure that consists of grants and subsidies.

However, if a comparison is made with the Italian economy as a whole, the size of the sector is modest. Employment provided by foundations does not even amount to 0.3 per cent of total employment (agriculture excluded as marginal) and 0.4 per cent of the services sector. The cost of labour (intended as a measure of added value) is less than 0.2 per cent of total value added and is only a little higher compared to the services sector.

Before describing the particularities of the areas in which Italian foundations operate a distinction should be made between operating foundations (which not only make grants to other non-profit organizations but also produce goods and/or services) and purely grant-making foundations.[2] Table 16.1 summarizes the economic and human resources of foundations in Italy and also gives the composition by sector of the different types of foundation.

The analysis of grant-making foundations is particularly interesting (27 per cent of total foundations), especially in economic terms. Whilst they make little impact on employment accounting for around 4 per cent, an examination of receipts and expenditure shows two traits: the greater size (27 per cent of receipts and 23.5 per cent of expenditure) and greater ability that these foundations demonstrate to accumulate funds.

Almost 47 per cent of the Italian foundations surveyed by the ISTAT were formed after 1990. These statistics show simply, but effectively, how Italian foundations have grown constantly in recent decades. With regard to the so-called foundations of banking origin, numerically speaking, not many foundations were formed in this way (a total of 89). Their assets, however, account for a very large part (more than 63 per cent) of the total assets of Italian foundations (Acri 2002). Most of their grants go to the cultural and artistic sector (more than 34 per cent of total grants in 2001). This is followed by education (down from 14.8 per cent in 1999 to 13.4 per cent in 2000 and 12.8 per cent in 2001) and welfare assistance (12 per cent, but fluctuating in recent years). There are also grants to support the voluntary sector (mostly grants to the *Centri di servizio per il volontariato* – voluntary work service centres), which amounted to more than 10 per cent in 2001 (Table 16.2).

Foundation roles

All of the interviewed foundations[3] professed a very high opinion of their usefulness to society, and their contribution to the well-being of the local community in which they operate. They instinctively perceived themselves as organizations located within and as part of a broader non-profit sector and as instruments that can contribute to its professional and financial growth. They see themselves as players that can also identify with the specific sector in which they operate, both in the case of foundations with a mission rooted in a single area of activity and in the case of those that operate in more than one area of activity.

Table 16.1 Percentage distribution of human and economic resources of Italian foundations (1999)

Typology	Sector	Institutions	Receipt	Expenditure	Employed (full-time work equivalents)	Remunerated staff (full-time work equivalents)	Volunteers (full-time work equivalents)
Operating foundations	Culture, sport and recreation	27.8	29.3	30.3	16.6	18.4	5.6
	Education and research	27.3	10.9	11.1	21.4	14.6	83.2
	Health	7.3	44.8	44.4	43.0	48.5	2.0
	Social services	22.5	10.7	10.3	14.8	14.8	6.2
	Environment	0.5	0.0	0.0	0.0	0.0	0.1
	Economic development and social cohesion	3.2	2.4	2.1	2.0	2.3	0.1
	Civil rights defence and political activity	0.7	0.8	0.8	0.1	0.0	0.1
	Philanthropy and voluntary service promotion	4.4	0.3	0.3	0.7	0.6	0.5
	International cooperation	0.6	0.3	0.2	0.2	0.0	1.3
	Religion	4.4	0.3	0.3	1.0	0.5	0.9
	Other	1.3	0.2	0.2	0.2	0.2	0.1
	Total operating foundations	**57.3**	**67.0**	**70.6**	**93.9**	**95.0**	**93.5**
Mixed foundations	Culture, sport and recreation	40.3	4.3	4.6	12.4	11.9	38.2
	Education and research	13.5	12.2	12.2	18.2	22.2	6.3
	Health	2.7	3.9	3.8	12.8	11.2	2.0
	Social services	29.3	13.8	13.1	45.0	50.3	31.0
	Environment	0.5	0.0	0.0	0.0	0.0	0.1
	Economic development and social cohesion	1.8	0.1	0.1	0.2	0.1	1.0
	Civil rights defence and political activity	0.7	0.4	0.4	0.1	0.0	0.7
	Philanthropy and voluntary service promotion	2.3	64.1	64.6	1.7	0.6	2.3
	International cooperation	2.5	1.1	1.1	3.3	3.5	7.8

Religion	6.0	0.1	0.1	6.3	0.1	10.1
Other	0.5	0.0	0.0	0.1	0.0	0.4
Total mixed foundations	**15.7**	**5.6**	**6.0**	**1.9**	**1.3**	**2.1**
Grant-making foundations						
Culture. sport and recreation	24.0	26.9	24.6	11.8	9.8	20.6
Education and research	22.2	3.7	4.3	14.7	15.8	12.6
Health	3.5	2.1	2.4	20.1	26.3	3.1
Social services	30.4	18.2	15.2	36.6	36.6	37.2
Environment	0.5	0.0	0.0	0.1	0.0	0.7
Economic development and social cohesion	2.2	8.6	9.8	1.8	0.7	1.6
Civil rights defence and political activity	0.7	0.1	0.1	0.6	0.8	0.1
Philanthropy and voluntary service promotion	7.4	35.2	37.9	8.3	6.1	6.3
International cooperation	1.8	0.5	0.4	0.7	0.3	3.0
Religion	6.4	2.6	3.1	3.0	1.5	6.0
Other	0.8	2.1	2.2	2.3	1.9	8.7
Total grant-making foundations	**27.0**	**27.4**	**23.5**	**4.3**	**3.7**	**4.3**
Total foundations						
Culture, sport and recreation	28.8	27.2	27.4	16.4	18.0	7.0
Education and research	23.7	9.0	9.6	21.1	14.8	78.5
Health	5.5	30.8	32.1	41.4	47.2	2.1
Social services	25.7	13.0	11.6	16.3	16.1	8.0
Environment	0.5	0.0	0.0	0.0	0.0	0.2
Economic development and social cohesion	2.7	4.0	3.8	1.9	2.2	0.2
Civil rights defence and political activity	0.7	0.6	0.6	0.1	0.1	0.1
Philanthropy and voluntary service promotion	4.9	13.5	12.9	1.0	0.8	0.8
International cooperation	1.2	0.4	0.3	0.3	0.1	1.5
Religion	5.2	0.9	0.9	1.2	0.5	1.3
Other	1.0	0.7	0.6	0.3	0.3	0.4
Total Foundations	**100**	**100**	**100**	**100**	**100**	**100**

Source: data processing IRS based on Istat statistics 2001.

Table 16.2 Percentage distribution of grants for sector in Italy

Sectors	Number		Amount	
	Interventions	%	€ *millions*	%
Cultural activities and arts	7,984	37.3	331.6	34.1
Education	3,576	16.7	124.2	12.8
Social services	4,161	19.4	116.6	12.0
Philanthropy and voluntary service	491	2.2	104.2	10.7
Research	941	4.4	96.7	10.0
Health	1,233	5.8	93.6	9.6
Local community development and promotion	1,152	5.4	71.0	7.3
Sport and recreation	1,462	6.8	13.1	1.3
Environment	151	0.7	12.0	1.2
International activities	139	0.6	6.3	0.6
Religious activities	112	0.5	1.8	0.2
Civil rights defence and promotion	26	0.1	0.1	0.0
Total	**21,428**	**100**	**971**	**100**

Source: data processing Irs based on ACRI data 2002.

To summarize the stakeholders' opinion, foundations today "should act in a context of subsidiarity and complementarity" paying particular attention to "emerging needs in civil society". They should play an "innovative, pioneering role" assisted by their "ability to respond rapidly" and their "agility". It is right therefore for the government to address issues of general social and economic importance. Foundations feel that they share a mission of social utility with the government, but they inevitably channel their resources towards more specific targets. Whilst "government is a place for politics", the "world of foundations is an intermediate ground" where relations are basically operational and reciprocal, an expression of values that are not considered in economics and in politics. If we add to this that foundations are not obliged to be fair, impartial and democratic, this means, on the one hand, that they are independent, to a certain extent, and, on the other hand, that they have great flexibility in their actions. The freedom to autonomously pursue objectives defined in their statutes and contained in their established missions is a very strong feature of the foundation form, another factor that distinguishes them from the public sector and from other types of organizations, such as associations.

One distinguishing feature of foundations is that they possess assets and this gives stability to their organization. Foundations are perceived to "focus on long-term projects and are therefore able to guarantee that the objectives they have in sight are achieved because their action is continuous and they therefore seek to overcome the cyclical nature of their intervention". Another common trait is that they tend to have a "longer-term commitment than other social, political and private sector actors" because of the resources and wealth they possess, which allows them "to achieve higher standards of quality and professionalism" and "to act on a more permanent basis". In reality foundations that possess substantial capital are the exception rather than the rule in Italy.

It is also a commonly held opinion that it is difficult for foundations *a priori* to define a distinct role common to all foundations, because of the great variety and complexity of the cases in Italy. This is not only because, in the interviewees' opinion, the role depends on the field of activity and the specific and autonomously chosen mission of a foundation and must therefore be defined in relation to it. It is also because to label roles in civil society would crystallize the vision of a community, even though it is fundamental for a foundation to be able to listen and to be open towards the community in which it operates.

With regard to specific roles, the interviews revealed the following:

Complementarity

Bearing in mind that foundations in Italy have different aims and are at different stages of development, this is the role that was most commonly agreed upon by almost all stakeholders even if, in many cases, the concept of "subsidiarity" was felt to be more appropriate to describe the role of foundations in complementing the state. It was also underlined that foundations sometimes intervene alongside the state in relation to the same groups in society. However, even when they intervene in similar fields, they can allow themselves to respond to more heterogeneous needs because they are less subject to uniform or democratic constraints than government and public sector organizations. Consequently where there is varied demand, their autonomy and flexibility allows them to specialize and to produce innovative and different responses, with a philosophy of diversity that is free of a uniform approach. They do this, however, without ever allowing the state to unload its responsibilities in certain areas which remain the state's responsibility.

Substitution

Consistent with the findings in relation to the complementarity role, all interviewees agreed that the role of "replacing" the state cannot and must not be taken over by a foundation, above all because of the necessary and irreplaceable role of the public sector particularly in the welfare system.

Redistributive role

As opposed to the previous roles, the redistributive role did not meet with the same consensus of opinion. It may be an aspiration and an important component for some foundations (e.g. community foundations) but not for all. Much depends on the type of foundation and the mission. In fact in some cases a foundation's actions may have the opposite effect. Activity in the cultural field often has non-redistributive effects. Culture consumers typically come from high- to medium-income groups and action and stimulation in this field benefits them most. In any case it cannot be and is not the primary function of a foundation. It is seen more as an economic policy task, which falls more within the sphere of government responsibilities.

Innovation

Innovation is perceived to be a characteristic trait of a foundation that distinguishes the foundation form from public sector activity. From this viewpoint, foundations may be considered as "prophetic" in perceiving social demands, responding rapidly to emerging needs and providing innovative, progressive and high-quality responses. This is one of the greatest ambitions of foundations, although they are aware that they do not always meet these aspirations in practice.

Social and policy change

A role where foundations stimulate social change by addressing social and emerging needs is generally considered desirable, but this does not necessarily imply solely giving voice to the socially excluded. The latter function tends not to be covered so much by foundations. Advocacy is perceived to be a function for associations or for organizations which work within more politically oriented environments, in which the foundations interviewed declared that they do not operate.

Preservation of traditions and culture

This is one of the primary areas of activity for Italian foundations. In the current context of the tendency for the state to retreat from certain responsibilities, culture is one field in which this is particularly evident. It is also reflected in the large proportion of donations and grants destined to art and the conservation of cultural heritage. A foundation's role is to conserve the past as a system of values and to use these values to try and stimulate research and innovation. In this sense foundations are conceived of as centres of cultural initiatives, places for "battles" over ideas and promoting cultural patronage where the goals are to:

- strengthen the role and importance of research and culture in local experiences and international relations;
- develop positive relations between the public and private sectors

particularly in the field of safeguarding and valuing the cultural heritage and values as fully and as broadly as possible.

It is underlined, however, that in reality, Italian foundations do not tend to interpret cultural activity from an innovative point of view. Rather, they show a preference for conservative interpretations aimed at restoration, and protecting and conserving archives, libraries and cultural heritage.

Promotion of pluralism

In relation to this role, interviewees are aware of the importance of their actions along with the other institutions of the third sector and their value in developing social capital (Putnam 2000) (as well as relations, competence, ability to innovate) in the community. The transformation process of Italian society from welfare state to welfare society is rather slow. It has finally been set in motion and its goal should ideally be a pluralist society, where power and responsibility are broadly distributed between state, market and third sector.

The common starting point is that the suitability of a foundation to aspire towards certain roles must be assessed in terms of its original mission. Generally speaking, for all the interviewees, a role may not be appropriate if it is not suited to the purpose of the foundation, nor if the means necessary to fulfil certain roles are not available. Italy has neither a culture nor a tradition of foundations as, for example, the United States has. Foundations are too small in number and above all in terms of capital endowment and overall capacity to be very significant actors. While interviewees recognized that foundations are acquiring increasingly greater awareness and maturity, it was also found that some of them performed activities which are not always recognized as belonging to the non-profit world. For example, interviewees agreed that they found it difficult to view the banking origin foundations as authentically philanthropic foundations. Some of them still feel tied to the banking model and focused on their role as shareholders and investment bankers rather than operating actively in the non-profit sector.

Visions

The interviewees are aware that they are operating in a society which is transforming and in which responsibilities and opportunities are increasing. What today is considered "natural" for the public sector to provide, did not fall within its sphere of tasks in the past. So, many of the stakeholders selected for interview underline that foundations should therefore be very pragmatic in how they react to the apparent changes to the status quo and achieve the goals for which they were formed. A willingness to co-operate and to be more open are never intended by the foundation representatives to be interpreted as a willingness to infiltrate and replace public sector prerogatives. Again, a clear view emerges of foundations working in a (changing) context of subsidiarity and complementarity to the state.

The same approach that was used for roles was employed to explore if the various stakeholders' perception of a desirable society is reconcilable with the models that represent particular visions of state and society. Yet again, no single model emerges in the interviews as more dominant than the others. Rather, there is a mixture of various elements of one or the other, which largely reflects and confirms features of how roles are perceived as discussed in the preceding sections.

In short, the vision that is shared by the interviewees is that in Italy ongoing cultural changes will give more space to the third sector. The challenge for the foundations will be to benefit from new opportunities. Recent findings of research on the non-profit sector (Barbetta *et al.* 2003) place Italy in an intermediate position between a social-democratic welfare model, in which public sector service provision is consistent with a well defined space for other social actors, and a corporatist model where there is convergence between the state and non-profit organizations with high public spending and a substantial presence of third sector organizations.

Social democratic model

The welfare system is strongly based upon the public provision of services. Space for foundations is still rather tight, except for the areas which are not well covered by the state. Interviewees are aware that they are operating in a transforming environment in which the third sector is being called on more and more often to satisfy public needs.

Corporatist model

This vision is regarded as an aspiration among the interviewees. It may happen in the not too distant future in which subsidiarity forms are developed in favour of the third sector at both national and local level. The third sector, especially operating foundations (not only ex-IPABs), may become part of the social welfare or educational system. Grant-making foundations may be asked to support this transition with selective grants for specific projects.

State-controlled model

All actors interviewed agreed that this model was categorically not appropriate to the Italian context. The state must never be invasive and interfering in the management of foundations. They must operate independently and in complete autonomy. This was stated in the light of, and in conflict with, the recent (failed) attempt to draw the banking origin foundations back into the public sector sphere.

However, some respondents specified the need to introduce a system to guarantee transparency and the disclosure of information for the purposes of regulation (e.g. governing bodies, publication of governance rules, and of accounts and fundamental deeds) – more for the sake of the public than for the state. Currently there are no obligations in this respect with the exception of the banking origin foundations and those which have the status of ONLUSs (non-profit social utility organizations) for tax purposes. The introduction of an independent authority like the Charity Commission in Great Britain to act as a watchdog and guarantor appears highly desirable.

Liberal model

This model is perceived to be a long way from reality in the Italian case. Even when underlining their independence and self sufficiency from the public sector, none of the interviewees seems to share this kind of vision.

Peripheral model

It is true that there is still a long way to go in Italy for foundations to achieve a fully significant and visible role, but to describe them as peripheral is not always completely accurate. The size of the financial resources mobilized in some fields such as art and culture and for some welfare policies on a local scale is starting to become relevant compared to total spending in the respective sectors. This model is neither desirable nor descriptive of the current situation.

The business model

Over the last few years, the model of corporate social responsibility is spreading. This model strengthens the ties between the company and the community. In this environment, corporate foundations are taking on an ever more important role and this process will grow in the medium term. It is a new model, and has only recently aroused debate, but it has already started to characterize the visions of the sector.

Current development and emerging issues

The current debate on foundations in Italy is characterized by the following series of issues that also reflect the themes and questions that emerged from our findings.

First, our interviewees underlined the need for foundations to have a more stable legal basis; that replaces the current fragmented situation and gives order to the multitude of special laws and exceptions to these laws. Other legislative action is also desired:

- a reform of the tax regime that introduces tax incentives for dona-tions to encourage the accumulation of altruistic capital;
- legislation to introduce minimum requirements of transparency and information disclosure. The overall system of accountability should guarantee both within and outside foundation management, administrative and institutional transparency. To achieve this the entire system of foundations in Italy needs an independent supervi-sory and regulatory authority to help construct solid reliable organi-zations;
- since capital endowment is one of the distinguishing features of a foundation, it is only right that its capital should be sufficient for it to achieve its goals set out in its statute.

Second, the lack of umbrella associations for foundations in Italy has prevented any effective leadership from emerging. Today, only the banking origin foundations manage to put forward their views in a unified and effective manner with the Associazione fra le Casse di Risparmio Ital-iane (Acri is the association of foundations of banking origin). In the interviewees' opinion, some forms of aggregation (at least for different types of foundations or for areas of activity) which aimed to exchange and share strategies and experiences, would produce advantages in terms of the effectiveness of the activities performed, and of the visibility of founda-tions in society.

The third issue raised is the conflicting interests which can arise when members of administrative boards are connected in some way with those receiving grants. This problem should be solved via the implementation of transparent rules of assessment and selection in relation to projects (e.g. the peer review system of the large British charities). The introduction of some form of monitoring system is desirable for the proper pursuit of a foundation's goals. This could also provide feedback to understand what has really been achieved and what benefits have been produced. Italy is right at the beginning as far as the implementation of monitoring proce-dures is concerned. So far foundations have produced and developed pro-cedures with varying degrees of formality for the selection of applications. Therefore foundation representatives have underlined the need to intro-duce and use analytical and assessment instruments with a dual objective:

- to make their actions more transparent and communicable, so that they can be justified both in the eyes of the stakeholders and the general public;
- to produce useful information on results in order to be able to refine the way foundations work, make their actions more effective and to use resources more efficiently.

It is difficult in the current heterogeneous and changeable context to depict a single future scenario for Italian foundations. One imagines that the proliferation of growth patterns seen in the world of foundations in recent years will continue, leading hopefully to greater legitimization of the phenomenon and gradually to more stable and homogeneous organizations.

Conclusion

The key priority for all of the stakeholders interviewed is to be engaged in their complementarity/subsidiarity roles with respect to the public sector in the provision of services and to give support to the community when the state cannot act or fails to do so. This is regardless of the specific role played in terms of mission and operating area. In the stakeholders' opinion, foundations should pay particular attention to emerging needs in civil society. They should play an innovative, pioneering role assisted by their ability to respond rapidly. Yet, one of the main challenges for foundations concerns the system of accountability and lack of transparency as well as the disclosure of information that is not currently available.

The interviewees know that prevalent transformations in Italian society will bring about a wider role for foundations, both in providing welfare services and in supporting the third sector. This process increases the responsibility of foundations, which up until now has always been up to the standards that they have set for themselves.

Notes

1 See also the material published by the *Centro di documentazione sulle fondazioni* (various years).
2 Foundations were reclassified on the basis of the total spending on grant disbursements and the percentage of financial income designed to bring out the salient traits of the different types of foundation operating in Italy.
   The different combinations of the two variables gave the following classification:

   * operating foundations (both grant disbursement and financial income were less than 25 per cent of the total);
   * mixed foundations (grant disbursement and financial income were both between 25 per cent and 50 per cent of the total);
   * grant-making foundations (grant disbursement and financial income were both greater than 50 per cent of the total).

3 In order to acquire a representative profile of Italian foundations we selected a sample among 13 foundations. The selection criteria were designed to obtain an interesting and useful sample in terms of the research goals which would bring out the emerging trends of a complex sector that is changing rapidly and continuously.

References

AA.VV (2002) *Libro bianco sulle fondazioni in Italia*, Consiglio italiano delle Scienze Sociali, Roma.

Acri. (2002) *Settimo rapporto sulle fondazioni bancarie*, Roma: Acri.

Barbetta, G.P. (1999) "Foundations in Italy", in H.K. Anheier and S. Toepler (eds) (1999) *Private Funds, Public Purpose*, New York: Kluwer.

Barbetta, G.P., Cima, S. and Zamaro, N. (2003) *Le istituzioni nonprofit in Italia. Dimensioni organizzative, economiche e sociali*, Bologna: Il Mulino.

Barbetta, G.P. and Demarie, M. (2001) "Country Report on Italy", in A. Schulter, V. Then and P. Walkenhorst (eds) *Foundations in Europe. Society Management and Law*, London: Directory of Social Change.

Centro di documentazione sulle fondazioni (1999) *Fondazioni: il settore si espande*, "Network", n. 4, Torino: Fondazione Giovanni Agnelli.

Demarie, M. and Cima, S. (2003) "The Italian Third Sector: An Overview at the Beginning of the Century", in M. Di Matteo and P. Piacentini. *The Italian Economy at the Dawn of the 21st Century*, Ashgate, Hampshire, UK.

Istat (2001) *Istituzioni nonprofit in Italia*, Roma.

Putnam, R.D. (2000) *Bowling Alone*. New York: Simon and Schuster.

Ranci, C. and Costa, G. (1999) *Dimensioni e caratteristiche delle Ipab un quadro nazionale*, Roma: Presidenza del Consiglio dei Ministri.

Ranci, P. and Barbetta, G.P. (eds) (1996) *Le fondazioni bancarie italiane verso l'attività grant-making: tendenze, modelli e prospettive*, Torino: Contributi di ricerca della Fondazione Giovanni Agnelli.

Ruotolo, A. (2001) "Il nuovo regime per il riconoscimento delle persone giuridiche private", *Notariato*, n. 4.

17 Netherlands

B.M. Gouwenberg, C.E. Van der Jagt and Th.N.M. Schuyt

Introduction

The Dutch foundations (or *funds*) prefer a society in which they can operate independently from government and the market. Less regulation and autonomy are key issues. Out of the variety of roles foundations can fulfil, the most commonly accepted were those of complementarity, innovation and pluralism. The role of social change is considered for those foundations active in the provision of international aid. Regarding the foundations' visions of society, most foundations saw themselves as fitting under the liberal or social democratic model. Thus, the outcome of the analysis suggests that they favour independence vis-à-vis state and society, allowing for a high level of autonomy for decision-making. Any forced regulation will not be appreciated: the majority of the foundations feel that they are highly capable of making their own decisions in a responsible manner. First, we provide a brief insight into the historical and legal issues underpinning the Dutch foundation sector, followed by the analysis of the roles and visions of foundations in the Netherlands. The chapter concludes by reviewing the pertinent issues and challenges confronting foundations in the Netherlands today.

A profile of the Dutch foundation sector

Defining characteristics

The Netherlands has a large number of foundations. There are some historical and legal reasons for this (Burger *et al.* 2001: 193). For example, the religious fragmentation ('pillar-structure') has stimulated the development of an extended and diverse non-profit sector. In addition, legally, it is very easy to establish a foundation in the Netherlands. Actually a foundation is first and foremost understood as a non-profit organisation rather than primarily as an asset. The majority of the Dutch foundations are operating foundations (schools, hospitals, nursing homes) financed mainly through revenue from taxation and social insurance.

Foundations that are primarily concerned with transferring (private) money for public purposes are called *funds*. Funds are a subset of foundations. The Dutch definition of a fund is actually more in line with the working definition of a foundation outlined at the outset of this book than with the broad interpretation of a foundation outlined above. Therefore we exclude the non-profit organisations, labelled foundations, with close state links. Nevertheless we will still use the word 'foundation' in this chapter, because this term is recognised internationally.

The funds in the Netherlands are generally classified in four groups, according to their source of income:

1 Fundraising foundations (*geldwervende fondsen*)
   Fundraising foundations like 'Greenpeace' seek first and foremost financial support from the general public, government and business for their (own) purposes. They are almost exclusively dependent on annual fundraising to obtain the funds that they will, in turn, distribute each year.
2 Endowed foundations (*vermogensfondsen*)
   Endowed foundations like the 'Van Leer Foundation' do not seek public support, they manage the proceeds from assets that have been given by a donor. The donor tends to be an individual, a group of people or a corporation, who established a foundation and provided it with capital.
3 Foundations with other fixed sources of income
   Foundations such as a lottery-resourced foundation or a governmental foundation are included in this category. The former receives proceeds from a national lottery, provided to the foundation through an agreement with the body that organises the lottery. Regarding governmental foundations, like the 'Prince Claus Foundation', government bodies provide initial capital or make grants to the foundation on a periodic, usually an annual, basis.
4 Hybrid foundations
   These are foundations with a combination of the above sources of income, for example the 'Prins Bernhard Cultuurfonds', one of the major foundations concerned with arts and culture. Sources of income may include endowment revenues, funds raised from the public, corporations or additional sources, such as the proceeds of a national lottery or structural government support.

Historical developments[1]

The position of charitable foundations in Dutch society is defined by changes that have occurred and, indeed, continue to occur in the relationship between government and private initiatives. Three principal 'waves' or phases of change have occurred in the history of foundations in the Netherlands.

The 'first wave' shows how social care and charity in society has long been a matter for churches and private initiatives. During the first half of the twentieth century government played only a marginal role in the well-being of citizens. Government only interfered when churches and other organisations failed in fulfilling what was essentially a subsidiary role. The 'second wave' began with the rise of the welfare state after the Second World War. The roles were slowly changing because of the need for wide-spread poor relief, the high costs and the lack of cooperation between the different organisations involved in welfare provision. Churches and private initiatives were no longer able to perform their tasks in an optimal manner. The financial responsibility for non-profit purposes was trans-ferred from private initiatives to semi-governmental institutions. The efforts of churches and private initiatives assumed a new role in society. From the 1970s onwards, churches concentrated on groups in society that could not be helped or reached by public sector institutions, such as refugees, drug addicts, the homeless and so on (Burger *et al.* 1997). The private foundations, however, no longer concentrated solely on social needs. Their fields of activity broadened; donations in the areas of inter-national aid and environmental issues, for example, increased. Since the 1980s, the third wave can be identified. The Dutch government has been making drastic cuts in expenditure in the fields of social welfare, educa-tion and health. Concepts such as privatisation, marketisation, and effi-ciency have been embraced by successive governments. Due to this changing role of the state, private support for public purposes has increased (Schuyt-Lucassen *et al.* 1997: 12).

Legal issues

The Netherlands has a very liberal civil code on foundations. The official description of a foundation is: 'a legal person, created by a legal act that has no members and whose purpose is to realise an objective stated in its statutes using capital (property) allocated to such a purpose' (Civil Code, Book 2, art 285). To establish a foundation, the civil-law notary executes a deed containing the personal data of the founder and the articles of association. In addition the foundation must be registered at the chamber of commerce. If the foundation is not registered, the board members are personally liable for any debts of the foundation. In contrast to other countries, there is no minimum asset required; the mission and goals of the foundation are not checked and verified, and there is no approval necessary from the authorities (Van der Ploeg 1999: 67–68). Foundations can also obtain certain tax advantages. In general, 'public purpose' foundations enjoy favourable tax rates on gifts and inheritances.

The Dutch government is in principle not involved with the founding of non-profit or other organisations. There is, generally speaking, no active (preventive) supervision of the activities of organisations. This attitude is based on the idealistic vision of a pluralistic and tolerant society, with a minimum of bureaucratic interference (Van der Ploeg and van Veen 2001: 22–23). Future regulations are likely to be made through self-regulation by the sector.

Empirical Profile

From the official registration at the website of the Chamber of Commerce over 142,000 foundations are registered (as of July 2003). Most of these foundations are operating foundations, active in the fields of health, education, culture and social services. Unfortunately, a selection of *funds* (primarily concerned with raising money and donating money for public purposes) cannot be made from this database. Although nobody knows how many charitable funds are active in the Netherlands, there is some summary data available on the sector. In general, there is some information available on around 1,000 funds (endowed foundations and fundraising foundations) from the umbrella organisations like the FIN, VFI and CBF. However, these funds only make up a small group of the total amount of charitable funds in the Netherlands, since many foundations operate anonymously.

Endowed foundations

Endowed foundations have been the subject of two research projects that made a first attempt to map the field of endowed foundations (see Gouwenberg and Schuyt 2000; 2004)). The participating endowed foundations ($n = 312$) in this 2004 research project gave a total amount of €900 million in grants to 'good' causes in the year 2001. More than €100 million originated from the endowed foundations and more than €750 million originated from multiple resourced foundations (excluding grants made by fundraising foundations).

More than 50 per cent of the 312 participating funds are active in the field of social services. One third of the funds are active in the fields of education/research, culture and health.

Fundraising foundations

The 'Centraal Bureau Fondsenwerving' (CBF) collects information on more than 400 nation-wide operating fundraising foundations. These foundations spent a total of €1,750 million on their missions and goals in 2001 (see CBF report 2002). Although the grants made by endowed foundations are spread over eight categories of recipient organisations, the fundraising foundations only provide information on four categories.

From the total amount of expenditure, 39 per cent of the grants were directed to international aid, 27 per cent to health, 20 per cent to environment/animals and 14 per cent to support the welfare of individuals.

Foundation roles

In general, foundations believe that their position in society is autonomous and that they exist alongside the government. One of our respondents mentioned that foundations function as 'lubricants' in society, allowing small and innovative initiatives to be developed, without having to take the broader political agenda into consideration. The main advantage foundations have in relation to the state is the possibility to set their own agenda. They have the autonomy to decide which project is important enough to be granted funding, without having to consider whether the project is for the good of the people as a whole, if it is politically correct, whether it is likely to be successful and so on. Government, on the other hand, has to address the political ideals of those elected, and is accountable to the major groups in society. In what follows, we provide a summary of the roles the foundations we interviewed believe they fulfil, in addition to the comments of experts in the philanthropic sector (representatives of the umbrella organisations, grantees, policy makers, private bankers).

Complementarity

The complementarity role is associated with the way in which foundations provide an alternative source of funding in addition to the standard government subsidies. This role has gained importance in recent years, due to the withdrawal of government from certain sections in society. Examples of the effects of this policy by the government can be found in all fields, such as research, welfare, education and healthcare. Non-profit organisations are currently forced to seek several sources of income in order to keep their services both available and affordable for their clients. In doing so, in addition to governmental support they seek support from foundations and commercial enterprises.

An example of a foundation engaged in the complementarity role is given by one of the interviewees from a foundation which supports cultural programmes for the elderly as a means of supplementing stretched budgets in homes for the elderly. The importance of the complementary role played by foundations was underlined by a locally operating foundation, whose budget for culture exceeds the budget of the local government by four times!

Although the experts interviewed agreed with the foundation representatives' interpretation of this role, they also underlined that although the foundations do help groups of individuals, they also expect some action from other parties too. The experts emphasised that it should not be the main goal of foundations to enter fields where the state should provide support.

Substitution

It can be argued that the foundations generally do not want to fulfil this role, since they feel that they will be forced into a certain role in society by the government. Another reason for refusing to fulfil this role is that foundations wish to maintain a clear distinction between governmental functions and private functions in society. If government is no longer willing to fulfil certain tasks, they cannot expect other institutions such as foundations to simply 'fill gaps' that are not addressed by the government.

An example of the substitutive role is given by one of our respondents, who mentioned that they organise the maintenance of a particular statue in their city following the withdrawal of the local authority from this responsibility due to lack of funds. Perhaps more importantly, in the social welfare and research fields, foundations provide universities with support for projects on loneliness amongst the elderly or for research on cancer or other diseases.

The views of the experts on this role were more mixed than those of the foundation representatives interviewed. On the one hand, nobody is of the opinion that the foundations should take over tasks that were originally performed by government. On the other hand, if government withdraws from certain tasks, other institutions like foundations should take over in order to ensure that prevalent needs in society are being met.

Innovation

Most of the interviewed foundations believe it is important to encourage innovative projects. In some cases, it is even clearly stated that innovative projects have a better chance of receiving grants than more traditional projects. However, they also point out that it is difficult to find innovative projects. The different actors in the field had different definitions of innovation. In general there are two directions that can be identified: new solutions for new problems or existing solutions applied to new areas. The first definition narrows the field for projects: it is extremely difficult to be *that* innovative. The second option offers more chances for success: for example, the operation of farms as part of a programme of care for the elderly who suffer from mental illness is adapted to the provision of day care on a boat for retired sailors. However, most grant-requests are 'more of the same', as one of our respondents mentioned. Generally it can be stated that all foundations identify this role as one of the more important roles they have to fulfil in society.

The reaction of the experts in relation to the innovative role is somewhat ambiguous. There is agreement that the role of stimulating innovation in society is a role that should be fulfilled by the foundations. There is, however a difference between the desire to innovate and the actual encouragement of innovation. Most foundations want to innovate, but do not see how they can reach this goal within their present organisation. According to the experts' views, the 'new' foundations are very innovative. This is mostly due to the fact that they have an open mind to society, and that the founder is personally working and guiding these foundations towards an innovative outlook, that has not been tarnished by many years of experience in the foundation sector!

Promotion of pluralism

Another important role for foundations is the promotion of pluralism in society. Pluralism is expressed in the variety of small foundations for very specific issues. Next to that, many foundations support minorities in society in building and strengthening their own identity. Examples can be found in the support given to cultural festivals that are organised by minority groups in society, thus maintaining their own identity in a foreign country.

Similar to the foundations, most experts also are of the opinion that foundations have an obligation to stimulate pluralism in society. One of the reasons for this is that the foundations are operating independently compared to government bodies.

Social and policy change

When foundations speak about social and policy change, they aim to help the minorities in society to speak for themselves. Most foundations mentioned that they should fulfil this specific role, but they are unsure as to how they should integrate this role in their actions. Others are unsure of their ability to fulfil this role. The majority of the foundations however approach this role from a positive point of view: they see themselves as involved in initiating changes in society via the structural stimulation of improvements in society as a whole.

According to the experts, the stimulation of social and policy change is highly dependent on the mission and goals of the foundation. In addition to this, most endowed foundations give grants to other organisations, not to individuals. Foundations active in the field of social welfare are supposed to have a higher need to stimulate social change than foundations active in the field of arts and culture.

Preservation of traditions and culture and redistribution

The foundations do not often mention the last two roles. In relation to the preservation of traditions and cultures, none of the foundations mentioned this as an active role to be fulfilled by them, although most interviewed foundations felt it to be an important role. Actually, the preservation of their own traditions is a part of their culture and identity. The last role that was mentioned in our research is the role of redistribution. None of the foundation representatives interviewed mentioned this as an appropriate role for them. One of the reasons is that the Dutch tax system has proven to be a very efficient way of redistributing money to society. The foundations prefer to work on their own projects, without being influenced by the government or the public in the selection of those projects.

Summary: different roles from different perspectives

Although most foundations have not given the issue of their place in society much thought, the information gathered from the interviews provides an image of a highly diverse philanthropic sector. Not only are the projects the foundations support highly diverse, there is also a clear distinction between the different foundations and their approach to achieving their goals. The most important roles of the foundations lie in the fields of complementarity, innovation and the promotion of pluralism. None of the foundations find the role of substitution necessary to fulfil, although we expect that in the future there will be a trend that the foundations take over tasks from government.

In general it can be concluded from the experts' interviews that the foundations fulfil the roles that they identified with in the interviews. There is however one remark to be made: although the foundations fulfil these roles, they can do a much better job than they think they are doing. The self-image of the foundations is more favourable than the image the experts have of foundations. The foundations are of the impression that they make a major contribution to society. In practice the foundations are only a small part of society and they are visible to just a few people active in the same fields as the foundations.

Foundation visions

Although the exploration of the roles of foundations in society was difficult, the investigation of the visions of foundations proved even more complicated. We found in our interviews that foundations have no clear vision of society, neither of an ideal society, nor of how they can contribute to a better society. The original reasons for creating the foundation by the founder guide its future direction and activities. These in turn provide an indication of the vision of society underlying the actions of a specific foundation. Another indication of the vision of foundations is given by the roles they fulfil, or want to fulfil. The general role-pattern from the previous section of the chapter provides some indication of the vision(s) the foundations have of society. A social democratic and a liberal vision are in evidence. However, the high level of autonomy and the attitude towards government clearly indicates a stronger liberal vision.

Social democratic vision

This vision assumes an important position for operating foundations, which either complement or supplement state activities. When taking the Dutch charitable fund sector into consideration we can posit that the social democratic vision is applicable. Most of the interviewed funds fulfil a complementarity role, presenting themselves as a partner in society next to government and other actors. What is more, several funds fulfil the role of substitution and fill the gaps that are left by the government.

State-controlled model

This vision of society is not one of the basic visions followed by the Dutch foundations. On the contrary, the foundations are completely opposed to this vision, cherishing their independence and the ability to decide for themselves what is important. This aversion towards the state-controlled model is particularly evident in the extent to which the innovative and complementary roles are awarded such importance. Although the foundations do not easily accept the state-controlled vision as a possible scenario for them to operate within, there is a certain need for more (government) interference. The general opinion of the foundations and the experts is that foundations should be more open and transparent. This is presently an issue of debate, and will be discussed in the next section.

Corporatist model

The corporatist model maintains a subsidiary relationship between the foundations and the state. The corporatist model is characteristic of the foundation sector in the Netherlands as a whole, but not for the charitable fund sector. As a result of how Dutch society has developed, there are many operating foundations active in the field of education, health and social welfare. These foundations are controlled and paid for by the government, with no grant-making roles for the individual foundations. However, the operating foundations suffer more and more from the withdrawal of the welfare state. This has resulted in operating foundations seeking grants from other sources, for example the funds sector in the Netherlands. In this somewhat indirect way, the corporatist model is gaining relevance since the endowed and fundraising foundations are getting more involved with other actors in society who have traditionally enjoyed a close and privileged relationship with governments.

Liberal model

The liberal vision of society is expressed in the independence of the philanthropic sector. In general, the Dutch foundations have the freedom to act as they like. This implies that they operate autonomously in accordance with their mission and goals. Many foundations seek to stimulate social equality in society, for example through giving minorities a voice, or stimulating alternatives to the generally accepted opinion. Based on the liberal society they are part of, they have the possibility to take greater risks in their grant-making than the government or even commercial enterprises.

Peripheral model

In general, none of the interviewed foundations or experts felt that this vision is applicable for the Dutch situation. Foundations are seen as small, though important for the welfare of society in general; despite the fact that the general public is not really aware of the existence of foundations. The larger fundraising foundations are known and accepted, the endowed foundations are largely invisible to the general public. The majority of the foundations are however pleased with this situation: they find it important to be well known by their target groups rather than by the general public.

Business model

The business model makes foundations instruments of corporate citizenship in society. This vision is supported by the idea that foundations should cooperate more with the for-profit sector in the field of social welfare and the public good. In practice, almost all foundations feel that they should cooperate more with the commercial sector in society, albeit under strict conditions. Foundations can take more risks than commercially operated enterprises, since they do not have to fear negative reactions by the public to their actions. Commercial enterprises are more likely to give consideration to the commercial effects a specific action of 'doing good' can have for them, and will be especially concerned to avoid any possible scandal that can damage their reputation. Risk-carrying projects are likely to be avoided.

Summary: clear visions?

In general there is no clear picture available on the visions of foundations of society. Most foundations or experts on the field of foundations have never given their vision of society much thought. However, when the actions of foundations and the philanthropic sector are examined, there are some indications of the visions of foundations. Based on the roles the foundations fulfil, a social democratic and liberal vision can be distinguished. The difference between the two is only minor, it is more a matter of interpretation than fact-finding.

Current developments and emerging issues

Recently, economic and social changes have either had, or have the potential to have, an impact on the work of foundations. These include: downturns in the world economy, government cut-backs, globalisation and the movement for more localisation, increased personal wealth, the disproportionate increase of the aging population and finally the change from a welfare state into a 'civil society' where different parties in society take responsibility for the public good. All of these developments have more or less some impact on the work carried out by foundations. In this section, we will focus on the likely impact of two key developments, but will also address some of the key themes which are topical within the foundation sector too.

The transformation of a Dutch welfare state into a civil society?

There are indications of a change in culture and shifting responsibilities. The general opinion in Dutch society has long been that government is responsible for the tasks that are derived from our welfare state. However, due to the withdrawal of government from certain sections of the welfare state, Dutch society is changing into a society where, in addition to government, other actors will have to take responsibility for public purposes at the national and local levels. This of course may result in the growth or expansion of civil society. Other actors, such as charitable organisations, churches, companies and citizens, are facing a situation where in the future only basic support is provided for by the state.

Another development in society is globalisation and localisation. The world is getting smaller due, for example, to the technical developments in the media and the internet. Globalisation is creating a counter-movement: a need for more local involvement. One of the effects is the introduction of the community foundation concept in the Netherlands. This 'new' concept allows civilians and enterprises to get involved in their local society and through this involvement, to the development of a civil society.

Growth of personal wealth

A second long-term development is that the growth of individual wealth – despite economic fluctuations – has been increasing over the past 100 years. In particular, the post-Second World War generation has had the opportunity to build up large assets. One of the effects of this growth in wealth is that many people find it important to make a difference in

society: they create their own foundations, based on a major private donation by themselves or their relations. The number of new foundations that
are emerging and many of the existing foundations (especially in the
1990s) have built up considerable financial reserves due to economic circumstances. Many new foundations are setting a trend in the professionalisation of the foundation sector.

Professionalisation and transparency

One of the main issues the foundations and the experts mentioned as
necessary for the survival of most foundations is the need for a more
professional approach within their organisations. Foundations are giving
greater consideration to the contribution they make to society. In
particular, new foundations are now making clear efforts to establish
their name and purpose in the public eye and are seeking ways in which
their funds can be made available to society and various good causes in a
responsible manner. In order to ensure a more efficient use of their
funds, the foundations are looking at what their counterparts do. They
can then work more effectively and in a more targeted manner. Concepts such as cost-effective operating, cooperation, the exchange of
information, monitoring and evaluation, advice and openness are
becoming more significant. The emerging governmental interest in the
foundation sector is also indicating a certain need for professionalisation: as long as the foundations can work out a code of conduct and regulations by themselves, these measures will not be forced upon them by
other bodies.

Another emerging issue in philanthropy is the call for more transparency and visibility among the different actors in society. The general
public and the government are regularly asking for more information on
foundations, especially on the fundraising foundations. Gradually, foundations are becoming more visible in society and concepts such as transparency and visibility are becoming important to them. In order to spend
the revenues generated in a more effective way, it will be necessary for
some foundations to make themselves known to the public.

A role for Europe in Dutch foundation sector?

The subject of the European Union and its influence on the environment
of the foundations is not recognised in the Dutch context. Given the
absence of knowledge and interest in the European Community and its
actions, most foundations are not interested in the activities of the European Foundation Centre (EFC). Only two of the larger internationally
active foundations did mention the EFC as an actor of influence in future
developments for the sector, but only one of them was familiar with the
output of the EFC.

Conclusion

In the Netherlands, the foundation sector has a centuries-old tradition. This is one of the main reasons why the Dutch foundations are so extremely varied in nature. The range of activities of the foundations is also expressed in the roles they adopted. Of the variety of roles foundations fulfil, the most commonly accepted were those of complementarity to the state, innovation and pluralism. When the roles were presented to the foundations, it emerged that the average foundation has never given their place and position in society much thought, let alone that they had considered the issue of roles and visions in society. It was only after discussion that the foundations could place their organisation in a societal perspective regarding roles and visions. Concerning the visions of foundations in society, most foundations see themselves as fitting under the liberal or social democratic model. Less regulation, autonomy, a position as a partner in society next to the government and with other actors are the most important elements in their visions of society. The Dutch foundations prefer a society in which they can operate independently of government and the market.

The Dutch endowed foundations have not maintained a very visible presence in the public eye despite full and active involvement in a large number of areas. Although for many foundations the decision of operating in anonymity is a conscious one, concepts such as professionalisation, cooperation, transparency and visibility are gradually becoming of more importance. The Dutch foundations are attempting to find a balance between dependency and autonomy, between openness and reticence. On the one hand foundations cooperate with each other to work in a more effective way, but on the other hand they are reluctant to lose autonomy.

Based on the findings of this research project, the perspective of foundations on their functioning should be further reviewed. The following questions are arising and worthy of more investigation. How do the Dutch foundations struggle with this ambivalent development? What are foundations afraid of? What explanations can be given for their strong craving for autonomy? How can this be interpreted? Sociologically? Historically? Besides, which exogenous and endogenous forces influence the emerging process of professionalisation? Theories of organisational behaviour and inter-organisational processes will be useful in addressing these questions. The social invisibility of the Dutch foundations is reflected by the lack of academic knowledge in this field. Actually, there is still a lot of work to do for researchers specialised in foundation-related topics. The research questions mentioned above are the subject of ongoing research in the Netherlands at the moment. Although this present chapter contributes to the enhancement of what we know, and understand of foundations in the Netherlands, there are still many gaps in the existing knowledge of foundations that remain unfilled.

Appendix

We used the following procedure to select foundations for interviews. Due to the uncertainty about numbers of endowed foundations (funds) and the exclusion of operating foundations (in the broad sense of the word) we selected 16 foundations for this project in advance. As two foundations were difficult to approach, we eventually had a sample of 14 foundations. These 14 foundations were all studied via annual reports and other published material. Eight of these foundations were interviewed. Next, we interviewed six experts in the philanthropic sector and we organised a workshop with 13 participants.

Note

1 This section is (partly) drawn from a paragraph of the article 'Charitatieve Vermogensfondsen in Nederland en de Naaste' by Gouwenberg (2000a).

References

Anheier, H.K. and Toepler, S. (eds) (1999) *Private Funds, Public Purpose: Philanthropic Foundations in International Perspective.* New York: Plenum Publishers.
Burger, A., Dekker, P., Ploeg, T. van der, and Veen, W. van (1997) *Defining the Nonprofit Sector: the Netherlands.* Working papers of the John Hopkins Comparative Nonprofit Sector Project No. 23. Baltimore: Johns Hopkins Institute for Policy Studies.
Burger, A., Dekker, P. and Veldheer, V. (2001) 'The Netherlands', in Schluter, A., Then, V. and Walkenhorst, P. (eds) *Foundations in Europe: Society, Management and Law.* London: Directory of Social Challenge.
CBF (2002) *Jaarverslag Fondsenwerving 2001.* Amsterdam: Centraal Bureau Fondsenwerving.
Gouwenberg, B. (2000) 'Charitatieve Vermogensfondsen in Nederland en de Naaste', in *Sociale Interventie 2000–2,* Den Haag: Elsevier.
Gouwenberg, B.M. and Schuyt, Th.N.M. (2000) *Vermogensfondsen in Nederland: een Verkenning.* Amsterdam: VU.
Gouwenberg, B.M and Schuyt, Th.N.M. (2004) *Vermogensfondsen in Nederland: Nader Onderzocht.* Amsterdam: VU.
Leeuwen, M.H.D. van (1998) 'Armenzorg in Nederland na 1800', in Gerwen, J. and Leeuwen, M.H.D. van (eds) *Studies over Zekerheidsarrangementen, Risico's, Risicobestrijding en Verzekering in Nederland Vanaf de Middeleeuwen.* Amsterdam: NEHA.
Ploeg, T.J. van der (1997) 'Overheid en Particulier Initiatief, Enkele Juridische Aspecten', in Schuyt, Th.N.M. and Hoff, S.J.M. (eds) *Filantropie en Sponsoring.* Amsterdam: VU.
Ploeg, T.J. van der (1999) 'A Comparative Legal Analysis of Foundations: Aspects of Supervision and Transparency', in Anheier, H.K. and Toepler, S. (eds) *Private Funds, Public Purpose: Philanthropic Foundations in International Perspective.* New York: Plenum Publishers.
Ploeg, T.J., van der and Veen, W.J.M. van (2001) 'Juridische Aspecten van de Non-Profit Sector', in Burger, A. and Dekker, P. (eds) *Noch Markt, Noch Staat: de*

Nederlandse Non-Profitsector in Vergelijkend Perspectief. Den Haag: Sociaal Cultureel Planbureau.

Prewitt, K. (1999) 'The Importance of Foundations in an Open Society', in Strübin, M. and Walkenhorst, P. (eds) *The Future of Foundations in an Open Society.* Gütersloh: Bertelsmann Foundation.

Schluter, A., Then, V. and Walkenhorst, P. (eds) (2001) *Foundations in Europe: Society, Management and Law.* London: Directory of Social Change.

Schuyt, Th.N.M. (2003) *Geven in Nederland, Giften, Legaten, Sponsoring en Vrijwilligerswerk*, Houten/Mechelen: Bohn Stafleu van Loghum.

Schuyt-Lucassen, N.Y., Leene, G.J.F. and Houben, P.P.J. (1997) *Hofjes met Perspectief.* Bussum: Coutinho.

Soetenhorst-de Savornin Lohman, J. (1990) *Doe Wel en Zie Om, Maatschappelijke Hulpverlening inRelatie tot het Recht.* Lisse/Amsterdam: Swets en Zeitlinger.

Vereniging van Fondsen in Nederland (2002) *Fondsenboek 2002–2003.* Zutphen: Walburg Pers.

Young, D.R. (1998) 'Complementary, Supplementary, or Adversaries? A Theoretical and Historical Examination of Nonprofit – Government Relations in the United States', in Boris, E.T. and Steuerle, C.E. (eds) *Nonprofit and Government. Collaboration and conflict.* Washington: The Urban Institute Press.

18 Norway

Håkon Lorentzen

Introduction

In Norway, the term *voluntary sector* has been used to describe civic activities during the last 50 years. Within the voluntary sector, the membership-based *association* (*forening*, a word that originates from the German *Vereinung*) has been the core unit. Until recently, foundations have not been included in the voluntary sector, most often they were regarded as a type of 'private' ownership, together with limited companies and other for-profit ownership forms.

As a consequence, foundations as a group have been less influential than in other Scandinavian countries. Unlike its Nordic neighbours, whose foundations primarily were built on wealth and family fortunes, the foundation sector in Norway developed mainly from moderate or small middle-class giving. For a long time there was, and still is, a political tension between ideals of collectivism, and philanthropic ideas of individual responsibility. During the 'golden age' of social democracy, which had begun to diminish by the 1980s, the legitimacy accorded to the private welfare contributions of foundations and other civic actors was rather weak. At the *legal* level, definitions of foundations have been rather strict, excluding assets that are included in many other countries. In 1997, the foundation sector consisted of around 9,000 registered units (NOU 1988: 7). This number has been relatively stable during the last ten years.

The neo-liberal economy that emerged internationally in the 1980s resulted in a general trend towards the separation of state services from political influence and control. In this process, where institutions and activities needed to be more autonomous, the foundation form was perceived to be a suitable tool for ensuring equality among the variety of emerging actors involved in service provision and also as a means of weakening the direct influence of external actors, notably the government.

As a field of its own, the foundation sector is composed of a mix of institutions with different origins and goals. This makes it difficult to identify common visions and roles. The purpose of this chapter is to describe the somewhat unclear identity of foundations in Norway. The case studies examined in this study reveal that grant-giving foundations in Norway do not share a common understanding of their purpose, role or function in society. We did not find shared platforms of philanthropic, religious, liberal or other ideological values. For many actors, the choice of foundation as a legal form was due to opportunistic, rather than ideological motives. Rather than having a sense of being part of a family of foundations, each one had bonds to a market niche, culture in general, public policies or the geographic community. The result is a sector where a collective consciousness and feelings of identity are more or less absent.

During the last 20 years, new types of foundations have emerged. First, there are those set up by *public authorities* to realize public goals, second, those which emerge when *collective fortunes*, from municipalities, saving banks and collectively owned insurance companies are converted into grant-giving foundations. Today, these are larger and more influential than most of those that originated from private fortunes. They also contest our traditional understanding of philanthropy as something 'private'.

In Britain the existing legal form of foundations is characterized as a nineteenth-century creation (Anheier and Leat 2002). This is probably true also for Norway. But this fact has not prevented interests very different from those of early industrial capitalists to use the foundation form for their purposes. This chapter will show that regarding the combination of flexibility, autonomy and vertical coordination that is needed in the post-industrial society, the 'old-fashioned' foundation appears to be a highly adequate ownership form.

A profile of foundations[1]

Historical development

The first foundation in Norway grew out of a power struggle over the ownership rights to a hospital between the King and the Church in the thirteenth century. A hospital for the poor was established without the King's permission, and this private ownership was contested. Ultimately the King chose to abandon his claim to the property and the property rights were related to those who, at any time, were administering the hospital (Grankvist 1982). This establishment later came to be regarded as the first foundation in Norway.

During the years between 1500 and 1900, the number of foundations increased, particularly in larger towns along the coast. Here, merchants accumulated private capital, which subsequently laid the ground for gift-letters and foundations. Some foundations were independent and were mainly poor houses, hospitals or homes for elderly people, but many were administered by members of the local community (Frimann 1774).

During the eighteenth century, and as a result of a growing middle class, a large number of *legacies* were established in the larger cities. Most often they provided minor economic support for vulnerable groups, for the education of individuals, or simply for basic necessities of the daily life. These legacies reflected good intentions and civil spirit rather than the wealth and fortunes of the Norwegian society (Backe and Krøvel 1940).

The industrialism of the twentieth century did not produce a new, influential class of wealthy capitalists. Moreover, those who were well off seemed to lack the kind of civic spirit that is evident in new foundations (Rudeng 2000: 228). However, during the years between the First and Second World Wars, large profits within *shipping* laid the ground for large, private fortunes in several of the smaller cities along the coast. Land-based industry also created new fortunes in this period, particularly in the city of Oslo. These individuals were often very generous, and gave large donations, particularly to cultural purposes. Their ideological frame of reference – if one may use such an expression – seems to have been the community or the *city*, rather than the social class or the nation.

In the twentieth century, the ideas of solidarity and collectivism undoubtedly formed the most important ideological cornerstone of the Norwegian society. As a consequence, the ideas and practical solutions of philanthropy and charity were suppressed and stigmatized as attempts to cushion the effects of an exploitive capitalism.

The new liberalism that emerged around 1980 marks the end of the collectivistic, social democratic era. As mentioned earlier, by establishing new foundations, rather than by legitimizing charity, some public authorities sought to disconnect specific state activities or interests from political control. In 1998, 240 foundations with some kind of relation to governmental authorities were registered (Statskonsult 1998). 65 of these (or 27 per cent) were private schools and research institutions. Symphony orchestras, museums and coordinating organs between state and civil society were also among these organizations. In 70 cases, governmental departments had an opportunity to appoint board members, and in approximately 60 the right to approve changes of the rules of the foundation. Many were also heavily dependent upon public financing.

Legal issues

The Norwegian Constitution of 1814 declared that foundation property may be used only in accordance with a foundation's stated intentions (paragraph 106). The Norwegian legislation on foundations is rather recent. *Stiftelsesloven* (Foundation Legislation), the first legislation on the subject of foundations, is dated 12 May 1980. Before this date, the law on foundations had been based on a mix of court practice, legal practices and administrative regulations. A national register of foundations still does not exist.

The law on foundations from 2002 states that the core feature of a foundation is a unit that has its legal base in a disposition: placing an object of economic value at the independent disposal of a defined purpose. A legal subject that fulfils these demands constitutes a foundation, independently of whether it is called a legacy, an institution, or anything else. (Woxholt 1998, *Stiftelsesloven* paragraph 2). Legally, the asset must be of some permanence, a requirement that excludes time-limited arrangements and assets for ad-hoc purposes. This requirement excludes activities such as mass meetings and campaigns, or money collected for a special purpose such as aid to earthquake victims, which are not on-going activities.

A key element here is the *requirement of independence*. According to the law, a foundation should have a *board*. However, no single individual, legal entity or interest outside the foundation is allowed to have the opportunity to influence the dispositions of the board. There is, however, considerable doubt about the scope of this paragraph, and what types of external influence are acceptable.[2]

The criterion of independence is usually assumed to exclude the possibility for a foundation to have internal *members*, or to establish formal relations between an external membership unit and the foundation. Still, such relations exist in the Norwegian case. In our sample, the Health and Rehabilitation Foundation has 22 organizational members, all with the right for the largest entities to appoint members to the board of the foundation. In this particular case, the rules of the foundation state that the board stands above the member. Still, it is a controversial issue as to whether foundations can include members. The law also excludes assets controlled by membership organizations, a limitation that places a considerable number of units outside the foundation sector.

The Norwegian law draws a distinction between *corporate* (nærings-drivende) foundations and *common* (alminnelige) foundations; the latter category will in practice include all non-corporate foundations. For operating foundations, the original asset should not be less than NOK200,000, (or approximately €25,000), while all other foundations can be established with half of this amount. This demand does not have legal validity prior to the enactment of the legislation, and does not include older foundations.

As of 2004, no authority has had the responsibility of ensuring the units that call themselves a 'foundation' satisfy the legal demands. The new law states that whether an asset is covered by the law or not does not depend upon what it is called. This means that units that call themselves foundations do not necessarily fall within the present legal frame, and units that call themselves something else may be classified as foundations. Diffuse legal demands create a huge grey zone of assets that may, or may not belong to the foundation sector. One illustrative example is the Government Petroleum Fund, established by the Parliament in 1990, with the intention of safeguarding long-term considerations in the application of central government petroleum revenues. In 2004, the Fund's portfolio totalled approximately NOK1,000 billion (or approximately €125 billion). Also the recently established National Research Fund can be mentioned here. In 2002, the Research Fund had assets of NOK13 billion (€1.6 billion) and distributed grants for NOK780 million (€97 million) in 2002. Legally, it is quite unclear whether assets like these are covered by the new law or not.

Empirical profile

It is very difficult to obtain a full picture of the present purposes fulfilled by foundations in Norway. *Statistics Norway* classifies foundations according to area of activity, but these categories do not correspond very well to the stated purpose of foundations. What is more, not all foundations are registered and part of the official statistics. Table 18.1 sets out the size of non-commercial foundations in Norway. Approximately one-third of all present foundations are public, common purpose and ideal/service producing types, while the rest have commercial purposes, providing research, cultural and social services, education or material goods for a market. In 1998, the average amount of grants per foundation was NOK204,000, or approximately €26,000.

Table 18.1 shows that 43 per cent of all foundations (and 56 per cent of all grants) in Norway belong to the *social service* category, indicating that 'social' activities are the most important category for grant-giving foundations. The second largest group, *education and research*, comprises 21 per cent of the total, or approximately 600 of the grant-giving foundations. The average size of distributed grants are NOK211,000, or €26,000 per year, slightly less than the 'social' category alone. The third largest category, *not elsewhere classified*, covers 20 per cent of all foundations, and 17

Table 18.1 Grant-giving legacies and foundations: numbers and grants in Norway, 1998 (€1,000)

Purpose	Number	%	Grants	%
Culture and recreation	153	5	160	2
Education and research	616	21	1,631	21
Health	28	1	4	<1
Social services	1,286	43	4,281	56
Environment	81	3	30	<1
Development and housing	25	1	50	<1
Advocacy, supporting employees	182	6	226	3
Not elsewhere classified	618	20	1,268	17
Total	2,989	100	7,650	100

Source: *Statistics Norway* (Statskonsult) 1998.

per cent of all grants. This category consists mainly of foundations with mixed purposes. Many, and particularly the larger ones, engage in humanitarian, social as well as cultural activities.

The remaining five categories (*culture and recreation, health, environment, advocacy and development/housing*) together make up 16 per cent of the total. With the exception of culture and recreation, these categories represent issues of interest for foundations that have emerged during the last 30–40 years, and that have not yet grown to a size that corresponds to the traditional *social* category. This means that the sector of grant-giving foundations is still dominated by 'traditional' or 'conservative' foundations, and more or less explicitly reflects established traditions of philanthropy.

Service-producing foundations exist within all sub-sectors of society, but they are not dominant in any field. Most of them are integrated in public welfare production and receive public support for their services. Grant-giving foundations in the social field are numerous, but in financial terms their contribution is marginal. This picture of foundations that are more or less absorbed by public welfare reflects the *traditionally* strong ideological position of social democracy and the absence of a distinct spirit of charity in the Norwegian society.

Foundation roles and visions

Do foundations share common roles? A 'role' in this context should mean a common way of acting for a group, observable from outside, but not necessarily consciously expressed by the actors themselves. A common role implies that foundations within a field or subfield perform certain tasks, or share common functions, in ways that make it reasonable to talk about a common role. Roles can exist on the societal level, and role identities can be traced as part of the strategic consciousness of individual foundations.

In our sample, some foundations within the large social service category perceived their role as one of supplying public welfare. This role demanded flexibility, a capacity to trace needs and to identify innovative projects. In the search for new, innovative projects, very few followed an explicit strategy. At times, the identification of projects originated from the personal network of board members rather than from written applications. As a strategy, these efforts tended to channel resources towards well-proven fields of philanthropy, such as marginal groups, international aid, the preservation of cultural treasures, support of culture, music and voluntary associations and support of religious activities and projects. In interviews, board representatives stressed the importance of loyalty to the donors' original intentions, and for them, it was important to form a role that was consistent with these intentions. When the donors' intentions were rather vague and unspecific, considerable room for interpretation occurred. Nonetheless, board representatives tended to underestimate, or to downplay the opportunity for them to express their own judgements, in favour of stressing the consistency between allocation of grants and donors' original wishes

Roles emerged as the sum of donative acts, and in most cases, they were not reflected as an explicit understanding of filling particular functions in society. As most of the foundations worked according to the 'mailbox principle', meaning that donations were distributed among incoming applications, there was no apparent need for a proactive strategy. There are important exemptions from this general impression. In the recently established Cultiva foundation, roles and visions were related to future perspectives for the city of Kristiansand. The intention of the foundation was to stimulate cultural activities and to place the city on the European map as an innovator in relation to arts and culture. The Freedom of Expression foundation has also sought out new ways of realizing their role as a watchdog for the free word.

A recent generation of foundations in Norway originated as a side effect of the transformation of collectively owned capital into limited companies. In these cases, there was neither an original donor nor a stated will, nor a tradition that the board could relate their activities to and with which they could clearly identify. Here, the absence of pronounced roles was particularly visible. One example is the UNI foundation, a formerly collectively (e.g. membership) owned insurance company, which was divided into a for-profit insurance firm and a grant-giving foundation. Another is the Cultiva foundation, a result of the city of Kristiansand's sale of stocks in electricity-producing waterfall rights (2002). Rooted in collective traditions, both of these foundations expressed an ideological distance to foundations that had their origins in private fortunes. These foundations were also reluctant to express general visions for foundations as such, visions that transcended their own particular role.

A general impression that followed from interviews is that visions are *particularistic*; they are related to each individual foundation and its surrounding economic, social or cultural context. Moreover, few of those who were interviewed stated that their foundation had laid explicit strategies for the future. For the older and established foundations, *continuity* and loyalty towards the intentions of the donor was, as mentioned, an ideal. Most often, strategic considerations were related to investment strategies and similar, more 'technical' matters. Few, if any, had developed scenarios or general visions of the future, where the roles of their own foundation had been debated. The absence of dependency upon external actors can be seen as an important explanation in relation to this scenario. Grant-giving foundations are autonomous and self-supplying entities and, as a consequence, the planning of strategic behaviour is not perceived to be an urgent necessity.

Visions for the future were not related to the status of being a foundation, but to the specific field(s) to which the foundations belong. The actual field may be the segment of the market from which the preceding fortune was made, community life or simply the goals stated in the statutes of the foundation. Bonds of identification, loyalties and personal relations to these fields resulted in identifications that hindered the further development of common foundation identities.

A reason for the absence of common identities may be that most grant-giving foundations live a life of their own with few, if any, relations to other foundations. A collective consciousness of foundations as a condition for collective strategies did not, with some few exceptions, exist among those who were interviewed. Private endowments were anchored in the will of the donor, and amongst those who administered these wills today we found strong feelings of loyalty towards the original deeds. The result was foundation strategies that, with few exceptions, defended the label 'conservative' or 'traditional'. Although many supported new initiatives, these were rarely disputed or controversial. For example, the administration of many elderly legacies, founded on charity ideals of the nineteenth century, has been modernized. One example is the UNIFOR foundation, established in 1993 with the purpose of administering the assets of around 200 smaller legacies and foundations that are at the disposal for purposes at the University of Oslo. Here, one common board makes final decisions, based on proposals from each of the underlying legacies. Today, these assets represent a supplement to ordinary budgets and have created additional opportunities for scholarships and research funding.

Until 2003, there did not exist any common meeting place or associations for foundations that could have weakened this strong impression of foundations as a fragmented field, more rooted in private than in societal considerations. There are several explanations for these conditions of 'particularism' among foundations. The weakness of a historically anchored *liberal*, political tradition is pointed out above. This is partly a result of a wealthy middle class, the absence of nobility and a state church with little or no distance from the welfare state. Another reason can be traced back to strong *communitarian* traditions, where civic engagement historically has been anchored in local communities rather than philanthropic ideals. Although civic good-doing is most often inspired by civic spirit, it is most often realized within a local context, which adds meaning and reference to the acts.

Lack of identification with a foundation society can also be traced back to the *institutional autonomy* of foundations. Foundations are, according to their legal definition, self-owned. As such, they are supposed to have a high degree of autonomy, working independently of external sources and influences. Their activities should follow from their own statutes, and not from regulations or demands from 'above', or anywhere else. Rather than being a result of political regulations, shared roles should probably follow from the fact that those who established or administer foundations see their societal missions in similar ways. Living up to these ideals means that external influence ought to be kept to a minimum. Moreover, since most foundations are financially independent, the need for strategic alliances is low.

In the literature, foundations are at times described as tools for innovation and change. But in our sample, most of the actors interviewed expressed their strong loyalty to the founders' visions, and the engagement of the donor. Most of these original intentions were neither particularly innovative nor directed towards radical types of change, but rather directed towards more modest complementary roles. A conclusion drawn by Nielsen (1972) and cited by Anheier and Leat (2002: 92) suits the bulk of Norwegian grant-giving foundations: The profile of their activities is largely conventional, not reformist. They are carriers of social continuity, not change. Some foundations stand out as exceptions to this observation. The Freedom of Expression and the Cultiva foundations, mentioned above, have developed active strategies for change.

Most foundations in our sample supported activities, ideas, arrangements and projects which had difficulties in getting sufficient public support. The preservation of cultural memorials, the restoration of ancient buildings, economic support for festivals, instruments, cultural activities, a particular service within a public institution, communal volunteer centres, self-help groups or wage support for a particular position within public welfare institutions are examples. At times, such support can be labelled innovative, but again innovation seemed to be more of a consequence than an intention; few, if any foundations stated innovation as their explicit strategy.

Our interviews showed that boards of grant-giving foundations rarely follow explicit strategies in their distribution of grants. Some aimed at a balanced distribution of grants between several stated purposes. The number of self-initiated projects was generally low. For the most part foundations spread their grants in response to incoming applications. In some foundations, particularly those where the donor was present and alive, a considerable degree of individual discretion regulated the selection of supported applications. A general impression was that the degree of formalization increases with the age of the foundation; time makes the original will of the donor fade away, and subsequent administrators tend to replace the personal engagement of the donor with strategic, or rational calculations.

In all cases, the board took the final decisions about the distribution of grants. Only two foundations had formalized the treatment of applications, so that a statement or a comment from an external or independent source followed the application to the board. Most often, the director or the daily leader of the foundation handled applications and selected those who were regarded as worthy of support.

Summing up, visions and roles of Norwegian foundations leave a somewhat diffuse impression. The majority of foundations do not share a common identity, a feeling of belonging to a sector of foundations. Their visions and roles are *particularistic*, they are loyal to the intentions of the donor, his or her life and intentions. Some, but very few, have identified particular roles related to their purposes: promoting cultural activities, political discourse and freedom of speech. But the majority of foundations is loyal to the original intentions of the donor, and makes a deed of their individual, non-political charity activities.

In Norway, elderly foundations tend to be rooted in the philanthropic tradition, while more recent entities in some way or other stem from collective traditions: saving banks, collective insurance companies, municipal ownership, voluntary associations or public oil revenues. These actors perceive their status as foundations as a pragmatic choice, a way of ensuring stable activities, free from political fluctuations. The visions of these units form part of a broader picture of structural changes and the shift from hierarchical command to the decoupling of public activities.

Conclusion: current developments and emerging issues

In the European context, the case of Norway will probably stand forth as a deviant one. Norway appears to be lacking in the most important historical preconditions for an influential foundation sector: a liberal political tradition and a wealthy upper class with a philanthropic spirit. Traditional, philanthropic foundations of the nineteenth and twentieth century were numerous but with few exceptions tended to be small.

In our sample study, we found that among *traditional, philanthropic foundations* a collective consciousness, a feeling of belonging to a sector of foundations was absent. Rather than being orientated towards other foundations, loyalties and accountabilities were directed towards the field from where the foundation originated, its public sub-sector (like culture, health or social affairs) or the donor's original intentions. Foundations tended to look at themselves as private actors, anchored in the history and will of the donor, rather than belonging to a common field of foundations. They perceived their role as one of pursuing welfare and cultural activities within the community, and with reference to the donor's original intentions. As fragmented and traditional, representing small or moderate assets, it is not relevant to talk about common roles or strategic visions for this group.

There are some exceptions to this general picture: the philanthropic foundations with a strong feeling of autonomy, carriers of a liberal tradition who underline the position of foundations as something different from 'state' and 'market'. These actors were attempting to improve cooperation among foundations by being an active counterpart in the law-making process and promoting the general interests of foundations towards public authorities. It should also be mentioned that, as a result of interviews and the perspectives of the project behind this article, several foundations started processes of modernizing their identities. This was primarily done by defining new strategic roles, which then altered their grant-giving profiles.

A group of foundations originate from the *collective* tradition and activities such as cooperative insurance, saving banks, municipal ownership, membership associations and state petroleum funds. The general marketization of society, together with the transformation from hierarchical to horizontal coordination, have motivated a change of ownership forms among these actors. For several, the commercial parts of the activities were marketized, while their collectively accumulated capital laid the ground for new, common good foundations. These foundations, rooted in the collective tradition, do not share the historic experience of the philanthropic foundations, and they do not always share their liberal perspectives. An ideological cleavage seems to part foundations from the philanthropic and the collective tradition. More often than not, the latter regards the foundation form as a pragmatic choice given the need for autonomy and the continuity of an activity. Some foundations within the collective tradition have articulated visions related to their field of activity. In some cases, these visions were formulated in the political process on the national or local level and then given as the strategic goal of the foundations.

Community foundations stand out as a particular sub-group of the collective tradition. The number of locally-oriented/based foundations has been steadily increasing during the last ten years. Most often, the choice of the foundation form is a pragmatic one, determined by the need for horizontal cooperation among actors from state, market and civil society. The foundation form secures independence and equal influence among the participants. At times, the choice of the foundation form is motivated by the need for a *buffer* between state or local public agencies and civic interests.

In the 1990s, public authorities regarded the foundation form a suitable tool for decoupling formerly state-controlled activities like cultural services, research and other specialized and professional activities. The roles and visions of these actors are related to their particular sub-field, their status as foundations is most often not given any particular meaning. These foundations do not share a common identity or common goals for the future, and they have no ties of identification with the philanthropic part of the foundation sector. In the late 1990s, a report criticized the government for not respecting the autonomy of these foundations: by controlling their incomes, the government also controls their activities, and this is a break with their legal demand for autonomy. Following this report, the ownership form of *limited company* (aksjeselskap) was chosen as an ownership form of these quasi-autonomous state activities.

A final conclusion from these studies is that the foundation sector in

Norway stands out as divided between foundations rooted in the *philanthropic* tradition, those which have their origins in civic, *cooperative* or *communal* activities and foundations established *by public authorities*. Differences in history and traditions are the main reasons for the absence of common visions, roles and perspectives among these actors. In the Norwegian context, the symbiotic ties between 'foundation' and 'philanthropy' are broken. According to those interviewed, the foundation was regarded a value-free ownership form, suitable for purposes when autonomy, independence and continuity were important, less suitable in 'dynamic' landscapes or when political responsibility is needed.

Notes

1 Evidence in this chapter originates from the analysis of a sample of 20 Norwegian grant-giving foundations, where data about their visions, strategies and practices are collected from written information as well as interviews of board and staff members.
2 In 1998, the Auditor General pointed out that controlled goal-setting for public foundations may conflict with the basic requirements for autonomy and self-regulation referred to in the legal regulations of foundations (Riksrevisjonen 1998–1999). An 'active ownership' from governmental authorities may undermine the autonomy of the foundation. The state's right to spend public money in accordance with public and political goals may be conflicting with foundations' legally instituted right to pursue their own goals, specifically as enacted under legislation in 1980. This dilemma has been pointed out in several reports, resulting in a higher degree of reservation in the use of foundation as a tool for governmental authorities (Statskonsult 1998, NOU 1998: 7, Riksrevisjonen 1998–1999: 3).

References

Anheier, Helmut and Leat, Diana (2002) *From Charity to Creativity. Philanthropic Foundations in the 21st Century*, UK: Comedia.
Backe, J. and Krøvel, A. (1940) *Legat-register*, Oslo: Cappelen.
Frimann (1774) *Foundations and Gift-letters in the Bishopric of Bergen*.
Grankvist, R. (1982) *Nidaros Kirkes Spital 700 år. Trondheims Hospital 1277–1977*, Trondheim: F. Bruuns bokhandel.
Nielsen, W. (1972) *The Big Foundations*, New York: Columbia University Press.
NOU 1998: 7 *Om stiftelser*.
Rudeng, Erik (2000) *Allmennyttige stiftelser i det sivile samfunn*, Oslo: Stiftelsen Fritt Ord.
Statskonsult (1998) *Riksrevisjonens undersøkelse vedrørende bruken av stiftelser i statlig forvaltning*, Oslo: Riksrevisjonen: Dokument 3: 6.
Woxholt, Geir (1998) *Nonprofit Law in Norway*, Oslo: Institute for Social research, Report 98: 12.

19 Poland

Jerzy Krzyszkowski

Introduction

This chapter examines the roles and visions of foundations in Poland, one of the countries of Central and Eastern Europe that began the process of political, social and economic transition from socialism to democracy and capitalism in 1989. The first part of the chapter presents a profile of Polish foundations which includes a brief account of the historical development of foundations, the legal environment and some empirical data. The second part of the chapter discusses foundation roles, visions and policies and concludes by exploring the current developments and emerging issues facing foundations in Poland today. In Poland, there is a divide between the powerful, wealthy grant-making foundations, who are in the minority and tend to favour a role as agents of social and policy change, and the smaller, operating foundations, which constitute the majority. Their focus on the complementarity role (and, ideally, on innovation) is evident in the close relations many of these foundations have with the state. In spite of these divisions, the improvement of regulation and transparency poses a challenge for all foundations and policy makers alike. Foundations are also grappling with the opportunities and challenges regarding funding and cooperation which have been generated by Poland's accession to the European Union.

A profile of foundations

Historical development

Poland has never had a strong tradition of self-organization, due mainly to the partition of the country in the nineteenth century, the two World Wars in the twentieth century and the period of the communist regime. The presence of foundations has always been connected with the activities of the Catholic Church, particularly during the nineteenth century. The Communist regime de-legalized foundations and nationalized their assets in 1952. The reactivation of foundations as a legal form of organization began in 1984, but again this mainly affected Catholic Church foundations. In addition, at the end of the 1980s (1988) one of the most influential grant-making and operating foundations, the Stephan Batory Foundation, was established by George Soros.

The transformation which began in 1989 was dominated by foreign grant-making foundations that provided substantial funding for rebuilding Polish civil society. The most important actors were the American foundations (National Endowment for Democracy, Ford Foundation etc.) and the German foundations (Alexander Humboldt Stiftung, Bosh Stiftung, Friedrich Ebert Stiftung). Nonetheless the majority of foundations in Poland today are operating foundations without significant financial resources. Indeed, one of the main reasons that these entities possess the status of a foundation can be linked to the ease with which foundations could be established at the beginning of the 1990s.

Legal issues

Foundations are regulated by the Law on Foundations 1984, the Law on Income Tax of Legal Persons and their own statutes (Kwiatkiewicz 2002–2003). Nonetheless, in Poland foundations are not defined clearly by law. Various provisions of the law suggest that a foundation is broadly understood to be a non-membership based entity, created by a donor for the purposes of 'economically and socially beneficial objectives subject to the essential interest of the Republic of Poland such as: health care, development in economy and science, education, culture and fine arts, welfare, environmental protection and protection of national monuments' (Law on Foundations, Article 1). Foundations can carry out economic activities to achieve their goals but these activities must be sanctioned by the foundation's statutes. In effect, the foundation must legally serve a public benefit purpose, but as is evident from Article 1 this is also not comprehensively defined by the law. However, under the Law on Public Benefit and Volunteerism, introduced in 2003, foundations can also apply for Public Benefit Organization (PBO) status. One benefit of this status is that it lists 24 public benefit activities in total and makes clear that PBOs do not have to pay corporate tax on income which is directed towards their public benefit activities. Of course, this also means that different legal statutes have different interpretations of what constitutes public benefit. The act has also sought to improve the regulation and supervision of foundations and other non-governmental organizations in Poland as PBOs must meet certain requirements regarding accountability and transparency.[1]

An empirical profile

Prior to 1989 there were only 277 foundations registered in Poland. The most dynamic patterns of growth were observed in the first years of the transition to democracy from 1990 to 1995. In 1995 there were approximately 4,700 foundations and in 2002 approximately 6,000 foundations. They employ more than 13,000 people which equals 0.1 per cent of national employment. Full-time employees can be found only in one in every three foundations. One in every four foundations is located in Warsaw. Health, culture and recreation, education and research and social services constitute the main areas of foundation activity. As stated above, operating foundations without reasonable financial resources constitute the majority of foundations in the Polish context, whereas grant-making and corporate foundations are in the minority.

The largest grant-making foundations have been created by foreign capital (e.g. Polish-American Freedom Foundation), banks (e.g. Kronenberg Bank Foundation) or the state treasury (e.g. Polish Science Foundation). The absence of more grant-making foundations can be attributed to the lack of significant wealth in society as well as the low costs required to set up a foundation. One needs to declare only a little more than €200 in capital to set up a foundation. For instance, the results of research carried out since 1991 by the Bank of Information Klon/Jawor show that more than 25 per cent of foundations have an annual income lower than €2,000 and only 8 per cent have an income of more than €200,000. For the larger foundations, public means provide twice as big a source of income as for the small ones. In 1997 public subsidies were received by 45 per cent of big foundations and by only 20 per cent of smaller ones.

Roles

The roles of foundations in Poland were assessed based on the extent to which the interviewees displayed awareness of the different roles which are associated with foundations. The extent to which the interviewees felt that particular roles reflected what was both feasible and desirable in practice was also explored. The main research findings show that foundation representatives and policy makers are aware of the various roles of foundations and agree with the relevance of most of the foundations roles presented in the research.

Foundation representatives and policy makers are aware of the complementarity role of foundations. This role is fully accepted by the stakeholders and policy makers. Foundations are seen to be engaged in identifying and addressing gaps in services provided by the state. They not only meet neglected needs but provide savings for the state budget as well. There is much evidence that this complementarity role is performed by both grant-making and operating foundations, such as the Nobody's Children Foundation which provides support for children who are victims of family violence. Grant-making foundations, such as the prominent Stefan Batory Foundation, engage in a complementary role in that they often provide foundations and associations with the financial resources that are necessary for their activities through grants and awards.

Foundation stakeholders and policy makers are much less aware of the substitution role of foundations. The role of a foundation as a private provider of public and quasi-public goods is not as popular as the complementarity role. The apathy towards the substitution role could be explained by the fact that this is not a role that is associated with foundations, as well as the lack of financial capital that would allow foundations to 'replace' the state in its functions.

Although the foundation stakeholders and policy makers perceive foundations as being representative of individual acts of voluntary wealth redistribution, the majority of foundation representatives interviewed did not see the relevance of this role in the Polish context, given the economic weakness of the foundation sector. The only exceptions were the two corporate foundations included in the study (the Polsat Foundation and the Leopold Kronenberg Bank Foundation): these foundations identified with this role in terms of how a share of each company's profits is allocated for public purposes.

Foundations are very often seen as engines of social innovation and sources of renewal in areas that are addressed by neither government or market. Foundations are considered to have such a role by both foundation representatives and policy makers. The popularity of the innovation role can be explained by the perceived lack of efficiency on the part of the Polish state. Innovation and complementarity are sometimes combined, such as in the example of the Incubator Community Foundation, created by the Lodz City Council and the Lodz Agency of Regional Development in 1992. Its aims include support for entrepreneurship and fighting unemployment. It has helped to create over 90 small businesses and nearly 1600 new jobs. The majority of foundation stakeholders and policy makers were also aware of the importance of the role of foundations in generating social change. Foundations should be political agents voicing opinion and providing resources, promoting socio-political changes, creating a more just society by recognizing new needs, expressing their beliefs and empowering the socially excluded. There is much evidence of the presence of such a role in practice. For example, the Joint Programme 'Against Corruption' is implemented by two foundations, namely the Stephan Batory Foundation and Helsinki Foundation of Human Rights. The main aim of the programme is to fight corruption with anticorruption legislation proposals, supporting independent media, monitoring actions, education campaigns, local leader training and legal aid for victims of corruption.

The preservation of traditions and cultures is mainly of relevance to foundations from the field of culture and those with links to the Catholic Church. The main actor in Poland performing the preservation role as its statutory mission is the Culture Foundation. It is a state foundation established by the Ministry of Culture and Art in 1990. The mission of the

Foundation is to support national culture and art development including arts activities, publications, education and culture heritage preservation. During the period 1992–2001 the Culture Foundation co-financed over 1000 cultural projects to the total of €5 million.

The role of foundations in the promotion of pluralism is emphasized mostly by liberals, people whose life experience and political activities were connected with anti-communist movements. The Helsinki Foundation of Human Rights, for example, was established in Warsaw in 1989 as a continuation of the Helsinki Committee that had worked against the Communist regime since 1982. After the fall of communism in 1989, the Helsinki Committee members decided to work in the area of human rights education and studies. At present the Helsinki Foundation of Human Rights receives substantial funding from foreign foundations (the Ford Foundation, Open Society Institute, Charles Stewart MOTT Foundation, Friedrich Naumann Stiftung, Freedom House), as well as Polish grant-making foundations (the Stefan Batory Foundation) and political institutions such as the Council of Europe and the United Nations.

The analysis of foundation roles permits the assessment not only of the extent to which foundation representatives and policy makers are aware of the various roles, but also of how these roles are feasible and reflected in foundation visions and practice. Complementarity, innovation, social policy change, preservation of traditions and cultures and pluralism are roles that foundations most easily identify with (see Table 19.1). The roles of substitution and redistribution were mentioned less often. Perceptions of the roles of foundations are different for grant-making and operating

Table 19.1 Roles of foundations in Poland: a summary

Roles	Awareness	Visions	Practice	Feasibility	Overall assessment
Complementarity	Total agreement	Yes	Yes	Full	Excellent
Substitution	Medium agreement	No	Yes	To some extent	Good
Redistribution	Some agreement	No	No	No	Not relevant
Innovation	Total agreement	Yes	Yes	Full	Excellent
Social change	Total agreement	Yes	Yes	To some extent	Good
Preservation	Total agreement	Yes	Yes	To some extent	Good
Pluralism	Medium agreement	No	Yes	To some extent	Good
Other roles	Total agreement	Yes	Yes	To some extent	Good

foundations. Whilst grant-making foundation representatives are much more often in favour of substitution, redistribution and social policy change roles, representatives from operating foundations emphasize complementarity, innovation and pluralism as the main roles of foundations. These different perceptions of roles are generally consistent with the practice of foundations. There is a clear division between powerful and wealthy grant-making foundations that act as social and policy change agents and small operating foundations that concentrate on complementarity and (ideally) innovation roles.

According to the interviewees the ideal foundation should be apolitical, independent, and transparent for donors and society. It should be an integral element of civil society open to innovations, active, tolerant and appreciating education. In such a society foundations could cover areas and problems neglected by the state. Foundations should educate people on how to protect the environment, monitor government, and support citizen initiatives. Visions of the roles of foundations in society include the cultivation of good relations with the state, business, third sector and the whole of civil society. Foundations should however protect their independence in their relations with all of the partners mentioned above. It is viewed as particularly important to maintain independence from the political influences of changing governments and from the economic pressures of sponsors. Foundations should make information about their activities and finances more readily available to the public. At the same time it was felt that the government should support foundations in their actions by clear legislation and user-friendly reporting systems. The business sector ought to be provided with encouraging conditions for philanthropy (tax reductions etc.). The visions of foundation roles are correlated with the types of foundations. Private and corporate foundations' representatives emphasize that relations with the government should not be too close so as to protect their roles as civil society representatives. By contrast, foundations in receipt of public funding underline the benefits of close relations with the state. The analysis of foundation visions and practice has shown that the main problem seems to be feasibility in terms of resources and capacity. The majority of foundations fall into the operating type with limited resources and unclear prospects in terms of legal and financial stability. Nowadays this instability makes rational planning as well as implementation difficult. Overall the accepted or envisaged roles for foundations are complementarity, innovation, social change and the promotion of pluralism. The main roles that are actually performed are complementarity and innovation.

Visions

The most popular vision amongst the foundation representatives was the liberal model. Supporters of this model are representatives of all types of foundations. This reflects how although some may favour close relations with the state, they still value their independence. Policy makers who are members of liberal political parties, such as the Union of Freedom and Citizen Platform, also supported this model. This position can be explained by how the foundations were originally established as an alternative or complementary organization to the state and its institutions. Less popular was the social democratic model, the supporters of which are representatives of public foundations established and subsidized by the state budget (the Culture Foundation). Representatives of operating foundations that cooperate with the state, especially in the field of social services, using mainly public money (e.g. Food Bank and Nobody's Children Foundation) also identified with this model, as did corporate foundations' representatives (Polsat Foundation). The relevance of the social democratic model is rooted in the role of the state in funding some of the foundations mentioned above (the Culture Foundation) but also in the interest shown by others in cooperating with the state. Similarly, the corporatist model has found support among representatives of operating foundations interviewed in our research particularly those who have acted in the field of health protection and social services. Thus, the visions of those interviewed in many respects reflect the broad support for roles such as innovation, on the one hand, and complementarity, on the other.

There is a striking difference between foundations representatives and policy makers in their opinions about the business model. Whilst the majority of foundation leaders support close cooperation between business and foundations, policy makers are against such a relationship with the corporate sector. To understand negative opinions about the business model among politicians one should note the weaknesses of legal regulations and state institutions in post-communist countries like Poland, which led to foundations and other non-profit organizations being used as an instrument for strictly economic enterprise. Both foundation stakeholders as well as policy makers rejected the state-controlled model. There is widespread acceptance of foundations as an integral part of the civil society among policy makers and foundation representatives in Poland, though foundations face clear challenges in consolidating their position

Current developments and emerging issues

One of the key political issues for the majority of foundation representatives is the establishment of new legal regulations for the functioning of foundations. The most important legal instrument for the future of foundations is the Law on Public Benefit and Volunteerism passed in 2003, which as mentioned above aims in part to provide for better regulation and supervision of foundations and non-governmental organizations more generally. Relations between third sector, political parties and policy makers are also the subject of popular debate. Foundations have become popular forms of self-promotion and political marketing among political leaders. The influence of policy makers on foundations' operations is evident in the case of operating foundations that have to cooperate with central and local authorities, for example in the field of children and family services.

Economic growth has a decisive affect on the development of founda-tions, especially grant making foundations. It should encourage the estab-lishment of new grant-making foundations and increase the involvement of local businesses in philanthropic giving. One of the outstanding experts in the field of the third sector in Poland, Ewa Leś expects that the Euro-pean Union (EU) will encourage civil society building via EU develop-ment programs (e.g. fighting long-term unemployment and social exclusion). Others, like an active third-sector leader Ewa Szymczak, expects that the role of foundations will decrease because of the financial crises experienced by non-governmental organizations. This is due to the absence of significant wealth in some sections of Polish society, underde-veloped local business and the withdrawal of foreign foundations. In con-sequence, there will be two kinds of foundations that will survive, namely small, local organizations based on voluntary work, and the largest and the most powerful organizations.

In all, there are two broad types of factors that are likely to influence the future development of foundations: internal, national factors related to regulation, on the one hand, and external factors related mainly to the European Union, on the other. Key internal factors include the legal reg-ulation of foundation status, national economic growth and improving the public image of foundations that have no public confidence and are popular targets for media attacks. The regulation of relations between public administration, business and politicians should allow for founda-tion development as an integral element of civil society development. External factors that affect foundations' development are evident mainly in EU integration. The involvement of the EU in the third sector is gener-ally expected among foundation representatives. In their opinion it will have a positive influence on the status of foundations. It will make politi-cians treat foundations as a serious partner in the social dialogue with the government and as an integral element of civil society. At the same time integration with the EU and the new sources of funding that are likely to follow will be a real challenge for foundations. Foundations will have to maintain standards concerning professionalism, transparency, ethical codes, financial records, etc. in order to receive European funds. This could help to eliminate false foundations that currently exist and which have been the subject of investigation and scandal. At the same time foun-dation representatives fear that the government could keep control over the European funds and, as a result, have financial power over founda-tions. The government could create quasi-foundations so as to absorb the EU money. This could make foundations more sensitive towards political influence and generate real competition among them. EU integration will be a decisive factor for the future of foundations, but it is likely to cause a real division or polarization among them. There will be a split between the powerful, effective foundations and small community foundations organized at the local level to solve particular local problems. In all, the division between large and small foundations permeates all aspects of foundations' roles, visions and future scenarios. Building bridges across these divisions appears to be one of the most important challenges facing Poland's foundations.

Note

1 See www.usig.org/countryinfo/poland.asp.

References

Kwiatkiewicz, A. (2002–2003) 'Endowment Building in Poland: A Favourable Environment?' *SEAL (Social Economy and Law Journal)*, Winter 2002–2003. Available at: www.efc.be/publications/sealabstract.html.

Leś, E. (2000) *Od filantropii do pomocniczości* (From Philanthropy to Subsidiarity), Warszawa: Elipsa.

Leś. E. (2001) *Zarys historii dobroczynności i filantropii w Polsce* (Charity and Philantrophy in Poland: an Outline), Warszawa: Prószyński i s-ka.

Leś, E. and Nałęcz, S. (n.d.) '*Fundacje w Polsce: stereotypy kontra fakty*' (Foundations in Poland: Stereotypes and Facts), Unpublished.

20 Spain

Miguel Ángel Cabra De Luna and
Berta Fraguas Garrido

Introduction

At present, there are approximately 6,000 foundations in Spain, 4,000 of which are fully active. The non-active entities are very old foundations, or foundations that were created for a specific period of time; for instance, a foundation created for a certain event. Nonetheless, as no quantitative studies have been carried out in recent years there remain significant gaps in our knowledge about the Spanish foundation sector. Historically, the period of the Franco regime notwithstanding, strong patterns of growth in the number of foundations can be attributed to broader patterns in the social and economic evolution of the twentieth century. These historical changes have been accompanied by legal changes. Over the last few years several laws have been enacted, not just at a state level but also at a regional level (autonomous communities), thus clearly showing the government's interest in regulating foundations. Unfortunately, foundations do not find the scope of these laws sufficiently satisfactory, despite the efforts that have been made to improve them.

This study has been carried out taking into account the characteristics that are typical of foundations in Spain, which differ from those in the rest of Europe. In Spain there are almost no grant-making foundations. Spain has a significant number of operating foundations, i.e. those which develop their own projects using internal or external financing. In fact, the small number of purely grant-making foundations that do exist are becoming operating foundations as they aim to take part in projects and to move beyond making grants. Thus, in the case of Spain, it must be noted that the foundations referred to in most cases are operating foundations, although we have also interviewed and assessed grant-making foundations.

What is more, amongst the foundations, there is a lack of common identity, which is reflected in difficulties encountered in uniting interests, achieving inter-foundation cooperation and defending common positions. Nonetheless, the foundations' vision of their role in society and their position as an alternative to the state is quite clear. Most believe that their role is to be complementary to the state and to be innovative. Foundations also believe that their position allows them to be more flexible than the public sector. They can provide "answers" in a more efficient manner and have better links with society at large. Thus, foundations claim to have the advantages of both the public and private sector – providing a service to society and supporting dynamic initiatives – but without the apparent disadvantages of the public administration.

A profile of foundations in Spain

Historical development

Foundations have existed in Spain since the Middle Ages but their history has been affected by their relationship with the state, which has exerted considerable control over the establishment and functioning of foundations (Vázquez *et al.* 2001).

Although the first foundation to appear in the records of the Protectorates (supervisory authorities) was set up in 1120, the origins of the concept of a non-profit entity date back to the sixth century. Spanish foundations were created thanks to donations made by wealthy citizens to churches and other religious authorities, which allowed them to set up schools, hospitals and hostels for the poor. It gradually became popular amongst the bourgeoisie of the time to fund all sorts of charitable institutions. Thus the number of foundations gradually increased.

After the industrial revolution in the middle of the nineteenth century, social pressure encouraged the government to take on private social welfare services. Both the predominance of socialist ideology and the Franco regime then encouraged public rather than private action. It was only in 1978 with the new Spanish Constitution, which recognises the right to set up a foundation, that these bodies were accepted by society. In 1994 the Law on Foundations came into force and further promoted their development.

Legal issues

The right to set up a foundation is laid down expressly in article 34 of the Spanish Constitution and developed in Law 50/2002 on Foundations of 26 December. This law defines foundations as "organizations established with a non-profit motive whose assets are permanently earmarked for the performance of activities in the general interest, in accordance with their creator's will".

The basic legal regulation of foundations is to be found in the general rules governing legal entities in the Spanish Civil Code (articles 35–39) which establishes their powers and working regimes as well as rules for amendments and dissolution. However, specific aspects regarding regulation appear in other legislation.

Several Autonomous Communities in Spain have their own independent civil legislation, apart from State regulation. Foundations that carry out their main activities in more than one Autonomous Community or throughout Spain, must also adhere to Autonomous Community regulations. At present the Canary Islands, Castilla y León, Catalonia, Galicia, Madrid, Navarre, Basque Country and Valencia all have their own law governing the foundations that carry out most of their activities within their territory.

Regarding state regulations, the following apply:

- Law 49/2002 of 23 December on the tax regime of non-profit entities and tax incentives for sponsorship;
- Law 50/2002 of 26 December on Foundations, which annulled and updated Law 30/1994 of 24 November on Foundations. This new law remains to be implemented in the form of regulations.

The new law is largely based on the previous Law 30/1994 and maintains the same structure. The two main features of the reform are legal security and flexible functioning. According to the Preamble, it has three main objectives:

- "[T]o reduce the involvement of the public authorities in the functioning of foundations...;
- to make procedures more flexible and simple, especially those of an economic and financial nature...; [and]
- to promote the foundation phenomenon as a channel through which civil society can help the public authorities in achieving ends in the common interest."

The trends of the reform of the law on the fiscal regime of non-profit entities and fiscal incentives for sponsorship (Law 49/2002 of 23 December) did not amount to a break from the previous Law 30/1994, but rather aimed to continue finding solutions and resolving technical aspects in a simpler and clearer framework. The first measure was to separate basic foundation regulations from those of the special fiscal regime for non-profit entities.

In all, although the new laws have modified some of the most controversial aspects of the previous legislation, these amendments have not been as in-depth as the foundations expected. The sector still considers it necessary to promote a greater degree of trust in foundations, in the activities they develop and the services they offer in the general interest. The provision for legal and tax measures should facilitate and support their role(s).

An empirical profile of Spanish Foundations

The almost 6,000 foundations in Spain can be broken down by type as shown in Figure 20.1.

Spanish foundations working on a national level have accumulated assets of approximately €2.33 billion. In the case of cultural foundations, only the initial assets have been calculated, and there is no market price valuation of the movable and immovable property of the older foundations which would considerably increase this amount.

Foundations whose main activities are focused on education are the ones with the largest assets (€1.448 billion), followed by foundations working in welfare (€601 million) and foundations focused in the area of culture (€282 million).

Roles and visions of Spanish foundations

There is a distinct lack of consensus regarding the way foundations see themselves. Almost half of the foundations that have taken part in the project see themselves exclusively as entities that are part of the field in which they act (education, culture, health, etc.). However, an important part (20.83 per cent) also believe that they could identify with any of the roles depending on the definition applied and the context referred to.

Furthermore, a small part believes they belong to a civil society in general, and 25 per cent consider that they belong to the non-profit sector. This lack of feeling of belonging to a group could be the reason for the lack of coordination and heterogeneity many refer to in their interviews. Indeed, one of the greatest existing problems one encounters when defining the non-profit or third sector in Spain is the disparity in opinions, not only from society in general and politicians, but also from the actual entities in the sector.

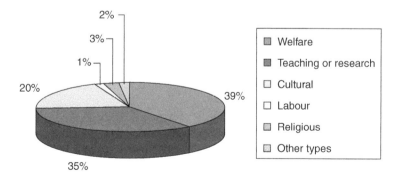

Distribution by foundational area

2%
3%
1%
20%
39%
35%

- Welfare
- Teaching or research
- Cultural
- Labour
- Religious
- Other types

Figure 20.1 Foundations in Spain.

Roles

Foundations mainly consider that their distinctive role is complementarity (80.95 per cent), followed by innovation (71.42 per cent) and political and social change (71.42 per cent). Subsequently, they claim a role involving the promotion of pluralism (61.9 per cent) and a redistributive role (57.42 per cent).

As regards to the role of preserving culture and traditions, they all claim that they only agree with this statement in the case of those foundations that really class this mission among their objectives. It is not viewed as a role that can be attributed systematically to all foundations.

Moreover, it is also important to state that opinions regarding the role of substitution are balanced between interviewees: the same number agree and disagree with the importance of this role. However, it is relevant to point out that it generates a substantial degree of controversy as those who do not agree with this role vehemently oppose it, while those who are in favour vehemently agree. Thus, it is a role which leads to the polarisation of positions between foundations.

Experts believe that the differences in the roles performed by the state and those fulfilled by foundations lie in the way foundations carry out their mission. Foundations have a higher degree of freedom; they are more flexible, operational, less bureaucratic and respond more directly to the needs of the civil society. Foundations are more in contact with "the people", thus they act more rapidly and are more efficient. Therefore, they possess the advantages of both the public sector – service to society – and the private sector – but are not burdened by their apparent drawbacks: red tape, slowness, low degree of flexibility, profit-minded and benefit of a few. Nonetheless, interviewees also point out that foundations still have to comply with too many administrative procedures, which sometimes makes them slower and more bureaucratic.

As regards the role of complementarity, the majority of experts and foundation representatives identified with this role. They aspire to fulfil this goal of complementing the state by attending to the special needs of certain groups that are not satisfied by other organs. But as foundations' resources cannot be compared to the state's resources, most of them say that their *level* of complementarity depends directly on their financial capacity. In figures, 45 per cent of the foundations interviewed would like to fulfil the role of complementarity, 27 per cent the role of innovation and 18 per cent the role of redistribution. The foundations' opinion does not differ from that of the experts from the public administration, although – as mentioned before – it is not possible to compare the expenditure produced by the state and that of the foundations. Unfortunately there is no specific reliable study on the expenditure of foundations in Spain and the impact of foundation's spending on the activities they develop.

Indeed, following the analysis of the documentation of the foundations (e.g., reports, websites), it appears that they do carry out the role of complementarity. However, this role is somewhat clearer in foundations with social purposes related to those on the margins of society, than in cultural or educational foundations dedicated to the general public interest. As the public administration also acts in these latter areas, the foundations' role may not be complementing that of the state but duplicating it. These opinions were reaffirmed in the meeting of experts that was held following the interviews.

A representative of the public administration verified the general belief that foundations exist because the state does not do its duty properly and that if the state did a good job foundations would not exist. However, she believes that this idea should be discarded because there must be a certain degree of collaboration between society and the state and one of the best ways for the state to remain accountable to its citizens is through non-profit entities. Once again, it is very interesting to see that there is no unique role attributed to foundations as a group. Instead, the role they play depends on the type of foundation in question.

Another factor that influences the classification of this role is the size of these foundations in terms of their "purchasing power" and "real power". The interviews indicate that large and powerful foundations want to take on a role that focuses mainly on substitution and the preservation of culture and traditions. Cooperation-oriented foundations aim to develop a more redistributive role and small foundations aspire to take on a more innovative role.

It was also suggested that operating foundations should take on a substitution role to guarantee their financing. This is due to the fact that administrations ever more frequently announce aid and subsidies for the implementation of actions that they themselves carried out traditionally, for example for the rehabilitation of drug addicts. The state commissions this task to non-profit entities and, therefore, the state acts in the same way as the private sector by hiring or outsourcing external services.

It is precisely this need for financing that prevents foundations from taking on a more innovative role which would contribute to the social change that many of them aim to achieve. The lack of resources means that the role they carry out is not exactly the role they aimed for. Moreover, the effectiveness of a role they play may be diminished by the lack of resources. The lack of professionalism or technical incapacity are also factors listed as causes that make it impossible for foundations to fulfil their roles.

Nonetheless, the competition established between the different foundations is also seen to have the potential to increase their effectiveness and, in fact, promote a greater fulfilment of the foundation's mission and, consequently, of the role for which they were created.

However, one of the key issues underlying the experts' contributions is the suggestion that there is no way to measure, either quantitatively and/or qualitatively, the extent to which foundations really fulfil the aforementioned roles.

Visions

The foundations interviewed set out various ideal scenarios of their vision of society. Foundations should support and represent the civil society before the public powers, acting as a counterweight to the private sector. The idea that foundations and the non-profit sector in general should act as a link or intermediary between the different sectors was also mentioned on numerous occasions. Some of the opinions voiced by interviewees when questioned about the ideal mission foundations should fulfil in a model or ideal society include:

> "Support and represent the civil society before the public authorities, acting as a counterweight to the private sector."

> "Social assistance requirements should be covered by foundations and not by the state."

> "Foundations should promote social and cultural values and should know how to channel private funds, thus encouraging more solidarity-minded societies."

> "The ideal role for a foundation is to be able to foresee the needs of the different groups for which it was created and propose innovative projects."

Foundations are not perceived to exist because society has failed or because it is not appropriately configured, but rather due to the need of civil society itself to participate in the actions that affect it. It is more a form of commitment or social co-responsibility on the part of the citizens.

As regards the relationship foundations should have with the other sectors (public, private, NGOs, civil society in general, etc.), the general feeling among the interviewees is that this relationship should be based – in all of the cases – on the principle that each party retains their autonomy. There should be a desire to cooperate between all parties, without aiming to claim more power over the rest of the sectors. At the same time, there should be a heightened interest by civil society to actively participate in all issues that concern it.

Regarding relationships between foundations and other NGOs, cooperation is viewed by the interviewees as the only way to achieve success. There should be more coordination between non-profit entities, given that – according to statements in interviews – there is too much dispersion and an absolute lack of common goals. Many of the interviewees believe that the task of the Association of Foundations could prove essential, but that at present they do not unite a sufficient number of entities. Once again, the heterogeneity of the sector acts against its best interests.

In relation to the models we used to frame our discussion of the visions of foundations, all the interviewees agree that the liberal model is the most appropriate for the development of the foundations (95.23 per cent). That is to say, the foundations must be an independent visible power, and offer alternatives to the mainstream, thereby safeguarding minorities. To the other extreme, we find the peripheral model (foundations are minor institutions, yet are ultimately worthwhile institutions as long as they do not challenge the status quo), that is widely rejected by the interviewees (85 per cent). They also agree to an extent with the social-democratic model (foundations should be part of a larger welfare system and have well coordinated relationships with the state in order to either complement or supplement state activities in meeting needs) (77.27 per cent), but add that this only works for social action oriented foundations.

A total of 63.63 per cent of the interviewees do not agree with a model which is controlled by the state, although many believe it to be part of the situation we are experiencing in present-day Spain, with its restrictive laws, complicated administrative procedures and strict and inflexible control 69.56 per cent support the corporatist model and 59.09 per cent support the business model.

With a view to confirming the results stated above regarding the models, the foundations were questioned about the following statements.

Foundations should have greater responsibility before the government   86.36 per cent of the interviewed foundations are completely against this idea.

Foundations are basically non-democratic institutions that have too many privileges
This matter raised a very high level of controversy because it was considered an ambiguous statement. Many believe that foundations are in fact non-democratic institutions but they do not think they enjoy too many privileges. 69.56 per cent support this statement.

Foundations should be more professional in the way they act   Only 8.6 per cent believe foundations already act in a sufficiently professional manner. It became clear that the lack of professionalism is one of the factors that will require the greatest effort on the part of all actors so as to improve the sector.

Foundations should spend a minimum percentage each year for the fulfilment of their activities (70 per cent stipulated in Spanish legislation)   Only 4.3 per cent believe that this should be different. The majority supports the notion that foundations should not consist of capital in idle hands as they were conceived originally. This idea is still present in some sectors of Spanish society, although the current legislation actively strives to avoid this occurring.

Foundations should only be constituted for limited periods of time 91.30 per cent do not agree with this statement. It is precisely their durability through time that makes the distinction greater between associations and foundations, in accordance with the Spanish laws.

Foundations are sufficiently represented in the political arena Only 4.3 per cent consider themselves to be well-represented. In fact, Law 30/1994 on Foundations foresaw the creation of a Higher Committee of Foundations, composed of different public entities and representatives of the foundation sector. However, it was never created and foundations currently call for the creation of this organisation. However, there are similar organisations in some Autonomous Communities.

Foundations have little influence in Spain 70.8 per cent consider this statement to be correct. Nonetheless, they believe it is due to the fact that they do not have a sufficient social basis to support their capacity to be more representative.

There are not enough foundations in Spain Opinions regarding this statement are curious to say the least, as Spain is one of the European countries with the highest number of registered foundations (approximately 6,000). However, only 16.6 per cent believe there are enough foundations, whilst the rest, 83.3 per cent, think there are not. One reason why respondents believe that there are enough foundations relates to the observation that some of the existing foundations do not carry out activities or are not operational. They believe it is necessary to remove or merge those foundations that are not fulfilling their original goals. This statement basically refers to the amount of old foundations (created over 100 years ago) that exist in Spain.

Foundations are very modern institutions 91.66 per cent think this is untrue, Spanish foundations will have to make a considerable effort in the coming years if they want to reach the same level as foundations in other countries. As a consequence, this will lead to some foundations ceasing activities, due to the increase in competition.

The public in general does not understand the role of foundations Only 8 per cent of the interviewees believe Spanish society understands the role of foundations and know they have a clear mission. Thus, one of the challenges the sector will have to face in forthcoming years will be to promote a greater presence and transparency before society.

Politicians do not understand what foundations can and cannot do   84.3 per cent agree with the opinion that politicians do not have a clear idea of the mission of foundations.

The leaders of the private sector and of foundations should work closer together Over 90 per cent agree with this statement. The possibilities of achieving funding for projects and of attaining a higher level of professionalism and efficiency between both sectors would increase, and companies would also fulfil the goal – a strong trend in forthcoming years – of social co-responsibility.

Europe and the Spanish foundations

There are more foundations carrying out their activities in Latin America – given the historical links – than there are within Europe. Nonetheless, there is a trend towards increasing the number of activities performed in collaboration with other EU countries. Foundations are undoubtedly encouraged by subsidies and the possibility of financing projects, rather than by a "European conscience", although there are some exceptions to this rule, for example Foundation Vodafone and Foundation ONCE. Most foundations interviewed are active on a national scale, although a small percentage is active on an international scale. However, none states that they are active on a European level.

Pursuant to the question of whether this will change in the future, a little less than half of the foundation representatives interviewed state that they will progressively start to develop activities with a pro-European trend, and the rest say they have not considered it. With the exception of those engaged in development cooperation, the financing of projects in other countries does not make up a large part of their budget. However, they do indicate that their aim is to increase their funding of these projects.

Foundations encounter many challenges when carrying out and financing international projects. Foundations for development cooperation underlined the need to promote long-lasting and self-sufficient development, to adapt projects to the needs of each country and to find non-profit partners in the countries in question. However, according to the interviewees there are many obstacles in playing a role internationally. It is very costly to fulfil the goal for which the project was created due to difficulties encountered in countries such as a lack of suitable infrastructure. Not only do foundations believe the follow-up and assessment procedures are very complex, but also once the project is completed, they find it costly to verify the number of beneficiaries, results obtained, etc. Interviewees from corporate foundations indicated that performing non-profit activities in particular countries is a more useful and cheaper marketing tool than a simple advertising campaign when aiming to demonstrate that the company is socially committed. All interviewees working on European or international projects stated that one of the main challenges was finding a partner to cooperate with. They deem the management of projects to be complicated. If more procedures, assessments and controls could be performed in source countries, many tasks could be simplified and deadlines reduced, thus resulting in increased efficiency.

Despite the challenges foundations face internationally, the opportunities to be had were also discussed. Entities that carry out international activities are held in high regard as they address the obstacles presented by the aforementioned difficulties. Thus they enjoy greater social prestige and appear more often in the media. Cross-border activity creates opportunities for foundations to increase their experiences and to contrast ways of working (benchmarking). As occurs in other sectors, exchanging experience and know-how between non-profit entities and other agents is always beneficial for both parties. Working via networks, will not only improve processes but could also cut foundations' costs and make them simpler. Foundations must start to get used to this procedure. This adaptation to a networked working-style is appearing more sluggishly than in the private sector, but it is occurring.

The lack of awareness among Spanish foundations of European issues is definitely undeniable. They do not appear to be affected by the workings of the EU, which is perceived as something distant and far-removed. New European Foundation initiatives are only likely to arise if progress is made in the European Statute for Foundations, if the European foundations association (the EFC) establishes more of a presence, and only if the foundations begin to perceive the EU as having an effective added value with a direct impact on them. However, another key issue is the securing of an explicit legal recognition of the role played both by Foundations and by the entities that compose the conglomerate of Social Economy as a whole.

The European issue seems to be an unresolved question, but it is widely acknowledged, as stated beforehand, that the Community dimension of Spanish foundations (at the least that of the large ones) will grow over the coming years.

Current developments and emerging issues

We find that when asked about how they see the horizon from here to ten years, interviewees concur in the belief that the sector will increase in number and size. This will partially be due to the new legislation, which will be more beneficial, and an increased awareness of philanthropy amongst companies, promoted by an increase in social responsibility, which will lead to the creation of foundations. Foundations will have more recognition and their role as an integrating agent will be vital.

However, on the other hand, they believe that there are already enough, or even too many, foundations in Spain and that this atomisation will lead to the closure of many foundations and the creation of larger and more powerful entities, something which will repeat itself at a European level.

There will also be a clear trend regarding the increase in the number of operating foundations, and the transformation of grant-making foundations into operating foundations. Furthermore, this is likely to lead to a debate on unfair competition between the non-profit and private sectors.

One issue that is clear is that the immediate and medium-term future will bring about the need for foundations to become professional, both as regards to staff and the performance of their activities, in order to fulfil more goals and to obtain, most importantly, greater recognition and social esteem.

For medium-operating foundations, Europe will entail a reduction of subsidies and a higher degree of competition. In general, there is a feeling of scepticism as regards the benefits of active participation in Europe, mainly due to the hindrances of working via networks and the aforementioned heterogeneity of the sector. However, large foundations see Europe as an opportunity to maintain their leadership and promote their actions internationally.

This will have the same consequences as in any other sector; the more professional and competitive foundations will survive over the rest. These foundations will take on their roles more efficiently and improve their role in society, although this will obviously occur gradually.

Above all, the key challenges and opportunities that Spanish foundations have to face include the following:

First, they have to better communicate to society in general who they are, what they do and what their mission is, thereby reducing the lack of information and unawareness. This could be considered the most important goal for the forthcoming years, as this lack of information and unawareness in society implies that the sector remains a mystery; that policies are not adapted to needs; measures needed for their development are not implemented; insufficient donations are received, and that, in all, their work becomes more difficult. In Spain, foundations are often in the news for scandals or malpractice, but it is unusual or almost impossible to find information on results or fulfilment of goals.

Second, there needs to be greater inter-foundation cooperation. The isolation many foundations experience makes them waste a lot of time and effort – both economic and personal – in performing tasks that are much simpler when carried out collectively. Optimising the existing resources for all foundations could mitigate this extra effort that has to be carried out individually, for example regarding applications before public administrations. In Spain there is a low degree of inter-foundation collaboration. Certain initiatives are promoted by foundation associations with the creation of thematic groups in terms of the scope of action, but at present their development is very sluggish. A code of practice could be created by the foundations themselves. In Spain there is no code of practice for foundations given that the actual laws establish guidelines quite systematically and appropriately. However, foundations would welcome the creation of their own code of practice especially in order to avoid cases of corruption and malpractice, which damage the whole sector and generally grab the attention of the media.

The promotion of greater transparency is a salient challenge. The Spanish legislation strengthens foundations' accountability and establishes that accounts should be available to the public. However, there is still much work to be done given that complying with administrative procedures is one thing but the general exposure of the actions and activities performed by each foundation is something else entirely. Attention should be paid to a new phenomenon that is appearing as an instrument to promote transparency: social auditing. Foundations that have started to use it even as a measure for quality management are ahead in improving foundation management and implementing mechanisms traditionally used in companies in non-profit entities.

The professionalisation of volunteers (in terms of both management and training) will be one of the main issues to tackle in forthcoming years, as more than goodwill will be needed. In many cases volunteers will be expected to have basic knowledge, and advanced knowledge in others, in order to carry out their task in non-profit entities. Similarly, there is a need for more board member training. The new law is now stricter with regards to the mission and responsibilities of Patrons in Foundations, it seems that previously this went unnoticed. This is an emerging issue. Foundations cannot be solely in professional hands. The Board cannot be just a gallery of the illustrious without a clear role. Some of the roles they must assume are: select professionals, define and evaluate the mission, create a strategic plan, control the budget, supervise the director's management, fundraise, insert the foundation in society. Control techniques and tools to ensure efficiency and good quality management, as implemented in the private sector, should be applied to these entities so as to professionalise management.

Improving the legitimacy of foundations (by strengthening their social basis) is also a challenge. Foundations should become rooted in society, and to do so they must have a greater social base in terms of their mission and activities. Achieving a stable dialogue with the public powers may be important in this respect. This lobbying task should be performed systematically by foundation associations or any other interlocutor that appears. This is the only way to properly defend the sector's interests and promote greater cohesion from plurality.

Conclusion

Foundations have a long tradition in Spain as they have existed for many centuries. Although foundations have quite a clear idea of their role in society, society is not as aware of them. Much work must be done in this sense; the challenge of better communication must be a priority in the forthcoming years. This is the only way for this sector to find more opportunities to develop its activities, encounter less obstacles and distrust, and find more support for its projects. At the same time, public administrations will also become more aware of the need for policies that are adapted to the sector's requirements and its specific nature, relieving interventionism, excessive bureaucracy and deficient fiscal benefits. Transparency and the reporting of the use made of funds, as well as the attainment of goals, with specific results, should be among the top priorities foundations set themselves.

The dominant social trend involves co-responsibility and participation, thus the sector must be able to answer society's needs and have the free initiative to answer present and/or latent needs. To do so, it seems essential that foundations professionalise their management, implementing techniques used in private companies and guaranteeing the quality of their services. Nonetheless, companies also seem more interested in participating directly in the execution of non-profit projects as a means for social co-responsibility. This joint collaboration and action should be encouraged progressively to benefit both parties.

As regards their role as rival to the state, the study has shown that the role of complementarity takes priority over others, although this does not seem to be due to the fact that the state has failed or is configured unsuitably, but rather because the existence of non-profit entities is a form of participation for civil society. The role of foundations, in particular as an independent power that provides alternatives to the main trends and safeguards minorities based on professionalism and efficiency, is the main challenge for the coming years.

When speaking of Europe, Spanish foundations' individualism and heterogeneity is even clearer. It is hard enough to find common points in Spain and issues become even more complicated from a European point of view. Many foundations are completely unaware of the sector outside Spanish borders, which may be due to the excess of obstacles to be addressed: fiscal, legal harmonisation, etc. However, there is a trend towards change in this respect encouraged by the need to attract European funds. The enlargement of the EU generates uncertainty rather than perspectives of change in the sector. Nonetheless, Spanish foundations will have to adapt to this new reality of a common European space, which seems to extend beyond the concept of the single market.

References

Cabra de Luna, M.A. (1998) *El Tercer Sector y las fundaciones en España hacia el nuevo milenio*, Madrid: Escuela Libre Editorial.

Schlüter, A., Then, V. and Walkenhorst, P. (eds) (2001) *Foundations in Europe*, London: Directory of Social Change.

Vázquez, I.D., Allende, J.C. and García, I.G. (2001) *La Realidad de las Fundaciones en España: Análisis sociológico, psicosocial y económico*, Santander: Fundación Marcelino Botín.

21 Sweden

Filip Wijkström

Introduction

Sweden has a long and rich foundation history, but foundations are also found in the midst of a number of challenging societal transformations. Excluding the absolutely smallest foundations, there exist some 15,000 larger ones today. I will focus on the approximately 11,500 larger public benefit foundations. Swedish foundations can be grant-making or operating and administered either autonomously by a board of their own or via another organization's board. They represent an important element of the nonprofit sector economy and their economic importance must be underlined. However, foundations are not only of economic interest. The dominant role for Swedish foundations seems to be one of *complementarity* to the public sector. Foundations directly *substituting* public welfare arrangements are less frequent. Other roles discussed refer to foundations as *organizational tools* and *governance instruments* for economic control and ideological governance. Foundations are often created by wealthy people and rooted in a more conservative or liberal tradition. Still, large segments of the foundation population today can be understood as *embedded in a social-democratic vision*. A number of *alternative visions* are examined, with the *liberal vision* emerging strongest among these.

A profile of foundations in Sweden

Historical development

Economic surplus is crucial to explaining the existence of foundations. Since the industrialization period, economic wealth has accumulated and been retained nationally. It was initially private but, as a result of the Social-Democrats' dominance in government and subsequent high-tax regimes during the twentieth century, this wealth also found its way into the public sector. Three other principal historical developments of importance will be outlined briefly.

The Reformation led to a somewhat different situation in Sweden compared to many other countries. When a religious monopoly was granted to the new national church in 1593, the only major independent force outside of the nation state (i.e. the Catholic Church) was forced to leave the country. Elsewhere, the Catholic Church and its various educational and care institutions have been involved in the development of society. The Catholic Church and a number of associated fraternities and monastic orders were also active in Sweden at least since the twelfth century (Härdelin 1998). Throughout the Reformation, all social and charitable institutions of the Catholic Church were transferred to the Swedish Crown. These were the institutional seeds – in education, social services and health care – which were to become part and parcel of the young nation state, and later also integrated into the welfare state.

During the rise of the institutional 'social democratic' welfare state regime in the second half of the twentieth century, social rights were extended to the new middle classes in Sweden (Esping-Andersen 1990: 27). General welfare programmes were developed to satisfy all groups and delivered by the public sector. Only in a few limited welfare fields, such as the rehabilitation of drug-abusers or adult education, are major providers other than public bodies found (Lundström and Wijkström 1997; Stenius 1999). Sometimes, foundations and other nonprofit actors are described as an avant-garde (for an example, see Wisselgren 2000). The most obvious picture today, however, of private nonprofit institutions in welfare provision is one of the small marginal providers of either limited services or economic support. This marginal or complementary position seems to be the result of two processes. The first refers to older institutions that, from an earlier central position, were turned into marginal providers. The other process refers to education or social welfare foundations created later on, when a comprehensive public welfare system is already established. These new actors were created as an alternative to an already dominant welfare state system and charters, structures and boards are adapted accordingly. We thus have a situation where either earlier foundation arrangements are transformed, or later foundations have developed, into marginal actors.

Finally, the foundation is a nonprofit organizational form. The other major form found in the Swedish civil society is the modern association, often referred to as the popular movement association (*folkrörelseföreningen*). During the twentieth century, a popular movement tradition has emerged as the most dominant civil society paradigm. It has in many situations replaced other traditions as *the* form in which to organize nonprofit or voluntary activity and foundations have even been understood as being used in opposition to the popular movements. Often, this understanding has had to do with the people or values associated with foundations seen as the power instruments, or insignias, of the wealthier segments of the population. Also the non-democratic and member-less character of the foundation are viewed negatively by government agencies, in public debate and as well as in the legal arena (Wijkström and Lundström 2002; Wijkström, Einarsson and Larsson 2004).

Legal issues

The most important and recent legal event for foundations is the introduction of a Foundation Law (1996: 1220), understood as a codification of earlier case law and legal doctrine. A foundation exists only if: (1) an asset or property (2) has been set aside from the donor(s) (3) to be administrated separately and permanently (4) with the aim to serve a specific purpose. A Swedish foundation is described as 'self-owning' (*självägande*) and has no owners or members. A foundation must have a board and the word *stiftelse* in its name. Foundations can be administered through one of two arrangements: an autonomous board (*egen förvaltning*) or through the board of another institution (*anknuten förvaltning*), for example a municipality, a bank or an organization like the Red Cross. The law also requires larger foundations or enterprise foundations to register with their County Administrative Board (*länsstyrelsen*).

To receive tax-exempt status in Sweden, a foundation must belong to one of two categories: (1) charitable foundations or (2) the 'Catalogue'. To be considered charitable, a foundation must comply with three prerequisites: (a) the purpose should be considered a 'qualified' public good; (b) about 80 per cent of its income over a five-year period should be spent; and (c) its main activity should be in line with the purpose stated. *Qualified* purposes include health care, the strengthening of the national defence, relief work among the needy, to further child care and upbringing or education, promotion of scientific research, and the furthering of cooperation between the Scandinavian countries (Law 1947: 576). The 'Catalogue', finally, contains a number of institutions, for example the Nobel Foundation, with special tax privileges.

The law introduces several foundation types. The main form (*allmän stiftelse*) covers some 9,000 of the larger foundations. A special form recognized is the new fund-raising foundation (*insamlingsstiftelse*). Unlike all other foundations, no initial donation is needed. A public call for donations suffices for it to carry legal capacity. Two other special types are the pension and personnel foundations (*tryggandestiftelserna*) found in a separate law since 1967. A pension foundation (*pensionsstiftelse*) is set up by an employer with the exclusive purpose of safeguarding a pension commitment to the employees, while a personnel foundation (*personalstiftelse*) is created for staff recreational purposes. Also recognized is the collective-agreement foundation (*kolllektivavtalsstiftelse*), based on an agreement between the employers and the trade unions, with the purpose to contribute to the economic security of the employees. Neither of these labour-market foundations are primarily set up for 'public good' purposes and thus are not included in the present study.

Foundations operating some kind of enterprise are particularly mentioned in the law. They are required to register and have also been the topic of legal debate (see Olsson 1996 for an excellent overview). Approximately 2,000 Swedish foundations were in 2002 considered by the County Administration Boards to be enterprise foundations (*näringsdrivande stiftelser*). This form comes close to the international understanding of an operating foundation, although there is a difference. An enterprise foundation can, as defined by Olsson (1996), operate or be the owner of any kind of commercial activity or enterprise. An enterprise foundation will only be defined as an operating foundation if the enterprise also is related to, or part of the purpose of the foundation. Our estimate is that there were some 1,500 operating foundations in 2002.

Empirical profile

The exact number of foundations in Sweden in the early twenty-first century remains unknown, but we have identified some 15,000 larger foundations. Already in the early twentieth century, 12,000 to 13,000 foundations existed, and by 1976 the total estimate was 51,000 foundations with a combined wealth of €2.4 billion. About 48,000 were classified as charitable (*ideella*) while the rest were 'family' or labour-market foundations. A later survey found 16,169 foundations registered with the tax authorities in 1990 (SOU 1995: 56–57).

In December 2002, data on nearly more than 15,000 foundations were imported from the registers of the Swedish County Administration Boards into a research database at the Stockholm School of Economics where the data have been substantially improved. Total 2001 book-value assets for the foundations were close to €27 billion. Rough estimates of actual wealth (valued at market prices instead of book value) run into at least twice that amount (Birath *et al.* 2001: 11), indicating total foundation wealth surpassing €50 billion. The wealth of the smaller foundations is still unknown but it is unlikely that it is larger than €1.2 billion (Wijkström 2001a, 2001b).[1]

The Swedish foundation population can be divided into three major sub-populations along two main dividing lines (Table 21.1). The *first* line (horizontal) is drawn between public good foundations and more narrowly defined labour-market foundations. Approximately 3,000 labour-market foundations control substantial wealth, close to €12 billion (SEK120 billion), representing nearly 44 per cent of total foundation wealth. The *second* dividing line (vertical) is separating autonomous foundations from those 6,000 foundations administered through attached administration. Fields with many attached foundations are education, research and social services. However numerous, their combined assets represent only some 20 per cent of the foundation wealth, labour-market foundations excluded (Wijkström and Einarsson 2004).

Table 21.1 The Swedish foundation population in 2002

	Autonomous administration		Attached administration	
	Number	Assets (mkr)	Number	Assets (mkr)
Normal	3,571	94,373	5,971	30,677
Fund-raising	352	556	57	153
Operating	1,506	27,051	40	654
Public good	5,429	121,980	6,068	31,484
Pension	2,391	111,351	–	–
Personnel	586	2,086	–	–
Collective A.	20	5,134	–	–
Labour-market	2,997	118,571	–	–
Total	8,426	240,551	6,068	31,484

Nearly 75 per cent of all existing foundations and more than 80 per cent of the assets in the early twenty-first century originate in the twentieth century. During the twentieth century, research became the most popular foundation field. Some 20 per cent of all new foundations established are research foundations, with combined assets representing 45 per cent of total public good foundation wealth. Between 1980–2002 alone, approximately 3,800 new foundations were created with a combined book value of some €5.2 billion. The assets found in research foundations set up during these years well surpass 50 per cent of the new capital. There are still some 2,500 social service foundations in existence from previous periods, but they only hold some 15 per cent of total wealth; similar to the field of education with some 1,600 foundations. However, an interesting development can be traced in education where there appears to be a downward trend in terms of the relative number of foundations as well as in total foundation wealth. But these crude aggregated numbers hide a more qualitative shift; where an increasing number of operating foundations in primary, secondary as well as higher education were created in the 1980s and 1990s (Wijkström and Einarsson 2004).

Foundations of the state

During the 1990s, the unrestricted number of appropriation foundations (*anslagsstiftelser*) set up by public sector bodies and the political battles around the wage-earner-fund foundations (*löntagarfondsstiftelser*) have led to growing irritation and increased debate around the role of foundations in relation to government.

The appropriation foundation was discussed as a special form prior to the foundation law. It would not require an initial endowment to sustain its purpose but was instead to rely on annual grants or appropriations.

Although never instated, a number of operating foundations already have this character, many established by public sector bodies. This form has subsequently been seen to decrease the governmentability of government. Understood to limit the possibilities of new governments to implement their politics, a number of state agencies issued recommendations against government use of foundations in general, and the appropriation form in particular (Riksrevisionsverket 1990; SOU 1994; Statskontoret 1997; Riksdagens Revisorer 2000). These foundations were not considered flexible enough for a political system, which is a development similar to the one reported for Norway (Lorentzen 2004).

The wage-earner funds were established in 1984 to transfer profits from large and successful corporations. The creation of these funds by a Social-Democratic government met with severe criticism. The right-wing government in power during 1991–1994 dissolved the funds and almost SEK2 billion were transferred to a number of new foundations. Two were earlier public sector universities turned into appropriation foundations. Official reasons given by the conservative government were that foundations allowed for a more flexible way to organize and operate, and that the foundation form already was well tested in distributing resources for research. Later, the independent position of the foundations and the fact that they were so tightly bound by their original missions were argued to secure stability and a long-term perspective. The new foundations have been hotly contested and, in 1994, the newly elected Social-Democratic government met with foundation representatives. The aim was to secure a promise to contribute resources to compensate for cut-downs to come in the research budget. None of the boards were at that time willing to comply (Riksdagens Revisorer 2000).

The debate around the government's use of foundations stands at the very centre of a transformation and shift of responsibilities in society where both the role and governance of foundations are salient. The use, influence and resources of foundations have also spurred increased activity in re-drawing the map of responsibilities, for example in the academic world (Wijkström and Einarsson 2004).

Roles of Swedish foundations

In general, foundations do not have a strong common identity in Sweden, in line also with how Lorentzen (2004) describes the situation in neighbouring Norway. Where a foundation 'belongs' is instead described in different ways and it is also necessary to acknowledge the existence of *multiple roles*. Foundations are often associated with either (a) a *type of institution* (museum or school), or with (b) a *particular activity*, e.g. fund-raising or grant-making. Sometimes they are understood as (c) *part of the same field as the recipients* of grants or services. For example, the Association for the Visually Impaired (SRF) Foundation is clearly posited within the movement for the visually impaired. This is true also for The Gustav V Foundation, a royal foundation distributing cash-grants to youth organizations, as described by its secretary Lennart Elbe:

> We are definitely one actor among others in our field, the youth sector. The most important objective for us is to support nonprofit youth organizations. We are on the same half of the playing field as the nonprofit organizations engaged in those matters. I would be very sad if we are not seen as a part of the nonprofit youth sector.

Foundations are sometimes also associated with a particular 'family' or group of other organizations. A family metaphor is for example used in the case of the SRF, when they describe the foundation as part of the 'SRF Family', where the other two family members are the IRIS Corporation owned by the foundation and the 'Mother' Association itself (SRF 2000).

Complement or substitute?

A surprisingly strong common picture emerged during our interviews, where foundations were described as a complement to the (welfare) state or municipality arrangements. None of the other roles received the same level of general support. The distinction between the complementarity and substitution roles often proved to be ambiguous and controversial, in particular when tracing older foundations over time. Foundations in Sweden are not, as a rule, allowed to change their original mission. On the contrary, unless the mission is considered fulfilled or impossible to fulfil, the original one must be adhered to. Older foundations might, for example, very well have had an innovative role. Over time, however, the foundation and its originally innovative operations can be understood both as a complement or a substitute in relation to later welfare state arrangements. Changes to how we label the role of foundations, then, are not dependent on the operations of the foundations, but rather on what has happened in the wider society. Whether we understand the role of the foundation as, for example, innovative could thus better be understood more as a reflection of the changes in the society *around* the foundation, rather than a particular character or role of the foundation. Thus, a foundation's role in society can shift over time although it does not change at all itself.

The role of complementarity also appeared to be the most generally preferred choice of the interviewees. Foundations were described, metaphorically speaking, as a 'lubricant or oil in the machinery' (*olja i systemet*) where machinery indicates larger society, or as something 'extra to top up with' (*grädde på moset*). Foundations were also described as 'filling gaps' in society's fabric, or identifying shortcomings in the existing system. In these two latter cases, the role could also be understood as one of innovation.

The substitution theme was on the minds of many people interviewed. Several had recently been discussing the obligations of their foundation on the one hand, and that of government on the other. Sometimes, the discussions included elements of a critique of public sector reforms and government policies. There was in some cases a feeling of unjust treatment, of the politicians changing the rules of the game, and some pointed to a more general policy shift whereby the welfare state was retreating from earlier responsibilities, leaving the foundations – set up to complement but not to replace the welfare state – to assume a larger and more burdensome task than intended.

Respondents meant that the local tax authorities (LTAs) more actively than before have tried to find new objects to tax. The LTAs have the power to enforce fiscal legislation from the 1940s in a tougher and more narrowly interpreted way than earlier. This increased attention seems to be an indirect and probably unintended effect of the new law and the registers set up (see above). Through these registers, the LTAs are able to extend their reach further into the foundation world, as one person expressed it. This is particularly clear in fields like social services for people in need or research and higher education, where it was felt by some of our respondents that the other hand of the government – the tax authorities – is reducing the available resources of the foundations and also *de facto* trying to more narrowly define their degrees of freedom.

The situation confronting some Swedish foundations today is described as somewhat paradoxical. Many representatives see the foundation as a complement to more general welfare arrangements. At the same time, a recent trend is identified, where they are expected to take over or replace what is understood to be government or municipal responsibilities. For some, this development represents a clear conflict of interest in itself. However, foundations who are indifferent or at least not necessarily negative to these new substitution expectations also seem to be frustrated. At the same time as they are expected to do more, they also experience a tougher tax climate. It was expressed by some that these policy changes were not really coordinated or even intended, but nonetheless pose a challenge which they report difficulties in addressing.

Organizational tools and instruments of power

Some clearly viewed foundations as organizational tools, which is one of the most interesting findings. Foundations as organizational building blocks seem to at least partly contradict the practice of furnishing foundations with some kind of personality or identity, to treat and discuss foundations as if they have an independent 'life'. Lars Jonsson viewed both the Foundation for the Visually Impaired and its business group as means to an end, rather than having an identity or vision of their own. This view is also supported by board member Dan Berggren. In a similar vein, Katarina Olsson also pointed to the use of foundations within a movement or organization to separate out more business-like operations, for example conference centres, so as not to risk the tax-exempt status of other operations of the organization. In a similar understanding, Marianne af Malmborg in our interview stresses the use of foundations to secure assets for a certain cause. This is done to protect them from misuse, but also to make sure the resources are used for that particular purpose and not appropriated or taxed away by government.

Close to this instrument role is the idea of governance foundations (*maktstiftelser*). Several respondents immediately recognized this role and even put names on such foundations associated with famous and wealthy Swedish industrial or trading families, for example the Wallenberg, Axel Johansson or Kamprad families. These foundations are sometimes understood to be part of a corporate governance or control system through their ownership of stock, a Swedish practice discussed recently both in the national and international business press (Brown-Humes 2004; Nachemson-Ekwall 2005; Steneberg 2004). The CEO of *Sparbankstiftelsen Nya*, offered us an example of this governance role:

> The foundation's primary mission is as an owner of *Föreningssparbanken* to make sure that the old values and ideals of the old savings bank sector survive and develop. This means that we first and foremost are an owner foundation. This is something that the public is not always aware of. They often think that our purpose is to hand out grants. But that is only our secondary role.

Governance foundations are often understood to exercise their control in an economic sense, which is also the most common understanding in Sweden. But sometimes, this role of control and power is exercised in more of an ideological sense. For example, the three foundations, set up to own and control the liberal UNT newspaper (*Upsala Nya Tidning*), were created when the founder of the newspaper, Axel Johansson, wanted to secure its continued existence and liberal profile, even after he no longer could function in this capacity himself. In our set of case studies, the SRF foundation identifies with this role most clearly. One important function was initially to receive gifts and endowments. When the foundation was set up in 1954, it was seen as a strategic issue to take care of the assets and to secure these resources for the organization (SRF 2000: 27). However, as explained by Per-Arne Krantz on the foundation board:

> Today, through the foundation as 100 per cent owner [of the IRIS corporation], we have an impact on where the company is going, a capacity to carry through corrections and exercise control through the decision on what people we shall have on the board of the corporation.

Redistribution of wealth

The argument could easily be made that the people establishing foundations in general have more resources than those benefiting from these
foundations. Few cases present themselves where the recipients have more
money or resources than the founder. Whether or not these people who
benefit from the foundations in their turn are better or worse off than
other people in the world is another issue, as is the question of whether
this was the intention behind the foundation.

A strong negative attitude towards charity is clearly important when discussing the role of re-distribution of wealth in Sweden. Lars Jonsson
immediately reacted against the positive way to frame this practice and the
phrase, 're-distribution of wealth':

> I would never have expressed it in that way, but there is some truth to
> it. This is very much of a top-down approach where a wealthy benefac-
> tor donates his money to a foundation that can be used for the poor
> people. This is not the way I would like to see changes in society, or a
> more equal distribution of wealth, come about.

Also interesting is whether re-distribution of wealth is an intended role or
not:

> This [re-distribution of wealth] might not be the primary purpose
> when establishing a foundation; that the intention of the donor is to
> re-distribute his or her wealth. I do not believe so. But if you look
> strictly only at the economic reality of the foundation, this might very
> well be the case. But this is not the guiding principle behind a dona-
> tion, nor is it an argument for more favourable tax treatment of
> foundations.
>
> (Richard Arvidsson)

> If a very rich person makes the donation, a re-distribution of wealth is
> in the nature of the transaction in itself. And it is this re-distribution
> that constitutes the basis for tax-exemption for foundations. This is
> the reason why they are tax-exempt; it is a way of paying your taxes.
> The law requires some kind of re-distribution to grant the foundation
> tax-exemption.
>
> (Jan Lindman)

Innovation, change, preservation and remembrance

On the one hand, a foundation could be innovative only by being set up
in a new field or by using new methods. On the other hand, some respondents referred to the foundations themselves working in an innovative

way, dealing with their mission and field of operation in new, inventive ways. Foundations were further said to be better suited for innovation than other actors since they were quicker and more flexible than public sector institutions in addressing new issues or problems. Marianne af Malmborg also meant that the innovative dimension of a foundation might be enhanced, since foundations can concentrate in a very narrow field or on a specific issue, without any wider responsibilities. In comparison to business actors, foundations were said to have more stamina. Rolf Kjellman made a comparison between a foundation and a traditional company:

> If the investment [of a company] is not successful within 2–3 years, it will be discontinued, while for example the Wallenberg Foundation [i.e. The Knut and Alice Wallenberg Foundation] in their investments in science and research is an excellent example of endurance in the longer run.

The innovation role was almost as positively understood as when discussing foundations as complements. Sometimes these roles also seemed to overlap, for example when the innovative role was described as 'filling gaps' or identifying shortcomings that should be taken care of. This language also signals a complementary role. Research foundations were expected to have the innovative role built into their very raison d'être. In an interesting version of the innovative role, Gunnar Hambraeus, chairman of the Scandinavia-Japan Sasakawa Foundation, mentioned the transfer of knowledge and cultural patterns between these two regions as one important task for this particular foundation but otherwise our respondents gave us very few examples of innovative foundations.

Related to the role of innovation is social or political change. A handful of our respondents agreed with the suggestion that this could be a role for foundations. As an example, Lennart Elbe said their role in the foundation sometimes was to try to create opinion, and to put pressure on local politicians in the field of voluntary youth work. But even more people said they could not see this as a main role for foundations. In general, social or political change was instead associated with associations, in particular with the popular movements. Foundations are thus in general better understood as 'carriers of social continuity, not change', as expressed by Lorentzen (2004: 41).

About half of our respondents could associate foundations with the preservation of values and traditions. The foundations taking this role can, for example, have some similarities with another role – the establishment of 'free zones' (see below). There is a major difference, however, when listening to our respondents' examples. The establishment of free zones can refer to any kind of community or value system, also new or foreign ones. But the preservation role relates to values and traditions that have for long existed in Swedish society but are for one reason or another threatened or fading away. Carl-Olof Nilsson used the image of the last bastion to fall:

> I would say preserve values, but I would like to sharpen that formulation a little. In a society where values age fast it can be important to have institutions or organizations that are able to safeguard their survival. Using foundations can be one way to do this. There are several lifestyle associations that have a hard time getting funds today, the temperance movement for example, but it would be much easier if they had access to a foundation. I mean, the foundation is one of the last bastions to fall.

Foundations are often set up in memory of a family member lost or to commemorate a private anniversary. This role was not originally included in our list of roles, but was spontaneously mentioned when we asked for other roles for foundations. The foundation could be established in memory of oneself when it is time to pass on or in memory of one's parents. This is not a way to preserve traditions or values, but rather a tradition in itself, like the use of tombstones in a burial site. Whether a foundation should be understood as a vehicle primarily to preserve a personal memory or for example to replace government is indeed difficult. The interpretation depends on the way we frame our understanding of what a foundation role is and I chose to interpret the answers of our respondents as indicating a *role of remembrance.*

Pluralism or establishment of free zones

Foundations do not, in general, have built-in correctives to change their values or operations, to adapt and change their ideology in a response to a changing world, where their religion or political agenda would be the only existing or dominant one. It is therefore difficult, except in a very small number of truly pluralistic foundations, to find a role like pluralism adhered to by individual foundations.

A single foundation can be established within a firm liberal political ideological framework to preserve and develop the liberal press. This could be done in an attempt to counteract an expansion or dominance by social-democratic newspapers. This foundation is not however set up primarily to promote pluralism, but to enhance and strengthen the liberal voice. As long as social-democratic newspapers exist, a liberal foundation contributes to pluralism. But if the social-democratic press would disappear to be replaced only by other liberal newspapers, this foundation would no longer be supporting pluralism but rather be part of a liberal hegemony. The same logic is also true for most religious schools and foundations promoting alternative pedagogical methods, for example in kindergartens.

Instead, the role of pluralism seems to be relevant to discuss, at least in Sweden, only for foundations *as a group*. When it comes to most other roles it is possible to discuss the role of an individual foundation, be it as substitution, innovation or instrument of control, without taking into account the wider population. This seems not to be the case when we talk about pluralism. Instead of pluralism, a role perhaps better used to describe this phenomenon is that of using foundations to establish free zones. Foundations are used to create openings for alternative ideologies, methods, or ways to reflect or operate. This role does not demand the creation of the foundation to be based in a quest for pluralism, but rather in the intention to set up an institution to support or guard a particular community or to maintain certain values.

About half of the respondents in our study could see or identify this free-zone role as one performed by foundations. Mikael Wiman mentioned the existence and expansion in Sweden of both Catholic and Muslim schools in the form of foundations as possible expressions of this role. In a special version, the use of foundations can be seen as establishing a space in society, free from both market and state, as expressed by the *Antroposofiska Sällskapet*:

> The Society wants to defend the time-honoured free zone that always has been open for the popular movements through the possibility to establish foundations and associations. . . . For the part of the Society, the foundation form has been the most appropriate.
>
> (Ds 1992: 70–71)[2]

Visions of Swedish foundations

The idea of foundations as elements in larger visions was crucial in the research, but was also the most complicated part of the interviews. The borders between roles and visions are often blurred. The challenge could be formulated as to whether to understand visions as something inherent in the character of the foundation, thus *leading up* to a situation where they assume particular roles, or if these visions are more the *analytical tools* derived from the roles of the foundations. We might also need to distinguish between two approaches. Visions can be of interest as they might appear *in one particular foundation*, but foundations held together *as a population* can also be assumed to have, or to be part of, a certain vision. In the latter case, the challenge is how to aggregate something like a vision of society for a group of foundations.

Several respondents expressed doubts as to whether the average founder really had such a grandiose agenda as a vision for society. 'They just wanted to do something good for society' or 'He just wanted to be remembered after he died', were comments received. I would still like to argue that many Swedish foundations, on a more implicit level, might be understood as part of (or embedded in) a wider Social-Democratic system. Some of the discussions on the roles of foundations were framed in such a language, although no explicit reference to any over-arching vision was made. In this section, however, foundations are discussed and understood mainly as key ingredients in a liberal civil society tradition, but it is also necessary to address the use of foundations in the establishment and defence of *small pockets of minor or alternative visions.*

Foundations with clearly expressed larger visions are, according to Mikael Wiman, usually small and isolated. Other respondents gave examples of smaller and more recent foundations. Their missions often include some kind of alternative vision of what society could or should be, as if in opposition to the current situation. The purpose of the Foundation A Non-smoking Generation (*Stiftelsen En Rökfri Generation*) established in 1978, is to combat the use of tobacco.[3] Another example is the Foundation Women Can (*Stiftelsen Kvinnor Kan*) established in 1982. The explicit aim is to show how women's values and knowledge can improve and reinvigorate society, with the overall ambition being to work for women to achieve a fair share of power.[4]

According to Henning Isoz, a group of foundations where the ideological or political vision often stands out clearly are newspaper or publishing foundations. As discussed earlier in the section on roles, the daily newspaper UNT in Uppsala is such an example. Mikael Wiman also specifically mentioned the use of foundations within the Rudolf Steiner tradition as an example of foundations as part of a larger vision. Other respondents referred to religious foundations. Carl-Olof Nilsson, for example, explained that their foundation is firmly based on a Christian value system with an ambition to carry those values into society. Foundations associated with the cooperative movement were also mentioned, as well as foundations attached to the market-economy ideology. Jan Lindman spoke about the KAW foundation (the major foundation within the Wallenberg family sphere) as a foundation where the vision is the well-being of the nation (see also Hoppe *et al.* 1993).

In some interviews, more explicit elements or fragments of a liberal vision were present. This was the only, and certainly the most elaborate and coherent, larger alternative ideological framework presented explicitly to us. In particular one of our respondents helped us to pull the bits and pieces together to form a more coherent picture, here used to frame the discussion. Richard Arvidsson viewed foundations and the legislation surrounding them as part of a larger system and the basic story is very much one of liberal coinage. The dominating vision in Sweden can still be described as a classical social-democratic vision. Government and municipalities bear the overall power and responsibility in a number of welfare areas. This power and responsibility runs all through the regulatory and legislative systems, via the funding of the services (through taxes) down to the actual provision of services. On all of these levels, government and public sector bodies are the only relevant actors. In this model, the role of foundations is inferior or marginal. The language (as visible in practice and regulations) in which foundations are framed is thus one of complementarity.

Arvidsson argued that this situation now is changing, at least partly because of Sweden's EU membership. The Swedish welfare state may have to withdraw or retreat from a number of earlier assumed responsibilities which it, according to the argument, will not be able to keep since this would require a high-tax regime not in line with the other EU countries. The reduction of services will, partly, have to be met by increased foundation activity, not only in a complementary function but also in direct substitution of earlier government arrangements. The development was compared to the American situation, where foundations are much more active both in financing and operating welfare services. A development like this would in a next step also require tax reductions, to be able to finance the increased responsibilities assigned to foundations, as argued by Arvidsson. Foundations must be granted larger tax benefits and the possibilities to operate must be expanded. The general level of income tax must also be reduced in this model and the will to donate private money encouraged instead of distributing available resources through taxes (see also Braunerhjelm and Skogh 2004).

Conclusion

Foundations offer an interesting but challenging alternative to government tax or market solutions for the (re-)distribution of wealth. Foundations are further used in the provision of welfare services outside the public sector, and might be understood in line with a more liberal tradition. The popular movement form, with open democratic member-based associations, is today the dominant civil society framework in Sweden. In combination with a high-tax regime and the lion's share of welfare services provided by the public sector, this tradition might be seen as a key element in a social-democratic vision of society.

The dissolution of the wage-earner funds and the establishment by government of a number of foundations as non-public entities, for example in culture, research and higher education discussed earlier, could be described as a form of state philanthropy (*statsfilantropi*). At the same time, an increased use of foundations in the provision of welfare might call for more private donations. Also a new role for large corporations is being discussed in Sweden today, for example in the recent debate on Corporate Social Responsibility (CSR) and sometimes foundations are used. This development might be considered as a wave of private new philanthropy (*nyfilantropi*). These two developments could be viewed as part of a larger change in society, where earlier roles of foundations are renegotiated within an experienced wider liberal or conservative shift during the final decades of the twentieth century.

I stress the connection between a certain political or ideological vision and a particular organizational form. This is an over-simplified story with a number of clear exceptions and the evidence is of somewhat piecemeal character. Consciously stretching the analysis further and being slightly more speculative than our data can sustain, I am however confident that the foundation form represents a challenge to established civil society policy and thinking in Sweden. It also offers a transformational vehicle in the current re-negotiation of the roles of different sectors in society. In its very form, but also in the practice found in many foundations, this legal institution differs not only from available for-profit solutions or public bodies, but also from traditional popular movement associations.

Notes

1 This is a maximum estimate based on 50,000 Swedish foundations in total, with each of the 35,000 small foundations (50,000 − 15,000 larger foundations) with assets of a maximum book value of SEK350,000 each.

2 Med den konservatism som ofta finns inom statlig/kommunal förvaltning respektive det rigorösa skatteregelsystem som finns för aktiebola har det inte varit möjligt att skapa den nödvändiga och relativt stora kapitalbildning som i många fall behövts för att bygga upp de antroposofiskt orienterade allmännyttiga verksamheterna ... Genom stiftelseformen vill vi vad beträffar produktionsmedlen komma bort från både privatkapitalismen och den statliga ägandeformen. (Remissvar, Ds 1992: 36, 70–71)

3 *Att bekämpa bruket av tobak, särskilt att påverka barn och ungdomar att aldrig börja röka.*

4 *Att visa hur kvinnors värderingar och kunskaper kan förbättra och förnya samhället ... att verka för att kvinnor får rättvis del av makten och beslutsfattandet i samhället.*

References

Birath, E. *et al.* (2001) *Det mesta om stiftelser i teori och praktik*, Stockholm: Kommentus.

Braunerhjelm, P. and Skogh, G. (eds) (2004) Sista fracken inga fickor har, *Filantropi och ekonomisk tillväxt*, Stockholm: SNS Förlag.

Brown-Humes, C. (2004) Can the next generation Wallenberg maintain its status and influence? *Financial Times*, July 12, 2004.

Ds (1992) Stiftelser. Sammanställning av remissyttrandena över departementspromemorian (Ds Ju 1987: 14). Stockholm: Justitiedepartementet, Regeringskansliet.

Esping-Andersen, G. (1990) *The Three Worlds of Welfare Capitalism*, Cambridge, UK: Polity Press.

Hirschfeldt, L. (1994) De Johanssonska stiftelserna, Uppsala, AB Upsala Nya Tidning.

Hoppe, G., Nylander, G. and Olsson, U. (1993) *Till landets gagn. Knut och Alice Wallenbergs Stiftelse 1917–1992*, Stockholm: KAW-stiftelsen.

Härdelin, A. (1998) 'Kloster och konvent i den tidiga medeltidens kyrka', 222–227; in B. Nilsson *Sveriges kyrkohistoria. Missionstid och tidig medeltid*, Stockholm: Verbum.

Lorentzen, H. (2004) 'Philanthropy and collectivism – grantgiving foundations in Norway', *ISF rapport 2004*: 015, Oslo: Institutt for samfunnsforskning.

Lundström, T. and Wijkström, F. (1997) *The nonprofit sector in Sweden*, Manchester: Manchester University Press.

Nachemson-Ekwall, S. (March, 2005) 'Special Wallenbergstiftelserna', 30–37; Stockholm: Affärsvärlden.

Olsson, K. (1996) *Näringsdrivande stiftelser*, Lund: Lund University.

Riksdagens Revisorer (2000) *Statligt bildade stiftelser*, Stockholm: Sveriges Riksdag.

Riksrevisionsverket (1990) *Stiftelser för statlig verksamhet*, Stockholm: Riksrevisionsverket.

SOU (1994) Former för statlig verksamhet. (Statens offentliga utredningar 1994: 147) Stockholm: Finansdepartementet, Regeringskansliet.

SOU (1995) Översyn av skattereglerna för stiftelser och ideella föreningar. (Statens offentliga utredningar 1995: 63) Stockholm: Regeringskansliet.

SRF (2000) IRIS-utredningen, Stockholm: SRF.

Statskontoret (1997) Statens samverkan med andra parter i aktiebolag eller ideell förening, Stockholm: Statskontoret.

Steneberg, K. (September, 2004) *Forskning utan penga*, Stockholm: Dagens Industri.

Stenius, K. (1999) *Privat och offentligt i svensk alkoholistvård. Arbetsfördelning, samverkan och styrning*, Lund: Arkiv förlag.

Wijkström, F. (2001a) 'Om svenska stiftelser', *Social ekonomi i Sverige*, in H. Westlund (ed.) Stockholm: Fritzes.

Wijkström, F. (2001b) 'Sweden', in *Foundations in Europe. Society, Management and Law*, A. Schlüter *et al.* (eds) London: The Directory of Social Change.

Wijkström, F. and Einarsson, S. (2004) *Foundations in Sweden. Their Scope, Roles and Visions*, Stockholm: The Economic Research Institute, the Stockholm School of Economics.

Wijkström, F., Einarsson, S. and Larsson, O. (2004) *Staten och det civila samhället. Idétraditioner och tankemodeller i den statliga bidragsgivningen till ideella organisationer*, Stockholm: Socialstyrelsen (*The National Board of Health and Welfare*).

Wijkström, F. and Lundström, T. (2002) *Den ideella sektorn. Organisationerna i det civila samhället*, Stockholm: Sober Förlag.

Wisselgren, P. (2000) *Samhällets kartläggare*, Stockholm/Stehag: Brutus Östlings Bokförlag Symposion.

22 Switzerland[1]

Robert Purtschert, Georg Von Schnurbein and Claudio Beccarelli

Introduction

Switzerland's foundation sector is undergoing a period of change as new tasks and expectations emerge alongside traditional values and customs. At the present time, a revised version of the country's liberal foundation act is being discussed in parliament, and the foundations are organizing themselves into new associations. The number of foundations devoted to charitable causes has increased in the last few years, as have the assets they possess. Debate about the roles and abilities of foundations has brought together politicians, foundation representatives, researchers and other stakeholders. Indeed, Switzerland has been described as 'a particularly enthusiastic country when it comes to foundations' (Riemer 2001b: 512). Although a rather small country, Switzerland has a disproportionate number of foundations. Nonetheless, conducting research on foundations is no easy task. Information and data about foundations is scarce and the sector as a whole lacks transparency. Against this background, the principal aim of this chapter is to address the information gap in terms of what we know about Swiss foundations, using what existing material is available, but also drawing upon new findings gathered through interviews with foundation leaders, stakeholders and experts.

A profile of foundations in Switzerland

Legal issues

The liberal foundation act has led to a large number of special forms of foundation. The Swiss foundation act forms part of the Swiss Civil Code, namely Articles 80 to 89. The loose-knit and liberal foundation act has not been amended since 1911. Along with generous tax breaks, it has sustained growth and activity amongst foundations in Switzerland. The idea of 'being able to draw upon these benefactors as an alternative, or in addition to the State and the business community for a wide variety of worthy causes' (Riemer 2001b: 512) is also firmly anchored in Swiss society.

Since 1950, there has been a steady rise in the number of 'classic'[2] charitable foundations, thanks to a climate of political and economic stability. This climate has also led many foreign nationals to set up foundations in Switzerland (Riemer 2001b: 512).

Although, or perhaps because it is small in scope, the Swiss foundation act has been the subject of much discussion and interpretation (Riemer 1981, 2001a, 2001b; Schmid 1997; Sprecher and von Salis-Lütolf 1999; Riemer and Schiltknecht 2002; Hopt and Reuter 2002). The act fails to provide an unambiguous definition of the term 'foundation'. Instead, Article 80 of the Swiss Civil Code stipulates the following with regard to setting up a foundation: 'The setting-up of a foundation requires the dedication of assets for a particular purpose.'

Many foundations are set up due to the special treatment they receive under tax legislation. In this regard, it is important to bear in mind that the Swiss federal government and each of the 26 cantons have their own tax legislation.

To be granted tax-exempt status, the foundations have to demonstrate to every canton and the federal government their potential public benefit, e.g. by proving that they fulfil the two requirements of public interest and altruism (Maissen 1992: 6).

There are no pay-out requirements set up by law, but foundations that do not distribute donations at all are forbidden. Encouraged by the liberal legislation, several special types of foundation have evolved in the course of the last few decades. There are foundations that benefit the public by maintaining a company and others that act, and appear to be more like an association than a classic foundation.

Two features of the Swiss foundation sector require further explanation. Staff pension foundations (PVS) are a special type of classic foundation in the form of a separate estate administered by the employer. Within Switzerland's three-pillar social security system, the PVS, as sponsors of occupational retirement, survivors' and disability pension plans (Riemer 2002: 515), represent the 'second pillar' and enable employees to make sufficient provision for their own care and retirement (Helbing 1989: 22).

The second special type is the company foundation. This type is a variation of the classic foundation, which rather than being defined in law has evolved in practice. Company foundations can be subdivided into operating foundations and holding foundations. Whilst a company operating foundation manages a commercial enterprise itself, a holding foundation owns shares in one or several companies (Schmid 1997: 96).

The purpose of a company foundation can be charitable, purely financial or a combination of the two (Riemer 1981: ST N 386). Therefore, it is often difficult to distinguish between company foundations and classic foundations, as many classic foundations operate a commercial enterprise in order to improve their usefulness for the benefit of the public.[3]

This study took only classic foundations for the benefit of the public into account. Therefore, company foundations which are not primarily for the benefit of the public and the special legal forms of classic foundation (family foundations, church foundations and staff pension foundations) were disregarded.

Current debate: revision of the foundation act

Following the introduction of new legal and tax regulations for foundations in Germany, Italy and Austria, Switzerland decided to revise its Foundation Act. The aim of completely revising the act is to provide greater legal security, as the existing foundation act is considered to be too rudimentary (Riemer 2001b: 516). Following a parliamentary initiative[4] in December 2000, a revised version of the foundation act was introduced with the aim of further liberalizing the existing legislation (WAK-S 2001: 6). After passing through both chambers of the parliament, the legislation is expected to be enacted in January 2006. The main points of change in the revised law are:

- an obligatory auditor with responsibility for monitoring the foundations;
- an option to change the purpose of the foundation as long as the deed of the foundation makes provision for such a change (for the first time after ten years); and
- an increase in the tax relief on donations from 10 to 20 per cent (von Schnurbein 2004: 4).

Empirical profile

Current knowledge of the size of the foundation sector in Switzerland is restricted to classic foundations and staff pension foundations. According to the Swiss Federal Commercial Registry Office, 20,021 foundations were entered in the cantonal commercial registers in 2001. If we exclude the 8,914 staff pension foundations, a total of 11,107 foundations remain, including some registered church or family foundations and quasi-commercial company foundations. As there are no more specific data available, we can only estimate that the number of classic foundations is around 10,000.

The first data on the foundation sector were recorded after the Swiss Civil Code took effect (31 December 1911). These data cannot be reconstructed for each year, which is why Figure 22.1 (figures by Federal Office for Statistics (BfS), 2003) provides an incomplete timeline.

Whilst the number of staff pension foundations continues to fall as a result of corporate mergers and tie-ups, there has been a continuous rise in the number of charitable foundations. An even more startling picture emerges if we examine the economic impact of charitable foundations.

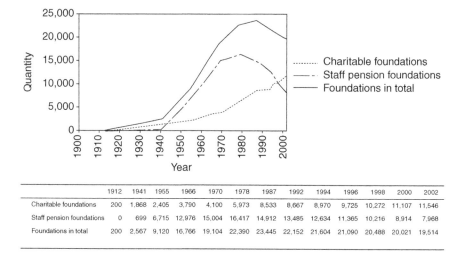

	1912	1941	1955	1966	1970	1978	1987	1992	1994	1996	1998	2000	2002
Charitable foundations	200	1,868	2,405	3,790	4,100	5,973	8,533	8,667	8,970	9,725	10,272	11,107	11,546
Staff pension foundations	0	699	6,715	12,976	15,004	16,417	14,912	13,485	12,634	11,365	10,216	8,914	7,968
Foundations in total	200	2,567	9,120	16,766	19,104	22,390	23,445	22,152	21,604	21,090	20,488	20,021	19,514

Figure 22.1 Growth of the Swiss foundation sector.

According to the register of enterprises and companies (Betriebs- und Unternehmensregister) maintained by the BfS, in 2001, 2.95 per cent of all employees work in foundations, an increase of 17.1 per cent since 1995 (during the same period, general employment rose just 3.4 per cent).

In terms of primary activity, the majority of the Swiss foundations were quite clearly set up as grant-making foundations (95 per cent under federal supervision and 63.4 per cent under cantonal supervision). In accordance with the International Classification of Non-Profit Organizations (ICNPO) classification scheme, most of the foundations are active in the area of 'social services' (group 4), followed by 'culture and recreation' (1), 'education and research' (2) and 'health' (3). Reflecting this situation, foundations active in these areas account for two-thirds of the total number of foundations selected for interviews and analysis in this study.

The lack of comprehensive data mentioned above means that we can only estimate the foundations' total capital. With the exception of the information on staff pension foundations, there are no sufficiently precise figures regarding either the foundations' financial situation or the total amount of annual pay-outs. Switzerland's national supervisory authority for foundations estimates that the reported assets of the charitable foundations amount to around CHF30 billion. Annual pay-outs are likely to total around CHF1 billion, equivalent to around 2 per cent of the federal budget. Added to this sum are the disbursements of foundations under public law, e.g. the national fund with annual pay-outs of around CHF400 million (Purtschert *et al.* 2003: 18).

The foundations regulated by the national supervisory authority were recently examined in more detail for the very first time. The findings reveal that 10 per cent of the foundations account for 83 per cent of the capital, whilst 50 per cent of the foundations share almost all, i.e. 99.4 per cent, of the assets (Rüegg-Stürm 2004: 85). These figures indicate how there are some big players which dominate the foundation landscape in Switzerland, and a vast quantity of small and medium-sized foundations.

Roles of foundations

One of the main features of foundations in Switzerland is their obligation to formulate a purpose. The founder's wishes are hardly limited at all. Moreover, the legal limitations are not very tight. In the following section we explore which aims and roles the founders pursue through their activities (Prewitt 1999; Anheier 2000). Generally speaking, the roles favoured here by Switzerland's foundations are complementarity, innovation, social and policy change, and/or the preservation of traditions and culture.

Complementarity

Prior to analyzing the complementary role, we need to identify what is to be complemented. In this case, it is the public-sector budget for education, culture, social and health care. In 1999 the state spent CHF63.8 billion (€42.5 billion) in these areas. Government spending rose from 26.1 per cent in 1970 to 37.8 per cent in 2000. As greater responsibility was assumed by public-sector authorities, foundations became complementary in fields where they had previously worked independently. For example, through their activities and projects aimed at reducing environmental pollution, foundations such as the World Wildlife Fund (WWF) and Greenpeace worked in areas in which there was no government interest. However, the success of these organizations contributed to the public-sector authorities' decision to put in place environmental protection programmes. Today, the WWF organizes projects together with public-sector institutions such as the Swiss Agency for the Environment, Forests and Landscape (SAEFL).

According to foundation leaders and experts, the complementarity role is the most important role of both their own foundation and foundations in general. More than two-thirds of the respondents regard complementarity as a specific role of foundations. By providing complementary support and projects, the foundations increase the services available to the public. Foundations see themselves in a complementary role in all areas of society, such as development aid, health care, education and culture. For instance, in recent years, the funding of new professorial chairs by foundations has become popular in universities, as they lack public-sector resources for such purposes. The Mercator Foundation Switzerland has funded several chairs and projects, such as a professorship for cardiology at the University of Zurich and the 'science and society' project at the University of Lucerne (Mercator Stiftung 2002: 729).

Innovation

Promoting innovation in social perceptions, values and practices has long been a role ascribed to foundations in general. One reason is the independence existing legislation gives to foundations. It allows foundations to take greater risks than companies or even public-sector authorities. In contrast, foundations are widely perceived to be fusty conservative organizations that spread their grant-making arbitrarily. Nonetheless, at the same time, the foundations are expected by the general public to provide innovative ideas.

In the interviews, innovation was also widely accepted as a role of foundations in Switzerland. However, the foundation leaders were much more persuaded by the innovative force of their own foundation, than of the foundations in general.

This difference essentially reflects the reality of the situation because the majority of foundations either do not encourage, or rarely encourage innovation. There are some exceptions, most of which – but not all – were founded in the last decade.

Since it was formed in 1997, the Gebert Rüf Foundation has sponsored the transfer of knowledge from universities to the business sector. Through its own projects and its donations to innovative initiatives and research projects, it paves the way for new collaborations between universities and the business sector.

In addition to research, the foundations also focus on the economy. Zurich's Technopark, which is led by a foundation, for instance, has led to the creation of over 60 companies since 1993. Young entrepreneurs in establishing their company on the Technopark receive assistance in the form of consultancy, contacts with clients, universities and venture capitalists, and the offer of training courses.

These examples show that foundations can take a greater risk than companies or even the state. Foundations are able to support long-term projects that carry an unpredictable risk.

Social and policy change

This role is accepted by the foundation leaders but not to the same extent as the complementarity and innovation roles. Only four respondents out of a total of 26 accept the relevance of this role. Similar to the innovation role, social and policy change is seen to be more evident within the interviewee's own foundation than it is in the foundation sector in general.

In recent years, foundations have started to become more active in public debates and political discussions. Avenir Suisse is a think-tank founded by 14 international Swiss companies. Independence was the deciding factor in favour of creating a foundation rather than an institute. The foundation's projects cover issues ranging from problems in society to economic development. Avenir Suisse aims to influence political decisions at an early stage and to play a role in informing public opinion. It also aims to inform the public about the outcome of policies in a comprehensible manner.

Social and demographic change is also viewed as another area where foundations must become more active. As our society ages, the Pro Senectute (Foundation for the Elderly) is faced with new challenges in addition to its original purpose, i.e. to offer social services to elderly people. Increasingly, it campaigns for a modern policy to address the needs of the senior population and better solidarity between the generations.

Preservation of traditions and cultures

The special legal position of foundations guarantees them a certain degree of stability. For this reason, foundations are well placed to maintain and preserve traditions. The majority of interviewees agreed that foundations preserve traditions and cultures. However, interviewees that rejected this role did so categorically. Many foundations are set up as a result of conservative values which are reflected in the purpose of the foundation. Often local and regional foundations are set up as a way of resisting the *zeitgeist*. For instance, in 1998, 90 communities in the Jura region in the northwestern part of Switzerland established the Fondation Bellelay. The foundation pursues several objectives, all of which are linked to its main objective: to preserve the culture of the region. It aims to promote tourism, maintain traditional horse-breeding and increase awareness of the specific geology of the Jura region.

Private support for the arts has a long history in Switzerland, ranging from the funding of artists and orchestras through awards and scholarships, to foundation-owned museum exhibits (Purtschert *et al.* 2003: 44). This is an area where foundations are highly active, promoting innovative projects that foster traditional values and sponsoring culture in very different ways. The Sophie und Karl Binding Stiftung launched the 'TransHelvetia' theatre project, not only to support young theatre directors, but also to promote the multilingualism of Switzerland. This project supports cultural exchange within the country and preserves its multilingual tradition.

Further roles of foundations

Our research found little support for any of the other roles amongst our interviewees. In contrast to the complementarity role, the respondents rejected the notion that it was the foundations' role to substitute state activities. Foundations are prepared to take on more responsibility in the future, but they feel committed principally to the intentions of their founders. Many see the 'assignment' of public-sector duties as leading to a reduction in their autonomy, as one consequence may be a greater obligation to follow official guidelines. One alternative option is for the state to set up foundations. The most prominent examples in Switzerland are Pro Helvetia (Arts Council of Switzerland) and the Swiss National Science Foundation (NSF). Both organizations respectively play a leading role in the arts and research funding in Switzerland.

In relation to redistribution, most stakeholders reject this role. As newly established foundations enjoy tax relief, this loss of potential income for the government has to be compensated for by their yearly donations to the public. But foundations are not seen to serve a redistributive role at all.

Another role rejected by the interviewees was the promotion of pluralism. The unique Swiss political system, the 'semi-direct democracy' (Linder 1999: 236), institutionalizes pluralism. The structural minorities are integrated by means of federalism and concordance and are sufficiently involved in power. Plebiscites and referendums enable efficient opposition. Therefore, the promotion of pluralism is not a stated aim of foundation activities. Moreover, pluralism is not promoted in general but in a specific field of activity such as culture or education. However, this role may become an increasingly important one for foundations because institutionalized pluralism is not able to solve some of the challenges posed by increased migration into Switzerland.

Visions and policies

Political stability and continuity has had a positive influence on the foundation sector in Switzerland, as is evident in the absolute number of foundations but also in the many foundations established by foreign nationals (Riemer 2001b: 512). In the interviews, both foundation leaders and experts affirmed the influence of the political model on the foundation sector. What is more, the liberal foundation act of 1911 has advanced the creation of foundations.

We understand the term 'policy' to mean the interactions and relations of public-sector authorities with their environment (von Prittwitz 1994: 11). The way in which these relations are structured determines how others within the State may develop. Therefore, the realization and implementation of foundation visions is related to political self-conceptions. In a previous study, 'Foundations in Europe' (Schlüter *et al.* 2001), the Swiss foundation sector was classified as part of a corporatist model due to the importance of operating foundations and the complex relations with the state and the business sector (Anheier 2001: 70). If we examine the sector more closely, we can differentiate between four different clusters, all inter-

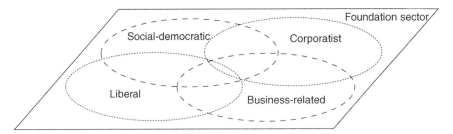

Figure 22.2 The four clusters of the Swiss foundation sector.

acting in various ways with the state (see Figure 22.2). Each one of the four clusters is related to one of the models surveyed in this study. Three of the four relevant policy models were viewed positively by the majority of the respondents, whereas the other models put forward were clearly rejected. The authors added the business-related model alongside the three other models, as the corporate foundations play an important role in the Swiss foundation sector – even though they are not entirely altruistic. In classifying the foundation sector using this pattern, there may be foundations that fit into more than one cluster or those that do not fit into any cluster at all.

It is easy to explain why the two other policy models, the state-controlled and peripheral models, were rejected. Switzerland is basically understood to be an extremely liberal country with minimal governmental regulation. The current revised version of the act does not tend towards more state control but towards even greater liberalism. The peripheral model envisages foundations in a minor role, but there are over 10,000 foundations in Switzerland that serve a public purpose.

The social democratic cluster

In a social democratic model, foundations often play a complementary role. Their contribution can take the form of providing financing, infrastructure, property or professional support. In addition, grant-making foundations join forces with public-sector programmes, as they lack their own experts with the ability to judge the quality of a project. Therefore, they safeguard their decisions by following a larger organization or public-sector institution.

When public-sector funding is tight, private contributions become even more important. Particularly within the social and health system, foundations work closely together with public-sector facilities or support them through donations or their own projects. Equivalent forms of cooperation can be found in research and in cultural contexts. The Helmut Horten Stiftung, one of the largest foundations in the Italian-speaking part of

Switzerland, funds projects in medical research and medical treatment on a national basis. In 2000 the 'Institute for Research in Biomedicine' (IRB) was established with a donation of CHF 10 million for the first five years. The IRB will help the Italian-speaking part of Switzerland to become more involved in national and international research. Through this institute the Helmut Horten Stiftung not only complements the national research institutions but at the same time serves cultural exchange and pluralism in Switzerland. However, foundations are resisting the government's attempt to engage them in long-term programmes in order to decrease government costs. This is viewed as a kind of 'hidden substitution'.

The corporatist cluster

Switzerland is often referred to as a corporatist country. However, it differs from the systems of neo-corporatism in Austria and Germany (Kriesi 1995: 335), such as the de-centralized structure of economic organizations and the fact that associational solutions can be found in all political areas (Linder 1999: 53).

In recent years, foundations have had to deal with, and adjust to processes of change within public-sector administration. By embracing the New Public Management concept, Switzerland's public-sector administration incorporates foundations as part of this new policy agenda. The Pro Senectute Foundation, for instance; cares for senior citizens by providing advice, courses, support services and training for service personnel (Art. 101[bis] section 1 AHVG). The foundation agrees a public service contract with the public-sector authorities covering not only the goods and services on offer per se, but also the supervision of the quality of the services provided.

Within the corporatist cluster, it is often difficult to separate the roles of complementarity and substitution. Foundations are deeply embedded into state systems. In particular, many operating foundations in the health and social system either play a complementary role or 'inherit' public services completely. The Inselspital, a university and cantonal hospital, is a key part of the health-care system in the canton of Bern. In return for the goods and services provided, the hospital received US$110 million of public funds in 2001. This relationship allows the canton to indirectly influence the foundation's decisions, as the hospital is dependent on public funds.

The liberal cluster

In a liberal environment, the influence of public-sector authorities over foundations is not significant. In contrast to the corporatist cluster, the foundations in the liberal cluster underline their independent position in society. Through their grant-making and projects, they pursue their own

goals, which do not necessarily overlap with the goals of public-sector programmes. Liberal foundations are able to promote innovative ideas and
social change, but as discussed in the previous section, these roles are not
sufficiently fulfilled. Rather, the foundations support a great variety of
activities *and* at the same time play a complementary role to the State.
Public-private partnerships are becoming increasingly common. One of
the promoters of this kind of collaboration is the Jacobs Foundation. Its
project 'MovingAlps', for example includes training programmes for
young people living in the alpine region and aims, first, to create jobs for
young people and, second, to diversify the business infrastructure in rural
regions. Although this project is complementary to public-sector offerings,
the focus is on the innovative perspective of the projects. The Jacobs
Foundation initiated the project on the condition that the public-sector
authorities also took part. Moreover, the project is also sponsored by Swiss-
com AG.

These foundations are more output-oriented than they are aimed at
common welfare, i.e. they evaluate the outcome of their work for society,
instead of acting solely for the common welfare of society. The roles
played by foundations in this cluster often include preservation, innovation or social and policy change.

The business-related cluster

The business-related cluster has developed out of the major philanthropic
activities of Swiss companies. Many corporate foundations make a significant contribution towards financing business-related activities such as
research and training. They are also active at a cultural, environmental
and social level. In contrast to a sponsorship scenario, the company has no
legal influence over the foundation but maintains links by appointing representatives to the foundation's board. However, given that the foundations are established by profit-driven organizations, their purpose is not
only philanthropic. In a more strategic context, the foundations serve as a
corporate communications tool. The literature suggests that corporate
philanthropy adds the most social value if it is related to the core business
of a company (Porter and Kramer 2002: 68). The Accentus Foundation
and Credit Suisse Group is just one example of this kind of working relationship. The foundation pursues its charitable purposes by accepting gifts
and establishing sub-foundations on behalf of private founders. The assets
are managed by the Credit Suisse Group, which also covers the administrative costs.

The relevance of the business model is generally rejected by our interviewees because it is believed that corporate foundations are not set up for
altruistic reasons alone. Taking a more pragmatic view, one can argue that
many cultural projects and institutions could not survive without the
support of companies. What may appear to be 'ego-driven' at first can

have a positive impact in society at large. Philanthropy in a competitive context increases a company's involvement.

Current developments and future trends in the Swiss foundation sector

Organization and management of foundations

In order to meet the public's expectations of their work, foundations have to become more management-oriented. Weak legal control mechanisms have recently led to scandals, proving that the principles of corporate governance are a necessity for foundations. The statement 'Do good but do not tell anybody' is not acceptable any more (Toepler 2000: 9). Foundations are neither restricted by the market nor by legal controls. This is due to the fact that at the time the foundation act was drawn up, it was assumed not only that their purpose would be altruistic but also that the work towards this purpose would be based on altruistic values (Littich 2002: 378). An open attitude can increase the credibility of foundations, thereby having a positive impact. First, if foundations gain trust, they will encourage imitators. Second, transparency will improve the foundations' image in society. Quality standards and certification, such as the NPO Label in Management Excellence (Purtschert and von Schnurbein 2004: 324), could help change attitudes.

Another important issue in the context of foundation management is supervision, e.g. internal supervision and project supervision. Internal supervision requires figures and key data on every unit of an organization, not only accounting figures (Schwarz *et al.* 2002: 130). However, in reality most NPOs restrict their supervisory activities to financial criteria (Schauer 2000: 28).

Projects have to be evaluated ex ante in order to ensure that grant-making is of a high quality. In many cases, a lack of personnel makes it impossible to evaluate projects diligently. Moreover, once a project has been completed, the foundation must clarify how it will measure output, as charity and philanthropy cannot be expressed in terms of 'hard' performance figures. Potential solutions include benchmarking systems and value-for-money reports (Schauer 2000: 115).

Agenda setting

In addition to the issues of foundation management, several issues on the political agenda are also of interest to the foundations. The State's rising expectations in relation to the provision of public services by private organizations forces foundations to be more aware of issues that may affect their activities. According to the foundation leaders interviewed, research and education are of particular importance – possibly due to the negative results achieved by Swiss pupils in the PISA study.[5] Political and social structures are ranked next, followed by the health system and our ageing society. Health will be one of the major policy issues for the society of the future (Nefiodow 2000: 135). However, there are also areas where foundations need to do more. For example, only three foundations have so far been involved in migration research (Steinert 2000: 99).

Cooperation

Since expectations by the state authorities and the general public are rising, foundations are trying to collaborate more closely with one other. Nonetheless, although nearly 50 per cent of the foundation managers indicated that they cooperate often or very often with other foundations, 41 per cent seldom work with another foundation. By pooling their knowledge and resources, foundations can become more efficient. Moreover, the number of foundations collaborating within umbrella organizations remains at a very low level, as can be seen in Table 22.1.

The foundation leaders monitor developments in the EU. It is expected that the EU's influence will increase in the foundation sector as well as at a political level, where bilateral agreements have led to closer relations between Switzerland and the EU.[6] The foundation leaders have positive expectations mostly at an operational level. Foundation assets may be used more efficiently if collaboration within Europe becomes more significant and more frequent. Therefore, both structural and operational collaboration should be encouraged.

Half of all foundations under federal supervision have an international focus. For example, the purpose of the Avina Foundation, established in 1994, is the sustainability of quality of life and future developments in Latin America, Spain and Portugal. The foundation supports private education initiatives and provides regional relief. In most cases, international giving is increasing. Consequently, these foundations face new challenges and problems. These problems include the cultural differences that arise with international initiatives, the supervision of international projects and the different legal regulations that apply from country to country.

Conclusion

Perhaps most importantly, this analysis has resulted in a better understanding of the foundation sector in Switzerland, which is currently undergoing a period of change. As the foundation sector grows – in terms of both absolute numbers and economic relevance – it becomes of increasing interest to the public, and to the political establishment.

In earlier analyses, the Swiss foundations were defined as part of a corporatist system. A deeper examination of the roles and visions of foundations allows us to differentiate between four clusters. The

Table 22.1 Data on cooperation within the Swiss foundation sector

Foundation associations

Association	Purpose	Number of members	Domicile
Pro Fonds (form. Arbeits-gemeinschaft gemeinnütziger Stiftungen AGES)	To serve as an umbrella organization for charitable foundations; to carry out lobbying and to exchange experience	Approx. 250	Basle
Swiss Foundations	To promote the idea of foundations and in particular the services of grant-making foundations	27	Bern
Association Genevoise des Fondations Académique (AGFA)	To support the University of Geneva	10	Geneva

social-democratic and corporatist clusters are orientated towards the aims of the welfare state and in some ways even merge with it, whereas foundations in the liberal and business-related clusters use the weak legal regulations to further their own agenda. This heterogeneity gives foundations the ability to strengthen civil society and influence the political agenda.

This study has contributed to addressing the information gap about what we know of the abilities of foundations and the contribution they can make to civil society. Nonetheless, we still lack a complete picture of the sector and there is still much work to be done.

Notes

1 The chapter is an extract from a country report on the foundation sector in Switzerland sponsored by SwissFoundations (Association of Grant-Making Foundations in Switzerland) and the Bundesamt für Kultur (BAK – Federal Office for Cultural Affairs).
2 In the Swiss Civil Code, charitable foundations as defined for this project are called 'classic foundations'.
3 For example, the foundation of the Swiss air rescue service REGA receives a third of its revenues totalling CHF85 million (1994) in the form of insurance payments (Schmid 1997: 32).
4 'A parliamentary initiative (Art. 93 Swiss Federal Constitution) is a general motion or specifically worded bill on which Parliament makes a direct decision, following consultation in an individual committee. This allows the normal initial parliamentary process to be bypassed' (Linder 1999: 206).
5 Program for International Student Assessment (PISA): a study provided by the Organization for Economic Cooperation and Development (OECD) on the educational systems of its member countries.
6 After the rejection of the European Economic Area (EEA) agreement in a referendum in 1992, Switzerland and the EU signed agreements for seven sectors (Free Movement of Persons, Trade in Agricultural Products, Public Procurement, Conformity Assessments, Air Transport, Transport by Road and Rail, Swiss Participation in the 5th Framework Programme for Research) in 1999 and for another nine sectors (Taxation of Savings, Fight against Fraud, Schengen, Dublin Convention and 'Eurodac', Processed agricultural products, European Environment Agency, Statistics, Media, Double Taxation) in 2004.

References

Anheier, H.K. (2001) 'Foundations in Europe: a Comparative Perspective', in Schlüter, A., Then, V. and Walkenhorst, P. (eds) *Foundations in Europe – Society Management and Law*, London: The Directory of Social Change.
Anheier, H.K. (2002) *Visions and Roles of Foundations in Europe – Project Overview*, London: CCS.
Badelt, C. (ed.) (2002) *Handbuch der Nonprofit Organisationen – Strukturen und Mangament*, 3rd edn, Stuttgart: Schäffer-Poeschel.
BfS Federal Office for Statistics (ed.) (2003) *Statistik Schweiz, Fachbereiche*, www.statistik.admin.ch (accessed 11 March 2003).
Bundesversammlung (ed.) (2003) *Bericht der WAK-S zur PalV 00.461 s*, www.parlament.ch (accessed 22 March 2003).

Centre for Civil Society (ed.) (2002) *Research Memorandum 1 – Definition, Classification, Roles and Visions*, London: Centre for Civil Society.

Egger, P. (ed.) (2004) *Stiftungsparadies Schweiz – Zahlen, Fakten und Visionen*, Basel: Helbing & Lichtenhahn.

Esping-Andersen, G. (1990) *The Three Worlds of Welfare Capitalism*, Princeton: Princeton University Press.

Helbing, C. (1989) 'Personalvorsorge und BVG', in *Schriftenreihe der Studiengesellschaft für Personalfragen*, vol. 2, 4th edn.

Helmut Horten Stiftung (ed.) (2003) *Helmut Horten Stiftung*, www.helmut-horten-stiftung.ch (accessed 14 March 2003).

Hopt, K.J. and Reuter, D. (eds) (2001) *Stiftungsrecht in Europa*, Köln: Heymanns.

Kriesi, H. (1995) *Le système politique suisse*, Paris: Economica.

Linder, W. (1999) *Schweizerische Demokratie – Insitutionen, Prozesse, Perspektiven*, Bern: Haupt.

Littich, E. (2002) 'Finanzierung von NPOs', in Badelt, Ch. (ed.) *Handbuch der Nonprofit Organisationen – Strukturen und Management*, 3rd edn, Stuttgart: Schäffer-Poeschel.

Nefiodow, L.A. (2000) *Der sechste Kondratieff- Wege zur Produktivität und Vollbeschäftigung im Zeitalter der Information*, 4th edn, St. Augustin: Rhein-Sieg.

Porter, M.E. and Kramer, M.R. (2002) 'The Competitive Advantage of Corporate Philanthropy', *Harvard Business Review*, Nov–Dec.

Purtschert, R., von Schnurbein, G. and Beccarelli, C. (2003) *Visions and Roles of Foundations in Europe – Länderstudie Schweiz*, Fribourg: VMI.

Purtschert, R. and von Schnurbein, G. (2004) 'Das NPO-Label für Management-Excellence als Instrument der Corporate Governance', in Voggensberger, R., Bienek, H.J., Schneider, J. and Thaler, G.O. (eds) *Gutes besser tun – Corporate Governance in Nonprofit-Organisationen*, Bern/Stuttgart/Wien: Haupt.

Riemer, H.M. (1981) 'Die Stiftungen, Systematischer Teil und Art. 80–89bis ZGB', in Meier-Hayoz, A. (ed.) *Berner Kommentar – Kommentar zum schweizerischen Privatrecht, Band I: Einleitung und Personenrecht, 3. Abteilung: Die juristischen Personen*, vol. 3, 3rd edn, Bern: Stämpfli.

Riemer, H.M. (2001a) *Die Stiftung in der juristischen und wirtschaftlichen Praxis*, Zürich: Schulthess.

Riemer, H.M. (2001b) 'Stiftungen im schweizerischen Recht', in Hopt, K.J. and Reuter, D. (eds) *Stiftungsrecht in Europa*, Köln: Heymanns.

Riemer, H.M. (2002) 'Wollen wir im schweizerischen Stiftungsrecht liechtensteinische Verhältnisse? Kritische Bemerkungen zur Parlamentarischen Initiative Schiesser vom 14. Dezember 2000', in Riemer, H.M. and Schiltknecht, R. (eds) *Aktuelle Fragen zum Stiftungsrecht, unter Einbezug der geplanten Gesetzesrevision (Parlamentarische Initiative Schiesser)*, Bern: Stämpfli.

Riemer, H.M. and Schiltknecht, R. (eds) (2002) *Aktuelle Fragen zum Stiftungsrecht, unter Einbezug der geplanten Gesetzesrevision (Parlamentarische Initiative Schiesser)*, Bern: Stämpfli.

Rüegg-Stürm, J. (2004) 'Stiftungen im 21. Jahrhundert: Change Management', in Egger, Ph. (ed.) *Stiftungsparadies Schweiz – Zahlen, Fakten und Visionen*, Basel: Helbing & Lichtenhahn.

Salamon, L.M. and Anheier, H.K. (1992) *In Search of the Nonprofit Sector I: The Question of Definitions, Working Paper No. 2*, Baltimore: The Johns Hopkins Institute for Policy Studies.

Salamon, L.M. and Anheier, H.K. (1997) *Defining the Nonprofit Sector – A Cross-National Analysis*, Manchester: Manchester University Press.

Schauer, R. (2002) *Rechnungswesen für Nonprofit-Organisationen*, 2nd edn, Bern/Stuttgart/Wien: Haupt.

Schlüter, A., Then, V. and Walkenhorst, P. (eds) (2001) *Foundations in Europe – Society Management and Law*, London: The Directory of Social Change.

Schmid, R. (1997) *Die Unternehmensstiftung im geltenden Recht, im Vorentwurf zur Revision des Stiftungsrechts und im Rechtsvergleich*, Zürich: Schulthess.

Schwarz, P., Purtschert, R., Giroud, Ch. and Schauer, R. (2002) *Freiburger Management-Modell für Nonprofit-Organisationen*, 4th edn, Bern/Stuttgart/Wien: Haupt.

Sprecher, T. and von Salis-Lütolf, U. (1999) *Die schweizerische Stiftung – Ein Leitfaden*, Zürich: Schulthess.

Steinert, M. (2000) *Schweizerische Stiftungen – Eine Analyse des schweizerischen Stiftungswesen unter besonderer Berücksichtigung der klassischen Stiftungen*, Freiburg i. Ü: VMI.

Technopark Zürich (ed.) (2000) *Wir vernetzen Kompetenzen, Von der Vision zur Realität – Ein Statusbericht zum Jahr 2000*, Zürich: Technopark.

Toepler, S. (2000) *Das amerikanische Stiftungswesen in den 1990er Jahren: Wachstum und Problemstellungen*, Arbeitspapier für die Expertenkommission zur Reform des Stiftungs- und Gemeinnützigkeitsrechts Maecenata Institut/Bertelsmann Stiftung.

Voggensberger, R., Bienek, H.J., Schneider, J. and Thaler, G.O. (eds) (2004) *Gutes besser tun – Corporate Governance in Nonprofit-Organisationen*, Bern/Stuttgart/Wien: Haupt.

Von Prittwitz, V. (1994) *Politikanalyse*, Opladen: Leske + Budrich (UTB).

Von Schnurbein, G. (2004) 'Entscheid des Ständerats zur Revision des schweizerischen Stiftungsrechts', *Verbands-Management*, vol. 1/04.

23 Foundation roles and visions in the USA

Comparative note

Stefan Toepler

Introduction

Since the emergence of the "modern philanthropic foundation" in the wake of the Russell Sage, Carnegie and Rockefeller philanthropies in the early twentieth century, the question of roles and functions (if not necessarily visions) of foundations has always been a firm part of the American foundation debate, as well as of its rhetoric and mythology. Since then, the guiding foundation paradigm in the United States (US) has been that of the well-endowed grant-making foundation acting as social venture capital to foster social change. Early recourse to a role definition (e.g. the innovation or change agent role in particular) was a necessity to establish societal legitimacy for the "new" organizational form. This was perhaps less necessary in Europe, at least in those parts of Europe where the foundation survived the transition from pre-modern times to modernity. In fact, the very emergence of the modern philanthropic foundation was almost immediately contested in the progressive, anti-corporate climate of the early 1900s. Political challenges (albeit on very different grounds) reemerged in the 1950s and 1960s.

With new wealth flowing into the foundation field in the 1990s, foundations have once again become the beneficiaries of renewed public and academic interest in the form of significant criticism; new normative management prescriptions (e.g. venture philanthropy); and the spectre of new regulation. Accordingly, the turn of the millennium has apparently led to a re-appraisal of foundations on both sides of the Atlantic. But is this merely coincidental or an indication of a more fundamental re-thinking of the role of private, philanthropic intercession into the public realm? With the changing nature of European welfare regimes, is there a discernible trend towards convergence in European and American foundation debates? Particularly in view of the popularity of the liberal vision among European foundations, is the American model a useful guidepost for the future development and role definition of European foundations? Based on a review of the literature and the recurrent themes of the US foundation debate, this paper will seek to answer these questions by applying the roles and visions framework to the US case and comparing and contrasting the American experience to the European findings. Before discussing roles and visions, however, I will first briefly outline some conceptual/structural and regulatory differences, as these arguably have some bearing on the discussion of foundation roles. I will then summarize the recent growth, and main strands of criticisms, of US foundations.

A profile of foundations in the US

Historical development

Although many charitable trusts existed for various purposes in early American history and the foundations of Benjamin Franklin, James Smithson and George Peabody were of no small importance (Weaver 1967), the birth of the US foundation sector as we know it today is usually pinpointed around the beginning of the twentieth century. In an influential series of articles in the 1880s titled "Wealth," Andrew Carnegie began to argue in favour of an obligation on the part of the rich to devote excess wealth to public purposes and to help provide opportunities for the less fortunate to better themselves. Over the following decades, the traditional focus of charitable trusts on providing relief and amelioration was gradually supplanted by a new orientation towards analysing and addressing the causes of social problems rather than just addressing their effects. Using the emerging sciences to tackle the "root causes of social ills" set the ambitions and operations of the early twentieth-century foundations apart from earlier foundation activities in America and launched the "modern philanthropic foundation" sector (Karl and Katz 1987). The earliest of these new foundations included the Russell Sage Foundation (1909), the Carnegie Corporation (1911) and the Rockefeller Foundation (1913), which popularized the foundation idea and provided a blueprint that other wealthy donors began to follow in the 1920s and 1930s. High marginal tax rates that originated during the Second World War and continued into the post-war period, combined with relative lax regulation, further propelled foundation growth in the 1940s and 1950s. Financial advisers began to not only tout foundations as a tax planning mechanism, but also as a means to structure business ownership and business transactions (Rudney 1987). By the 1960s, however, perceived economic misuses of foundations led to a political backlash culminating in the introduction of the new and relatively stringent regulation of foundations by the end of the decade.

Legal issues

Beyond the general charitable trust law, foundations largely emerged in a legal vacuum at the beginning of the twentieth century. Typically using the corporation rather than the trust as a legal form, neither general nor tax laws made any distinction between foundations and other charities in stark contrast to the Continental European civil law tradition. Although Congress in various acts began to distinguish implicitly between public and private charitable organizations in the 1940s and 1950s (Edie 1987), foundations were not subject to special supervision and regulation until public and congressional interest and criticism intensified in the 1950s and 1960s. Congress finally imposed specific regulations on private foundations in the Tax Reform Act (TRA) of 1969, using tax law to distinguish between foundations and other non-profit organizations.

Legally, the term foundation is essentially a creation of the tax law, which considers this type of organization to be a donor-controlled (usually endowed) organization.[1] Foundations are therefore characterized by the dominance of a single source of income – provided by the founding donor – as opposed to public charities which have a more diversified income structure. Somewhat simplified, private foundations are a residual category comprised of those non-profit organizations that lack a certain measure of public financial support for their annual operations. The Internal Revenue Code grants a blanket exception from private foundation status to certain types of organizations, including hospitals and colleges, independent of income structure – meaning that some of these institutions, while functionally foundations in the European understanding, are not legally considered to be foundations in the US. It also outlines a number of rules to separate broadly supported organizations (public charities) from single donor-supported organizations (private foundations). Without a positive legal definition, tax regulation thus relies on various tests and exceptions to single out those "foundation-like" charitable organizations that Congress found in need of more stringent regulation and lesser tax privileges. Moreover, the TRA of 1969 also differentiated for the first time between operating and grant-making foundations, easing for the former some of the harsher regulations imposed on the latter.

One of the key provisions of the Act was the imposition of an annual pay-out requirement for grant-making foundations of either all income or the equivalent of 6 per cent of the asset value, whichever was greater. In essence, this prohibited foundations from retaining parts of their investment income to maintain the real value of their capital and forced them to draw on their assets for spending where investment yields remained below the 6 per cent mark. In combination with the stagflation of the 1970s, this is widely seen as the main reason for a decline of the US foundation sector in the 1970s. In the early 1980s, the pay-out requirement was changed to a flat 5 per cent of asset value, allowing foundations to retain excess income and to keep giving below asset growth. The growth of the foundation field then began to pick up again.

Beyond the pay-out requirement, a number of other restrictions were imposed on foundations that are generally not applicable to other charities.

- The TRA of 1969 introduced an excise tax, that is a levy on income, which was to be used to fund government oversight of foundations.
- Self-dealing (e.g. business transactions) between foundation and donors, board members, managers and certain other persons are generally prohibited, even if they were to the advantage of the foundation.
- Foundations may not own privately-held business or control public corporations; and are prohibited from engaging in any kind of political activity, including lobbying.
- In addition, donations to foundations have generally lower deductibility limits than donations to other charities. For example, a donor may deduct up to half of the donor's income for gifts to charities, but only 30 per cent for endowing a foundation.

Recent growth and criticisms of the US foundation sector

The foundation field began to recuperate from these measures in the 1980s. The 1990s saw a substantial growth in the number, assets and grants of foundations. According to data provided by the New York-based Foundation Center, there were close to 62,000 grant-making foundations in the US in 2001, holding aggregate total assets of close to $477 billion and spending $30.5 billion in grant and other expenditures. While the number of foundations had only doubled since the late 1980s (there were about 30,000 foundations in 1988), there was a dramatic acceleration of the financial means of the foundation sector in the space of only a few years (see below). More specifically, total assets in nominal terms essentially doubled between 1995 ($227 billion) and 2001; and grant dollars have almost doubled since 1997 ($16 billion).

Despite this growth, funding patterns have remained relatively stable (Table 23.1). About six out of every ten grant dollars flow into traditional welfare areas broadly defined: education received about a quarter of all foundation support (26 per cent) in 2002, health 18 per cent and human services 15 per cent. The other major funding areas are arts and culture (12 per cent) and public affairs (11 per cent). The remainder is distributed between environment, sciences, religion and international affairs. Although international affairs accounts for only 3 per cent of foundation grant-making, most of the largest US foundations maintain international programmes (if not offices) and it is likely that a share of the health and education spending also reaches international recipients.

There are a number of reasons for the considerable growth that the foundation field underwent in the 1990s. With their diversified investment portfolios, foundations profited enormously from the stock market boom

Table 23.1 Distribution of US foundation spending, 2002

Funding domain	Share of total foundation spending (%)
Education	26
Health	18
Human services	15
Arts and culture	12
Public affairs	11
Environment	6
Science and technology	4
Religion	3
International affairs	3
Social sciences	2

Source: *Foundation Giving Trends*, 2004 edn, New York: Foundation Center.

of the late 1990s. In addition, the hypothesized intergenerational transfer of wealth – estimated to be between $41 and $136 trillion over the next five decades (Havens and Schervish 1999) – may have begun to benefit the foundation field. To some extent, the conversion of non-profit health plans and hospitals to "for-profit" status resulted in the creation of new, mostly health-related grant-making foundations with significant endowments (since the charitable assets of the converted institutions must remain devoted to similar, charitable purposes). And finally, new post-industrialized wealth from technology (the Bill and Melinda Gates, David and Lucile Packard, and William and Flora Hewlett Foundations) and the media (Ted Turner's United Nations Foundation), for instance, has begun to flow into the foundation sector and will likely dominate the foundation field in the future.

At the same time, however, growing social, economic, and cultural problems have heightened interest in foundations again. This heightened attention has also come with renewed criticism. Although the asset values of foundations have increased significantly over the last decade, so have current needs. In particular, the largest foundations, it is often argued, have not adapted their spending policies, but have continued to observe strictly the current pay-out requirement of 5 per cent of asset value rather than increasing pay-outs to make additional resources available for current needs (Mehrling 1999). A second strand of criticism accuses foundations of over-professionalization and "administrative self-absorption" (Frumkin 1997; 1998). The argument here is that over the past 30 years, foundations substantially increased their staff, and thus their administrative costs at the expense of their grant-making budgets. Recent legislative proposals before the US Congress (H.R. 7 of 2003) threatened to prohibit foundations from counting any administrative expenses towards the calculation of the 5 per cent-minimum pay out. What is more, after a series of media coverage and growing criticism of payments to foundation trustees

(Ahn *et al.* 2003; Cohen 2003), the Senate conducted hearings on over-sight problems with foundations and charities in an effort to crack down on potential abuses.

Roles of foundations and European assessment

This brief review suggests that the foundation debate in the US is essen-tially squarely centred on the question of what societal roles foundations (should) pursue, and how well they perform in carrying out these roles. It is also indicative of major differences in the way the US and European foundation debates are currently playing out. Whereas Europeans seem on balance interested in encouraging foundations, many critical US observers take more of an interest in discouraging, if not foundations at large, then at least certain foundation behaviours. How well then does the conceptualization of foundation roles mesh with the American discussion? Before discussing roles and visions in the US, I will however first summa-rize the European findings.

As Anheier and Daly discuss in greater depth in their comparative analysis (see Chapter 2), the assessment of the various foundation roles varies greatly within Europe. For illustrative purposes, Figure 23.1 maps the European responses in a foundation roles continuum from irrelevant to highly relevant. The individual roles are positioned according to the degree of agreement across countries that a given role is fully or at least somewhat applicable. As Figure 23.1 shows, there is near universal agree-ment that European foundations perform the complementarity role. Like-wise, there is a similar consensus that fostering innovation constitutes an important role for foundations, although the interpretation of this role occasionally merges with complementarity to the extent that Europeans sometimes define the role vis-à-vis government. At the opposite end of the continuum, the substitution and redistribution roles emerge as barely rel-evant from the findings of the European research, with the proviso that European foundations apparently feel increasing pressure to step into substitutive functions. Social and policy change, preservation and plural-ism receive somewhat mixed assessments. In each case, these roles are rated as somewhat, but not very strongly, applicable by about half or more of the countries.

Roles of American foundations

While the respective salience of these seven roles received varying assess-ments across Europe, there are not all equally useful as a yardstick for assessing US foundations, or as a means of capturing the sector's self-identity either. As suggested in the US foundation role relevance contin-uum of Figure 23.2, four of the roles have little, if any, salience in the US context, while one is modestly, and two are highly relevant. In particular,

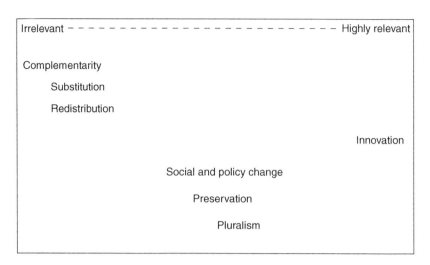

Figure 23.1 Relevance of foundation roles continuum, Europe.

the substitution and preservation of tradition and culture roles have neither resonance nor relevance in the US context at all, as evidenced by a near complete lack of a discussion of these roles in the foundation literature or policy debate. In terms of substitution, it is the case that funders occasionally worry about government cut-backs or other revenue shortfalls in particular fields of activity and the prospect of having to divert resources to help secure basic funding levels. However, such concerns relate for the most part to the perceived ability of foundations to maintain other roles over the short-run. They do not raise the systemic question of whether substitution may be an acceptable (or even debatable) permanent role.

At the same time and in contrast to Europe, there appears to be little expectation by policy-makers that foundations would (or usefully could) step in and fill gaps left by the government's retreat from prior responsibilities. As perhaps best evidenced by the 1996 welfare reform effort, government "exit strategies" tend to focus on creating incentives for individuals or markets to address needs rather than creating incentives for philanthropic intervention.[2] Another reason for the virtual non-existence of a "substitution debate" in the US helps to explain why the preservation function also lacks relevance. Both functions in the European context highlight in some measure the roles of operating foundations. However, in the US, operating foundations (except for those that also maintain grants programmes) are largely absent from the foundation debate for conceptual as well as regulatory reasons, as discussed above (see also Toepler 1999a). Otherwise and similar to Europe, the preservation role could be tied with relative ease to a variety of existing operating

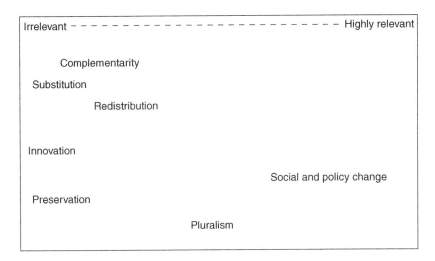

Figure 23.2 Relevance of foundation roles continuum, US.

foundations in the US as well (Toepler 1999b). Insofar as preservation can also be interpreted as maintaining the social status-quo, there is a persistent line of argument that views (grant-making) foundations as essentially hegemonial tools of economic elites intended to neutralize social change (Roelofs 2003). Some policy experts similarly ascribe to foundations an important role in shaping the policy formulation process in favour of economic elite interests (Dye 2001). This in turn mirrors the key political concerns at the beginning of the twentieth century. As historians Barry Karl and Stan Katz wrote:

> The criticism was ... based on the assumption that the foundations represented the investment of ill-gotten gains in a manner which threatened to subvert the democratic process by giving philanthropists a determining role in the conduct of American public life.
>
> (Karl and Katz 1981: 248)

However, the hegemony critique remains largely marginalized and outrightly rejected by the foundation field.

In terms of redistribution and complementarity, these roles are traceable within the US foundation discourse without, however, having gained a definitive status. The redistribution role is occasionally discussed, but has little bearing conceptually and is rather limited practically (Margo 1992; Wolpert 2004). In essence, that foundations support causes, such as high culture or elite education, which may benefit the affluent more than the disenfranchised is generally acknowledged, but not perceived as a significant problem. Complementarity, by contrast, presents a more complex picture. In the defining early years of the ascendancy of US foundations, both the Rockefeller and Carnegie philanthropies relied heavily on working with and through public institutions, which arguably contributed to the success of their work in the first half of the twentieth century (Flexner 1952). The complementary nature of foundations was also a staple in the arguments in favour of foundations in the course of their critical examination through Congress in the 1960s. The 1965 Treasury Department's assessment of the foundation field allowed for their "vital role" in "providing for areas into which government cannot or should not advance" (Treasury Department 1965: 13).

Likewise, the "Petersen Commission" asserted that a diversion of funds from the treasury (e.g. tax exemption) is "strongly justified when private philanthropic money is used, not as a substitute for tax dollars, but as a supplement of a special kind that serves the public interest in ways in which the government itself is under various operational constraints" (Commission on Foundations and Private Philanthropy 1970: 15). Since the 1970s, however, the complementarity role has largely disappeared from the foundation discourse, although it is still traceable in foundation practice. The Annenberg Foundation's arts education initiative, a challenge program to reintroduce arts education into public school systems is an example of the complementary role with some substitutional element to it (since the initiative reacted to arts education cuts in public school budgets). But perhaps the most explicit and prominent example of complementarity is the United Nations (UN) Foundation, established by the media executive Ted Turner in 1997. The UN Foundation pursues a two-pronged strategy which involves advocating on behalf of the United Nations in the US (which the UN as an international governmental institution cannot do itself), on the one hand, and influencing policy priorities within the UN through grant-making, on the other (Toepler and Mard 2003).

The pluralism argument was a corollary to the references to the complementarity role in the 1960s and 1970s. In contrast though, it has retained a measure of relevance in the foundation discourse, primarily with reference to foundation support of the private non-profit sector (Prewitt 1999). However, given the relatively small contribution of foundations to overall non-profit sector revenues the pluralism case is inherently weak (Nielsen 1972). The proliferation of foundations may thus be seen as a sign, rather than a cause, of pluralism and societal openness.

Apart from pluralism, most foundation roles are given little credence in the US. However, the societal "change agent" function, that is either the innovation or the social/policy change role of foundations, is probably the most recognized and widely discussed function. The idea that foundations should serve as social "venture" or "risk" capital can be traced back to at least the 1920s in the US literature (Kiger 1954). In one variation or the other (Reeves 1970; Letts *et al.* 1997) it has continued to play an important role in legitimizing foundations. At a basic level, the appeal of this role lies in the unique characteristic of the foundation form – its virtual lack of dependence on external economic resources. References to this characteristic and its implications are ubiquitous in the foundation literature.

Moreover, the relative centrality of the change agent function to the self-identity and the external assessment of the foundation field is widely reflected in the critical discussion of foundation work. Many observers, for example, bemoan an apparent short-term focus within foundations. The trend in the field has been towards funding short-term projects and specific programmes rather than committing to long-term general support of potentially highly innovative organizations. This problem has frequently been associated with the emergence of a "programme officer profession." The argument is that foundations have become more risk-adverse and less innovative, because professional foundation managers prefer to fund smaller and safer programmes so as not to have to take personal responsibility if larger and riskier projects fail (Nielsen 1972; Frumkin 1998). The proposal that foundations should act within the non-profit sector like venture capitalists do in the business sector (Letts *et al.* 1997) has thus sparked a broad debate and considerable soul-searching among foundations leaders. Nonetheless, making requisite investments in staff to be able to work closely with grantees over the long-run may potentially further spark criticism of over-professionalization and undue administrative spending.

Another line of perpetual concern is a lack of recent success stories. Buttressing the professionalization criticism, risk-taking, innovation and the willingness to experiment with new ideas are seen to be in danger of becoming mere myths. The US foundation community has indeed found it difficult to point to far-reaching social, medical, cultural or other societal breakthroughs that can be attributed to early foundation funding and that are equal to those from the early part to the middle of the last century. The principal foundation umbrella group, the Council on Foundations, maintains a "Great Grants" section on its website, which is intended to highlight significant foundation contributions to societal change and innovation:

> The developments described here have touched the lives of nearly every American. Yet many Americans don't know that foundation grants helped make these successes possible. Because foundations serve as society's research and development arm – by funding programs that explore new problem-solving approaches – much of value is learned from those foundation-funded experiments that don't work out as well as the wide-impact successes reflected in these grants.[3]

The list covers a gamut of significant achievements, ranging from the development of rocket science to the invention of polio and yellow fever vaccines, and the creation of the public library system and public television. However, the most recent of the ten highlighted foundation successes date back to the early 1970s – rather underscoring the critique that foundations have little to show for over the last 30 years and may have lost their innovative touch. Is this a function of the failure of foundations to communicate more recent "success stories" better? Is it a function of a more complex policy infrastructure in which increasing numbers of other private policy actors drown out the contributions and impacts of foundations? Or, is this situation indeed indicative of a failure to perform the distinctive roles the foundation community has long claimed for itself? These questions must remain the subject of further debate.

While the dominance of the innovation or change function within the American foundation discourse is undeniable, it is worth noting that there are undercurrents in the debate that aim to locate foundations in supplementary or complementary role contexts. Both the over-professionalization and the pay-out critiques can be interpreted in this way. Reducing the number of professional grant-making staff would inevitably lead to less systematic and more ad hoc funding decision-making, carried out by (part-time) trustees. While this might reduce bureaucracy and perhaps increase faithfulness to donor intent, it would also be likely to lead to more traditional support for charities without larger change agendas. Likewise, current efforts to increase foundation pay-outs are largely motivated by the desire to increase funding for the financially stressed non-profit sector (Toepler 2004). Insofar as the non-profit sector essentially serves as an alternative to government in the American system, efforts focusing on increasing foundation funding for non-profits per se (rather than change) do fall within the scope of the complementarity function.

Comparative assessment of foundation roles and the question of visions

Although the European and US foundation role relevance continua are merely illustrative, the discussion nevertheless suggests that there are some commonalities between the United States and Europe. At the same time, it also underscores some fundamental differences in foundation role assessments and outlook. The commonalities include a clear rejection of substitution and redistribution as appropriate roles for foundations; a half-hearted acceptance of the pluralistic function; and a full embrace of innovation as a role to which foundations should aspire to fulfil. Although the innovation role defies precise definition, there nevertheless appear to be some differences in the way the role is contextualized on both sides of the Atlantic. In the United States, the focus is on societal innovation with little apparent cross-references to the role of government. While foundations have in the past worked with or through government agencies, and continue to do so, the relationship with the public sector remains largely undefined. Much of the innovation discussion largely treats foundations as operating in an institutional vacuum, set apart from the non-profit sector as the implementation mechanism of foundation work. Moreover, many, if not most, foundations tend to shy away from engaging government, which is in part due to concerns about potentially violating the prohibitions on political activities imposed in the TRA of 1969.

In Europe, by contrast, the state does serve more explicitly as a reference point for the self-definition of foundations in the innovation role. Critical views of government as bureaucratic, slow, inflexible and unresponsive provide an opportunity to define foundations in a positive light. The pursuit of innovation is therefore less of a desiderata per se. Rather, the raison d'être of foundations lies in providing a counterpart to, and compensating for, the institutional-operational drawbacks of the public sector – a line of argument that remains largely unexplored in the American context. This difference in the way the role of the state flows into the self-understanding and self-definition of foundations also underlies the single most important divergence in role assessments concerning the importance of complementarity. While European foundations tend to feel comfortable describing their work as a complement to the state, complementarity has largely become a non-issue in the US debates.

How do these commonalities and differences mesh with the question of vision? Casting the question of vision in the form of various underlying models raises a number of interesting questions in the American context. Three of the six vision models that Anheier and Daly (see Chapter 3) identified have little apparent relevance in the US context (corporatist, peripheral, business). Beyond that, however, a valid question could be raised about a partial applicability of the state-controlled model. While American foundations would not perceive themselves as subservient to government and contrary to widely held perceptions, aspects of the existing legal framework suggest a certain measure of state control. In Anheier and Daly's conceptualization, the state-controlled model comprises restrictive laws, complicated administrative procedures and extensive oversight. The main case for this model rests with the restrictiveness of US foundation regulation after 1969, when taken in comparative perspective (Toepler 1998). In particular, there are two crucial dimensions of foundation regulation where the US tax framework seems less than enabling compared to Europe: provisions about foundation control of business corporations, which is essentially prohibited (Fleishman 2001); and the regulation of foundation spending policies as defined in the pay-out requirement (Toepler 2004). In addition, while procedures for incorporation and tax exemption are relatively straightforward, foundations faced new calls for, as well as hearings in the US Senate on, tightening oversight provisions in 2004. They are also struggling with anti-terrorist financing guidelines resulting from the Patriot Act, particularly in relation to international funding programmes.

Historically, there is some evidence for the social-democratic model, particularly during the progressive period of the early twentieth century. As this model is closely associated with the complementarity role in Europe, however, the lack of awareness of this role in the American discourse limits the model's applicability to the contemporary foundation sector. In essence then, the American experience centres around the liberal vision, in which foundations (and the non-profit sector) are frequently perceived as parallel to, or as an alternative to government. The vast majority of foundation funding flows to private non-profit organizations rather than public institutions. Many foundations view heavy financial dependence of grantees on government as a negative. The general liberal outlook also meshes well with the dominance of the innovation, change, and – to some extent – pluralism roles.

Conclusion

In the past, discussions about the societal roles and position of foundations in the US and Europe have rarely overlapped. The prevailing presumption has been that the American "philanthropic advantage" is such that there was little possibility for a meaningful exchange (beyond exporting concepts and a degree of technical know-how). Indeed, comparing the level of sophistication of the respective analytical as well as critical discourses suggests that the US does in fact maintain a considerable advantage, at least in the way that the impact of foundations on policy and polity has been evaluated. In some ways, many European countries have yet to tackle issues that were subject to significant debate in the US a good three or four decades ago. In part, this is due to the fact that foundations in Europe have largely confined themselves to the social and political sidelines in the past – content "to do good quietly."

Only very recently did foundations move more squarely into the political and policy mainstream. European governments have traditionally been ambivalent, if not hostile, towards foundations. But in the context of fiscal retrenchment beginning in the 1980s, the US model has become more appealing and there has been a considerable shift in policies and government postures since. At present, foundations are drawing new policy interest in the United States as well. Curiously though, as governments in Europe strive to deregulate and liberalize legal and tax frameworks for foundations, the US is poised to tighten regulatory control once again. After three decades of relative calm in the government/foundation relationship subsequent to the Tax Reform Act of 1969, new attempts to control foundations and foundation spending have moved to the Congressional agenda. New legislation is under discussion to force foundations to spend more on charitable grants; and recent media coverage of financial abuses may well lead to tighter supervision and more stringent disclosure and conflict of interest rules in the near future.

Accordingly, a fundamental re-thinking of the roles of foundations is underway on both sides of the Atlantic, but it is based on very different premises. While the political ambivalence towards privately controlled wealth deployed for public purposes is waning in Europe, it appears to be on the increase again in the United States. This perhaps reflects the differences in the respective development stages. While Europeans still perceive the need for more enabling environments, the US foundation sector is established and mature enough to be able to weather a further round of restrictions. But it likely also reflects fundamentally dissimilar postures among policy makers. Despite protestations about the importance of foundations for creating a new European civil society, the core policy interest seems to be to facilitate the commitment of private means to public responsibilities, thereby relieving the existing burdens on financially strapped European treasuries. A similar intent, by contrast, is barely discernible in the American context. Politically, foundations remain tolerated – rather than actively welcomed – social actors; and a perhaps better understanding of the financial limits of the foundation sector precludes viewing it as a potential panacea for fiscal malaise.

While the US does in many ways symbolize the liberal vision that many European foundations tend to aspire to, its usefulness as a guidepost for charting the future course of European foundation development should be assessed with care. European foundations will have to continue to define their roles and visions in relation to the state in a way that American foundations do not have to. The crucial conflict between the substitution and complementarity roles is something that is easily sidestepped in the US by focusing foundation programmes and funding on the non-profit sector. While comparative research has shown that the non-profit sector is all but an exclusively American phenomenon (Salamon *et al.* 1999), some of the most important funding domains, including education and culture, still remain more state-centred and less institutionally varied in Europe than in the United States. This is, however, something of a mixed blessing for US foundations as well. The absence of pressure to clarify the foundation/government relationship has allowed the foundation sector to fully adopt the higher ideals of fostering societal innovation and change. But with the difficulties of actually measuring and convincingly demonstrating the somewhat elusive objectives of this role come attendant problems when accountability for the use of resources is being called in. In times of periodic political scrutiny, new arguments based on a nuanced assessment of the complementarity role may have their uses in the American context as well.

Notes

1 Donor control in this sense refers to the ability of the donor to structure the organization, determine purposes and governance. Since foundation boards are self-perpetuating and thus principally able to retain control within the donor's family or within the circles of persons that the donor initially appointed into the future, US tax laws consider foundations donor-controlled even after the donor ceased active participation.
2 It is important to keep in mind though that many US foundations may still perform a substitution role even if it is not discussed and thematized.
3 www.cof.org/index.cfm?containerid=133 (accessed 09/18/2004).

References

Ahn, C., Eisenberg, P. *et al.* (2003) *Foundation Trustee Fees: Use and Abuse*, Washington, DC: Georgetown University Center for Public and Non-profit Leadership.
Cohen, R. (2003) "Time to Stop Excusing the Inexcusable: Foundation Trustees Who Play by Their Own Rules," *Non-profit Quarterly*, 10 (4).
Commission on Foundations and Private Philanthropy (1970) *Foundations, Private Giving, and Public Policy: Report and Recommendations of the Commission on Foundations and Private Philanthropy*, Chicago and London: University of Chicago Press.
Dye, T. (2001) *Top Down Policymaking*, New York: Seven Bridges Press.
Fleishman, J. (2001) "Public Policy and Philanthropic Purpose – Foundation Ownership and Control of Corporations in Germany and the United States," in A. Schlüter, V. Then and P. Walkenhorst (eds) *Foundations in Europe: Society, Management and Law*, London: Directory for Social Change, 372–408
Flexner, A. (1952) *Funds and Foundations: Their Policies Past and Present*, New York: Harper & Brothers.
Frumkin, P. (1997) "Three Obstacles to Effective Foundation Philanthropy," in J.W. Barry and B.V. Manno, *Giving Better, Giving Smarter: Working Papers of the National Commission on Philanthropy and Civic Renewal*, Washington, DC: National Commission on Philanthropy and Civic Renewal, 84–104.
Frumkin, P. (1998) "The Long Recoil From Regulation: Private Philanthropic Foundations and the Tax Reform Act of 1969," *American Review of Public Administration* 28 (3): 266–286.
Frumkin, P. (2004) *Trouble in Foundationland: Looking Back, Looking Ahead*, Washington: Hudson Institute Bradley Center for Philanthropy and Civic Renewal.
Havens, J. and Schervish, P. (1999) *Millionaires and the Millennium: New Estimates of the Forthcoming Wealth Transfer and the Prospects for a Golden Age of Philanthropy*, Boston.
Karl, B. and Katz, S. (1981) "The American Private Philanthropic Foundation and the Public Sphere 1890–1930," *Minerva* 19 (2): 236–269.
Karl, B. and Katz, S. (1987) "Foundations and Ruling Class Elites," *Daedalus* 116 (1): 1–40.
Kiger, J. (1954) *Operating Principles of the Larger Foundations*, New York: Russell Sage Foundation.
Letts, C., Ryan, W. *et al.* (1997) "Virtuous Capital: What Foundations can learn from Venture Capitalists," *Harvard Business Review* (2): 36–44.
Margo, R. (1992) "Foundations," in C.T. Clotfelter, *Who Benefits from the Non-profit Sector?* Chicago: University of Chicago Press.

Mehrling, P. (1999) *Spending Policies for Foundations: The Case for Increased Grants Payout*, San Diego: National Network of Grantmakers.

Nielsen, W. (1972) *The Big Foundations*, New York: Columbia University Press.

Prewitt, K. (1999) "The Importance of Foundations in an Open Society," in *The Future of Foundations in an Open Society*, Gütersloh, Verlag Bertelsmannstiftung: Bertelsmann Foundation, 17–29.

Reeves, T. (ed.) (1970) *Foundations under Fire*, Ithaca: Cornell University Press.

Roelofs, J. (2003) *Foundations and Public Policy: The Mask of Pluralism*, Albany: State University of New York Press.

Rudney, G. (1987) "Creation of Foundations and Their Wealth," in T. Odendahl, *America's Wealthy and the Future of Foundations*, New York: Foundation Center, 179–202,

Salamon, L.M., Anheier, H.K. *et al.* (1999) *Gobal Civil Society: Profiles of the Non-profit Sector*, Baltimore, MD: Johns Hopkins Center for Civil Society Studies.

Toepler, S. (1998) "Foundations and their Institutional Context: Cross-Evaluating Evidence form Germany and the United States," *Voluntas* 9 (2): 153–170.

Toepler, S. (1999a) "On the Problem of Defining Foundations in a Comparative Perspective," *Non-profit Management and Leadership*, 10 (2): 215–225.

Toepler, S. (1999b) "Operating in a Grant-making World: Reassessing the Role of Operating Foundations," in H.K. Anheier and S. Toepler, *Private Funds, Public Purpose: Philanthropic Foundations in International Perspective*, New York: Kluwer Academic/Plenum Publishers, 163–181.

Toepler, S. (2004) "Ending Pay-out As We Know It: A Conceptual and Comparative Perspective on the Pay-Out Requirement for Foundations," *Non-profit and Voluntary Sector Quarterly*, 33 (4).

Toepler, S. and Mard, N. (2003) *The Role of Philanthropy within the United Nations System: The Case of the United Nations Foundation*. Paper prepared for the International Network on Strategic Philanthropy (INSP) sub-group on the Role of Philanthropy in Globalization.

Treasury Department (1965) *Treasury Department Report on Private Foundations*. Written Statements by Interested Individuals and Organizations on Treasury Report on Private Foundations. Volume 1. t. C. Committee on Ways and Means. Washington, DC: Government Printing Office.

Weaver, W. (1967) *U.S. Philanthropic Foundations: Their History, Structure, Management and Record*, New York: Harper & Row.

Wolpert, J. (May, 2004) *Redistributional Effects of America's Private Foundations*. The Legitimacy of Philanthropic Foundations: US and European Perspectives. Paris.

Index